D0768918

out on assignment

Out on Assignment

newspaper women and the making of
modern public space

# # #

ALICE FAHS   The University of North Carolina Press *Chapel Hill*

This volume was published with the assistance of the
GREENSBORO WOMEN'S FUND
of the University of North Carolina Press.

Founding contributors: Linda Arnold Carlisle, Sally Schindel Cone, Anne Faircloth, Bonnie McElveen Hunter, Linda Bullard Jennings, Janice J. Kerley (in honor of Margaret Supplee Smith), Nancy Rouzer May, and Betty Hughes Nichols.

The paper in this book meets the guidelines for permanence and durability of the Committee on Production Guidelines for Book Longevity of the Council on Library Resources. The University of North Carolina Press has been a member of the Green Press Initiative since 2003.

Library of Congress Cataloging-in-Publication Data
Fahs, Alice.
Out on assignment : newspaper women and the making of modern public space / Alice Fahs.
p. cm.
Includes bibliographical references and index.
ISBN 978-0-8078-3496-1 (cloth : alk. paper)
1. Women journalists—United States—Biography.
2. Women in journalism—History—United States—20th century.
3. Women and journalism—United States—History—20th century. I. Title.
PN4872.F35 2011
070.4082—dc23
2011022142

15 14 13 12 11   5 4 3 2 1

for Charlie and Mimi

Contents

Illustrations

out on assignment

Introduction

In 1891 Margherita Arlina Hamm began writing "Among the Newspaper Women" for the New York *Journalist*—the first newspaper column ever devoted to newspaper women as a group. Chronicling the work of women newspaper writers around the country, but especially in New York, Hamm conjured up a world of public sociability. "There were some four or five newspaper women met accidentally Thursday evening at a restaurant on Broadway," she began her first column; "they all became confidential in a short while, as is the habit of newspaper women. Not confidential about their inner lives, but about their business I mean." On the face of it this was a casual statement about a casual meeting of women in public, but it also deliberately laid claim to a public community of independent women in one of the most famous public spaces of New York.[1]

With her column, which she continued to write weekly over the next two years, Hamm publicized the activities of some of the hundreds of women who were entering newspaper work nationwide at the turn of the century. But she did more, as well: by writing about what newspaper women were thinking and doing, by reporting their conversations in the printed columns of the *Journalist*, Hamm also created a new public space for women within the world of print culture. As she did so, her column joined the work of numerous other newspaper women, who at the turn of the century wrote widely of new work opportunities for women, developed new newspaper genres such as advice columns and interviews, explored new living arrangements for women, advocated extensive travel, and covered and promoted women's political activism. Their work shaped new public spaces for women within the physical pages of the newspaper, while also writing into being a far-flung new public world of women.[2]

We get some sense of newspaper women's active creation of this new public realm when we examine the career of the ambitious and prolific

Margherita Hamm herself. Starting out at the *Boston Herald* at age sixteen, by age twenty she was briefly working for the *New York World*, as well as writing her column for the *Journalist*. She wrote "specials" for New York newspapers—like numerous other women in a newspaper world that offered few regular, full-time staff positions to women.[3] Traveling to China, Japan, and Korea in the mid-1890s, Hamm claimed to be the "first woman war correspondent" in the 1894–95 Sino-Japanese War. On her return she successively became editor of the *Journalist*, editor of the "woman's department" of the *New York Mail and Express*, head of what she called a "suffrage department" for *Peterson Magazine*, and editor of *Clubwoman Magazine*. Traveling to Cuba, Puerto Rico, the Philippines, and Hawaii during and after the Spanish-American War, she wrote newspaper articles as a "war correspondent" in addition to four popular books on America's "new possessions." She then turned to history, publishing a book on the "first families" of New York (still used by genealogists), as well as a volume on the "builders of the republic." Drawn to the theater, she brought out a volume of sketches of "eminent actors in their homes." All the while she occasionally published (quite bad) poetry—and in the early 1900s fulfilled a dream by publishing a collection of short stories about the Lower East Side, *Ghetto Silhouettes*, and several short stories on New York's "Egyptian colony" in the elite *Century Magazine*. No doubt she would have published more, but Hamm died suddenly of pneumonia in 1907. She was thirty-six.[4]

Hamm is not remembered today as part of journalism history, much less the history of women. But in this neglect she is far from alone: we know little about most of the women who took up newspaper work at the turn of the century and created new public spaces for women in print. Instead, the history of newspaper women follows well-worn grooves: it highlights the daring of the pioneering and influential Nellie Bly (Elizabeth Jane Cochrane); it discusses the so-called sob sisters who covered the notorious 1907–8 trials of Harry K. Thaw for the murder of architect Stanford White. These were prominent newspaper women, to be sure. But in between we have missed an entire generation of female journalists and a richly networked public community.[5]

Many of the women who are the subjects of this book have been hiding in plain sight for over a century. They achieved a measure of fame in their own day; enlivened the pages of metropolitan mass-circulation papers that sometimes reached hundreds of thousands of readers; innovated across a variety of new genres, developing styles of newspaper writing that in some cases remain startlingly fresh today; and created a rich set of public conversations within the public spaces of the newspaper. Thanks to the rapid growth of newspaper syndication, some of them reached a national reader-ship in addition to local audiences.[6]

Not only were their writings vital in shaping and disseminating ideas regarding women's changing lives, but they also created a set of public con-versations about the cultural politics of modern life. Publication—the rai-son d'être of newspapers, after all—gave these women new access to the power of publicity, which they could use to circulate their ideas. Publicity was itself a rapidly evolving term and set of practices in American demo-cratic life at the turn of the century; its positive connotations included pub-lic attention, access, and knowledge. Publicity could act as a "searchlight" that exposed areas of American life in need of reform—an important as-pect of a democratic culture, many newspaper women agreed.[7]

Yet newspaper women did not have unlimited access to the power of publicity; there were numerous constraints on women reporters such as Hamm, as we shall see. Likewise, publicity was by no means always a posi-tive good in women's lives: publicity could also imply notoriety, and it in-creasingly referred to practices of promotional manipulation. Still, there is no question that newspapers were a significant new public space for women in American life, one in which they discussed, shaped, and imagined new public lives—even as they became public figures themselves.

# # #

When Margherita Hamm arrived in the rapidly expanding metropolis of New York City in the late 1880s, she entered a fast-changing newspaper world. Among the established major newspapers were the *Sun*, the *Her-ald*, and the *Tribune*, all lively papers rooted in the penny-press era, with plenty of front-page attention to murder and other crimes. More sober, re-spectable papers included the *Evening Post* and the pipsqueak *Times* (with a circulation of only 9,000 in 1896). Then there were the splashy new sensa-tional newspapers—Joseph Pulitzer's illustrated *World* in 1883, followed by William Randolph Hearst's *Journal* in 1895.[8] These mass-circulation news-papers achieved phenomenal growth during the 1880s and 1890s—with the *World* reaching over a million readers in 1897.[9]

Energized, vital, cacophonous, Pulitzer's and Hearst's innovative mass-circulation newspapers were new print spaces that must be seen as part of the larger creation of diverse, congested, contested urban public spaces at the turn of the century.[10] Locked in intense rivalry during the late 1890s, the *World* and the *Journal* expanded on and experimented with the very con-cept of a newspaper: they were part of a much-discussed "New Journalism" in this period. Following in the tracks first laid down by the penny newspapers of the 1830s, the *World* and the *Journal* provided startling headlines and visually striking layouts.[11] But they also added and continually tinkered with new features and sections, including sports sections, woman's pages, comics, and Sunday editions. With their "human interest" stories of ordinary people's lives, their close attention to crime and scandal, and their intense engagement with readers through puzzles, contests, and advice columns, mass-circulation newspapers were an important part of the public texture of modern urban life, creating what one historian has called "word cities."[12]

Though other papers may have decried the most sensational, crowd-pleasing tactics of what they pejoratively referred to as "yellow journalism," they did not escape its influence. During the 1890s more traditional newspapers underwent substantial change in response to the "New Journalism" of the *World* and *Journal*. They added new features including woman's pages, sports pages, and Sunday editions in order to stay in the competitive fray. At the same time, reflecting the possibilities created by New York's population increases in this period, new newspapers sprang up—including the lively and literary (but unfortunately short-lived) *Recorder*, begun in 1891.[13]

As newspapers expanded dramatically, seeking new readers and hoping to satisfy their advertisers' demands for more customers, it became possible (although never easy) for women to enter several different types of newspaper work. The extraordinary expansion of the great metropolitan papers in the late 1880s and 1890s often meant that the pressing demands of commerce—the need to fill newspapers with lively material on a daily basis—outweighed even the most conservative editors' staunch belief that women should stay in a private sphere. The creation of woman's pages and special woman's features, for instance, allowed many women entry into newspaper work, as many editors assumed that women would be best at covering "woman's concerns." (Many editors also believed that "woman's stuff" was *all* newspaper women were fit for.) As Mary Twombly wrote in 1889, "The easiest, and, as a rule, the only, way through which a woman can make a beginning on the press is through writing on what men regard as distinctively feminine topics,—dress, millinery displays, household matters, etc."[14] Of course for women with ambitions beyond the "woman's department," this was a source of exasperation rather than a cause for celebration. As Margherita Hamm commented in disgust, "The average managing editor or city editor will not believe that a woman is capable of handling anything but the latest parties, the latest dresses, the newest bonnets, the latest weddings."[15] It was virtually impossible for a woman to avoid the woman's page entirely over the course of her newspaper career—even if she was hired as an "all round" reporter or as a "stunt" reporter.

Yet women directly assigned to the woman's page were not necessarily entirely confined there. Marie Manning remembered that she and two female colleagues not only "got out the woman's page of the *Evening Journal*" in the 1890s, but also "did general reporting, wrote book reviews, produced thrillers for the Sunday edition and added the 'woman's angle,' whatever that is, to murder trials."[16] Producing "thrillers" meant that newspaper women sometimes even wrote fiction for the Sunday papers.

The demands of newspaper work inevitably undercut editors' desires to "contain" newspaper women—although editors often attempted to cloister women within the physical spaces of the newspaper office. (Marie Manning sardonically labeled women's segregated space at the *Journal* the "Hen Coop.") But being sent out on assignment to get the "woman's angle" (a phrase many newspaper women disliked) exposed one of the paradoxes of journalism at the turn of the century: the same editors who believed women could not cover "news" and should be confined to reporting on frills and fashions, often sent them out into a world that offered a revelatory and expansive education in an array of urban social problems. Outside the newspaper office, as women reporters traveled throughout the city, they not only gained new experiences directly related to their assignments, but also necessarily experienced the serendipitous and the unpredictable as they became part of a larger city life.

An expansion of the idea of "news" in this period gave newspaper women additional opportunities for work. As the "quirks" of human nature were redefined as part of daily news within "New Journalism," brief stories of "human interest" became a mainstay of Pulitzer's and Hearst's papers in particular.[17] Newspaper women quickly developed a reputation for their abilities in this area. As Helen Hambridge recounted, "editors and publishers" came to "recognize a woman's remarkable faculty of interesting woman readers and men readers alike in treating the so-called human interest and emotional phases of newspaper topics."[18]

Newspaper women disagreed about whether women had special abilities for a "woman's style" of newspaper work. Margherita Hamm argued that although the "brain in itself, so far as science can judge, has no sex," women had special abilities for "emotional" work.[19] Marie Manning had never "been able to discover what the Woman's Angle really means. Unless you're writing about puddings or petticoats, a story is good or bad without regard to the writer's sex."[20] Whatever their views on this question, by the turn of the century newspaper women were closely linked with several newly developed genres of popular writing, including interviews, advice columns, and urban "sketches." They also wrote book reviews and Sunday "specials"—as well as, of course, "woman's feature" work such as fashions, cookery, and society and women's club notes.

"Sensational" exploits provided other, controversial opportunities for newspaper women. In the wake of Nellie Bly's pioneering "stunts" in the late 1880s, numerous women obtained similar work, including a variety of daredevil feats with the appeal of public circus acts. Sensational newspapers quickly realized that they could reach a large audience with women's personal accounts of such escapades, especially when accompanied by illustrations of their bodies exposed in "dangerous" situations.[21] Such sensational work is still often dismissed as merely exploitative of and "degrading" to women—echoing criticisms made in the late 1880s and 1890s. Yet a number of newspaper women clearly thrived on the excitement of such work, at least in the short term. As Ada Patterson remembered, "The first chance I got I left off chronicling society notes for the Salt Lake *Herald*, where I began." After becoming a reporter for the *San Francisco Call*, she had her "fill of fights and frenzies," she commented with satisfaction. "Every day, nearly, had its exciting adventure, and the 'yellower' the assignment was, the better it pleased me. Once I rode on an engine cab through a particularly dangerous region of the really Wild West, when every moment we expected a hold-up, for those were the days of genuine train robberies."[22] The so-called Nellie Bly of the West, Patterson eventually made her way to New York City and the sensational *American*, where her first assignment was to "go down in the caisson of the bridge being built across the East River"—a classic stunt.[23] Patterson flourished on this public exposure.

Stunt work was, in fact, part of an emerging culture of leisure and entertainment that included the nickelodeon and amusement parks like Coney Island. Newspaper stunts also drew upon an earlier melodramatic literature and, with their emphasis on "plucky" heroines involved in urban adventures, were a major precursor to popular film melodramas of the 1910s featuring adventurous and endangered "Perils of Pauline"–style heroines.[24] A series of articles in 1896 in the *New York World*, for instance, featured the adventures of newspaper woman "Kate Swan" (probably Kate Swan McGuirk) and included "Kate Swan Scales Harlem River Bridge" and "Kate Swan as a Snake Charmer"—among many others. In each article, Swan provided personal descriptions of her exciting adventures in a variety of titillating and quasi-dangerous situations. The novelty of these stories lay in their public exposure of a woman in situations usually off-limits to women; their offense, as far as many critics were concerned, lay in that same exposure. The *Chicago Times-Herald*, in reviewing the "abominations" involved in sensationalism's "depths of degradation," specifically cited a "Kate Swan" article as an example of the "squalid enterprises of women reporters."[25]

There were numerous "Kate Swans" in the 1890s. Their articles, featuring independent heroines reflecting on urban adventures, were part of a new articulation of modern life in which newspaper women became performative public figures. Going "undercover" in "detective work" even allowed them to enact dramatic cross-class fantasies of being working girls and beggars. Nell Nelson, for instance, first made a splash in Chicago with her 1888 undercover series on the "white slave girls" of Chicago—an exposé of the conditions of working girls in factories. Her success in this series caught the attention of the *World*, which brought her to New York to write what Margherita Hamm called "heart-breaking stories" on urban poverty.[26]

We tend to assume that newspaper women wrote either such "sensational" pieces or woman's page material. In fact, however, numerous women engaged in both kinds of work over the course of their newspaper careers and cannot be so easily pigeonholed. Elizabeth Jordan, who later became editor of the woman's page of the *World*, told an admiring interviewer in 1891 that "the piece of work" of which she was "the proudest of all" in her newspaper career was watching over the deathbed of a woman dying of consumption. This assignment was classic sensational work, although Jordan might have denied it; she knew only too well that sensational work often carried the hint of scandal.[27]

Not all newspaper women approved of sensational work, as we shall see. Indeed, such work created great controversy among newspaper women. But with a range of other types of assignments available—from book reviews to woman's page articles to "all round" reporting—newspaper work offered a welcome alternative to such occupations as teaching. Margaret H. Welch, who wrote the column "Her Point of View" for the *New York Times*, noted that "newspaper work seems incomparably easier than teaching, notwithstanding the three months' vacation of the schoolmistress. Life with a copy-pad or wielding a blue pencil can never, to my mind, touch the routine drudgery of over and over drilling of the young idea." Newspaper work was "never monotonous," whereas "ten years of teaching, it is said, finishes a woman's usefulness in it. She is worn out in nervous force."[28] This assessment reversed critics' often-expressed worry that a newspaper job would overtax women because they did not have sufficient "nervous energy" or stamina to do the work.

Although many women chronicled the difficulties of obtaining and doing newspaper work, over and over they also talked of its fascination. As newspaper woman (and prominent suffragist) Ida Husted Harper wrote, journalism had "less monotony and more novel experiences, perhaps, than any other legitimate business"; "its own peculiar attractions" made "it as hard to 'let go of' as the handles of an electric battery."[29] Anne O'Hagan wryly observed that "to say that it has a fascination is to say no more than may be said of opium by the opium eater, or of the car of the great god Juggernaut by its victims. It has such a fascination, one that is inexplicable."[30] Elizabeth Jordan agreed that "it is a peculiarity of the work that its slaves are willing slaves, who would not throw off their shackles if they could. Even the failures, and there are many of them, feel the fascination of the life."[31]

One of the chief fascinations of newspaper work was the wide public exposure it gave women. Involving an expansive relationship to public space, turn-of-the-century newspaper work was dramatically different from women's mid-nineteenth-century literary and journalistic work, which had emphasized privacy and the home.[32] Numerous newspaper women reflected on this fundamental aspect of their work. "If a woman counts wide experience of life as gain, it is hers," Anne O'Hagan wrote of newspaper work in 1898. "She knows the teeming sweat shops of the East Side, and she sits at banquets where clever men and women make epigrams. She gauges the depth of the visiting foreign poet's soul, and she accurately reckons the length of his hair. She visits sinners in their cells. She finds saints in unexpected places. She meets shams at every turn and gradually she comes to recognize them. She is forced to regard the world objectively, and that for a woman is a blessing too great for easy measuring."[33]

Women "out on assignment" became urban explorers who crisscrossed cities in search of their "stories," observing and interviewing men and women from every walk of life. Elizabeth Jordan remembered that for her 1891 *New York World* series "True Stories of the News," she "became a daily frequenter of the Tombs, of Bellevue Hospital and the Charity Hospital on Blackwell's Island, of the Police Courts and the city prisons." Sometimes she found her story "in the underworld; sometimes in the Chinese quarter; sometimes among the tenements; occasionally on Fifth Avenue." "The series took me into all sorts of places and among all types of human beings," she said.[34]

Such work created a new engagement between women and public life, one centered around active participation and observation. Newspaper work, in fact, required new modes of seeing and observing—new modes of gaining and producing knowledge. If the tropes of "innocence" and an "averted gaze" had structured Victorian women's selfhood, now "experience" and an alert, forthright, all-seeing gaze reorganized ideas of what constituted appropriate knowledge for newspaper women. As Edna Ferber wrote of her time as a reporter, "I wouldn't swap that year and a half of small-town newspaper reporting for any four years of college education." In those eighteen months "I learned to read what lay behind the look that veiled people's faces, I learned how to sketch in human beings with a few rapid words, I learned to see, to observe, to remember."[35]

Being "out on assignment" was an experience that many women remembered as a new and exciting phase of their lives. "But the city, how fascinating that was," Neith Boyce Hapgood wrote, "seen from my viewpoint, a reporter going out for a story—every day a different story in a different quarter."[36] "I never shall forget my thrill at the phrase *cover it*," Pulitzer Prize–winning author Zona Gale said of her early newspaper work in New York from 1901 to 1903. "When I was actually a reporter, I used to go about my work saying to myself, 'I'm out on an assignment!' People talked about the *newspaper grind*. But I was more than happy in it. I was ecstatic."[37]

Yet by the time Gale made these remarks, she had long since left newspaper reporting behind, having found that it could not be easily combined with her love of writing fiction. Other women, too, left newspaper work as they discovered that they had no chance of advancement, that the work was unsatisfying or too grueling over the long term, or that they could not make ends meet when they had to scratch out a living by the published column inch. Newspaper women's creation of a new public sphere was thus not permanent, but ever-shifting, as successive new waves of women moved into, and out of, newspaper work. The public sphere they created needed to be remade over and over again—much like the daily newspaper itself.

# # #

Most of the women who populate this book have dropped out of the historical record. Why? Given the prominence of many of them—some were nationally syndicated columnists—they might have been surprised by their invisibility today. After all, they were not powerless: they were overwhelmingly white and therefore racially privileged in American society; they were largely though not exclusively middle-class; and, crucially, they left behind a substantial body of published writings in their newspaper articles. Yet we know more about the few female columnists and writers of the mid-nineteenth century, such as the wonderfully acerbic Fanny Fern (Sara Parton), than we do about the hundreds of women who entered the newspaper world at the turn of the century.

There are often powerful political and cultural reasons for erasure from historical memory, and the case of newspaper women is no different. Indeed, it is almost overdetermined that they and their writings have not received the attention they have deserved. Let us start with the odd position of mass-circulation newspapers within American cultural history. Despite reaching an extensive audience and despite offering a host of innovative features that even included fiction, mass-circulation newspapers have rarely been considered a form of popular literature to be studied on a par with magazines and books. We almost never think of newspapers as a site where interesting writing took shape that has much to tell us about contemporary culture. Even at a time when we appropriately celebrate "literary journalism" and "creative nonfiction," we notice turn-of-the-century newspaper writing only if, as in the case of Stephen Crane, it was a "precursor" to later novels.

Our low regard for the turn-of-the-century press has long roots. In the 1890s and early 1900s, genteel critics launched a fierce attack on "sensational" newspapers, one that has had a lingering effect, down to this day, on our attitudes toward all newspapers. Working hard to shore up an older cultural hierarchy in which elite magazines and book publishers retained their prestige in American society, critics characterized sensational newspapers as degraded, beyond the pale. By the early twentieth century, "vicious" was an adjective commonly used to describe them.[38]

This successful genteel attack on sensationalism had a variety of consequences. The label "sensational" became a shorthand not just to describe the blaring headlines of the front page, but to dismiss entire newspapers—as though every aspect of these great, inventive, energized, visually arresting, and experimental publications could be summed up in one word: "sensational." We can quickly get a sense of how limiting this term has been in allowing us to *see* these newspapers by comparing the critical paths taken in the history of film with those taken in the history of newspapers. Many film critics point out that early films were deliberately sensational and even compare them to newspapers—but as a matter of interest leading to further analysis, and certainly without the negative judgments so often attached to sensational newspapers. Within the history of film, films are understood to have been primarily a form of entertainment from the start—while it has often been seen as somehow disreputable that newspapers at the turn of the century engaged in entertainment in addition to providing news. Applied to newspapers, the term "sensational" has been used as a summary and preemptive judgment that has limited and blocked analysis: sensational papers were "merely" entertaining; they merely wanted to create "sensation." But why not instead explore newspapers as one of the great public spaces of entertainment in turn-of-the-century cities? Why not explore *how* they created "sensation" and how they fit into a larger emerging culture of leisure?

There is perhaps no better proof that the genteel attack on sensational newspapers was effective—not only in its own time but down to our time as well—than the wholesale destruction of the paper copies of such great, color-filled newspapers as the *New York World* during the era of enthusiastic black-and-white microfilming in the 1960s and 1970s, when almost all libraries threw out their heavy, cumbersome bound volumes of these newspapers with abandon, or sold them to dealers who snipped them up for sale by the page. Nicholson Baker has documented in arresting detail his quest to save virtually the last complete paper run of the *New York World*—a newspaper read by hundreds of thousands of readers in its heyday, yet saved from destruction only at the last minute through Baker's personal efforts. (Anyone who has squinted at smudgy and streaked black-and-white microfilm images for hours, wistfully trying to imagine what the Sunday newspapers must have looked like in their original color, can only be grateful.)[39]

It is not that there wasn't much to criticize in sensational newspapers, as numerous historians and critics have pointed out. Indeed, the point is not to be *less* but to be *more* critical—meaning that newspapers deserve our full critical attention, not just offhand dismissal. But the long-lived assumption that they were merely sensational has blinded us to the riches of these cultural sources, including, for the purposes of this book, the writings of newspaper women. To turn the pages of any random *New York Sunday World* from 1899, or 1900, or 1901, for instance, is not just to find the "screaming" headlines and "vicious" features that offended critics, but also to discover a notably diverse group of writings by a wide variety of authors. Among them are talented newspaper women such as the satirical Jessie M. Wood, who illustrated her drama criticism with caricatures; Kate Carew (Mary Chambers), a witty interviewer and cartoonist; and Nixola Greeley-Smith, whose sharply observed columns on men and women led her inexorably toward feminism. There are many more.

The genteel attack on sensationalism has had far too much power in organizing, and erasing, our memories of turn-of-the-century newspapers—and, as a result, erasing the work of female journalists who worked for newspapers such as the *New York World* or the *New York Journal*. Similarly, early attacks on newspaper women have had far too much lingering power in organizing our understanding of their work. Almost every history of turn-of-the-century newspaper women moves from Nellie Bly to the much-attacked "sob sisters" (including Greeley-Smith) who covered the Harry K. Thaw murder trials in 1907–8. Of course, there are reasons to study these famous newspaper women. They were celebrities in their own time; they became the subjects of intense criticism; their own work is fascinating. They are an important part of any history of newspaper women.

But telling the history of newspaper women by focusing only on the most famous and controversial among them has hidden costs. First, it elevates fame, celebrity, and controversy to primary organizing principles in narrating the stories of newspaper women—as though there were no others but a notable handful working across the country at the turn of the century. Such a narrative organization has obscured the wider culture of newspaper women who were working at the same time. It has limited our understanding of the trajectories of their careers, as well as their daily lives as women "out on assignment."

Second, allowing controversy to be the major organizing principle in telling their history has had the perverse effect of retrospectively empowering critics who first attacked newspaper women—as though there were no other story to be told but the controversies these critics themselves created. Instead of examining the entire career of Nixola Greeley-Smith, for instance—whose writings on men and women, suffrage and feminism are fascinating—we end up looking *only* at her role in the Thaw trials. The net effect is a diminution of our understanding of newspaper women and their public world.

We also need to look squarely at some of the long-accepted criticisms of newspaper women in order to reassess them. The usual critique of the so-called sob sisters, for example, was (and is) straightforward: that they "gushed" their way through the Thaw murder trial and as a result ruined the credibility of *all* newspaper women as capable, "objective" reporters for years to come. But we need to acknowledge the hidden politics of this account. Both newspaper men and women wrote emotion-laden reports of the trial; they also employed emotion in other parts of the newspaper (for men, often on the sports page, just as today; for women, often on the woman's page). Emotion was an accepted and valued "tool" of both male and female journalists. Thus it was not just the "emotional" style of newspaper women that brought them under attack: it was the spectacle of their accrued power, made visible by their sitting in the public space of a courtroom together—a space that only a few years before had been off-limits to them. It was their perceived "invasion" of public space that invited scrutiny and triggered attacks meant to diminish their power.

Finally, another reason newspaper women have not received sufficient attention has to do with their devaluing of their own work. Like their male counterparts, newspaper women valued "front page" stories over all other kinds of work at the turn of the century: in the newspaper world, then as now, the reporting of front-page news stories was given more respect than any other form of writing except editorials. Yet few women had the opportunity to appear on the front page, much less the editorial page. At most mass-circulation newspapers, staff openings available to women were mainly on the "woman's page" or writing for the "woman's department" or providing the "woman's angle." True, some women were hired as "all round" reporters, and even the women hired for the woman's page often managed to leverage their initial assignments in order to do other kinds of work. They were sent out to cover crime stories by the largest mass-circulation papers (though often to obtain the "woman's angle"); they received "general" reporting assignments; they wrote "specials" for the new Sunday sections of newspapers. Nevertheless, most newspaper women either began on, cycled through, or remained stuck on the woman's page. Such work was hardly the first choice of most newspaper women, but it was the reality for many at the turn of the century.

Looking back over their careers, newspaper women tended to downplay their work on the woman's page; they were embarrassed by its "fluff" and "gush" and seemingly endless features about society women or its silly decorating projects that involved making furniture out of boxes. The woman's page was not the invention of newspaper women, after all, but instead was the creation of male editors seeking an expanded female readership. Thus even the foremost historian of turn-of-the-century newspaper women, Ishbel Ross, whose 1936 *Ladies of the Press* has never been superseded, talked disparagingly of the woman's page. A reiterated theme of her work was the pride women took instead when they achieved a front-page story. That pride was real, and justified, in a world in which male reporters and editors circumscribed women's work.

Yet we neglect the "woman's page" at our peril. For it is precisely because most newspaper women were hired to write "woman's features" that we find there a rich collection of these ambitious and intelligent women's writings about women's changing lives—on topics *not* limited to "jam and cookery." Likewise, we need to pay attention to women's special features—their pictures of urban life and personalities, their sketches and profiles, their interviews and "human interest" columns. All of these stories offer compelling insight into a lost world of women's writings that placed women at the heart of a new public life. To find these writings, we have no choice but to ignore newspaper women's own disparagement of their early work.

If we do pay attention to newspaper women's work, we discover a world surprisingly different from that of either the "New Woman" or the working girl of many histories of the turn of the century. Newspaper women of that era emphasized new forms of selfhood centered around freedom and independence (even if that freedom was often a fantasy). They rejected much of earlier sentimental culture, with its emphasis on the importance of a domain of privacy for women. Through their work they instead sought to live their lives in public—both the public spaces of the city and the public spaces of print. In the process they created distinctive modes of modern selfhood.

Newspaper women especially celebrated "experience"—which forces us to rethink some of our assumptions about turn-of-the-century literary history, as well. We often tell a narrative of "masculinization" in this period, pointing out that numerous male authors embraced new values of rough readiness and the strenuous life, even as they repudiated an earlier sentimental literature they associated with female authors.[40] But newspaper women, too, embraced a strenuous life; they, too, rejected an earlier Victorian sentimentalism; they, too, explored an expansive new relationship to public space. In articulating the value of experience, newspaper women helped to define a modern gendered selfhood. And they took this sense of modern selfhood into their fight for suffrage, as well. For many newspaper women, suffrage was not the culmination of an older sentimental maternalism, but instead the political expression of their new modern gender identity.

###

There are multiple ironies in writing a history of newspaper women at a time when our great metropolitan papers are under threat. But perhaps the greatest paradox is this: The very technologies that have forced newspapers to reinvent themselves in an ongoing struggle for survival have suddenly enabled us to bring back from the dead a host of newspapers that seemed long extinct. Who knew that by the end of this project easy access online would exist to far-flung papers stretching from Galveston, Texas; to Atchison, Kansas; to Portland, Oregon, among many other places? Newspaper research has changed dramatically over the last few years.

As recently as a decade ago, a research project like this one would have been possible only by painfully scrolling through a few select newspapers on microfilm. Because most newspapers have no index (with the prominent exception of the *New York Times*), searching for articles on microfilm was the newspaper equivalent of looking for the proverbial needle in a haystack.

The emergence of newspaper databases, as well as the increasing digitization of individual newspapers, has led to a changed world of research. Through the use of databases, it is possible to discover that the articles of a newspaper woman like Eliza Putnam Heaton—who wrote not just for a Brooklyn newspaper but also for a prominent newspaper syndicate—were reprinted around the country. Suddenly what had seemed merely a local story takes on national dimensions in new ways.

But databases, as helpful as they have been, currently offer only a partial view of newspaper women's writings. Databases such as the Library of Congress's wonderful *Chronicling America* series are still in relatively early stages—they include only selected newspapers and for selected periods of time. Thus the picture of newspaper women offered here is necessarily limited by the databases available: it can be no more than a "snapshot," recording a distinct moment in the present as well as the past.

This book is a "snapshot" in other ways, as well. My interest throughout is in how newspaper women shaped public lives and embraced and shaped new public spaces. I have been less interested in pursuing topics such as beauty, fashion, decorating, and cooking for their own sakes (although clearly these so-called typical woman's page concerns are also worthy of sustained attention). I focus on newspaper women's bylined feature writing rather than their unbylined (and therefore often-impossible-to-identify) news writing. My focus on mainstream, mass-circulation newspapers has meant that ethnic, foreign-language, and "race" newspapers get short shrift here, although throughout I am attentive to the politics of race in newspaper work. Finally, this is a story of major metropolitan newspapers—especially in New York, the acknowledged center of newspaper publishing at the turn of the century. Yet thousands of local papers are also worthy of study. I am only too aware that there are many more stories of newspaper women to tell.

# # #

If we begin to think about newspapers as a richly articulated public world at the turn of the century, we can also begin to view newspaper women in a new light. We might do well to remember that the physical artifact of the newspaper—a freshly inked, perhaps somewhat smeary, black-and-white printed paper that we might have picked up at a city newsstand on a spring evening in 1900, say, before boarding an elevated train—was in fact part of a larger public process. The physical page men and women held in their hands was the result of a complicated set of actions that included the hiring of women, whether as on-staff reporters or as "special" writers; the devising of ideas for and assignment of stories; the traversing of the city to conduct interviews or to do special research; the actual writing of stories; and the rewriting of those stories in "conversation" with an editor or fellow writer— not to mention all the actions involved in the physical production and dis- tribution of the paper. At the end of that process, the paper belonged to its readers, who were invited to register their responses in letters that poured in to advice columnists and would shape new cycles of production.

When we shake the newspaper loose from the idea that it was merely a static physical location in print, but instead see that it involved mobility and circulation on a daily basis, we can begin to discover the "story behind the story" of newspaper work. We can also begin to discover the daily lives and writings of newspaper women, who created new lives in public even as they brought to life a new public world in their writings.

## chapter one

Among the Newspaper Women

As early as the mid-1880s, women began moving into metropolitan news-paper work in increasing—and increasingly visible—numbers. "There is a large number of women in New York who support themselves by writing for the newspapers, daily and weekly," wrote Martha Louise Rayne in her 1884 guide *What Can a Woman Do; or, Her Position in the Business and Literary World*.[1] The *Journalist*, a New York trade journal, estimated in 1888 that about two hundred women were working for New York newspapers alone,[2] and many commentators noted that most local papers employed one or two women during the same period. By 1889 women had become so visible in newspaper work that the *Journalist* devoted a special issue to their achievements.[3] Women were "firmly established in their position in jour-nalistic work," the same periodical commented in 1891.[4] Four years later even Charles A. Dana of the *New York Sun*, a paper known for resisting the regular employment of women, observed that "there are now a great many ladies employed on the newspapers, not only in New York city, but, I dare say, almost everywhere else. They are employed as reporters, writers, as art-ists, and they are valuable assistants in almost every department."[5]

Census figures underlined this increase in newspaper women: in 1870, only 35 women were recorded to be working as editors and reporters; in 1880, 288 women; in 1890, 888 women; and in 1900, 2,193 women out of 30,098 total journalists.[6] In twenty years women had moved from being 2.3 percent to 7.3 percent of the journalism workforce.[7] Yet such numbers considerably underrepresented the number of women working in journal-ism, as many women worked for newspapers on "space" rates rather than on salary as regular reporters.

Word traveled fast that major metropolitan newspapers were hiring women to write articles and "specials" not only on "space rates" or as "correspondents" but even sometimes as regular staff members. Beginning in the mid-1880s, newspaper women were the subject of articles that not only gave them additional publicity, but also frequently received national circulation through syndication (newspaper syndicates were themselves a new development of the mid-to-late 1880s). Fiction, too, began to incorporate the newspaper woman as a new figure of publicity. In Henry James's *The Bostonians* (1886), for example, newspaper man Matthias Pardon remarked that male newspaper correspondents "suffered a good deal to-day from the competition of the 'lady-writers': the sort of article they produced was sometimes more acceptable to the papers." Newspaper women "certainly made lovely correspondents," Pardon said. "They picked up something bright before you could turn round; there wasn't much you could keep away from them; you had to be lively if you wanted to get there first."[8] Meant as a form of satire, this commentary might have described Margherita Arlina Hamm, who worked for Boston newspapers in the mid-1880s and wrote "correspondence" from summer resorts.

A surprising number of newspaper women became public figures at the turn of the century. Women columnists discussing suffrage or female occupations—or perhaps providing "bright chat" from New York—created ongoing discussions that were picked up by a variety of newspapers around the country. Many newspaper women gained a measure of fame, themselves becoming subjects of public discussion. Indeed, the principle of publication permeated newspaper women's lives. Not only did they publish their own writings, but also in a variety of ways they themselves were published—made public. Even as they became subjects of public interest, they necessarily became part of a larger public life as they searched for work, interviewed various subjects, and themselves became the subject of newspaper profiles. To become a newspaper woman, it turned out, was a very public process.

#

"From the South and the West an army of talented and ambitious young women came on to New York," remembered newspaper woman Kate Masterson in 1902. Many women had their first taste of newspaper work on local dailies but were then drawn by the greater perceived opportunities at metropolitan newspapers, especially in New York. The newspaper woman "usually comes from the West or the South," Haryot Holt Cahoon said, and as a result of "some little experience in the office of a village paper or county weekly," she is "determined to try her skill in the field of journalism in New York."[9] Mary Gay Humphreys simply commented that women were arriving in New York "from the West in regiments, and from the South in brigades."[10]

Jennie L. Hopkins, for instance, had a successful career as a reporter in Denver before venturing east in the late 1880s. Having started with the "inevitable 'society column,'" as she noted wryly in an 1890 article for *Harper's Weekly*, she then "little by little, inch by inch" worked herself into the "position of general reporter on the staff of a large and enterprising" newspaper (the *Denver Republican*). She even "enjoyed the somewhat lurid reputation" of being the "smartest girl reporter in the Union," she said—and indeed, in late 1887 and 1888 numerous papers variously reported that Hopkins had "held her own against all the male talent in the town," was versatile enough to cover a "baseball match or a murder," and went "everywhere" and was "afraid of nobody and nothing." A description of Hopkins as the "best newspaper man in Colorado" was reprinted in papers from St. Louis to Boston to Portland (Oregon) to Milwaukee to Bangor (Maine)—there was even a mention of her in New Zealand. Eventually, however, Hopkins became one of the hundreds of women who sought to make a living in New York.[11]

Established newspaper women in New York could not help but take note of the "army" of women who were looking for newspaper work. Laura Holloway, for years employed by the *Brooklyn Eagle* and "a striking demonstration of the possibilities of a woman's success in newspaper work," reported in 1887 that she "had upwards of 200 letters from strangers, accumulated within two or three months, all asking for criticism, opinions, help toward making a living by the pen." A "large proportion" of her letters came "from the South," she explained, "partly because of the new activity of Southern women" and partly, she supposed, because she was a Southerner herself. These women were "seeking employment on the best-known magazines, weeklies, or dailies." Was there "a future for women on the newspapers?" Holloway was asked. "Certainly," she replied.[12]

A spirit of adventure animated many of the women who sought metropolitan newspaper work in New York, but financial need was also an important factor. Margherita Hamm described meeting a "tall, dark, thinly-clad woman walking relentlessly back and forth" in front of the Pulitzer building one afternoon in 1891. The woman, who had "two great tears streaking down her cheeks," told Hamm: "I am most distracted. I don't know what to do. You see, I'm from the West. I left a good position there to come here. I have been a newspaper writer for a good while, but I can't seem to do anything here." She added that "I haven't a cent to my name and I don't know what to do."[13]

"Intensely interested," Hamm asked the woman her name and "remembered of reading extensively about her work on one of the Western sheets." She suggested that the woman "take a nice dinner, get a good sleep and then make another journey of all the newspapers." Hamm concluded triumphantly that the woman had done so and "sold a good Sunday story, for which the editor gave her an order for half the money coming to her. She was delighted with her success."[14]

Florence Finch Kelly asserted that her career in journalism was "born out of economic necessity, and economic necessity kept it going."[15] Accounting for her own early search for newspaper work, Jennie Hopkins wrote that she "simply found myself obliged to earn my own living." While the "rosy lasses of the country-side wisely" preferred to "get married or teach school," she drily noted that she was "not particularly well calculated to fulfil the duties incumbent upon either position. Evidently there was but one thing to do, and that was to seek employment on newspapers."[16]

Not only did single women who needed to earn a living move into newspaper work, but so did many women who were widowed or divorced, or who were refugees from unhappy marriages. Fannie Brigham Ward, for instance, claimed to be a widow, although federal census records show that Ward was actually divorced. Rheta Dorr, who moved from Seattle to New York, left an unhappy marriage and was determined to support herself through newspaper work. Dorothy Richardson took care of a younger brother and two younger sisters in New York, as well as her mother—it is unclear what had happened to her father.[17]

The drastic economic fluctuations of the 1890s, including the panic of 1893, also forced many women to seek work. Elizabeth Garver Jordan, a successful New York newspaper woman who started out in Milwaukee, remembered that her father, a well-to-do businessman, "lost practically everything he had" in the panic; her family was suddenly dependent on her, to her obvious surprise. After "years of regarding it as a trivial detail," Jordan said, "the amount" she earned "had suddenly become important." All "that was left" to her parents "from the wreck" was their house. Although her "father was full of plans for a fresh start," the "depression was still on and life's thumb was turned down against him." His "health failed steadily," and he "never got back into the current of affairs." In this crisis Jordan asked for a significant raise from her newspaper, the *New York World*—and got it.[18]

Just as women sought newspaper work for a variety of reasons, they

Newspaper women of the New York World. *In this rare group photograph,*
Elizabeth Jordan is seated at the desk in back. In the front, from left to right, are Marie Manning
(holding a kitten), Grace Gould, Olivia Dunbar, and famous beauty editor Harriet Hubbard Ayer.
(Marie Manning Papers, Sophia Smith Collection, Smith College)

also came from a variety of backgrounds. Many were turn-of-the-century
"New Women"—that is, they were recognizably middle-class, embraced
having an occupation, lived independently rather than with their families of origin, and celebrated being able to explore the public spaces of the
city as they went about their work. After all, "it was inevitable," Mary Gay
Humphreys wrote of women's new working lives, "that in time ambition
should quicken, and that the desire to try conclusions with the great world
should stir in many breasts." In earning her own living a woman gained
"the realization of independence and power," she noted in her 1896 article
on "Women Bachelors in New York."[19]

College women were especially interested in newspaper work. In 1893 Margherita Hamm noted that "I was up at Vassar College this week and some of the girls whom I met, hearing that I was a journalist besides a college graduate, gathered round me and asked me so many questions about newspaper work that I almost wished I didn't know anything of it."[20] The movement of young college-educated women into journalism had become so prevalent by 1898 that Anne O'Hagan of the *New York Journal* reported receiving a questionnaire from the Association of Collegiate Alumnae asking, "How many women journalists are there?" "What dignities have they attained?" "Are many of them managing editors or city editors?" "What advice should be given to young women ambitious to be journalists?"[21] Immediately after college, many women, such as future author Olivia Dunbar (who graduated from Smith), went to New York to find newspaper work. This trend only intensified in the first decade of the twentieth century.

The late 1880s and 1890s, in fact, marked a significant generational shift in newspaper work, as "new" newspaper women began to replace established writers of an earlier age, some of whom had been born in the 1820s and thus were in their fifties or sixties by 1885. Dynamic young newspaper women like Elizabeth Jordan began to speak with reverence of famous "pioneers in the work"—most notably Jennie June (Jane Cunningham Croly), who at the time of the Civil War had "climbed the dingy steps that led to the editor and fame and a 'new field for women.'"[22] Croly was far from a relic in the 1880s and 1890s—her famous "Jennie June" column was still widely syndicated—but the rising generation began to treat her as someone whose day was now past. Helen M. Winslow, for instance, paid tribute to Croly in 1896 by conceding that "the newspaper woman is not entirely a modern innovation." But Winslow insisted that "the evolution of the woman journalist, pure and simple, was left for this age—women regularly on a daily newspaper; women to take editorial and reportorial positions and stand side by side with the men with whom they compete."[23]

This generational shift among newspaper women sometimes excited controversy: Margherita Hamm, already an experienced reporter at twenty, was indignant when she heard a speaker at a woman's club meeting say that young newspaper women destroyed "the eminent standard of newspaper women's work" on "account of their age." "You must take this for granted," Hamm asserted, that the woman who spoke was "old" and had become "embittered on that account."[24]

Hamm felt it was her "duty to deny such maligning statements." "No woman," she argued, "be she as young and fair and beautiful and as marvelously fascinating as Venus," could "earn her way in newspaperdom without real merit." While Hamm "freely" gave "great credit to the elder women" who had been "few and far between" in past years, she also gave "the greatest possible credit to the young newspaper women of to-day." They not only elevated the profession but also adorned it "with their ability, scope and experience of human nature." The young newspaper woman was "pretty, stylish, brave, courageous, dauntless, the personification of personal honor and shrewdness."[25]

Younger women began to chafe at what they considered the old-fashioned standards for membership in "Jennie June's" Woman's Press Club, founded in 1889, which included some women who dabbled in poetry, wrote only occasionally for magazines, or had engaged in "press work" by once having published a "sketch" or two—but were not involved in daily newspaper work.[26] In an 1887 article on "Women in Journalism," Ida M. Tarbell had ridiculed the notion that "a good journalist is one who is able to say bright things, make rhymes, and write essays. Now 'essay writing,'" she believed, "however admirable, will not make a journalist."[27] Newspaper women began what became a perennial, long-term lament: "Real" newspaper women needed a professional organization of their own, not a club devoted to "tea and tattle."[28]

Was a woman who worked for the newspapers a "newspaper woman" or a "journalist"? As Helen Winslow made clear, the term "newspaper woman" had particular resonance in a turn-of-the-century world beginning to professionalize through courses in, and schools of, journalism. "There is a story of a certain editor who was asked to define the difference between a 'newspaper man' and a 'journalist,'" Winslow said. "He replied that the newspaper man was one who had worked for years on the press, writing editorials, criticisms, literary articles, and everything else that goes to make up a great paper; while a journalist was a young man fresh from college, with no experience of his own and usually too conceited to profit by that of others. After he has worked a few years, gets some of this self-esteem rubbed off, and learns to estimate himself at something like his true value, he becomes a plain, ordinary newspaper man." The "same definition," Winslow noted, "will apply to women with equal force. It is the young girl fresh from school who insists upon her title of journalist; the woman who has labored side by side with men for years and whose work will stand the strain of comparison is content to be a 'newspaper woman.'"[29] Women embraced the term "newspaper woman" precisely for its lack of pretension, the sense it gave them that they belonged to the real, gritty world of the newspaper. They had pride as "newspaper women" in joining a long-lived fraternity of men.

Younger women also pushed for a new definition of who qualified to call themselves "newspaper women." The "crucial test," Elizabeth Jordan declared, was whether women were able to "earn their living with their pens." There was "a distinction between newspaper writing and writing for the newspapers, and the young lady who 'does a little space-work' in the intervals of her social or business engagements" could not be regarded as a bona fide newspaper woman. Those who could be considered "newspaper women in the best sense of the words," she said, held "staff positions on journals of good standing, or they have had experience which fits them for such positions."[30]

Of course, Jordan made these observations from the inner sanctum of her own staff position on the *New York World*: she had quickly risen from "all-round reportorial duty" in 1890 to "editor of the woman's and child's pages of the *Sunday World*."[31] Energetic, indomitable, with obvious executive abilities and striking self-confidence, Jordan would later become the editor of *Harper's Bazar* and was the author of numerous novels and plays.

But most newspaper women did not have regular, salaried positions on newspapers; many of them moved rapidly in and out of newspaper work, patching together writing careers. Nor were they all college graduates or recognizably middle-class. There were several "bohemian" routes to newspaper jobs that make class identifications slippery. Zoe Anderson Norris, for instance, came from Kentucky to New York and wrote occasional urban sketches and features for the *New York Times* in the early 1900s. She was well known as a New York bohemian—although, like most newspaper women, she is little remembered today. Norris published the fascinating and idiosyncratic radical magazine *East Side* at the turn of the century and formed a club of like-minded bohemians she called the "Ragged Edge Klub"; it was composed of "writers of radical tendencies and their sympathizers, who met monthly at downtown restaurants." Norris was distinctly *not* a professionalizing "New Woman."[32]

Another "bohemian" pathway into newspaper work was through acting. Several prominent newspaper women in the 1880s and 1890s, including Viola Roseboro' and Winifred Bonfils Black, who used the pen name Annie Laurie, were members of touring companies before they wrote for newspapers. Kate Field, who worked for a variety of papers until starting her own weekly, *Kate Field's Washington*, was both an actress and a lecturer at various points in her career. And a number of famous full-time actresses— including Olive Logan, Lillian Russell, and May Irwin—parlayed their theatrical careers into ongoing newspaper columns.[33]

While some women moved into journalism from acting, others took the opposite path, deciding to become actresses or "elocutionists" (dramatic lecturers) after a stint of newspaper work. "She is an all-round good newspaper woman," Margherita Hamm noted of "Marjory Daw" (Grace Drew) in one column, "although she has of late taken to the stage."[34] The *New York World* announced in 1892 that "Mrs. Margaret M. Merrill, the well-known journalist, has decided to give up newspaper work and enter the field of elocution."[35] The fluid connection between acting and the public drama of newspaper work was clear to many women: after all, going "undercover" was not just an attractive alternative to the theater—it *was* a form of theater, albeit played before a wider public audience and situated on the street rather than in a bricks-and-mortar theater. This connection between newspaper work and acting even took an institutional form in the Professional Woman's League, which included both prominent female journalists and actresses.[36] The class status of many of these women defies easy description, reminding us that the term "middle class" was not yet fixed at the turn of the century.

While middle-class and "bohemian" women moved in and out of newspaper work in the 1880s and 1890s, only occasionally were working-class women able to find jobs at major metropolitan newspapers. Lack of education, lack of resources (including, for factory workers, the time to write), and discrimination by the press were all powerful barriers. For working-class immigrant women, language could be an additional hurdle—they were more likely to be employed by ethnic newspapers (most of whose stories remain to be told). A notable exception was Eva Valesh, a prominent labor activist and speaker who moved from a Wisconsin newspaper, to the American Federation of Labor in Washington, D.C., to a stint as "all-round" reporter for the *New York Journal*.[37]

A rare working-class newspaper woman who briefly crossed the line between ethnic and mass-circulation newspapers was Rose Pastor Stokes, who began working for the *New York Jewish Daily News* in 1903. There she produced urban sketches and columns that included "Just between Us Girls," an advice column she wrote in the character of "Zelda" (see Chapters 3 and 6). Stokes achieved a striking measure of success at this ethnic newspaper, but her writings became of interest to mass-circulation metropolitan papers only when she became engaged to millionaire James Graham Phelps Stokes in the spring of 1905 and thus enacted in real life the working-girl fantasy—stuff of dozens of dime novels—of marriage to a rich man.[38] Dubbed the "Ghetto Girl," Stokes became a press sensation across the country. The *New York World* quickly hired her to write an "exclusive" series on her life; it also republished several of the short stories she had written for the *Jewish Daily News*. But this interest was short-lived, and in some sense

Stokes is the exception that proves the rule. Aside from Stokes and Eva Valesh (see Chapter 6), both newspaper women who identified themselves as working-class (Stokes's autobiography was even titled *I Belong to the Working Class*), working-class women remained few and far between on metropolitan newspapers.[39]

Still, there were no absolute barriers to working-class women on mass-circulation newspapers. There *were*, however, absolute (if unstated) barriers to African American women on the major metropolitan papers. Initially, in the late 1880s and early 1890s, it seemed that the burgeoning world of the metropolitan press might be open to all women; after all, in 1889 the *Journalist* ran a special feature on "colored women journalists" as part of a larger issue on women in journalism. In the late 1880s Gertrude Bustill Mossell wrote optimistically of the many opportunities for African American women, including on white newspapers. Her *New York Age* woman's columns represented the first woman's department in an African American newspaper. Then, too, Margherita Hamm, in her first column on newspaper women in 1891, mentioned that "the cleverest colored woman in newspaper circles in Boston is Miss Lillian Lewis," who edited a society page. This notice of a "colored woman" seemed to signal that there could be room for some African American women on mainstream newspapers—or, at the very least, acknowledgment of their work in a wider public arena.[40]

But this was the only mention of "colored women journalists" Hamm ever made. After 1891 the *Journalist*, and Hamm herself, were silent on the subject of African American women journalists—even Ida B. Wells's famous antilynching newspaper campaign received no mention whatsoever. This did not mean, of course, that black newspaper women were themselves silent. During the 1880s and 1890s a prominent group of African American women contributed to race newspapers: among them were Ida B. Wells, Victoria Earle Matthews, Gertrude Bustill Mossell, Mary Church Terrell, Fannie Barrier Williams, and Josephine St. Pierre Ruffin, the founder of the *Woman's Era*—the first national African American women's newspaper. But it was impossible for these talented women to obtain regular positions on metropolitan mass-circulation dailies.

It was also difficult for African American women to publish articles in the mainstream press. In her memoir *A Colored Woman in a White World*, Mary Church Terrell remembered the extraordinary trouble she had in placing her articles on the "Race Problem" in mass-circulation newspapers at the turn of the century. Though Boston papers occasionally printed her pieces, the *Chicago Tribune* held on to her article "How, Why, When and Where Black Becomes White" for "a year before it was released." When she asked that the article be returned so she could place it elsewhere, the editor told her he intended to print it, but "he would have to wait a bit" until "the psychological moment arrived because the paper had a large southern clientele which he did not want to offend."[41]

In an 1886 column titled "Some Painful Truths," Gertrude Bustill Mossell explored the many barriers she faced in newspaper work: "Said a gentleman to me a few days ago, a white man, editor of one of the white weeklies, 'I find a great difficulty in disposing of articles relating to the Negro, especially when the showing is creditable to him. A colored editor warned me that this would be my experience.'" Mossell related that "a few weeks ago I prepared an article on the Negro in our higher grade white institutions, and sent the manuscript to a western paper that occasionally prints my articles. It was returned with the following reply: 'I don't believe the "niggers" are making any such progress, and I decline to print the article.'" Another time, when she applied "for reporting on a daily in a certain city," the editor said that "'we have a full quota of our own reporters,'" but if she could tell him "'where we can find a voodoo doctor,'" she would be paid just as though she had reported it.[42]

Regardless of its political affiliation, "a white man's paper is for the white man of whatever party, more than for the Negro," Mossell asserted. Editors gave her the runaround, telling her "'I cannot find that article. It is well-written and readable. I will gladly give you an introduction to such an editor of Weekly, Sunday, Daily, Monthly, etc.'" They said, "'If you can make the matter local in some way; if you can bring out more humorous points, it might be available.'" "The fact is," Mossell concluded, "if we could and would continually write columns of scandals on our own society, or ridicule our race, should show them up in their ignorance and superstitions, we could find a ready sale; but the facts of value, the truths about the white man's treatment of us can find no sale with large numbers of white editors."[43]

Given that newspapers were "looked upon as much as a matter of amusement as instruction" the "spicy scandal, the comic story, the old story of Negro superstition, ignorance and comicality" were a "better paying investment than the sermon or the lecture of some colored divines, or the moral truths enunciated by some enthusiasts, or the great reform questions of the day." The "moral of all this is that there are certain facts of value to the colored people known by them, and that can be written by them alone. There is no white editor so liberal, or that possesses so liberal a mass of readers that he can afford to publish these articles." It was thus doubly important that African American newspapers continue to develop, especially "to secure to ourselves the services of the young, ambitious, talented ones of our race."[44]

Nevertheless, in late 1886 Mossell thought it was at least conceivable that white newspapers would be more and more receptive to African Americans. "The white papers in all the cities are opening up and soliciting specials and reports from the colored writers," she said. But as the cultural politics of Jim Crow intensified in the late 1880s and early 1890s, there were fewer, not more, opportunities on the white metropolitan press for black men and women. Only race newspapers were consistently open to articles by African American women—and there, black women sometimes faced the same kind of discrimination from male editors that white women encountered on mass-circulation papers.[45]

Yet this by no means finishes the story of the relationship between African American newspaper women and the mass-circulation metropolitan press—as the career of Ida B. Wells showed. Wells's ability to use the power of mainstream newspaper publicity in her antilynching campaign is well known—especially her clever strategy of rousing the English press on the subject of Northern acquiescence in American lynching, forcing many Northerners for the first time to account for their lack of outrage—or even simple response—to Southern lynching. But Wells was not the only accomplished newspaper woman to deploy the publicity of the mainstream press. We need to reassess African American women's relationships to mainstream newspapers by acknowledging that, through a variety of protests, they were able to be in *dialogue* with the mainstream press—even as they were shut out from writing their own articles for metropolitan newspapers. Thus we find Fannie Barrier Williams—whose work appeared in a variety of black periodicals as well as the *Woman's Era*—as the subject of a number of *Chicago Daily Tribune* articles during the 1894–95 controversy over her proposed membership in the Chicago Woman's Club (see Chapter 2). We find Victoria Earle Matthews the subject of an extended 1895 interview in the *New York Times* about the Malby Law (requiring hotels to accept African American patrons).[46] We find Ida B. Wells-Barnett writing a heated letter to the *Chicago Daily Inter Ocean* in response to a column by prominent Chicago newspaper woman Mary H. Krout (see Chapter 7).[47] And we find Josephine St. Pierre Ruffin the subject of respectful profiles at the time of her exclusion from the General Federation of Women's Clubs in 1900. These were fleeting moments of public exposure, to be sure, but they remind us that for some African American women, one means of "writing for the papers" was through acts of resistance that drew attention and caused *other* newspaper men and women to write articles in which their views gained publicity. African American newspaper women's acts of resistance are an important part of the larger story of newspaper women's creation of public lives.

# # #

Even for racially privileged white women, breaking into metropolitan newspaper work was not easy. Women often started by peddling individual articles from newspaper to newspaper, hoping that some editor might buy one on "space rates." They sought commissions for "specials," which would only be paid for if the article was deemed acceptable. If they sold an article, their reward was to begin the process all over again. The successful newspaper woman—one able to support herself by her work—clearly needed a distinctly entrepreneurial spirit as she traversed the public spaces of cities. She also required knowledge of the various interrelated "markets" emerging in the turn-of-the-century newspaper world.

A number of guidebooks and manuals gave would-be female reporters advice in the late 1880s and 1890s, revealing a widespread national interest in newspaper work. But much of the advice they offered was too general to be of practical use. For instance, the chapter on "Newspaper Women" in *Occupations for Women* (1897), by Frances Willard (head of the Woman's Christian Temperance Union), stressed the importance of good work habits. ("You must prove your mettle before you are admitted fully to the inner circle and recognized as an accepted worker.") Willard warned "girls" that they must avoid sensational "stunt" work. ("If any girl who ever reads this is ever tempted to make her entrance into newspaper work through this unclean path, let her put aside the temptation and give up her fondest hopes of becoming a newspaper woman if they are to be attained at such a cost.")[48] But her counsel did not solve the problem of how to find work.

For ideas on how to obtain a job, would-be newspaper women were better served by reading the many fictional day-in-the-life stories of newspaper women that populated newspapers and magazines at the turn of the century. Even when written with a cautionary moral, such stories often took the reader imaginatively through a newspaper woman's day, step by step. Many of them were written by newspaper women and published on the woman's page of newspapers. Newspaper women also gave specific information about their work, including pay, in detailed "newspaper woman" articles.[49]

The truth was that newspaper women usually needed to cobble together a variety of assignments to make ends meet. This was evident even in a *Journalist* profile of Margherita Hamm that was meant to stress her success in journalism; the piece inadvertently revealed just how much sheer scrambling was involved in newspaper work. Hamm had first done "all sorts of newspaper work in Boston, from society news to police assignments, and after several years of this best-of-all training she came to New York and was taken on the staff of the World." (That staff position did not last, for reasons we cannot know—although, intriguingly, Hamm once commented that "I have nothing to love the World for, in fact there are many unpleasant incidents in my career for which I can thank the World.")[50] Since then, the *Journalist* noted, she "has done special work for most of the New York papers, writes a regular weekly letter for several Western dailies, conducted the women's department of the United Press Literary Budget, and has charge of the woman's pages of *The Journalist*." Yet it also pointed out: "This does not, by any means, cover the amount of work which she turns out every week, for with true newspaper instinct she catches a good story wherever she sees it, and places it in the most appropriate market."[51]

Hamm's newspaper work, in other words, involved selling articles to various New York papers (or being given assignments by them) in the form of individual "specials," writing her weekly column for the *Journalist*, and contracting with various "Western dailies" that were willing to buy a weekly "letter" from her directly. All of these activities clearly involved a public entrepreneurship of the self as she sought the "most appropriate market"— no wonder Hamm once stated that newspaper women needed to be "egotists," or that Elizabeth Jordan said that the woman with "little push" would "stand a hard chance of fame or money" in New York."[52] The need for "pluck" or "push" was emphasized by many newspaper women.

Rheta Childe Dorr, who later became a prominent labor activist, suffragist, and author, vividly remembered her early struggles to find a secure newspaper position. In the late 1880s and early 1890s Dorr had briefly lived in New York, selling "little newspaper stories" and a few fashion articles to the American Press Association (APA), a newspaper syndicate.[53] By 1893, married and living in the West (first Nebraska, then Washington State), she "sought to get into syndicate work again." Dorr wrote to Charles Dayton, "the only person now on the American Press who will be likely to remember me," in the hope that various topics related to Puget Sound could "furnish material for a few first-class articles."[54] Syndicate work was one way she could continue doing newspaper work—and earn some money—even while living away from New York. Eventually she had a "small success" selling stories of the Klondike to New York newspapers.

Having recently separated from her husband, and with a two-year-old child to support, Dorr moved back to New York in the autumn of 1898, determined to "try for a place in the newspaper world," she later recalled. Because the *New York Sun* had published some of her Alaska stories, she first went to the "dingy old Sun Building" and "was received in a small, dark, airless hallway where a young man in pink shirt-sleeves and nose-glasses informed me in tones of finality that the 'Sun' had no women on its staff and never expected to have."[55] (Nine years later the *Sun* continued to hold fast to its no-woman policy: when Agnes Ernst, fresh out of college, applied for a "regular job" in 1907, she was also told "We don't employ women on the *Sun*.")[56] At the *New York Evening Post* Dorr "had even a chillier reception. Mr. Clark was the most pessimistic newspaper man I ever met in my life. He despised his profession, or said he did," and "as for helping a woman to get a job in the accursed trade he would rather die."[57]

Nevertheless, Dorr "did not falter" until she had "visited every newspaper, morning and afternoon, in New York, and had been given to understand that Park Row was a masculine monopoly and meant to remain so as long as possible." While she knew there were women in the newspaper world, she wondered "with what burglar tools they had broken in." "I was appalled," she later wrote. "On the other hand, I was enlightened. I found out exactly the place women held in the social scheme. Not pretty girls, young ladies, protected wives, but women. They had no place at all."[58]

Realizing that she would be unable to get a staff position on a newspaper, Dorr determined to try to sell stories on space rates instead. After all, even the young man at the *Sun* had told her that "if women sent in contributions they were, of course, considered." Like numerous other women in New York, she began making the rounds of papers "day after day, week after week," trying to sell ideas for stories to Sunday and city editors whom she never saw, since she was relegated to dealing with an office boy. "I sent in a printed slip with my name and under the cold phrase 'Nature of Business,' the hopeful word 'story.' After that it was a matter of waiting in the unventilated, electrically lighted anteroom sacred to the office-boy until a supercilious youth appeared to represent the great invisible." Occasionally, Dorr would sell a news tip, but a salaried reporter would be sent out instead of her to "get the real story."[59]

"As the months wore on" and Dorr continued "her insistent siege," she began to have, "once in a while, a bit of luck." She sold a column a week of "fashion stuff to be made into boiler-plate matter for country newspapers" to the APA syndicate. She worked with a news photographer, supplying text for pictures that appeared on Sunday pages. Dorr finally received a fortunate break when she successfully managed a job supervising photographers of Teddy Roosevelt on the day of his nomination to the vice presidency.

On the very next day she had her "first salaried job on Newspaper Row," to "boss" a cameraman in order to get daily news photographs during the 1900 campaign. After "learning every day more and more about the newspaper game," she "felt confident now that I should get in"—and in the fall of 1900, she landed a staff position on the woman's page of the *Evening Post*. "At last I was a real newspaper-woman," she declared, "not an unwelcome hanger-on in editorial anterooms, but a reporter with a desk and a salary."[60]

That desk and salary represented a victory even though Dorr was on the "woman's page" rather than a regular "all round" reporter. And no doubt her desk was away from the "regular" newspaper men. Women's low status was, in fact, reflected in the spatial arrangements of many newspapers, which sought to maintain women's "privacy." At the *New York Sun*, Dorr noted, the one woman reporter was never "allowed to enter the city-room." Instead, "she got her assignments and wrote her copy in the office-boy's dark cubbyhole."[61] Marie Manning joked about inhabiting the "Hen Coop" at the *New York Journal*, a room at some distance from the city room where regular reporters sat.[62]

Like Dorr, most women began their newspaper careers in some way connected with the woman's page—one of only two departments of the newspaper where women could rise to editorships. The other department managed the new Sunday sections of many newspapers. Women were able to become Sunday editors there in part because these sections contained woman's pages, society pages, book reviews, and interviews—all features often assigned to women. As Anne O'Hagan noted in 1898, only a few women were in "small executive positions on daily papers," and they were either in charge of the woman's page—"sacred to currant jam and current gossip concerning subjects of no importance," she commented sarcastically—or a section of a Sunday supplement.[63] O'Hagan concluded that newspaper work did not "offer advancement sufficient to allure an ambitious and clever woman." There "are no managing editors among women," she said. "There are no city editors; there are no night editors. There is a rumor that on one Chicago paper—the *Post*, if I recall aright—a woman is employed as an editorial writer. With that the whole sisterhood comforts itself. There is a remembrance which it hugs to its heart—that once a woman was a Sunday editor on a New York paper. And it refuses to go on and admit that her day of glory was brief, that she now writes fashion articles for a syndicate, and that the paper that made the experiment was itself an experiment that failed."[64]

Confined to the Hen Coop, paid substantially less than men, often asked to cover news stories such as murders only in order to get the supposed

"Woman's Angle," women reporters, perhaps not surprisingly, tended to be committed suffragists and, later, feminists. "We three of the Hen Coop were all ardent feminists," Marie Manning said, adding, "You would think [women's] spirits must have been permanently broken by the slavery they have been subjected to, but nothing of the sort."[65] Manning could not quite hide her bitterness over the treatment of women reporters under the playful humor of her memoir. Dorr did not even try. "I used to watch the men on Saturday mornings, when the pay envelopes were handed around, counting out substantial sums to send to the bank," she remembered, and "I repeated to myself like a lesson: 'This is a man's world. You are an accident in it.' But something deep within me said, 'No! No!'"[66]

Even if a newspaper woman obtained a regular staff position, that *still* did not guarantee regular pay in the early 1890s. The *World* paid many men and women in the form of space rates rather than salaries—thus generously rewarding those workers who produced the most quantities of column inches, since pay was literally measured by the inch. (Newspaper men and women pasted their columns into "strings" to determine how many inches they had produced.) Not surprisingly, this system tended to reward top male reporters who received multiple assignments and were able to produce large quantities of column inches.[67] Newspaper women were rarely so lucky. When hired by the *World*, Marie Manning was given a choice of pay by salary or space rates—and naïvely chose the latter, in the belief that space rates would pay more than the small salary she was offered. She was wrong, she noted ruefully, about the "quicksands of space."[68]

It was true that space rates—being paid "not by the week, but by the piece, to speak in jobbing terms," as Anne O'Hagan put it—resulted in highly unpredictable and fluctuating pay. "The average rate a column" in 1898 was "about seven dollars," O'Hagan said, but she also pointed out that "a column a day is an unusually good allowance." More likely, "many days—sometimes whole weeks" would pass "without the space writer's happening upon a 'story' worth half that allowance in the paper."[69] No wonder that Lida Rose McCabe asserted, "Women dislike space work." In McCabe's view, women preferred "the certainty of a small competency to the uncertainty of large promise." Still, space work was usually a necessity. "Staff positions are rarely won by outsiders," McCabe said, "without a course of training in space work."[70]

The earnings of regular female staff members varied widely, as did their estimates of other newspaper women's earnings. In 1891 McCabe claimed that "there are several women now engaged in legitimate journalistic work in New York city who earn from fifty dollars a week to five and six thousand

of her need to remain in the South while she convalesced, is a chilling reminder that there were no financial safety nets for newspaper women when they became ill.[84]

We do not know whether the APA hired Fannie Thomas that summer, or what she managed to do if they did not hire her. Nor do we know whether the association gave assignments to Emily Verdery-Battey, though she did engage in newspaper work again. We do know, however, that syndicates were an important source of work for many women, especially those who had already gained a foothold in the newspaper world. Both Rheta Dorr and Margherita Hamm worked for newspaper syndicates intermittently: Dorr wrote "fashion stuff" for the APA, and Hamm provided material for the woman's department of the United Press Literary Budget. In the 1880s and 1890s prominent newspaper syndicates like the McClure Syndicate, the Bacheller Syndicate, and the APA, along with a number of smaller, often short-lived syndicates, provided "ready-plate" material or ready-made sheets that could simply be inserted in local papers around the country that subscribed to their services. Although they are most known for their syndication of fiction by authors such as Robert Louis Stevenson and Henry James, syndicates also supplied "woman's page" or "woman's department" material as part of their services—and as a result gave numerous newspaper women employment.[85]

Syndication operated as a new force in American newspapers at the turn of the century, allowing women as well as men a public forum beyond just one paper. A wide range of writers on women's topics first developed a local reputation in New York, then achieved a measure of national fame through syndication. Eliza Putnam Heaton, for example, was among an early group of newspaper women who were able to take advantage of the sudden rise in newspaper syndicates in the mid-to-late 1880s. The same article by Heaton might appear not just in her home paper, the *Brooklyn Times*, but also in Atchison, Kansas; Houston, Texas; Milwaukee; and Los Angeles. As one contemporary profile of Heaton put it, "Her entrance into the journalistic profession was almost coincidental with the rise to prominence of the newspaper syndicate idea and she was soon under a regular engagement with one of the leading syndicates"; this "gave Mrs. Heaton a much larger circle of readers than any one newspaper could afford."[86] The weekly columns of a writer like Heaton created a newly visible world of women within a public world of print.

Several syndicates hired women as editors to run their "woman's departments," thus giving newspaper women an additional public role. Eliza Archard Conner, for instance, was head of the woman's department of the APA; several letters to her indicate that she acted as the fulcrum in a wider public community of newspaper women. In October 1893 Ida Husted Harper, who had previously been a newspaper editor in Indianapolis and would become increasingly prominent through her writings about suffrage (among them, a biography of Susan B. Anthony), wrote to "My Dear Mrs. Conner" to ask for help in obtaining newspaper work. At the time Harper was living near Stanford University to be close to her daughter, a sophomore in college. "Will you add to your former kindness," Harper asked, "by asking Mr. Hill" if he could use articles about Stanford or an upcoming "'Midwinter Fair'?"[87] A few weeks later Harper wrote to Mr. Hill himself to say that she had received his letter and would send him "something in regard to the Midwinter Fair that I think will suit you."[88] Clearly Eliza Conner had smoothed her way; a large syndicate such as the APA allowed Conner to be both a clearinghouse for and a builder of public community among newspaper women nationwide. At the same time, her own syndicated articles reached a wide audience through local papers around the country.

But it was not just the major syndicates—like McClure, Bacheller, and the APA—that broke new ground in the concept of syndication at the turn of the century. Newspaper women themselves were important innovators in this area. Jennie June Croly was widely acknowledged to be one of the pioneers of the "syndication idea," having contracted to send the same weekly "letter" to a group of newspapers nationwide.[89] Fannie B. Ward boasted in a letter to her friend Clara Barton that she had some forty-two newspapers lined up for her travel articles—all obtained on her own. Self-syndication was an idea that a number of newspaper women used to establish writing careers that would pay the bills.[90]

When Ida Tarbell decided in 1891, at the age of thirty-three, to leave her editorial position at the *Chautauquan* magazine and embark on the great adventure of moving to Paris and attempting to make a living as a writer, she saw newspaper syndication as a crucial part of her "Plan." Tarbell wanted to write for magazines but thought the best way to achieve that goal was first to become self-supporting through writing newspaper articles. "I plunged gaily into planning for a career in journalism, self-directed, free-lance journalism," she remembered. "Surely I could find subjects enough in Paris to write about, subjects that would interest American newspapers. We were in the thick of a great agitation over the condition and the conduct of American cities. The *Chautauquan* had touched it occasionally. How did Paris keep house? I planned a syndicate of my own which would answer all questions."[91]

Tarbell had no experience as a newspaper writer. "Outside of my very limited experience on *The Chautauquan*," she said, "I knew nothing of the writing and publishing world, had literally no acquaintance among editors." But that did not deter her. If she "was not a writer," she had "certain qualifications for the practice of the modest kind of journalism on which" she had decided. She counted "no little on my habit of planning in advance what I was going to do," she said, and had "a strong conviction that a plan of my own was worth more than any plan which was made for me."[92]

As soon as Tarbell reached Paris she began writing newspaper articles: "If I did not have the documents to prove it," she later recalled, "I would not believe today that just a week after arriving, and in spite of the excitement and fatigue of settling, I had written and mailed two newspaper articles." Her doubts about whether she could "make something" from her articles were "set at rest some six weeks" after her arrival, when she "received a check" for her "first syndicate article—$5.00." It "was quickly followed by checks from two more of the six papers to which I had submitted my syndicate proposition—50 percent was not a bad percentage and they were good papers, the Pittsburgh *Dispatch*, the Cincinnati *Times-Star* and the Chicago *Tribune*. These three papers remained faithful to me until the election of 1892 compelled them to give all their space to politics, so they explained."[93] Self-syndication could give entrepreneurial women like Tarbell substantial freedom in devising their own writing careers.

Isabel Mallon, famous in her day for her "Bab's Babble" columns, syndicated herself by sending her popular weekly "letter" to a variety of newspapers. Her entrepreneurial story, and others like it, however, were later drowned out by the claims of male syndicators like Edward Bok, who after a brief career as a fledgling syndicator became the famous editor of the *Ladies' Home Journal*. In his remarkably self-serving memoir, Bok described having seen a "bright letter of New York gossip published in the *New York Star*, called 'Bab's Babble.'" Bok "saw the possibility of syndicating this item as a woman's letter from New York, as "he instinctively realized that women all over the country would read it." He "sought out the author, made arrangements with her," and the letter "was sent out to a group of papers." It was an "instantaneous success," and on the strength of this "a syndicate of ninety newspapers was quickly organized." What Bok failed to mention was that Mallon had already sold her columns to various newspapers, thus syndicating herself, when she accepted Bok's offer.[94]

Bok later hired Isabel Mallon to write the maternal "Ruth Ashmore" column for the *Ladies' Home Journal*. The differences between Mallon's "Bab's" columns and her "Ruth Ashmore" columns are instructive, reminding us that newspaper women created a variety of public personae in print, often shifting the personality of their writings to suit the market demands of differing publications—yet another crucial reason not to ignore the world of women's writings in newspapers. Indeed, it can be instructive to compare the humorous, splashy, sometimes racy writings of their newspaper columns to the more careful bromides of the pieces they published in genteel magazines. As the writer of the "Bab's Babble" columns, for instance, Isabel Mallon was witty, urbane, tongue-in-cheek. But in her "Ruth Ashmore" columns for the *Ladies' Home Journal* she assumed a more conservative, motherly persona.

Newspaper woman and author Zona Gale, for one, expressed astonishment that "Bab" and "Ruth Ashmore" were one and the same person. In a humorous column written while a newspaper woman in Milwaukee (she later went to New York to work for the *World*), Gale asked, "What can the young women who have been wont to subscribe themselves 'One of your girls,' or 'Anxious inquirer' or 'Violet,' and to proceed at length with some earnest solicitation as to their mentor's belief in the propriety of young women under 25 years receiving callers or presents or appearing alone in public—what can they say when it is borne in upon them that they have been trusting implicitly in the dicta of 'Bab'? Their ideal of propriety and prudishness whose very name created an imagery of forty years and black-bowed spectacles and caraway seeds to resolve itself into Bab—flippant and plain spoken and in some opinions very, very young!" Gale concluded that Mallon's "double role gives her credit for no small versatility and it is easy to see which vein of comment and opinion is lyrical, so to speak, and which is assumed."[95]

As Isabel Mallon's example shows, newspapers sometimes provided the opportunity for women to write in a bolder, more forthright, more radical style than that allowed by genteel magazines. We should acknowledge, however, that for some women the opposite was the case. While Ida Tarbell—soon to become one of the great muckrakers of the early twentieth century with her damning study of Standard Oil for *McClure's* magazine—published a variety of interesting newspaper stories on life in Paris during 1891–92, she also produced a few more conventional articles. Most surprising of these is what seems to have been her last piece as a self-syndicator. Her March 1893 illustrated article, "Egg-Shell Trifles: Pretty Things to Make for Easter," described some "charming egg-shell presents" that "skillful" French children had made and that "children anywhere" might make for Easter.[96] Even Ida Tarbell, it turned out, wrote for the woman's page.

On the other hand, a few newspaper women chose not to publish in magazines precisely because they thought most magazines were dull, conventional. In 1906 an interviewer asked Nixola Greeley-Smith, a *New York World* columnist and one of the most prominent newspaper women of the early 1900s, why she did not "break into the magazines" rather than work in "yellow journalism." Her answer was decisive: "Because I prefer to do journalism, cream, ecru, yellow or the deepest saffron, to the dim colored, drab gray hack work of the professional magazinist. Indeed, I consider myself a much more dignified person, and certainly an infinitely more useful member of human society, writing as I do for a live, up-to-date, honest newspaper than I could possibly feel were I manufacturing predigested fiction and doggerel such as litter the pages of the American magazines."[97]

# # #

Nixola Greeley-Smith was one of dozens of newspaper women who themselves became the subjects of press scrutiny and publicity at the turn of the century. Articles about newspaper women proliferated in both newspapers and magazines — and were often written by other newspaper women. Offering extensive advice about newspaper work, such articles connected newspaper women with a wider reading public of would-be women journalists.

Many newspaper women warned that their work was arduous and physically demanding. A newspaper woman put in "ten hours a day, six days a week, and fifty weeks a year; that is, 3,000 hours a year," said Anne O'Hagan. "She must be willing to wade through snow, to swim, if need be, overflowing gutters, to face cutting winds, to tramp in dog day heat, and at the end to write as sparklingly as nature and education permit."[98] Ida Husted Harper agreed: "The woman who desires to be a newspaper reporter should ask herself if she is able to toil from eight to fifteen hours a day, seven days in the week." "Is she willing to take whatever assignment may be given; to go wherever sent, to accomplish what she is delegated to do, at whatever risk or rebuff or inconvenience; to brave all kinds of weather?"[99] "That such an occupation requires women of strong physical and nervous constitution is sufficiently apparent," O'Hagan concluded.[100]

Such warnings carried a double message. At a time when a new athleticism was increasingly celebrated among women as well as men, the perceived hardships and possible adventures of newspaper work were part of its appeal. Elizabeth Jordan made this clear in her short story collection, *Tales of the City Room*. Jordan's fictional alter ego Ruth Herrick was the New York "Searchlight's" "leading woman" and a "resolute young person," who enjoyed a "good tramp" and "swinging rapidly across" Washington Square on her way home from Newspaper Row. Not only was there "keen satisfaction to her in the working up of a 'big story,'" but also Ruth "enjoyed the journeys and experiences it frequently included, and the strange characters among whom it often led her. Neither the experiences nor the characters were always wholly agreeable, but she never complained."[101] Through the character Ruth Herrick, Jordan laid claim to newspaper women's participation in the emerging 1890s ethos of the "strenuous life," which necessarily involved work in a public rather than a cloistered private domain.

But multiple writers also worried over the question of whether newspaper women's public work was too much of a nervous strain for them—a worry related to a larger turn-of-the century conversation about the effects of "modern life" on women's constitutions, including their ability to enter the workplace successfully. Anne O'Hagan, like numerous other women, frankly acknowledged that newspaper work was a job in which many women eventually "broke down." It was "an axiom on Newspaper Row that four years of journalistic work means an attack of nervous prostration for a woman," O'Hagan observed. "Some escape this by the simple process of having less momentous spells of illness, with their enforced rests, at briefer intervals. Occasionally one works for years with no breakdown and no sickness worthy of note. But she is regarded almost with awe as one slightly uncanny."[102]

O'Hagan's comments demonstrate that women reporters themselves internalized at least some part of a mainstream discourse regarding middle-class women's supposed susceptibility to nervous disorders. As the novelist Gertrude Atherton, who worked at the *New York World* in 1892, wrote to a friend about her various newspaper assignments, "I shall probably have nervous prostration between them."[103] Yet the well-known "fascination" of newspaper work also exerted its pull. Atherton temporarily shared space with Elizabeth Jordan to gather material for a novel. Jordan remembered that Atherton "was clearly fascinated by the atmosphere of a great newspaper," by the "rush and strain and excitement; by the fact that we all worked both day and night and never seemed to have time to eat or sleep."[104]

"Is Newspaper Work Healthful for Women?" asked newspaper woman Margaret Hamilton Welch in an 1894 talk before the American Association of Social Science. Welch's eventual answer was a resounding yes, but she began by acknowledging contemporary concerns about "nervous prostration" among women. "With two minutes' thinking" she could recall "a dozen newspaper women of my acquaintance who are struggling with some form of nervous exhaustion directly consequent upon their newspaper duties." She could think of "four or five more who are out of that and all work, completely broken down, with the story of their recovery uncertain"; "two other women," both "bright, gracious, lovely," lay in "untimely graves because of their labor in newspaper offices." With these cases in mind, she said, "the reply quickly suggests itself, 'No, the work is not healthful: it is killing.'"[105]

But Welch hastened to add that "there comes with equal promptness the recollection of a dozen other women of the craft who are in perfect health, and evidently at no odds with their occupation" even after twenty-five years. It was not "wholly the woman" but rather the work itself that needed to be considered. There were "places in the newspaper world" that were "well within the physical resources of any woman in normal health." Making a protofeminist argument, Welch pointed out that even when positions were not "wearing of themselves," they often were combined with "a difficult home life, the care of children or the sick"—some "necessary or assumed strain on time or energy that permits scant leisure or rest, yet keeps life at continuous high tension. When these women go under, as they often do, their newspaper work" was "frequently and misleadingly pronounced the only cause for it." In other words, it was not women's public lives that caused strain—but their private lives, where they received inadequate support.[106]

Asking the rhetorical question "whether journalism is a desirable occupation for women," Ida Husted Harper agreed that "we would answer this with a decided affirmative." Although for men it was often said that journalism did "not offer the rewards of either money or fame in proportion to the other professions," for women it was different. Men had "the world to choose from"; women, on the other hand, were handicapped by "tradition, prejudice, and inexperience." But women seemed "especially adapted to newspaper work," and there was "scarcely a department" in "which she has not shown her ability."[107]

Critics disagreed with these assessments, of course—including many newspaper editors. In 1887 Nellie Bly published an article in the *Pittsburg Dispatch*, based on interviews with prominent New York newspaper editors, in which she explored their views of women reporters. It was Bly's first foray into New York journalism, and it revealed her quick mind and entrepreneurial spirit. Bly had been trying—without success—to find a permanent newspaper job in New York. Frustrated in this quest, she decided to interview editors for an article—and suddenly had access to editorial offices that previously had been denied to her. It was a simple but brilliant expedient that allowed her to meet face-to-face with some of the most important newspaper men in the city—not as a job seeker but as a professional newspaper woman.[108]

The editors' extensive comments were revelatory. In answer to the question, "Do you object to women entering newspaper life?," the editor of the *New York Herald* told her that he did not object, "'but still there are many things about it not suitable for women.'" He "'could not think of sending one to the police or higher criminal courts,'" as he "'could a man.'" Even if he did, "'the officials there would give her as little information as they could, in order to get rid of her.'" Still, he said, "'crime and criminals, though important, do not engross all our columns, and there is much other work women can do, and do well. In this respect I might specify the gathering and writing of clerical, fashion and society news.'" Women, he explained, were "'unable to serve as all around reporters'" because "'the very sources from which we obtain a larger portion of our news render it an impossible field for a woman. On account of the sensations and the scandals which are demanded by the present popular taste, a gentleman could not, in delicacy, ask a woman to have anything to do with that class of news. That is what bars her from reportorial success, absolutely.'"[109]

It was true that regular coverage of the police or night courts remained a barrier most women could not cross in the early 1890s. Margherita Hamm, for instance, lobbied for the right to such coverage in one of her early "Among the Newspaper Women" columns. She recounted once asking a "well known newspaper man" what he thought of the idea of "sending a woman to police headquarters as reporter for a daily newspaper." He "burst into a contemptuous laugh, uttered the single word 'absurd,' and thus dismissed the subject."[110]

But Hamm made clear that newspaper women longed for the responsibility and public excitement of regular police reporting. On a "drizzly" New Year's Eve in 1891, she traveled downtown to the notorious Mulberry Bend neighborhood and stood transfixed—gazing with "sphinx-like intensity"—at the "green lights" of "Police Headquarters" on one side of the street and the corresponding lights of newspaper offices on the other, including those of the "'New-York Tribune,' 'O'Rourke's Bureau,' 'New York Herald,' 'Journal,' etc." This, as she well knew, was the public crossroads of the great metropolitan newspapers of her day: their satellite offices across from police headquarters were at the heart of urban news gathering and reporting.[111]

After she "quickly made" her way to their offices, Hamm was welcomed "right royally" by a group of newspaper men, including a "genial and clever"

"Trib" reporter. She immediately asked him a disingenuous question: "Are there any newspaper women here?" She already knew the inevitable reply, of course—No. "So sorry," she recorded herself replying. "What good work women could do here."[112]

Even as she stood there among a "host of other bright men who put themselves out considerably to give me a pleasant time," the "telephone rang and the alarm bells clashed" to announce a suicide. Coaxing the men to "let me go out on a 'suicide' with them," Hamm "went into the midst of the mess just like the rest, got some rousing good points, and caught the fever which permeated them." As she later waited for the men to make up "their copy," a "fine detective" explained "the intricacies of counterfeiting, gaming, and robbing safes." So "interesting were their accounts," Hamm commented, "that I forgot all my troubles the flight of time, everything, and I wished all the women writers of my acquaintance were right there at that time."[113]

Far from gesturing toward her own delicate sensibilities, as a mid-nineteenth-century "domestic" writer might have done, Hamm asserted that she "derived inspiration from that visit, loads of ideas, and an insight into the vital happenings of everyday life which I shall never forget." She demanded to know, "Why wouldn't a woman be good in that sort of special police work?" She wished that "some healthy, strong, clever woman writer would apply for a berth at headquarters. I would stake considerable on her making a success of it."[114]

In publishing the story of her visit to police headquarters in her *Journalist* column, Hamm transformed the physical space she was denied—a "berth" as a regular reporter at police headquarters—into a new physical space: columns of black-and-white print that appeared on the physical page of the *Journalist* and potentially disrupted accustomed gendered patterns of American life. She also continued to lobby for newspaper women's right to take on all kinds of newspaper work, without limitation.

She came to Nellie Bly's defense, for instance, after Bly was attacked for her "notoriety" in the wake of her celebrated trip around the world for the *New York World*. The *Herald* editor had told Bly that a "gentleman could not, in delicacy, ask a woman to have anything to do" with sensational newspaper work. But perhaps the editors of the *World* were not "gentlemen." At any rate, within weeks of Bly's published interviews with newspaper editors, the "sensational" *World*, always hungry for more readers, had no hesitation in asking her to undertake another sensational exploit—and she had no hesitation in agreeing to do so. Feigning insanity, Bly went undercover to write an exposé of New York's notorious Blackwell's Island Insane Asylum. The results, written in the first person in the detailed, breathless, self-absorbed, and oddly compelling style that would become Bly's signature, appeared under her name on the front page of the *World*. This undercover work (also called "detective work") was daring, original; the fact that it was undertaken by a woman made it sensational in a day when the very presence of women's bodies in public spaces was a form of spectacle.

Bly, who immediately followed up her first undercover assignment with more exposés, quickly became a lightning rod for the ongoing discussion of women's appropriate public roles at a time of visible change. In New York, some of Bly's newspaper colleagues admired both her daring and her results. As "Howard" (probably newspaper man Joe Howard) reminded readers of the *Daily Graphic* in 1888, Bly's initial reception in New York had been "courteously chilling." The editors she interviewed on the subject of "women in journalism" had expatiated on "how utterly impossible it was for a woman to succeed" except "when she wrote about fashions." Yet Bly had "produced fifteen columns of sensation, which none of her critics had thought of or could have accomplished if they had tried." Howard concluded that "there is no reason whatsoever, there can be no argument whatever against girls working on newspapers."[115]

But a number of writers vehemently disagreed with Howard, especially as Bly's fame spread nationally. The *Galveston Daily News* noted that the *New York World* was "getting some excellent work done by its female reporter, Miss Nellie Bly," but said that "the young lady herself pays dearly for her fame." It was "bad enough for a man to do such things, but it is simply outrageous for a woman to do the low detective work she has recently been engaged in, and no woman can long retain her self-respect or the respect of others who engages in such undertakings." Holding to a standard of gendered norms that saw woman's "purity" as always vulnerable, the *Galveston Daily News* saw a threat to women in their contact with the "impure" journalistic worlds of police, courts, criminals, and "slums"—not to mention insane asylums.[116]

Bly quickly became famous in 1888 and early 1889. But she became no less than a national phenomenon in late 1889 and early 1890 after undertaking, at the behest of the *New York World*, a trip around the world to beat the fictional Phineas Fogg's record in Jules Verne's best-selling *Around the World in 80 Days*. By steamship and train, Bly managed to "girdle the globe" in only seventy-two days, sending back necessarily brief telegrams that the *World* struggled to make into compelling, Nellie Bly–style articles. To compensate for this dearth of material, the *World* ceaselessly promoted her travels, encouraging readers to wonder "Where in the world is Nellie

NELLIE BLY, LAST TIE.

When Nellie Bly, the final Tie
That bound the earth had knotted,
The World looked on and cried 'Well done!'
The Globe was bravely trotted.'

Schenck's Mandrake Pills

Cure all Bilious and Liver Complaints.

Nellie Bly trade card. Bly's immense popularity inspired trade cards, among an array of other consumer items such as board games and puzzles. This advertisement for "Schenck's Mandrake Pills," which "Cure all Bilious and Liver Complaints," includes the verse: "When Nellie Bly, the final Tie / That bound the earth had knotted, / The World looked on and cried "Well done!" / The Globe was bravely trotted." (Author's personal collection)

Bly?" and to play a Nellie Bly travel game they could snip out at home from the pages of the *World*. Ultimately, Bly's popularity was too great to be limited to newspapers: it spilled over into advertising trade cards, board games, and other consumer paraphernalia that capitalized on her fame.[117]

Such celebrity for a woman attracted new critics. Even the *Journalist*, which prided itself on its support of newspaper women, criticized Nellie Bly. In 1891, almost two years after her most memorable "stunt," the *Journalist* introduced Margherita Hamm to its readers: she was a "clever young woman," a "bright writer and a young woman of ideas." But it cautioned Hamm not to become another Nellie Bly. "At present," the *Journalist* said, Hamm was "anxious to outdo Nelly Bly and work her way around the world on a cash capital of ten dollars. It might be an interesting experiment, but Miss Hamm is too young, too clever and too pretty to attempt such a scheme. There is nothing in it but notoriety, and young writers are too apt to forget that there is a vast difference between reputation and notoriety. It is easy to become notorious at a single stroke; solid reputation is more difficult to achieve, but it lasts longer."[118]

Within weeks of the *Journalist*'s paternalistic suggestion that she avoid the path of Nellie Bly, Hamm mounted a spirited defense of women's "sensational" reporting in her new column. In the process, she claimed newspaper women's right to *all* the public spaces of newspaper culture. "The school of sensationalism in journalism is constantly growing," she said, and acknowledged that "it is a question of many women writers whether it is a discreet and worthy department to embark in." But she argued, "It seems evident that if there is a good motive in an expose [*sic*], a woman is justifiable in entering any field of labor, which is necessary to such expose, no matter how common, degrading, or disagreeable." About Nellie Bly herself, she tartly observed, "A great deal too much unpleasantness in regard to this young lady has been indulged in by newspaper writers and others which does them no credit and which has caused her a great deal of unnecessary suffering. Miss Bly was always faithful, authentic and clever in her work, and she certainly accomplished what no other woman has been able to."[119]

Hamm clearly was responding both to Bly's spirit of adventure and to her ambition. But there was more to her response than first met the eye. The previous summer Hamm had experienced her own first brush with "fame" as a newspaper woman and now understood the kinds of attacks that could result. Hamm had obtained a "scoop" about the health of possible Republican presidential candidate James G. Blaine while she was employed as a newspaper correspondent in the seaside resort of Bar Harbor, Maine, where Blaine was vacationing. Newspaper rumors that he was in poor health were at a fever pitch that summer—and apparently Hamm obtained an interview with Blaine that "proved" he was recovering from illness. Instantly she became (momentarily, at least) famous herself: one newspaper sympathetic to Blaine said that "congratulations are offered to Miss Hamm on every side," that photographers had her portrait "in their shop windows," and that her name was "flashing on the many wires of the country and flowing from many a newspaper pen, while her portrait is being published in every important journal."[120] Later the *Journalist* would also crow about her accomplishment: she was a "plucky young girl" who was able to enter "into political questions with a thoroughly masculine zest." "Some of her best work," the trade paper concluded, "has been done in fair and square competition with men and in political interviewing where men are supposed to enjoy exclusive privileges." Male correspondents had been "ignominiously 'scooped'" by her on the Blaine story.[121]

But Hamm's journalistic triumph opened her to a variety of gendered attacks on her vulnerable position as a woman in public. One newspaper commented that though she came of poor parents she had "lived in style" in Bar Harbor and "had plenty of money," insinuating her involvement in some kind of scandalous impropriety. She was a "pretty girl of erratic habits and a love of notoriety."[122] According to the *Raleigh News and Observer*, she had "a particular penchant for being a Bohemian" and was "in constant grief that she is a girl."[123] By far the most vicious attack came from the *Boston Herald*, which called Hamm an "adventuress, prevaricator, and consorter with disreputable characters."[124]

Hamm threatened to sue the *Herald* for libel.[125] The lesson was clear: fame for a newspaper woman was potentially dangerous, particularly if she stepped onto the male turf of political reporting. Yet fame cut two ways for Hamm. Her well-known Bar Harbor triumph, trumpeted in newspapers around the country (and often mentioned by Hamm as an accomplishment in the various biographies she provided throughout her career), seems to have been her ticket into New York's newspaper world.[126] Within only a few months of her Bar Harbor scoop, she had her own column in the *Journalist*.

No wonder, then, that Hamm steadfastly defended Nellie Bly in her column despite Bly's "notoriety." Hamm understood that newspaper work was public work: not only did it take women into the public sphere, it sometimes made women into public figures. For many newspaper women, this was part of its appeal: newspaper work allowed them to participate in the new theater of modern urban life, to become actors (sometimes quite literally) on an urban stage. But a number of female journalists viewed the entrance of women into sensational reporting, in particular, as a distinct setback to their professional ambitions. Sensational journalism became a source of division within the larger world of newspaper women—with women lined up on both sides of the issue.

As Margaret Welch wrote, "The few sensational workers and adventuresses in the profession have made it a little difficult just now for the good average newspaper woman to take her rightful social position."[127] Cynthia Westover Alden, editor of the woman's department of the *New-York Tribune*, objected to sensational work on practical grounds: it used women without providing experience that could be employed in "legitimate" journalism. Alden commented that "the so-called 'yellow journals' delight in sending a woman to spend a night in the Morgue, or to interview a repulsive criminal, or to pry into some domestic scandal." Then "they print the matter turned in over the woman's signature, gratifying her vanity, and thereby aiding her to forget that she has been used purely in the interest of

Poster advertising New York Sunday World *for April 12, 1896. Both boys and girls sold newspapers in the 1890s. In this placard, which claims to have the "Best Woman's Page Printed," the newsgirl holds a copy of the* World *showing Kate Swan with a large spider. The copy also claims that the paper's Sunday circulation is 500,000. (Author's personal collection)*

sensationalism." Such reporting relied on a first-person voice "to take the place of originality of style," and as a result it was "of very little value as a training for the legitimate chronicling of legitimate news."[128]

Alden's concerns about sensational journalism were primarily practical and professional, although her distaste was clear. But other newspaper women used an older rhetoric of moral corruption and threatened purity to criticize sensationalism. Several wrote short stories or articles in which they imagined innocent young women dragged down to the depths by "gutter journalism," as newspaper woman Haryot Holt Cahoon (who had been head of the woman's page of the *New York Recorder*) called newspapers like the *New York World*. In a melodramatic 1897 article, Cahoon pictured a "fresh and fair" young girl who had come to New York, her eyes "bright with hope and credulity." A sequence of reporting assignments, however, steadily degraded her—from interviewing a prize-fighter, to a police court assignment, to "doing" the "filth of slum life," to investigating "the opium

Poster advertising New York Sunday World *for March 8, 1896. In 1896 the World engaged in a poster war with its rival, the* New York Journal. *Featuring a titillating image of a chorus girl, the notice announces "Articles by Nellie Bly and Kate Swan." (Art & Architecture Collection, Miriam and Ira D. Wallach Division of Art, Prints and Photographs, The New York Public Library, Astor, Lenox, and Tilden Foundations)*

den, Chinese vice, the brothel, and every other mysterious place in a great city that always stands ready to gratify morbid curiosity."[129]

The end result of such work, in Cahoon's view, was an intertwined moral and physical decline: the loss of "the bloom and delicacy" of "womanhood," along with a "blunting" of "moral sensibilities." Having been "disillusionized [*sic*] of every sacred ideal of her heart, having given all," she has "nothing left but ill health and experience."[130] For Cahoon, who adhered closely to Victorian ideals of womanhood, having "nothing left but experience" was a damning indictment: a woman's loss of the "bloom" of innocence could never be recovered. Her account reminds us that at the turn of the century older ideas of womanhood were competing with an emerging rhetoric of adventure, independence, and freedom.

"Is the Newspaper Office the Place for a Girl?" asked Edward Bok from the pages of the conservative *Ladies' Home Journal* in 1901. His answer, predictably, was a resounding no—but he did not rely on his own opinion, he

40 PAGES   280 COLUMNS

NEW YORK
SUNDAY JOURNAL

A New Dissipation
of New York City Girls.

THE FAVORITE MODEL
OF A POPULAR ARTIST.   THE PASSION OF LOVE
AS SCIENTISTS ANALYZE IT.

A Wonderful New Cure   All Night In A Room
For a Dreadful Disease.   Full of Writhing Snakes.

BEAUTIFUL ART SUPPLEMENT
"A WET NIGHT ON MADISON SQUARE."
FREE WITH EVERY COPY.

SUNDAY,   DON'T
MARCH 15.   MISS IT.

Poster advertising New York Sunday Journal *for March 15, 1896. This picture of a young woman seated alone in a café publicizes "A New Dissipation of New York City Girls" as an attraction of the upcoming Sunday edition. (Art & Architecture Collection, Miriam and Ira D. Wallach Division of Art, Prints and Photographs, The New York Public Library, Astor, Lenox, and Tilden Foundations)*

said. He had canvassed a number of newspaper women, asking them, "If you had a young daughter, desirous or forced to go into the outer world, would you, from your experience as a newspaper woman, approve of her working in a daily newspaper office?" Out of fifty women canvassed, he reported, thirty-nine said no while only three said yes (the remaining eight did not respond). One newspaper woman said, "It is the freedom which the work gives that is bad. With practically no definite hours, and a stipulation only that 'copy' shall be in in time for to-morrow's edition, there comes a dreadful sense of freedom which unconsciously deteriorates into all sorts of license and language and behavior, the combination that makes the world believe all newspaper women to be 'Bohemians.'" Another woman reporter stated that "a newspaper office certainly tends to make a woman too independent, too free, too broad. It establishes her on a footing with men that is not wise: it gives her opportunities of freedom that are not uplifting."[131]

Yet it was exactly this freedom and independence—combined with the new public experiences that newspaper work allowed—that most appealed to other newspaper women. According to Anne O'Hagan, newspaper work also permitted a new sort of camaraderie with men—if women could give up their demands that they be treated as "ladies." As she noted, the newspaper woman's "manners are not always what the editors of the etiquette columns and the gifted composers of the advice to debutantes would approve. The office life leads insensibly into tolerating a lack of punctiliousness from men." But there were benefits to be had as well: The newspaper woman "will, when she grows used to it, be not averse to the transformation of men from flatterers and cavaliers into friends and comrades."[132]

The public experience of newspaper work offered women valuable lessons, a number of female reporters insisted. "The training involved in the work is invaluable," Cynthia Westover Alden said: It was "more broadening in its influence on the mind than any other wage-earning industry that women take part in."[133] Newspaper work connected women to the greater life of cities, offering them an education unattainable in any other field. Ida Tarbell wrote that her brief stint in syndicate work gave her a connection to the greater life of Paris. "Enamored as I was of the city," she said, "no work could have been more satisfying than that I had laid out for myself. My little self-directed syndicate concerned itself with the practical everyday life of the city." After all, she explained, "one is always keen to know all the common things about the thing or person one loves. How did Paris keep herself so clean? What did she eat and drink, and where did she get it? How much did it cost her? Where did she go for fun? How did she manage it that even her very poor seemed to know how to amuse themselves? There were a multitude of things I thirsted to know about her. And if I could get my bread and butter in finding out, what luck! What luck!" Newspaper work offered Tarbell exposure to a broader life: "My manner of living, the contacts and circumstances attending the gathering of my material for my newspaper articles brought me for the first time in my life into daily relations with that greatest segment of every country's population—those whom we call the poor."[134]

Newspaper work demanded a new relationship to the public life of cities, one centered around active participation and observation. As Margherita Hamm wrote, the "business motto of the newspaper woman's life" should be "observation at any and all times." She advised women to "make your mind a beehive of information, not extracted from books, not through the middleman, the author, but from Nature herself." In "never tiring observation and experience will newspaper women find the clear road to the highest mark."[135] She returned to this idea several times in her columns, saying that it "is of great weight to the newspaper woman" to study "life closely," and to observe "the eccentricities and whims of all people, both high and low." Indeed, the "difference between newspaper women consists, in great measure, in the intelligence of their observation." Where "unthinking observers see nothing, women of intelligent vision penetrate into the very fibre of the phenomena presented to them."[136] Observation was the tool that would give newspaper women insights into all of human experience, including those parts of life that had previously been marked off-limits to them.

Newspaper women "out on assignment" were not, of course, free agents; they were limited by the demands of their editors, by the politics of their newspapers, and by the perceived desires of their readers. Anne O'Hagan acknowledged as much, commenting that a newspaper woman "sent to the scene of the coal mine strike in Pennsylvania" by a "clever organ of the capitalists" knew what she was supposed to find: "She has not been told what to find among the coal miners, but she knows. She is to find comfortable homes—owned by miners; flourishing schools, attended by miners' children; neatly dressed wives of miners, holding the fat babies of miners in their well developed arms." On the other hand, if she worked for the "'people's' paper," she knew she would find "a starving family in every block; hollow eyed mothers; and babies too feeble even to wail."[137]

In neither case was a newspaper woman guilty of "absolute falsity," O'Hagan believed. In each case she could find "instances of what she seeks," and she could "accentuate, not invent." Nevertheless, "the greatest harm that the journalistic life does women" was the "insincerity" that accompanied such writing, inevitably resulting in a loss of "clearness of vision and honesty of purpose." For O'Hagan, this was a far more serious issue than the supposed moral degradation of newspaper work deplored by commentators such as Edward Bok or Haryot Holt Cahoon.[138]

Yet what newspaper women observed when they were "out on assignment" could never be strictly limited to the work they had been assigned. O'Hagan grew uncharacteristically lyrical as she evoked the "trifles" that were some of the compensations of newspaper reporting for the woman whose eyes were "open always." "The newspaper woman," she said, "is watchful for pussy willows silvering a thicket on a late winter day in the country; she listens to the tune the street piano grinds, and she watches the tenement children dancing to it, when she climbs Avenue B stairs in search of her 'story.' Her eyes are always open for 'local color,' and so sometimes they catch a glimpse of what the godly might call divine radiance."[139]

In her 1893 "The Newspaper Woman's Story," Elizabeth Jordan took issue with the many rosy assessments of women's increasing success in journalism to be found in newspapers and magazines. Surveying the previous few years, she argued that "notwithstanding many claims" of women's progress in journalism, they occupied "practically the same position" that they had a few years earlier. "There is a vast difference between what has been accomplished and what is claimed," she said. "It cannot be pointed out too soon for the benefit of the ambitious girls whose pathetic little letters are filling our editorial waste-baskets." Looking back, she drily noted that "women stood at the door of the sanctums, so to speak, but their invitations to enter were not urgent." It might be true that they were "more numerous" and they were "further in," but "their tenure of office" was "distinctly open to discussion." Jordan, who wanted to count as "newspaper women" only those who had regular staff jobs on newspapers, took issue with numerical estimates of newspaper women as well. "It has been loosely estimated that there are several thousand newspaper women in this country," she observed; "in reality there are less than two hundred and fifty."[140]

But Margherita Hamm viewed newspaper women's status differently. Perennially an optimist, always attempting to boost the position of women in "newspaperdom," she saw much to celebrate in the changing position of women in metropolitan journalism. "The daily progress of women in the newspaper world is a matter of deep satisfaction," Hamm stated in 1896. "Not only are women succeeding in the profession, but they are rising up and are filling better places every day."[141]

Hamm strongly disagreed with all those critics who told "young women in the country" with "a taste for newspaper work to keep out of it" or "to steer clear of New York City." "What rot. What unkind discouragement. What individual jealousy," she declared. Such advice was "narrow, prejudiced and unreasonable." "We are looking for great minds among women and we should welcome a newcomer. There is field for all here, and success depends upon the individual." Hamm rebutted the idea that newspaper work would "degrade" women. "Do not be afraid of your moral character in New York," she urged. "If integrity is in you, it will not leave you in one part of the universe more than the other. Do not be afraid of starvation; you will not starve. Others have come here without a penny, and the impetus from the lack of funds made them work all the harder and more conscientiously."[142]

Hamm sought to stiffen the resolve and fire the ambition of her fellow newspaper women, claiming that "no woman need feel discouraged by the side of man." "Instead of brooding," she advised, "wake up to the facts of life. Realize opportunities. Determine to find a place in the newspaper market for your wares. If you can't write about music, art, or fashions, write about the sidewalks, the shops and signboards. Write something; at any rate, don't give up." With a touch of scorn she sketched the alternative: "Get married, and tell the same, hoarse and rheumatic old story, 'I got tired of trying to earn a living on the newspapers, so I got married.'"[143] "If a woman anywhere in America feels in herself the desire, the inspiration, the love to write so that she would peril everything," she concluded, "she should come straight to New York."[144]

It was both invitation and fair warning.

## chapter two

The Woman's Page

The woman's column of the *Brooklyn Times*, called "Readings for the Home" and offering "Gossip and Gleanings for the Family Circle," opened with its usual feature on October 23, 1886: an "Everyday Bill of Fare" that presented a menu and recipes by famous novelist Marion Harland (Mary Virginia Hawes Terhune). Harland had made a name for herself before the Civil War with best-selling popular fiction, but after the war she also branched out into domestic guidebooks and "cookery," sometimes in conjunction with her daughter, Christine Terhune Herrick. On this particular day, Harland proposed a breakfast consisting of ham breaded in flour, salted "slightly," and fried in lard, and a "Luncheon" of "Beef Balls, Corn Cakes, Potato Salad, Bread and Butter, Crackers and Cheese, Lemon Cream Toast, and Wilbur's Cocoatina."[1] It was only one of many such "healthful" meals (Harland even fried cucumbers in lard) that she proposed through the woman's department of newspapers in the spring and fall of 1886.

Harland was one of the most prominent of the antebellum "literary domestics" who continued to make a career after the war by celebrating the glories of home in the public spaces of print.[2] For Harland, home always came first: in her public persona, she questioned whether women's increasing professional attainments in the 1880s and 1890s were not taking too great a toll on their private lives. "In the haste to open avenues to women—many of which avenues have now become boulevards and crowded," she asked in 1892, "are we in danger of ignoring a heavenly-appointed highway? In asserting our right and ability to stand upon a level with man do we underrate the dignity of that which man cannot accomplish—the making and keeping of a home?"[3]

But while Harland questioned "professional" women's choices (and their homemaking skills), she continued to build a business empire around her domestic writings, skillfully combining novel writing with lecturing and extensive magazine work. Harland is not usually thought of as a newspaper writer, but in fact, as part of her larger literary career, she also became a syndicated woman's page writer during the first great wave of syndication. In 1886, for instance, her "Everyday Bill of Fare" column was sold to a variety of newspapers through the Bacheller Syndicate—and this was not her last significant press work.[4] She was affiliated with the *New York Herald* in the 1890s, and in 1901 she took on a syndicated woman's page established by the *North American* that she helped to make a nationwide force.

In her 1910 autobiography, Harland made clear that newspaper syndicate work was enormously satisfying to her. "I have been asked often," she wrote, "why I expend energies and fill my days in what my critics are pleased to depreciate as 'hack-work.' Nobody believes my assertion that I heartily enjoy being thus brought into intimate association with the women of America. The Syndicate has extended its territory into twenty-five States, and it is still growing. Women, boys, and girls, and housefathers—no less than housemothers—tell me of their lives, their successes, their failures, their trials, and their several problems."[5]

Harland received "thousands of letters" with "stamps for replies by mail" on subjects ranging from "Marmalade to Matrimony." From this "mighty mass of correspondence," she selected "letters dealing with topics of general interest, or that seem to call for free and friendly discussion, and base upon them daily articles for the Syndicate public." In addition, she worked with several volunteer societies that had emerged from "this germ of 'hack-work,'" as she put it—still obviously stung by that criticism. The "Helping-Hand Club," for instance, was an informal organization with no "plant" (building) other than Harland's own "desk and the postal service." "Quietly and without parade, our volunteer agents visit the needy and report to us," she wrote. "We distribute, by correspondence, thousands of volumes and periodicals annually" to the "indigent, the shut-in, the aged, and charitable societies."[6]

Harland framed this far-flung newspaper work—which used the modern channels of syndication for communication—in traditional terms of sentimental Christian womanhood: "'For Love's Sake' is our motto," she said, "and it is caught up eagerly, from Canada to California. 'The Big Family' they call themselves—these dear co-workers of mine whose faces I shall never see on earth. When, as happens daily, I read 'Dear Mother of us all,' from those I have been permitted to help in mind, body, or estate, I thank the Master and take courage."[7] Harland recognized the "direct lending of the Divine Hand" in this work and concluded "that I have never had such fullness of satisfaction in any other sphere of labor." To a friend who exclaimed "But it is not literature!," thus "voicing the sentiment of many,"

Woman's page announcement that "Marion Harland to Write Exclusively for the Tribune," by Mary Eleanor O'Donnell, Chicago Daily Tribune, October 29, 1911. (ProQuest Historical Newspapers, Chicago Tribune [1894–1987])

Harland replied "But it is *Influence*, and that of the best kind."[8] In invoking the power of women's influence, Harland evoked the rhetoric of domesticity, a discourse that had been a powerful force in antebellum American life—and never disappeared from some quarters of American culture.[9]

Harland's newspaper work—with its combination of sentimental, maternal, and Christian rhetoric; its provision of recipes and homespun advice; and its active do-gooding by a network of volunteers imagined as a "family"—represented one aspect of the woman's page that never seemed to lose its appeal. Indeed, so popular did Harland remain that in 1911, when she was seventy-one, the *Chicago Daily Tribune* picked up exclusive access to her syndicate work and excitedly trumpeted the news that "Marion Harland to Write Exclusively for the Tribune."[10] Publicity photographs of Harland for the *Tribune* showed a woman in strikingly old-fashioned dress, seemingly a relic of a bygone era. But that old-fashioned image was probably exactly what attracted her woman's page audience.

Harland's work is precisely what we imagine the woman's page to be: sentimental, reassuring, offering advice and recipes. By the 1880s, newspapers had in fact long included miscellaneous "household hints," recipes, and fashions. There had also been a steady trickle of female "domestic" columnists, ranging from the acerbic to the sentimental, starting in the mid-nineteenth century.[11] But what was different beginning around 1885 was the sudden expansion of the types and numbers of "woman's features" in mass-circulation newspapers, as well as the concentration of these features (often called "departments") on one page, or in one section, of the paper. Newspapers handled the new "woman's page" or "woman's department" or "woman's section" in different ways. In some papers an entire page or section devoted to women appeared in the Sunday edition or Saturday "supplement"; in others, it appeared only on weekdays. In some, women's concerns appeared under headings that changed from week to week, and even from day to day, such as the *New York World*'s "The Woman's Page," "The Interests of Women," "Woman's Latest Whims and Fashions," "The World of Women," "The Women Folk," "New Women and Their Doings," and "Woman and her Ways"—headings within a three-month period in 1896.[12] In other newspapers headings changed from year to year.[13] In still other papers, such as the *New York Sun*, no special masthead appeared to indicate that the reader was perusing the "woman's page" (only the content indicated this).[14] Newspapers continually tinkered with the woman's page and occasionally banished it entirely for a brief period, only to bring it back again later in new forms.

Starting around 1885, metropolitan newspapers began to hire more and more women to write or contribute to the woman's page; as a new generation of women entered newspaper work, the woman's page evolved as well. These new newspaper women brought lively minds to bear on the woman's page, where we can see traces of their influence not just in the abiding staples of fashion, beauty, home furnishings, and cookery, but also in features that increasingly focused directly on the status of women themselves in modern society. Many women began to provide not only the regular "stuff" editors demanded, but also what they thought women actually wanted and were interested in, including news of women's "progress"—a term often used by newspaper women.

In early 1887 twenty-six-year-old Eliza Putnam Heaton took over the *Brooklyn Times* woman's column "Reading for the Home," the column that had been the province of Marion Harland only a few months before.[15] We can easily guess that Heaton felt impatient with Harland's traditional fare—as appropriate to a woman's magazine of the 1850s as to a newspaper of the 1880s—when we look at her new version of the column. An 1882 graduate of Boston University, one of a new generation of college-educated women entering newspaper work, Heaton started her own "Reading for the Home" column not with a recipe but with a vigorous lesson in the history of women. "A notable event of the year 1846," she began without preamble, "was the appearance at a course of medical lectures of a young woman student named Blackwell." After briefly discussing the medical career of Dr. Elizabeth Blackwell ("the earliest woman physician of this country," Heaton reminded her readers), she then turned to the interesting fact that now, much younger women than previously—mostly in their twenties— were taking up the study of medicine in New York. "They believe it is a good thing for a woman to find herself a vocation," Heaton said firmly, in what would become a reiterated theme of her own newspaper work. Women medical students were "gathered from every nook and corner of the country," and "the women's colleges, of course, are responsible for the largest quota."[16]

It was women's professional progress, especially women's work, that most interested Heaton—and it would continue to interest her in a regular Saturday column, signed with her full name, which was quickly picked up through syndication (with the American Press Association) as a weekly "letter" by a number of newspapers around the country. Heaton wrote dozens of these columns over the next few years on a wide range of topics, from cooperative housekeeping to dress reform—but always with a special emphasis on women's work. As an admiring reporter said of Heaton in late 1887, "There are probably few persons living of either sex who are better informed than she upon the legal status, social environments, wages, health and general conditions of women not only in all the states of her own country, but in foreign countries as well."[17] In an extensive profile, another newspaper writer commented on her deep "interest in the progressive womanhood of the century."[18] Margherita Hamm observed that Heaton was "a power in her own way," with a "curt, terse, eloquent political pen." She was "one of the few brain workers among women whose writings ever live beyond a day."[19]

Though not all of her fellow newspaper women realized it, Eliza Putnam Heaton was also "Ellen Osborne,"[20] who produced a lively weekly column on fashion that was picked up for national syndication as well. By 1889, both of her columns sometimes ran side-by-side as a woman's feature in papers around the country. The Kellogg and Bacheller syndicate disingenuously advertised "Ellen Osborne" and Eliza P. Heaton as separate members of its stable of newspaper writers of "High Character."[21]

There was a certain irony in Eliza Heaton's "secret" identity as a fashion writer: she was not interested in clothes in the usual sense, at least according to one interviewer who has left us with a vivid portrait. At a time when women wore skirts that swept to the ground, the "decidedly small" Heaton always wore dresses that stopped "four or five inches above the ground"—the style of a dress reformer, or even a young girl, rather than a fashionable woman. "Her lack of size and unconventionality of attire sometimes lead to ludicrous results," this writer said, "as when on one occasion her butcher's boy invited her to go skating 'if her mother didn't object.'" If Heaton was sometimes mistaken for a child, she was in fact a "most uncompromising dress reformer." Although "for business reasons" she was "always well informed of the latest freaks of fashion," she herself was a "deadly foe to corsets, trains, high heels, paints, powders and all other adjuncts of the toilet which are of harmful or even questionable effect. Perhaps because of this unconventionality of attire," she could "row like a sailor, walk unheard of distances with enjoyment and without fatigue," and was an "expert canoeist."[22]

Margherita Hamm, initially ignorant of Heaton's dual identity, commented that Heaton was a "strong-minded, rather masculine woman." Hamm could "imagine nothing more discordant than Mrs. Heaton's idea on reception costumes"—this though Heaton was then writing descriptions of "reception costumes" to great success.[23] Hamm was astonished when "a bird" later informed her that "Ellen Osborne" was a "a nom de plume. The articles signed by this name are too clever to be printed in this way," she declared—meaning that they deserved to be printed with full attribution, not under a pen name.[24] Another newspaper writer informed readers of the *Brooklyn Eagle* that Heaton had once wanted to be a scientist, remarking: "The irony of fate never took a more eccentric turn than it did when it ordained that a student of Greek and Sanscrit, an investigator of polypi and queer wriggling things generally, should become one of the leading fashion writers of America." Heaton had "no sympathy" with the "fashionable foibles" she discussed. They appealed to her "only as business matters appeal to business people," furnishing her with "amusement." As this writer delicately phrased it, she was "inclined to attribute much of her success" to the fact that she was, "so to speak, a disinterested observer of fashionable antics from the outside."[25]

As Heaton's bifurcated career suggests, fashion and other "traditional" "woman's page" topics often offered the best—if not the *only*—opportunities for newspaper women to earn a living at the turn of the century. Yet on her own widely syndicated woman's page, Heaton brought an exceptionally lively mind to bear on "woman's topics" of her day. Like Heaton, many newspaper women managed to use the emerging "woman's page" or "woman's department" or "woman's column" as more of a public forum than has been recognized, writing articles that helped to establish and support new public roles for women.

In the late 1880s and the 1890s, newspaper women wrote hundreds of articles and columns exploring the subject of "progressive womanhood." By doing so they created an ongoing public discussion, one that frequently had a national reach through syndication. Newspapers became a significant means of creating, sharing, and spreading knowledge about women's status and prospects—with special attention to women's work, including what occupations were newly available to women, how best to obtain jobs, what qualities were needed to succeed, and how to avoid failure. Mixing information with a form of career guidance, such articles not only documented the "progress" of women across a variety of fields, but also reached out to women readers with advice and encouragement—and sometimes finger-wagging admonitions. Newspaper women created focused public conversations in which their readers were folded into larger communities; through "chats" and interviews, readers were invited to imagine themselves in direct contact with some of the most successful women of the day. The "woman's department" could even be used to discuss politics more generally.

It is thus a mistake to write off the woman's page too quickly—though it is certainly easy to understand why it has "flown beneath the radar" for so long. First, the woman's page perennially featured a number of articles that newspaper women themselves found unbearably silly. To cite one example among thousands, the "Only Woman's Page" of the *New-York Daily Tribune* for January 19, 1900, included such typical "jam and fashion" articles as "Pretty Things to Wear," "Incidents in Society," "The Tribune Pattern" (advertising a tissue-paper pattern for a girl's pinafore), and the "Tribune Sunshine Society," a recurring column that reported in saccharine prose the individual charitable work of its "members." The article "Homemade Dressing Table" advised readers that "a dainty piece of furniture" could be "constructed out of a packing box"—exactly the kind of long-lived woman's page feature that had already been satirized in the *Chicago Daily Tribune*. In 1895 that paper had remarked on the "delusion" and "snare" offered by "elaborately illustrated" woman's page columns that promised women they could make "comfortable pieces of furniture out of boxes and barrels"—but instead produced only "flush-faced women" after "hours of amateur carpentering."[26]

Yet on the same day, the "Only Woman's Page" included "Women of Many Lands," a report on a lecture by world traveler and newspaper woman Eliza Archard Conner; a piece titled "Progressive Western Women:

One Is Deputy Sheriff—Another Has Been Assistant Attorney General of the State"; an article on a divorce judge deemed overly strict in his requirements; and the short report "No Right to Practise [sic] Law in Delaware: Woman Lawyer Debarred from Arguing in Supreme Court of That State."[27] These articles clearly focused on women's changing public status at the turn of the century, offering an education beyond the local confines of New York—and certainly beyond fashion and cookery. The woman's page was both more miscellaneous and more diverse than we have given it credit for.

Yet newspaper women themselves have diverted our attention from the woman's page. After all, many women resented being relegated to woman's departments, which were first developed by male editors to appeal to a female readership, and which many newspaper women found both insulting and degrading. "This was not the newspaper work of my dreams," Elizabeth Jordan drily remarked of her short stint around 1885 editing the "new woman's page" of *Peck's Sun* in Milwaukee. Her editor "insisted on calling the department 'Sunshine,'" and "he wrote a flowery introduction for it which conveyed the impression that I would personally supply light and warmth to the universe. I myself was not a sentimentalist. It is a miracle that the stuff I had to carry did not permanently destroy my interest in newspaper work." At the end of a year she left the job with "vast relief."[28]

"It is humiliating to do no work worth being taken seriously," agreed Anne O'Hagan, who paid her dues on the *New York World* as a beauty columnist before taking up magazine work. "It is stagnating—and no one knows this more keenly than the woman's page editor—to have no more vital subject for thought, so far as her profession is concerned, than the presentation in new form of an article on chafing dish suppers or on Mlle. Lightfoot's complexion regimen." What's more, it was "debasing" to have to grovel before Congressmen's wives and other interview subjects to do "work either puerile or servile."[29] Margherita Hamm was even more acerbic, writing in 1891 that "if I were a cookery page reporter I would write such recipes that those who read to cook would poison themselves and make it possible for me to devote space to something else."[30]

Among both newspaper men and women, general reporting carried much higher status than "mere" woman's page work. As O'Hagan observed, "It is sometimes borne in upon" newspaper women's "minds that the management regards their departments either as an abuse of excellent space for the sake of a hypothetical circulation among women, or as a joke scarcely connected with real newspaper work."[31] Scorn for the woman's page was long-lived. Newspaper woman Ethel M. Colson Brazelton, who published

Writing and Editing for Women in 1927, talked of the "silly, sentimental slush once filling women's pages and publications."[32] As Ishbel Ross put it, The "woman's page" was "a department which once merited the scorn it received."[33] For many women journalists and writers, the woman's page has always been not just an embarrassment but also a source of understandable resentment.[34]

Given newspaper women's low opinion of much of the "woman's stuff" assigned by editors, perhaps it is not surprising that, as early as 1891, such criticism often appeared on the woman's page itself. The *New York Herald*, for instance, printed an article on women readers' estimation "of the reading matter ordinarily printed in the women's departments of newspapers." One reader, newspaper woman Elizabeth Akers, reported that "so exasperating is the drivel generally printed" under such headings as "What Women Should Know," "The Ways of Women," and "Women's Fancies," that she would quickly turn the page whenever she saw them to "avoid even glancing at the disgusting trash below." She could only account for this "persistent stuffing of trash down women's throats by supposing that it was begun, in one shape or another, in the days when women were merely chattels" and were regarded as "creatures which must not be encouraged to have choices of their own nor to know their own strength and capacity, lest they become insubordinate." She recounted a conversation with a male editor in which she asked, "Does your wife really like this trash that you deal out to women?" The editor "indignantly" replied, "'Why, no, she never looks at it!'" He claimed that his sister and mother did not read the woman's page, either—"'The idea of my mother reading fashion gossip!'" When Akers pressed him to explain why he "put this trash forward as the proper mental pabulum for other men's wives, sisters, and mothers," he simply responded, "'O, well, women in general like it, you know.'" Akers vehemently disagreed, contending that the woman's page was "insulting to the common sense of the average woman."[35]

Newspaper woman Helen Watterson also criticized the woman's page. Women "want more," she said. "They want to know, in the tersest and most accurate way the latest helpful discoveries of science and of art; they want to know what women are doing and thinking all over the world; they want to know what changes lawmakers are making that are likely to affect women." Watterson argued that women were "tired to death of the flood of stuff that is poured out these days, heavy laden with adjectives and lightly laden either with sense, truth, ideas, or morality." Women were "tired of being jeered at and ridiculed for every intellectual, social, or moral project they undertake."[36]

The fact that such criticisms appeared on the woman's page at first seems paradoxical: Why would editors print criticisms of their own newspapers? One possible answer, of course, is that editors did not believe such criticisms applied to the woman's page of *their* newspapers. But a more likely answer was provided by Edward Bok, the powerful and egotistical editor of the *Ladies' Home Journal*, who claimed in his autobiography to have *invented* the woman's page. Bok said that "the average editor" had "as a rule, no time to study the changing conditions of women's interests; his time is and must be engrossed by the news and editorial pages." (Note that in Bok's view, "women's interests" did not intersect with "news and editorial pages.") Having no time himself, the editor often "places the 'woman's page' in the hands of some woman with the comfortable assurance that, being a woman, she ought to know what interests her sex." (Note again Bok's dismissive "some woman.") "But having given the subject little thought," Bok wrote, "he attaches minor importance to the woman's 'stuff,' regarding it rather in the light of something that he 'must carry to catch the woman'; and forthwith he either forgets it or refuses to give the editor of his woman's page even a reasonable allowance to spend on her material. The result is, of course, inevitable: pages of worthless material."[37] In other words, women's criticisms of the woman's page could appear on the woman's page itself because male editors did not notice — or care.

While Bok saw "pages of worthless material" as the result of the male editor's inattention, we can use Bok's analysis to see something else: such inattention, in fact, gave some newspaper women scope and freedom for developing their *own* thoughts in print regarding women's affairs. Editorial inattention allowed these women a limited freedom. They often "flew beneath the radar" in writing for the woman's page precisely because in editorial terms it was the least important section of the newspaper — even if, paradoxically, the most important for attracting advertisers, especially the department store advertisers that major metropolitan newspapers hoped to please and appease.

We can thus see newspaper women's criticisms of the woman's page in another light as well: as a way of reaching out to other women as readers in a serious discussion. The woman's page, in short, could be a way of developing a woman's reading public, of connecting with other women in communities of conversation that sometimes had a national reach, and that continued from paper to paper as various newspaper women weighed in on a given topic.

Often the woman's page is mistakenly described as having *only* a consumer function. To be sure, Rheta Dorr's memories — among many others—underline the ways in which women's entry into journalism was tied to their growing importance as consumers. As Dorr commented about her tenure on the woman's page at the *New York Evening Post*, the "business office complained that [the paper] was not read by women. The department stores had the reprehensible habit of throwing their advertising where women would see it, and the business-office thought the 'Post' ought to make an effort to get more women readers." Every week, Dorr was required to produce two columns and a half about the women's clubs that "were just coming into prominence," as well as "about two columns a week of fashions and a column and a half of housekeeping stuff." Her boss "never let me forget that I had to do it well enough to attract department-store advertising."[38] Similarly, Edward Bok believed that "it would benefit the newspaper enormously in its advertising if it could offer a feminine clientele."[39] There is no question that the woman's page had a vital consumer function and purpose—newspaper women understood this.

But it would be overstating the case to say that the woman's page had only *one* function or meaning, or that its meanings could be strictly limited to newspaper editors' ideas. The miscellany of articles offered by woman's pages was various enough to defy tidy categorization: domestic hints were placed next to pieces on new occupations for women; a "squib" on lace might be next to an article on suffrage. Within just a single column, a newspaper woman might move from fashion to woman's rights to literature. Miscellany was itself a newspaper aesthetic at the turn of the century that structured individual columns as well as pages—not to mention entire newspapers. Such miscellany produced an abundance of meanings beyond the complete control of newspaper editors. Nor could the meanings of the woman's page be restricted to consumption alone: they spilled over into multiple public conversations as well.

Journalism historians have stressed that women's entry into the field had less to do with newspapers' interest in their position in society than with their position as consumers. From the point of view of most male editors, indeed, the woman's department had no serious goal, no serious topics— just fashion, beauty, and other "woman's stuff." What is forgotten in this version of newspaper history is that not all women agreed with this assessment of their work. Many newspaper women did not treat their columns as entirely without value. Instead, they saw that the woman's page gave them the opportunity to reach out to women readers in order to create a new public.

In 1899 Ida Husted Harper weighed in on precisely this point. She recognized that "unless a woman is in control of the paper it may not be possible to speak the desired word" on such issues as suffrage, a topic often banned by conservative male editors. "But even with this restriction," she said, "it is possible to give a vast amount of assistance to the progress of women" with newspaper work. "If the vital question of Suffrage is prohibited, there still are many chances to show the advancement they are making in the professions, the industries, the clubs, and the various associations." Then again, if editors "vetoed" even these topics as "too strong-minded," newspaper women could "encourage the great work" women were doing in "education, religion, philanthropy and the home." Such topics could "pass the censorship of the most conservative managing editor."[40]

Flying beneath the radar, then, newspaper women often published lively, opinionated columns—even under the silly headings established by male editors such as "Gossip" or "Chatter." Eliza Putnam Heaton, for instance, was particularly interested in the lives of independent young women in New York. Her "Reading for the Home" column had relatively little to do with such domestic topics as cookery or decorating. Instead, at a time of great change, when young women were entering the workforce as never before, she felt an intense curiosity both to see and to imagine a variety of women's lives in full. Like so many other young newspaper women, she was eager to observe and report on the new public lives of women for a large audience of newspaper readers. "Where do they come from?" she asked in an article on the young "medical students of the sex feminine in New York City." "How do they live?" If one "happens to run across them, their individuality marks them out at once, as a busy, cheery set, hard at work but usually ready for a frolic; much like other girls in their breezy, feminine ways, but holding their work foremost and keeping one object in life uppermost." "Each student is a marked individual," Heaton repeated later in the article. In age, she said, they ranged "from 22 to 26 or 27"—just about Heaton's own age. Though some of them were "decidedly pinched" for money, they managed a "homelike look" in their small furnished rooms with "a good picture or two, a comfortable litter of books and papers, blossoming plants," and "miscellaneous knick-knacks."[41]

Heaton was not interested in housekeeping or domesticity for its own sake; she did not adhere to the domestic pieties of the mid-nineteenth century, nor did she celebrate the "domestic angel" in her home. Instead she sought to prove in her columns that the independent young woman was *capable* of creating her own home—thus rebutting the many critics of the day who argued otherwise. She explored a variety of contemporary reform movements and ideas, especially as they might affect energetic, self-supporting young women. About the dress reformer Jenness Miller, who was about to visit Vassar College, she wrote: "Mrs. Miller's scheme is the most feasible one yet put before the feminine world; and it is to the younger women that any plan of reform ought to address itself. It is they who have the courage to break from the conservative lines, and they who have the grace and beauty to win favor for whatever guise they choose to assume before an indulgent public."[42]

Heaton was a strong advocate of the physical culture movement taken up by young women in the 1880s. Physical culture, she explained, meant "a gymnasium, of course, a gymnastic suit in which one can look much prettier, because freer and less restrained than out of it, and systematic exercise for the wholesome development of the body." She wrote of a "fresh-lipped girl with blowing hair and wind-reddened cheeks" who had "hurried along Thirty-third street the other day" on her way to the first gymnasium in New York City—then accompanied the girl inside to provide a quick tour for her readers in which they quickly became the gymnasium girl themselves. "Ready for business?" she asked. "Off comes the dress and the corset. A jersey and a short light skirt make all the costume necessary." Taking the reader from a rowing machine to weights, Heaton asked: "Did you ever see a woman handle a pair of Indian clubs? She touches them gingerly as if they were loaded and might go off at either end at first, but she catches the swing of that most graceful of all motions after surprisingly few trials."[43]

It was "high time," Heaton declared, that the "Yankee girl" was beginning to engage in physical culture. "This gymnasium training means not merely an hour or two of perfunctory exercise two or three times a week under supervision; it is a sign and a symbol of the whole tendency in favor of a more vigorous physical life that manifests itself in out of door abandon without limit in the lengthening summer vacation, in devotion to every winter sport within reach, and in the search for an in-door substitute and supplement that shall keep the blood moving and the eyes bright at every season and in all weathers."[44]

An athlete herself, Heaton applauded the "athletic movement" that had finally come to women and promoted "robust health." For too long standard books of etiquette had "erected debility into a sweet domestic virtue." She disapprovingly quoted one passage from Dr. John Gregory's *Legacy to His Daughters*, "the standard book of etiquette for fifty years." Gregory had asserted: "We so naturally associate the idea of feminine delicacy and softness with a correspondent delicacy of constitution that when a woman speaks of her strength, her appetite, her ability to bear fatigue, we recoil at the description in a way she is little aware of." Heaton's disapproval of such an old-fashioned view was explicit. "A gymnasium?" she asked. "The doctor's soul would have recoiled at it." But it was a "good thing for the New York damsel," who as an "average American girl" was a "good walker" but had a "flat chest, a small bust, and weak back." She was beginning "to realize her defects as a physical being" and was "giving a little time and attention to correcting them."[45]

Heaton's interest in independent young women extended to working women as well as college women. In 1887 this meant she joined a number of middle-class writers, reformers, and thinkers—from Jane Addams to Henry George—who sought to understand the "problem of poverty" and the "labor question." Quite striking in Heaton's many columns on working girls was her distance from those reformers who studied working-class conditions only to conclude that the "solution" lay in the help of upper-class, charitable men and women, who could lead the "ignorant," "prejudiced" poor. The reformer Helen Campbell, for instance, whom the *New-York Tribune* had hired in 1886 to write a series of articles about wage-earning women in the city, concluded in "Prisoners of Poverty" that only with the help of charitable women from the "better classes" could the lives of "degraded" working women be improved.[46]

But Heaton avoided such language of victimhood and degradation. In an article on shopgirls, she explicitly stated that "the salesgirl is not altogether a victim. She has a chance, from her involuntary post of observation, to learn a deal of human nature, and not infrequently she improves it." In an article on cooperative housekeeping—a reform idea bruited in the years just after the Civil War but receiving renewed interest in the mid-1880s— Heaton mentioned the failed scheme of department store magnate Alexander Stewart to provide a working woman's hotel. Heaton scornfully called it Stewart's "magnificent dunder," before adding: "What a rich man proposes to do for the working woman is one thing; what the working woman is doing for herself is, to me, a far more interesting thing."[47] Again and again, Heaton emphasized working women's own efforts, not the efforts of charitable women from the upper classes.

There was a "working-woman's hotel already in operation in New York city," Heaton said, "started by the capital of shop girls, which is run by shop girls and which accommodates shop girls. It keeps a roof over the heads of some seventy inmates, and it never asks the working woman to barter her independence for a home." Heaton provided an almost lyrical description of the pleasures working women had experienced in organizing their own space: on the day the "house" opened, one of the three organizers told Heaton that fifty young women ran through the house like "a flock of delighted children." They "ran upstairs and downstairs, and the homelier a nook or corner was the better they liked it. It was a camping-out frolic" for them: "To have a house to themselves where they could do as they pleased was a luxury that went to their heads." The building "in which this cheerful paragraph of the city's history is being written is a double brick house, abounding in a multiplicity of small rooms, in a quiet by street," Heaton said, adding that "it never tangles a woman in rules and regulations till she strangles for fresh air."[48]

If this boardinghouse sounded too good to be true—it probably was. Passionately interested in emerging cooperative ideas of all kinds—including cooperative boardinghouses, cooperative stores, cooperative housekeeping, and cooperative production—Heaton seems to have written a set of utopian fictions, or at least part-fictions, in her columns on these topics.[49] In this she was far from alone: both newspaper women and men often built upon "facts" in their writing to create compelling stories. Elizabeth Jordan, for instance, wrote her column "True Stories of the News" as a series of fictions based loosely on fact for the *New York World* in 1891. Newspaper men and women even invented conversations, or parts of conversations; it was often a matter of pride *not* to take extensive notes, but to re-create an interview from memory. Today we are distinctly uneasy with a genre of newspaper writing that is neither fiction nor fact, but at the turn of the century lines were often not clearly drawn between stories and "facts," particularly in columns, like Heaton's, that explored new ideas rather than actual news. What has been called the "myth of objectivity" was just emerging as a major journalistic value.[50]

In writing compelling stories—which often read like how-to accounts for setting up a cooperative store or cooperative housekeeping—Heaton was part of a wide-ranging group of reformers who were deeply interested in these topics in the mid-1880s, including author Edward Bellamy and settlement house pioneer Jane Addams. Notably, Bellamy's *Looking Backward* was published in 1888; Addams moved into Hull House in the fall of 1889. In other words, in 1887 Heaton was at the cutting edge in exploring and publicizing the idealistic visions of a cooperative commonwealth that circulated in the literature of the Knights of Labor, the writings of women reformers such as Mary Livermore, and the works of English reformers of the day, among others. The woman's page of the newspaper is not where we ordinarily expect to find such ideas circulated, but many newspaper women shared an interest in those reforms and must be seen as participants in wider reform movements.

Like Eliza Heaton, newspaper woman Florence Williams was interested in ideas of public cooperation among women. In a lively set of columns published during 1889 she explored the idea of forming a "co-operative society," or cooperative store, composed of fifty or more "good, earnest, working women" who would each contribute a limited amount of capital to the proposed venture. Williams imagined "dress and millinery departments" in the basement of a "house of four or five stories" in Manhattan: on the first floor would be "the display and sales department with counters, and cases filled with notions, such as linings, buttons, pins, cottons, sewing silks, ribbons, goods for aprons, white and colored muslins, trimmings of laces and embroideries, stationery, fancy goods, lamps, made-up garments, confections, and many other things too numerous to mention." Williams had "not the least doubt but that the society would be able to reap quite a sum from the enterprise" and invited her readers to respond, saying she "would be pleased to hear something upon this matter from well thinking women." A week later, delighted at the reader response she received to this idea, Williams urged the "co-workers" she had heard from to "call a meeting and get this association into working trim."[51]

Williams's advocacy of public cooperation was not unusual among newspaper women in the late 1880s and early 1890s; what *was* unusual was that she wrote glowingly of this utopian scheme in a lively, sharp-tongued column that appeared under her own byline during 1889 and 1890 in the African American newspaper the *New York Age*.[52] The subjects of her weekly column ranged from fashion to politics to working women's issues to humorous sketches of city life. Yet unlike the work of renowned African American newspaper woman Gertrude Bustill Mossell (Mrs. N. F. Mossell), who wrote the column "Our Woman's Department" for the *New York Age* in 1886 and 1887 and advocated "racial uplift," Williams's often biting, trenchantly observed column has virtually disappeared from historical memory. One reason may be that, like so many other newspaper women, Williams produced a miscellaneous column covering multiple topics, one that may have been hard for either literary critics or historians to categorize (or even to see). She sometimes wrote about such "woman's topics" as fashion, under such headings as "Fashion in Ball Costumes" or "Social Reflections" (titles possibly assigned to her by *New York Age* editor T. Thomas Fortune). But Williams was not a "society editor," as she was once described, nor did she explicitly advocate "true womanhood" — unlike Gertrude Mossell, who each week began her column with a header announcing that "the aim of this column will be to promote true womanhood, especially that of the African race."[53]

Williams never became well known outside the pages of the *New York Age*; she never published a book on the progress of African American women, for instance, as Mossell did. Nor was she named by her contemporaries as part of an emerging genteel black middle class—even though we can find her attending many of the same kind of literary club meetings, dinners, and soirees.[54] As with so many other newspaper women, her class identification may have been complicated by her need to work or her level of education or her family background, among other factors. Though she was an accomplished African American woman and a lively writer, Williams was never trumpeted by her editor, T. Thomas Fortune, as one of "our women" to be celebrated—as he did with Ida B. Wells and Gertrude Mossell. Nor did she appear in booster literature naming accomplished or elite African American women.

Like so many other newspaper women, Williams seems to have used newspaper work as a phase of her career rather than permanent work. Before starting her bylined column, for instance, she had been listed for several years on the masthead as the "only authorized collector" of "subscriptions, advertisements and other matter" for the *New York Age* (in its earlier incarnations as the *New York Globe* and *New York Freeman*), "whose receipts alone will be recognized by the publisher."[55] Soon after ending her column in March 1890, Williams was "off for the West Indies" as the manager of the "New York Concert Company," which was presenting the Tennessee Jubilee Singers in concert.[56] In short, she left newspaper work to become a theatrical impresario.

Forgotten by history, Williams's writings nonetheless compel our notice. From her very first column Williams created an animated public conversation, often deliberately engaging "racy" topics rather than domestic pieties. Her inaugural column led off with the distinctly nondomestic, even eyebrow-raising subject of "decollete dressing." "What is this complaint that goes out from the pulpit and press against this fashion?" Williams demanded. "We are told by some that it is immodest and an abomination." But "that depends entirely on how the minds of those run who gaze upon the dress," she said, in a pointed criticism of male critics. "American women have freedom and independence which they will exercise according to their judgment without the dictation of man," she declared. Besides, "these cavilers are a lot of cranks, who would not tolerate the interference of females with their style of trousers. O, no, but they feel it their divine right to pay strict attention to the garb of women." She urged, "Leave our women to decide what is modest and what is not. They are better able to judge on that point than man," and concluded sarcastically, "The next thing we will be asked to do is to exclude statuary and fine arts from our parlors for fear they might corrupt our morals."[57]

Here was a strong, biting, individual voice, established immediately without apology or sentimentalism—no "gush," to use the term that so often negatively characterized newspaper women's writings. In the same column Williams moved quickly to a paragraph on politics, offering the tart opinion that "there seems to be a lack of harmony in the different Republican clubs about town," as "every one wants a position and every one can't get a position." She then concluded with two adroit city sketches, based on observation of the city streets. In the first, she pictured "dudes in patent-leathers, kid gloves and silver-headed canes," who were standing "side by side of the park inspectors with red noses, bristling beards, ventilating hats, parted garments and sandals, exchanging breezy comments and attacking cold items from the free lunch reservoirs." In a quick sketch of children dancing on the sidewalks, she wrote: "Notwithstanding the cold winds of Monday afternoon a number of small and half grown children dived from back yards, alley ways, front houses, and in fact from every conceivable outlet in an uptown street, to enjoy the sweet strains of music set forth from a band of colored brethren consisting of a violin, banjo, guitar and clappers." Eventually, "their pent-up spirits found an outlet; away they went flying around and around on the sidewalk, feet keeping a patter patter with the music." Describing one little girl who "took up the sides of her dress with the grace of a duchess and set in," Williams exclaimed, "You should have seen the way that baby danced the shuffle, double and single, the curving and twisting of the body, the running on the heels, the side step"—in fact "all kinds of steps, that would have done credit to a minstrel performer."[58] This was a lively, street-smart urban sketch quite different from Gertrude Mossell's earnest columns of racial uplift and advocacy of new careers for women.

Williams's new column immediately received notice within the national community of African American newspapers communicating through "exchanges" (clipping and commenting on each others' articles)—notice that was swiftly reprinted as a welcome form of publicity in the *New York Age*. "Miss Florence Williams," Bruce Grit (John Edward Bruce) of the *Washington Bee* had written, "is now contributing a weekly letter to *The Age* on current events interspersed at odd intervals with real and imaginative descriptions of side-splitting and ludicrous happenings in and around New York City." Tackling the question of Williams's veiled criticism of Republican politicians, the *Bee* commented: "She is a pleasing writer and will be still more so when she learns to lay aside her prejudice against certain people whose portraits are between the lines of her biting sarcasm and invective." Williams was a woman with a "will of her own" and was "capable of saying sharp and pithy things."[59]

Williams quickly responded in her own column, noting that Bruce Grit "claims that I am prejudiced against certain people whose portraits gleam between the lines of my reference to the Cooper Union Emancipation Proclamation" (a meeting that had recently occurred in New York)—and that this is why I pounce upon the representatives sent from that meeting to Indianapolis to interview President-elect [Benjamin] Harrison." "Now, am I prejudiced or am I not?" she asked. "I am prejudiced against any action of colored men that places them or the race in a position of humiliation in the eyes of white men, be they millionaires or paupers; it is the same. If it be offensive to some to say so, so be it. Am I not right?" Mincing no words, Williams added that "I still maintain that the meeting was a white man's affair from beginning to end, and an insult to the emancipated people, who should not accept it as a compliment, but the reverse; in fact as an impertinence."[60]

What is one to make of a column like that of Florence Williams, in which fashion, politics, city "sketches," and humor intermingled? Clearly Williams, much like Eliza Heaton, used a "woman's column" to address issues of larger public significance. And like Heaton, she covered a range of women's concerns: Williams was strikingly feminist. In addition to urging cooperative stores among women, she advocated equal pay for women: "It is of no small interest to us as women to find that we figure on a large scale as wage earners," she began one column. "Many a woman is the head and support of a large family. Women are to be found in all sorts of occupations. They have the same hours and do the same kind of work as men; and yet it is not in three cases out of ten that they receive the same amount of pay for the same amount of work as a man. The unfairness of women's wages in comparison to men's wages is a puzzle to me. I cannot see why this difference should be made."[61]

African American newspaper women have often been portrayed as entirely different from their white counterparts of the same era—not only writing in a separate realm of black newspapers, but also writing exclusively about issues related to racial uplift. But as Florence Williams's work shows, metropolitan African American newspaper women sometimes addressed issues including, but not limited to, racial uplift. One of Williams's obvious goals was to entertain her newspaper audience—her columns were a form of theatrical performance.

African American newspaper women clearly read the mass-circulation metropolitan newspapers of their day, sometimes recycling the contents for their own readers: thus Gertrude Mossell quoted from Marion Harland several times in her *New York Age* "Our Woman's Department" columns. But she was far from an advocate of Harland's version of true womanhood. As Mossell said in one column, "The orthodox opinion concerning woman is that she should have a home and stay in it. Now we are orthodox, and then we go farther and fear some will cry unorthodox, for we believe in her place being at home and in other places, too."[62] No wonder Mossell also quoted extensively from the work of Eliza Archard Conner on the hopeful future of women in journalism and the training they needed to succeed.[63] Not only did she want to build up a "sisterhood" among her readers—a print community of shared information and goals—but also she strategically used the existing "sisterhood" among white newspaper women to find information for her columns. Many of Mossell's columns were devoted to employment opportunities for women—and a number of readers wrote to say how much they appreciated her efforts.

Although Mossell quoted extensively from works of "the other race," there was no reciprocity: white newspaper women never quoted from "race" newspapers and only rarely mentioned African American women in the woman's department. In her 1894 book *The Work of the Afro-American Woman*, Mossell put the best face on the barriers black women faced in newspaper work: "In the large cities especially of the North we have here and there found openings on white journals. More will come as more are prepared to fill them and when it will have become no novelty to be dreaded by editor or fellow-reporters." She also maintained that "in seven years' experience as an interviewer on two white papers I have never met with a refusal from either sex or race."[64]

Yet as she indicated in several columns, her interviews and articles were limited to African American topics. White newspapers employed African American women primarily to report on "colored" social events so they would appeal to an African American readership. The *Brooklyn Daily Eagle*, for instance, ran frequent brief notices of African American social events like the meetings of the Brooklyn Literary Union, which sometimes included newspaper woman Victoria Earle Matthews.

Not only is there no record of an African American newspaper woman being hired on staff by one of the major metropolitan newspapers during the 1890s, but most white newspaper women showed no interest in African American concerns or progress. As many scholars have shown, "progressive" womanhood was often predicated on implicit (and explicit) assumptions of white superiority, not to mention virulent racism.[65] Nevertheless, we can occasionally find the voices of African American women in the woman's pages of major metropolitan newspapers of the 1890s if we expand our ideas of what constituted "writing" in a world that denied African American women regular channels for placing articles. If we think of their writing as a set of interlinked actions—composing articles, submitting them to white newspapers, and using the power of mainstream newspaper publicity as a form of resistance—then African American newspaper women occasionally become visible in the woman's pages of the mainstream press. On several occasions African American newspaper women used newspaper publicity to test the "color line"—that race-based barrier to full inclusion in society. Their attempts to desegregate some of the major women's organizations of the 1890s and early 1900s are an example of this form of resistance.

The growth of the national woman's club movement was one of the major organizational stories for women in the 1890s, and "club notes" became a perennial attraction of the woman's page. Club notes were, in fact, a bread-and-butter feature for newspaper women—including accounts of such nationally prominent clubs as Sorosis, in New York, founded in 1868 by Jennie June Croly. Some newspaper women took middle-class clubs such as Sorosis quite seriously: Elizabeth Jordan of the *New York World*, for instance, often led off her woman's page of the 1890s with an account of the club's "doings." (Jordan was a member of Sorosis.) Other newspaper women despised the clubs for what they considered their vacuous tittle-tattle and elitist pretensions, and resented having to cover them. Nevertheless, coverage of the clubs remained a permanent assignment of woman's page writers. In 1914 Clara Savage, fresh out of Smith College and assigned to the woman's page of the *New York Evening Post*, wrote of the "sleek, fat clubwomen" wandering in to a club meeting half an hour late and then spending "an hour or so pitying the 'poor prisoner.'" "Oh! Those awful clubs!" she moaned to her diary.[66]

The club movement became a national force in the 1880s and 1890s, part of a larger drive toward professionalization and organization that took shape in multiple arenas of American life. State press organizations were founded in 1885 and 1886. The General Federation of Women's Clubs, a national organization of clubs, was formed in 1890, again inspired by Jennie June Croly, who invited club representatives from around the country to New York in order to create a national organization. It was a heady time for the founding of women's organizations that would engage in literary study, self-education, and—increasingly—social reform.

Most of these clubs, including new press organizations, were for whites only, with the exception of the New England Woman's Press Club, which admitted notable African American journalist Josephine St. Pierre Ruffin. Editor of the pathbreaking African American women's newspaper the *Woman's Era*, Ruffin was herself a vital force in the club movement. She founded the Woman's New Era Club in 1894 and the National Federation of Afro-American Women in 1895. The National Federation merged with another organization of African American women's clubs, the Colored Women's League, to form the National Association of Colored Women.[67]

Within the General Federation, and within most state and local clubs, the color line remained firmly in place. But the 1890s marked several attempts by African American newspaper women and women's clubs to break through the color barrier in white organizations—attempts that were often discussed on the woman's page of newspapers. And very occasionally progressive white women—though not necessarily newspaper women—took a stand against the color line. In 1894, for instance, African American artist, writer, and newspaper woman Fannie Barrier Williams was nominated for membership in the elite Chicago Woman's Club by its progressive club president. Williams was a seemingly unimpeachable choice to test the color line by the standards of this elite club, but the question of her admission turned into a protracted conflict. Chicago newspapers gave extensive coverage to the club's deliberations, which is how we know that one of the staunchest opponents of Williams's admission was Elia Peattie, a prominent newspaper woman who had first worked on the *Omaha World-Herald* before moving to Chicago and taking up work on the *Tribune*. She became that paper's foremost book reviewer in the early 1900s.[68]

Fannie Barrier Williams remembered her experience with the Chicago Woman's Club with understandable bitterness. "I allowed my name to be presented to the club," she wrote, "without the slightest dream that it would cause any opposition or even discussion. This progressive club has a membership of over eight hundred women, and its personality fairly represents the wealth, intelligence and culture of the women of the city. When the members of this great club came to know the color of its new applicant there was a startled cry that seemed to have no bounds. Up to this time no one knew that there was any anti-negro sentiment in the club. Its purposes were so humane and philanthropic and its grade of individual membership so high and inclusive of almost every nationality that my indorsers thought that my application would only be subject to the club's test of eligibility."[69]

Instead, Williams faced a grueling fourteen-month battle to win acceptance. As she wrote in 1904, "Before my admission into the club some of the members came to me and frankly told me that they would leave the club,

Mrs. Fannie Barrier Williams, member of the Chicago Woman's Club, newspaper correspondent, and author. (From A New Negro for a New Century [1900]; Manuscripts, Archives, and Rare Books Division, Schomburg Center for Research in Black Culture, The New York Public Library, Astor, Lenox and Tilden Foundations)

much as they valued their membership, if I persisted in coming in. Their only reason was that they did not think the time had yet come for that sort of equality." Williams would not back down. "I refused to recognize their unreasonable prejudices as something that ought to be fostered and perpetuated; beside, I felt that I owed something to the friends who had shown me such unswerving loyalty through all those long and trying months." She concluded that "whether I live in the North or the South, I cannot be counted for my full value, be that much or little. I dare not cease to hope and aspire and believe in human love and justice, but progress is painful and my faith is often strained to the breaking point."[70]

The Chicago Woman's Club controversy was picked up as a news story nationwide: it appeared in "regular" news sections in some papers, but on the woman's page in others. A few newspaper women took up Williams's cause. In Kate Field's view, it was to "the infinite credit of this club that its ablest members" were eager to admit Williams; after all, "no one questions her manners, her morals, or her brains. She seems to be the peer of most of her white sisters in all these respects, and the superior of many." But in scoffing at the fears of white clubwomen, Field revealed the limits of her own commitment to equality: "Those opposed to her admission fear to establish a precedent lest it open the door to scores of black women. Why hesitate to do right on the bare chance of an impossibility?"[71] In the end Williams won the battle, but she remained the only African American woman in the club. Most white newspaper women accepted segregation in their ranks—if not explicitly, then implicitly.

The 1893 Chicago World's Columbian Exposition, or World's Fair, was a defining moment for newspaper women as a group. The Woman's Press Congress, a daylong event of symposia and speeches in the midst of a week-long "Press Congress," brought together a national group of female press luminaries including Jennie June Croly, Kate Field, Eliza Archard Conner, Ida H. Harper, Mary H. Krout (described as "president of the National press league," one of many organizations newspaper women began in the 1890s), Helen M. Winslow, and, on the subject of "Women as Newspaper Proprietor and Editor," Mrs. E. J. Nicholson of the *New Orleans Daily Picayune*. Women from France, Sweden, Japan, and other countries also attended. Speaking at the newspaper women's first session, Susan B. Anthony proposed that women start their own daily newspaper, not limited to suffrage, but "edited and composed according to woman's own thoughts, and not as a man wants her to think and write." They should "organize a stock company and run a newspaper on their own basis," she argued. Her newspaper idea "was as catchy as fire in a dry prairie on a windy day," one reporter commented. "At the close of the session, every woman said, 'Of course we will; and we will make Miss Anthony managing editor.'"[72]

The Columbian Exposition not only firmed up white newspaper women's collective identity, it offered them many individual opportunities for work. With millions of people traveling to Chicago, the fair was a source of continuing national interest that provided numerous "woman's page" and "human interest" possibilities. Female reporters descended on the city, writing "Columbian correspondence" for their home papers. Catherine Cole (Martha R. Field) wrote sixty-four "letters" about the fair for the *New Orleans Daily Picayune*. Other women freelanced with human interest columns, such as Teresa Dean's "White City Chips" (see Chapter 3), which was a substantial hit for the *Chicago Inter Ocean*.[73]

African American women had an entirely different experience at the exposition. No black female journalist was invited to the Woman's Press Congress—not even Ida B. Wells, who had owned her own newspaper, the *Free Speech*, in Memphis, and whose extraordinary newspaper work against lynching was well known. That summer the *Chicago Inter Ocean* even commissioned her to write an investigative piece on a particular lynching—an unusual gesture by the progressive mainstream press acknowledging her authority on the subject.[74]

Wells was not the only prominent African American denied a place at the World's Fair. Frederick Douglass was invited to participate officially only by the government of Haiti, not the United States. Moreover, African American achievements were systematically denied representation; prominent African Americans themselves were denied any leadership roles on the Board of Managers and other governing committees; and African American women's work was not represented in the famous Woman's Building that showcased varieties of women's work, despite the efforts by many black women activists to obtain inclusion. Before the exposition began, African American newspapers had held extensive discussions on whether to participate in the fair at all.

Those discussions grew more heated after, in a supposedly placating gesture, an "African American Day" was designated at the fair that would include free watermelons offered at the gates. Ida B. Wells joined with Frederick Douglass in drafting a resolution to protest the fair. It began: "*Whereas,* It has been published that the 25th day of August has been set apart as colored folks, or jubilee day at the World's Fair; *Resolved,* That such resolution meets our most emphatic disapproval, and we earnestly recommend to the colored people throughout the country that no attention be paid by them to the setting apart of that day."[75] Although the African American press fractured on the question of whether or not to attend the fair, Wells went ahead with plans to coauthor, again with Frederick Douglass, a protest pamphlet to be distributed at the fair: *The Reason Why the Colored American Is Not in the World's Columbian Exposition.*[76] Ultimately, Wells handed out thousands of copies of this pamphlet at the exposition, but it attracted remarkably little notice.

The mainstream white press was not interested in celebrating or showcasing African American progress, as Gertrude Mossell had bitterly noted. But attempts to "break" the color line—at least if they involved an attempt to desegregate whites-only woman's clubs—continued to attract attention on the woman's page and elsewhere. Thus in September 1895, as the Atlanta Exposition drew near, the *Chicago Tribune* commented that the "'color line' among women" would not "obtrude itself into the Atlanta exposition." The "time-honored hospitality of the South" was the "saving force" that would keep the "vexed question under cover." The situation was after all "simplified by the official recognition of the negro in the negro building." But white Georgia clubwomen had made clear that they would leave the General Federation of Women's Clubs if any clubs containing "colored women" sent African American delegates to Atlanta. Newspaper woman Corinne Stocker, "one of the editors of the Atlanta Journal," explained that "in this matter Southern women are not narrow minded or bigoted, but they simply cannot recognize the colored woman socially."[77]

Again in 1900 another flurry of articles, many of them on woman's pages, surrounded Josephine Ruffin's attempts to have her Woman's New Era Club admitted to the General Federation. This time more newspapers—and newspaper women—covered the struggle. The "Only Woman's Page" of the *New-York Tribune*, for instance, featured an article titled "New-York Women Protest: They Declare that Colored Delegates Should Be Admitted to the Biennial." An anonymous female reporter had been enterprising enough to conduct a set of brief interviews on the color line with prominent New York white women. "For the life of me," Mrs. A. M. Palmer said, "I can't see any palpable excuse for a 'color line' to be drawn." Pointing out that there had already been "colored delegates" in the State Federation convention, she declared, "If a colored woman has the brains to keep pace with her fairer sisters, to write a brilliant paper and to read it intelligently, I would by far prefer to listen to it than to one-half of the 'twaddle' one is forced to hear at many club meetings during the winter."[78]

But in the event, the General Federation excluded Ruffin from its annual convention—news that many Northern mass-circulation papers reported as unfair. Yet even as they did so, they continued to exclude African American women from their workforce and to ignore their concerns.

# # #

The woman's page underwent a variety of changes between 1890 and 1915, many of which can be glimpsed if we focus initially on one newspaper, the *New York Evening Post*. A highly respected, "serious" paper at the turn of the century (compared, say, to the more "sensational" *New York World*), the *Post* had a wider circulation and higher status than the *New York Times*, which was only just coming into its own.[79] Luckily for historians, the *Post* maintained a handwritten index during the years 1892 to 1918, revealing a dramatic increase in stories about women at the turn of the century. Before 1900, such topics as "Women's Work in the Hospitals" (1892) or "Woman Suffrage—Not For" (1893) appeared only occasionally in the index. But in 1899 the index began to feature an entire section called "Women and Their Work," which itemized the titles of a new weekly woman's page column under that name.[80] It is not clear who began this column—whether it was initially the idea of a male editor or a newspaper woman—but, whoever started it, the result was that the *Post* now devoted dozens of articles every year to women and their changing status.

The "Women and Their Work" column underwent significant changes in the first few years of its existence. At first it dealt with topics that were little different from those discussed by elite women's magazines of a previous era, which focused on middle-class women's household issues. Thus, Margaret Hamilton Welch's October 1901 column, titled "Domestic Service Difficulties Growing Crucial," addressed the well-worn topic of the "servant problem"—by which she meant not the difficulties of work for domestic servants, but instead the supposed difficulties middle-class women had in hiring servants. The "servant problem" had been a mainstay of women's magazines for decades.[81] Welch, who during the 1890s wrote the column "Her Point of View" for the *New York Times* before joining the editorial staff of *Harper's Bazar*, assumed that her audience did not work for a living outside the home—this despite the fact that she herself had to do so after the death of her husband and staunchly defended newspaper work as a career for women. In an 1894 lecture she even asserted that there was "no career opening more of honor and of promise for a woman than in the field of newspaper work."[82]

But it would take a younger generation to press against the perceived limits of subject matter and style on the woman's page. Before Rheta Dorr was hired in a staff position by the *New York Evening Post* in 1900, it had not been clear that "the managing editor would consent to employ a woman," but he "needed someone" to edit the woman's page and thought she "could do the work." The paper "had a number of women contributors, and the management thought that if they could find exactly the right woman to edit this and write most of the purely 'woman stuff' herself, it might be advantageous." The managing editor informed her that she "would be given a few weeks' trial."[83]

Dorr's duties included following women's "club activities, local and national," and writing weekly columns about fashion and housekeeping. This was her "department" work, and her disdain for it was palpable. But she also wrote "editorial paragraphs and special articles of interest to women. These related to women's philanthropies, college women's activities and particularly to any profession or business in which women were beginning to shine." Close attention to emerging professions for women marked the woman's pages of many mass-circulation newspapers in addition to the *Post* at the turn of the century. Women "really were beginning," Dorr observed, but "in such small numbers that a single success was worth a special article. Even the newspapers were admitting that women were getting to have a certain news-value and one after another they began to take on women reporters. I found that I had quite a group of colleagues."[84]

Dorr clearly took pleasure in writing the "Women and Work" column, which ran every Wednesday and allowed her to interview women leaders and explore new reform movements. "I enjoyed this," she said, "because it brought me in contact with people worth knowing," including Maud Nathan and Florence Kelley of the Consumers' League; Lillian Wald, head of the Henry Street Settlement; suffrage leaders Carrie Chapman Catt and Dr. Anna Shaw; and author and lecturer Charlotte Perkins Gilman, who was an "object of reverence" for Dorr. The column also brought readers to the *Post*. "The business office let me know that I was getting results," she commented with obvious satisfaction.[85]

Dorr's column may have been "confined" to the woman's page, but the work it required actually liberated her from the "hen coop" and sent her out into the greater life of the city. After all, in order to write "Women and Work," Dorr needed to research potential stories and gather information about women's "doings," interview individual subjects, and attend meetings of women's organizations. Hers was physical as well as intellectual work, requiring her first to circulate physically through the city before circulating the information she had gathered in her columns.

Like so many newspaper women of the period, Dorr brought a keen intelligence to her work. But the topics she covered ranged far more widely than those of most newspaper women of an earlier era, who often had been limited to middle-class women's household concerns. In researching her column, she frequently encountered the new and unexpected — in fact, accident itself was an important way in which she gained new knowledge, something she later reflected on. She was "not unmindful of what the 'Evening Post' had done" for her, she wrote in her memoir, looking back on a rich career of social activism and writing. She was "taught to write good, clear English" and was "forced into habits of straight thinking and accurate statement," which "meant much" in her "life as a writer." But the "best that the 'Evening Post' did for me," she wrote, "was done accidentally."[86]

One day her editor had come to her "tiny office" with a "newspaper clipping in his hand," asking, "'What is a woman gold-beater?'" The clipping he held said "that the gold-beaters are going to strike and one of their grievances is that women have invaded their trade." Perhaps, he told her, there was a "Women and Work" story for her "in these proletarian Amazons." Dorr had "never heard of gold-beaters, male or female," but she soon discovered that gold beating was a "factory trade" involving the preparation of paper-thin gold leaf used in book binding. The gold-beating factory she visited employed "not Amazons but very meek, pale, undersized immigrant girls about fourteen years old."[87]

That visit changed her life. Why, she asked the shop foreman, did the men want to turn the "poor little girls out of the trade"? The foreman replied that "'they wanted to replace the girls with boy apprentices'"; after all, "'Girls just work temporary till they get married.'" "But what will these girls do if they lose their jobs?" Dorr asked. "'I dunno,'" was the "indifferent answer," she reported. "'Women don't belong in jobs nohow,'" the foreman told her. "'They oughtta get married.'" The story Dorr wrote as a result of her research told of "poor little immigrant girls who worked in cold, airless rooms for three dollars a week, which wealth was about to be taken away from them": it was "a new kind of a story" for the *Post* to publish. Not only was Dorr "commended" for it, but also her editor told her to "get another one of that sort once in awhile" (though he cautiously advised her to be sure to show it to him before it was sent to the composing room).[88]

Going after stories of "that sort"—whether about the female gold beaters or about the skilled women glassworkers at Tiffany's who were being driven from their jobs—changed Dorr's perception of the world around her, literally enabling her to *see* it in new ways. "I began to see them as never before," Dorr wrote of working women, "hundreds and thousands of women, every evening crowding the subways, the elevated, the surface-cars, the streets; hundreds and thousands of them going home from work. Were they all just filling in the time until some man offered bed and board, or were they, like myself, giving all their brain and nerve and muscle to earn their bread?"[89]

Dorr empathized with women workers across class lines: herself a divorced woman with a small son to support, she found that even in the "intellectual atmosphere" of the *Post*, the "same opinion prevailed" as that expressed by the gold beaters' foreman: women should be supported by husbands rather than work. When she asked for a raise after a year and a half, her editor refused, telling her not only that he could easily replace her with one of the many women trying to break into journalism ("and, as you know," he said, twisting the knife, "the positions are very few"), but also that women could never expect to be paid the same salaries as men. "Men are permanent industrial factors, women mere accidents," he told her. "Men work all their lives, women only until it becomes unnecessary for them to do so." Young men needed "higher salaries" than women because some day they would marry and have children and "must save money against that time."[90] It was a classic statement of "family wage" ideology that labor unions had been articulating for decades, and it enraged Dorr.

Eventually it would propel her out of newspaper work entirely. As she became more and more interested in trade unionism, Dorr began "to despise my own trade of writing" and found the "rarefied atmosphere" of the *Post* "almost unbearable." Her newspaper writing began to seem "thin and colorless" compared with the "tumult" of her own thoughts as she explored labor conditions for working women, moved to the Lower East Side in order to live among immigrant women, and began working with the Women's Trade Union League. When she asked her editor at the *Post*, "What is my future on this paper?" he "answered candidly: 'You have no future. There is no position open to you better than the one you now hold. You know yourself that a woman could never be a city editor, much less a managing editor.'"[91] With no possibility for advancement at the *Post*, Dorr left to write articles for magazines, to write books, to travel widely (she would report firsthand on the Russian Revolution), and to coordinate publicity for one branch of the suffrage movement, among other work.[92]

Other newspaper women, at other major newspapers, followed a similar trajectory. In Chicago, Wellesley graduate Ada May Krecker's first byline at the *Tribune* headed the "Household Hints" column: in early 1904 she alerted her readers that the "January cook" had a "good friend in cabbage, which may be transformed with delicate magic into many a fine dainty besides an accompaniment to boiled ham."[93] Though Krecker left no papers behind reflecting on her newspaper career, we can deduce from her contributions to the *Tribune* that provision of such "hintlets" to women was not the extent of her ambition. By 1905 she had supplied an article titled "Work Unnatural for Man: A Result of Evolution" for the "Workers' Magazine," a new Sunday section of the *Tribune*; in 1906 she began periodically supplying an editorial on the *Tribune*'s "Editorials by the Laity" page. Krecker's first editorial, "Muck Rake Is Emblem of a [sic] Era," reflected her avid and increasingly radical interest in reform.[94]

In 1907 Krecker began writing the column "What Women Are Doing in the World," which ran weekly on the woman's page under a cartoon illustration of a determined woman with her shirtwaist sleeves rolled up, using a long crowbar to lift the Earth. Along with providing brief discussions of new occupations for women such as the "woman mail carrier" and "women chemists," this column was unusual for discussing women's lives around the globe—perhaps a reflection of Krecker's upbringing in Japan as the child of missionaries.[95]

By 1908 Krecker was reflecting on the "modern" status of women in her editorials. In "Woman's Rise Parallels Masses," she argued that "the modern spirit is for elevating the position of woman, for making her a national as well as a domestic figure, for making her a ruler as well as a subject, for educating and enfranchising her, and for giving her positions of moment in public spheres which hitherto have been deemed above her." The "rise of women toward the dignities of men" was part of the "current tide toward democracy," she concluded.[96] From 1908 to 1911 Krecker continued to write about women's work and labor generally, with articles on child labor, work, and poverty, including the feature "How the Poorest Families Fight to Keep the Wolf from the Door."[97]

But in 1911 Krecker seems to have left the *Tribune*, for reasons we cannot fully discern. It is certainly possible that her ambition—or her vision of radical change—had moved beyond what could be expressed (or tolerated) at the paper. Interested in theosophy, fascinated by utopian visions, Krecker seemed to be moving beyond newspaper writing altogether. Her final *Tribune* piece—"Shall We Fly to Other Worlds?"—speculated on the possibilities of space travel, particularly to Venus. It concluded that by "traversing the celestial spaces of the firmament," we "shall be a new people" with "revolutions in our architecture and all our practical arts and sciences, in our foods, our dress, our language, music, our government, religion. In a word, there will be a new earth."[98] Such utopian speculation was no longer obviously newspaper material. In 1912 Krecker published an essay in Emma Goldman's anarchist journal *Mother Earth* titled "The Passing of the Family," in which she explored ideas of communal social arrangements that would enable women to have both careers and families: "For careers the mothers will have. Nothing can keep them out of careers."[99] Then Krecker, like so many other newspaper women, passed from view in the public record.

The woman's page could only briefly contain the radical energies that writers like Dorr and Krecker brought to it before 1910. But there is no question that the experience of working on the woman's page itself could be radicalizing. Such work often exposed women to social conditions and labor practices they might not otherwise have been aware of. As Marie Manning of the *New York Journal* wrote, "The first time I ever faced squarely the problem of girls patiently and gallantly starving occurred during the Theodore Roosevelt administration when I was sent to interview some young department store employees" who were struggling to live on scant pay. "How, when you came down to facts, did the three-dollar-a-week wage earner actually exist?"[100] Being sent out on assignment to get the "woman's angle" sometimes offered women a revelatory and expansive education in an array of urban social problems.

Few of the newspaper women who began their careers on the woman's page around the turn of the century stayed with newspaper work for the long haul. Many used their stints on the woman's page to find other newspaper work, whether as book reviewers, columnists, or editors of woman's pages (but never managing editors or city editors, positions reserved for men throughout this period). Other women "passed through" the woman's page on the way to becoming magazine writers, editors, novelists, press agents, and publicity agents.

Yet as successive waves of newspaper women left woman's page staff positions, new waves of women signed up. With ready infusions of fresh talent, the woman's page remained remarkably resilient; it continued to be a repository of cooking, fashion, beauty, and household hints through World War I. There was no wholesale revolution in the woman's page, nor did it disappear from most newspapers. In an era of department store advertising, after all, no page was more closely tied to the paper's main source of advertising revenue—in fact, it was often located next to a page (or pages) of department store advertising, underlining the point of who was the imagined shopper in the family.

The woman's page was hardly static, though. Coverage of women's activities shifted, sometimes dramatically, throughout this period, and the woman's page itself was perennially retooled and reinvented, both to take stock of women's perceived greater importance in contemporary life and to respond to the changing individual personalities of newspapers. Change itself, was, of course, an attractive commodity for newspapers to be able to sell, as well. In addition to new columns on women's "doings in the world"; regular household, cookery, beauty, and fashion features; and "fillers" (small squibs that literally filled the space between articles, and had titles such as "Can You Make a Salad Dressing?"),[101] the woman's page included a variety of articles that reflected women's changing status in society. Articles on suffrage increasingly formed a central part of this section; indeed, as the suffrage movement heated up around 1910, energized by the example of English radicalism, coverage of suffrage sometimes threatened to swamp the woman's page entirely.

Features related to women's occupations and public work were another important aspect of the woman's page in these years and continued to increase in number. By the 1910s formerly private household concerns were often reframed as topics for public discussion, part of an emerging new world of expertise that included domestic science, scientific management, and municipal housekeeping (the idea that women could use their housekeeping skills to clean up cities). In 1912 the conservative *New York Times* (which was antisuffrage, unlike, for example, the *Chicago Tribune* or the

New York Evening Post) announced that it would be publishing "a new kind of woman's page" for "the new kind of woman," one that would "reflect the new methods and new thoughts that make woman to-day a strong note in affairs." Promising that the new page would employ "an advisory board of women who are in the forefront of woman's work," including the celebrated muckraking author Ida M. Tarbell, former dean of Radcliffe College Agnes Irwin, and the *Times* "Woman's Department" editor Anne Rittenhouse, the paper claimed that "we have entered seriously upon the big 'business of being a woman'" (this last phrase a tip of the hat to Tarbell's popular 1912 book *The Business of Being a Woman*). Clearly intending to put the woman's page on a more "scientific" basis, the *Times* announced that "new methods are replacing the old, whether it be in keeping house by the Taylor system [a reference to scientific management] or selective marriage [a reference to eugenics]." Each Sunday "women and men who have made studies of the special subjects" would publish articles on "efficiency, domestic economy, social welfare, politics, eugenics, the care and training of children, and other vital subjects."[102] As lofty—or frightening—as this sounded, the updated woman's page offered only a mild revision of the previous page, revealing more reliance on "experts" than a wholesale change.

If the *New York Times* attempted to take the woman's page in a "scientific" direction, putting it squarely within Progressive reform movements of the day, other newspapers had different emphases for their woman's pages. One of the liveliest in the 1910s was the "Woman" page of the *New York Press*, with extensive coverage of women artists and the emerging feminist movement, a subject the *Times* sternly disapproved of. In 1914, for instance, the "Woman" page of the *Press* ran the feature "A Feminist Photographer of Feminists" as its lead article. This lavishly illustrated profile of photographer Nancy Shostac—who apparently is lost to obscurity except for this article—detailed her work as a photographer of "women who do things" and explored her views of other "new" women photographers. "Until women's lives began to take on broader aspects," Shostac asserted, "their photographs showed absolutely no individuality." The description of Shostac herself was telling. She was sitting "on her bamboo stool, her elbows resting on her knees" as she "gazed out at the October sunshine while she smoked languidly, with the deep-breathed inhalations of the woman who really enjoys a cigarette."[103] An approving reflection of "bohemian" women's lives in Greenwich Village, this was not the sort of portrait that could be found in women's magazines like the *Ladies' Home Journal*—not to mention the newly "scientific" *New York Times* woman's page.

The author of the profile, Yetta Dorothea Geffen—also apparently lost to obscurity—was remarkable for being the daughter of Russian Jewish immigrants who spoke Yiddish at home: few Russian immigrants could move easily into newspaper work in this anti-Semitic and anti-immigrant era.[104] Geffen, who listed herself as "reporter" for the *New York Press* in city directories of the period, by 1920 had moved to Washington Square—the heart of New York's Greenwich Village bohemia. Thus it seems likely that her newspaper work offered her a different sort of radical path than that chosen by labor and suffrage activist Rheta Dorr, one that led Geffen straight to the heart of feminism and artistic bohemianism. With a strong interest in theater, she would write a column and various features for *Theatre Magazine* before disappearing in the 1920s from the public record.[105]

By the 1910s, taking up work on a woman's page was a well-established career for women even if, admittedly, the very idea of a woman's career still occasioned disapproval among conservative pundits. The woman's page, too, was now well established, and at some newspapers, such as the *Chicago Tribune*, it employed half a dozen rather than just one or two newspaper women. When Fanny Butcher joined the woman's page of the *Chicago Tribune* in 1913 with the title "assistant to the woman's editor," she was chagrined to discover that there were several such assistants who worked for editor Mary Eleanor O'Donnell, all with the same title, and that Butcher was clearly "the bottom man on the totem pole."[106]

Her career at the *Tribune* underlines the fact that by the 1910s there were more opportunities for women beyond the woman's page at mass-circulation newspapers. During her first year Butcher's assignments ran the gamut of woman's page work. She began with the column "How to Earn Money at Home," a staple of woman's pages with its suggestions on how to sell "homemade 'goodies.'" Told to come up with an idea for this column on her first morning, she immediately "pounded out a half-column on the typewriter" about making "baby pillows out of worn sheets."[107]

Butcher's invaluable ability to "dash off quickly almost any kind of drivel with the aid of a little research" quickly landed her additional jobs on the woman's page, including editing "literally piles of 'Bright Sayings of Children,'" for which the *Tribune* paid a one-dollar prize for "any little monster's repartee." She rewrote the "almost illiterate" beauty advice of contributing columnist Lillian Russell, who had been an icon of 1890s hourglass-figure womanhood and who sent in her handwritten "literary efforts" in a "bulky envelope" every week to be deciphered by the woman's page staff. As "Sally Joy Brown" (one of several "paper names" the *Tribune* used to head its columns), Butcher "offered a helping hand to the needy poor"; under the name "Nancy Rudolph," she wrote about etiquette. She turned her hand briefly to a "column about women in business" and occasionally "wrote about fashions."[108]

But under the redoubtable Mary King, the successor to O'Donnell who would also become Sunday editor of the *Tribune* in 1915, the woman's page became a path to other work on the newspaper.[109] Butcher "had been working on the *Tribune* for a year" when she "got up enough courage to suggest writing a book review now and then." Immediately a "pile of books were thrust into" her "eager arms," and in 1914 she began her own bylined column, "Tabloid Book Review," from which she eventually graduated to become the *Tribune*'s chief book reviewer and a Chicago institution for decades.[110]

# # #

Perhaps it is overdetermined that the woman's page has not received much attention from literary critics and historians: after all, even women reporters themselves held the low-status woman's page in ill repute. And there is no question that for every woman's page feature that offered fresh insight into contemporary life, there were many other articles that were merely pedestrian or worse. Newspaper women were not wrong: there was plenty of "fluff" to be had on the woman's page. But that was not all to be found there.

As newspapers in the post–World War I era began to subscribe to an ideal of "objectivity," woman's page writing sank even lower in status (and into obscurity) because it was not "hard fact" and did not deliver a particular kind of "information." But as Michael Schudson has noted, "information" can be delivered in a variety of ways.[111] We still tend to privilege a particular version of the "hard-hitting news story" when we think of newspaper writing, but feature writing, of course, provides a different set of insights and different forms of knowledge.

Hidden between the miscellaneous articles that composed the woman's page were thousands of articles that provided vivid sketches of contemporary life, focused on women. The best of these stories, with their pictures of urban life and personalities, their sketches and profiles, offer insight into a lost world of women's work and women's writing that placed women at the heart of modern public life. Often using the vignette and the anecdote as forms of knowledge and information, reproducing snatches of conversation and overheard remarks, and relying on the interview for narrative shape, these articles formed a distinctive style of newspaper writing and a distinctive approach to modern experience.

Such woman's page articles were once dismissed as little more than an embarrassment. But with their reliance on the particularities of observation, their development of a range of writing styles, and their adherence to the complexities of stories, the best of woman's page articles reveal a surprising affinity with today's best feature writing. Much the same can be said of the "human interest" features that are the subject of the next chapter— and that often had their origins on the woman's page or in the "hen coop." When we tell the story of today's feature writing, in fact, we need to recognize that newspaper women's writings—including those that appeared on the much-maligned woman's page—are an important if unacknowledged part of its history.

## chapter three

Human Interest

In 1896 a witty, now-forgotten writer named Jessie Wood provided a spoof titled "The Newspaper Woman" for *Life* magazine. "In the vast advertising sheet which Americans—with their never-failing drollness—call a 'newspaper,'" Wood began, "it is sometimes considered necessary that a few items of so-called human interest should occasionally occur." On "every successful paper the spiciest of these items," she continued, "are supplied by a lady of great daring and enterprise, whom for polite reasons, and in spite of appearances, we should prefer not to call an adventuress, but a newspaper woman." Skewering the newspaper woman with a wicked wit, Wood called her "a woman of action, even more than" a "woman of words," which was "saying a good deal."[1]

The newspaper woman earned a "delightfully erratic income by doing things she shouldn't do, and telling about them afterwards," Wood explained. In "narrating her follies, a complete absence of such adult literary ingredients as grammar, style and common sense, united to a certain naïve but flamboyant egotism," convinced the reader that she "was an irresponsible little kitten" who didn't "know any better." She was also "extremely versatile," writing "syndicate fashion articles for the Western papers" in addition to her other work. These were "not mere treatises on bias folds and box plaits." Instead, millinery went "hand in hand with philosophy, and a strong outburst of morality" was "sandwiched in between a description of a collarette and that of a flannelette combing-jacket." This showed "the depth of the female literary mind," Wood said.[2]

Wood was a gifted satirist. But although one historian has assumed that Wood was a male critic who disapproved of female journalists, the truth could not have been more different.[3] Jessie Wood was in fact a versatile newspaper woman herself—not only a witty writer but also a superb caricaturist who illustrated her own articles. Born in London, Wood began her career in New York as a "cloak girl" in a famous dressmaking house. As she later remembered in typically tongue-in-cheek style, "I once tried being employed in a shop, but I found it irksome."[4] After breaking into print with a humorous submission to *Life*, she "threw down the cloak she was fitting" according to colleague Winifred Bonfils Black, and said: "'No more poor but honest working girl for me, thanks.'" From that minute on "she earned her living by her pen."[5]

Observing human foibles with a satirical and self-mocking eye, Wood wrote numerous lively sketches for the woman's pages of the *New York Recorder* from 1894 to 1896 before moving to the *New York World*, which also employed her as a drama critic. Next snatched up by the *New York Journal*, she became its chief drama critic by the late 1890s, with illustrated reviews featured on the editorial page under the bold heading "Miss Jessie Wood." As Winifred Black explained, "No matter what you knew about the new plays, or what you thought about the actors, you were not really up in things until you had read what Jessie Wood said in the evening paper." She "told the truth as she saw it, and she had a strange little knack of seeing the truth."[6] Although Wood has dropped out of historical memory, clearly she was a public figure in her own day, making a remarkable transition from unsigned articles on the woman's page to a place of honor on the editorial page.

Jessie Wood was one of many newspaper women at the turn of the century who explored "human interest" in reviews, urban sketches, advice columns, interviews, profiles, and other features. A defining factor of the "New Journalism," "human interest" was a capacious and flexible term. Most historians trace its first use back to Charles Dana, the influential editor of the *New York Sun* in the post–Civil War era. "The newspaper must be founded upon human nature," Dana famously said. "It must correspond to the wants of the people. It must furnish that sort of information which the people demand, or else it can never be successful." While Dana argued that the "first thing which an editor must look for is news," his definition of news was broad and far-reaching. "By news," he declared, "I mean everything that occurs, everything which is of human interest, and which is of sufficient importance to arrest and absorb the attention of the public or of any considerable part of it."[7]

An emphasis on "human interest" meant that mass-circulation newspapers had the potential for greatly expanded coverage. Not just politics, not just party concerns, not just foreign news—but all of the great life of the metropolis, even all of humanity, were potentially newsworthy. "Human interest" not only gave newspapers wider scope, it drew them closer to their audience: embedded in the very term "human interest" was the assumption that "news" should respond to the perceived "interests" of the reading public.

Newspapers created "human interest" in a number of entertaining new features. Celebrity interviews with actresses and other prominent people, profiles of murderers and murderesses, urban "sketches," advice columns, contests—all of these were attempts to entice readers, to capture their attention. Viewed through the lens of "human interest" journalism, almost any aspect of human experience could be an interesting story. As Marie Manning sardonically observed of Arthur Brisbane, her editor at the *New York Evening Journal*, he could "humanize a weather report." The "human interest angle was the secret of his unprecedented success."[8]

"Human interest" journalism is often treated as "merely" part of a newspaper's "entertainment function," dismissed out of hand as trivial or of little interest because it is not "straight news." Yet as an important part of an emerging culture of leisure, human interest journalism surely deserves more of our attention. Newspapers, after all, were arguably the cornerstone of a new world of mass popular culture that included amusement parks and movies—both subjects that have attracted the attention of numerous historians.[9]

Human interest journalism, in fact, created an important new social space within the pages of the newspaper. On the one hand, this was meant to be an interactive, participatory space: in various features readers were invited, urged, and cajoled to interact with the newspaper through letters, contests, "forums," prizes, and other devices. On the other hand, it was also a new representational space: features by writers like Jessie Wood both reflected and imagined a variety of new social worlds.

The new social spaces of human interest journalism had a distinct role to play in a commercial democracy. As Michael Schudson has observed, "Learning about our neighbors through the mass media, both news and entertainment," actually "serves a vital democratic function." Schudson has built upon the work of political philosopher Joseph Raz, who points out that "it is important in a democracy, and particularly in a pluralistic democratic society, for the media to portray and thereby legitimate various styles of life in society, giving them the stamp of public acceptability." Yet "journalists as well as media critics who urge news to serve democracy better rarely call attention to this sort of journalism, often not at all directly political."[10]

Schudson also calls our attention to the work of political theorist Nancy Rosenblum, who has argued that "'democracies should learn to cultivate in their citizens a set of virtues that people would manifest in everyday life.'" One virtue she has called for is that of "'easy spontaneity,'" a "'style of civility in which one treats other people identically and easily, without standing on ceremony.'"[11] That "easy spontaneity" was an important aspect of the new human interest journalism, which reached out to a vast realm of "ordinary people," representing and sharing their concerns, laughing at their absurdities—but always inviting readers to share the joke. With its eager, friendly style, and its offers to help, the New Journalism sought to enfold readers within a metropolitan world of lively incident and to make itself necessary to their daily existence.

We can see some of the new social spaces created by human interest journalism in the popular commentaries of Teresa Dean, who built a large following with her 1893 "White City Chips" columns about the Chicago World's Fair (the fair was called the "White City" because of its gleaming white architecture; "chips" was a slangy expression for tidbits). Dean had started out as an occasional "newspaper worker" (and also trained as an artist) in Oshkosh, Wisconsin, before moving to Chicago; like so many other newspaper women, she sought an independent urban life—to the consternation of her family. After first dabbling in art, she tried metropolitan newspaper work. When she succeeded in getting a "society" assignment from the *Chicago Tribune*, her family was appalled. "Whatever effect I had hoped for in my announcement," she bitterly remembered, "if I had hurled a bomb with a short, sparkling sputtering and fizzy fuse at their respectable family feet I could not have created more horror." Her brother informed her that there was already "more or less disgrace and recklessness in my having left home for an independent life in a city," even to pursue "elevating" art; but to "take the leap into newspaper work, with its unconventionalities, was really overstepping all bounds." Nevertheless, Dean pursued additional assignments from the *Tribune* and eventually caught the attention of "the big man of the *Chicago Herald*—James W. Scott"—who told her, "If you would write as you talk, I would give you a column on my editorial page and you could sign your name to it."[12]

Soon Dean was off and running with a column titled "Snap Shots," a series of miscellaneous observations and stories that ranged from brief sketches of people she had glimpsed on the street to reflections on marriage, to anecdotes ("I knew a woman once," was a typical opening), to pure gossip, to disquisitions on envy and "snubs," to chat about newspaper women and the press, among many other topics. Her column was anything but domestic—nor was Dean particularly interested in the tried-and-true woman's topics of etiquette and manners. "What an awful bore the perfectly proper person is!" she began one column—and took pleasure in telling stories that were somewhat racy.[13] In one anecdote, a drunken salesman at the theater suddenly got up in the middle of a performance, while the rest of the audience was "as still as a mouse," and announced loudly "'——— it! When I'm drunk I want music.'"[14] It was a scene that could have come straight out of Theodore Dreiser's *Sister Carrie*.

Like a good raconteur at a party, Dean enjoyed circulating stories she had picked up. She also sometimes engaged directly with her readers. "Well! Well!" she began one column, "In last Saturday's column I asked a question innocently, and here I am with a cudgel of defense raised high above my head." In the previous piece Dean had asked "how a clergyman who refused even to read criminal news, and who had no practical knowledge of the evil existing in the world, could understandingly and temptingly expound the good." The letter of a reader who vigorously objected to this idea, arguing that clergymen did not need direct knowledge of sin (such as might be obtained by reading the newspaper), became food for a new column by Dean. "The day has gone by when sins and temptations can be taught from allegorical perspectives," she retorted. "The fast growing intelligence of the universe demands practical, every-day illustrations." "Is an acquaintance with so-called sin a necessary part of a clergyman's education? You ask me directly," she said, "so I will say most decidedly yes, and I will say it with capital letters and three exclamation points."[15] Dean pounced on this opportunity to respond to a reader's letter: it allowed her to create an atmosphere of intimacy, a public connection to readers through public "debate."

The title of Dean's column—with its reference to the newly popular practice of taking "snap shots" with hand-held cameras—implied a new relationship to public metropolitan life that foregrounded human interest stories. For Dean, there was value in the fleeting impression, the photographic sketch, the quick study, the overheard conversation, the telling anecdote, the quickly limned profile of someone standing on a street corner. But if her "Snap Shots" column allowed her the freedom to explore the terrain of "human interest," it was her Chicago World's Fair columns that were most successful in creating an engaging metropolitan world— perhaps because they were focused on one long-running event (May– October 1893), which by its very nature was miscellaneous and played to her writing strengths.

Dean's style in "White City Chips" was irreverent and informal. Instead of giving readers earnest, lofty, guidebook-style reports on the fair's attractions, she portrayed herself as the reader's companion and friend, creating a world of intimacy by drawing close to her audience. Day by day, she pro-

vided an inside look at how ordinary people experienced the fair—how they got lost, where they ate lunch, what they said as they stood in front of paintings.

She shared the amusing and idiosyncratic incidents she observed. In one early fair column, she noticed a "crowd of men trying to get in" to the "International Dress and Costume Exhibit," with "not a woman among them." "It struck me as being strange," she commented wryly, "that men should be so eager to see costumes of the different nations." She asked a guard why. "It ain't the costumes," he answered. "It's the girls—they are beauties. And they are beauties, and don't you forget it."[16]

Each day Dean took readers with her to visit an attraction and on the way "listened" to visitors' conversations. She was amused by a mother who did not realize she had just drunk a beer in the German Village Garden, insisting to her two daughters that "'it was not beer, it was "Edelweiss," the man said so.'" "'Well, mother, we got a glass of beer down you, any way,'" one of the daughters said triumphantly. Dean made fun of fair-goers who were shocked by nudes in paintings or nude statues—"'Here's one of those perfectly disgraceful pictures in full view of everybody,'" one woman said.[17]

But Dean approved of the "elderly man" who went to the Art Palace every day. "'I never had lived where I could see paintings and sculpture,'" he told her wistfully.[18]

In collecting her columns into a book two years after the fair ended, Dean noted that she had had "one thought" in "giving the incidents of the days, as they rolled by so rapidly—to be only one of the people, to write my column for them, and from their standpoint." She wanted to explain why she had quoted so many "plain and unassuming people, those who have not had the advantages of metropolitan life." Their "homely sayings, controlled by the heart and hard common sense, were more to me, many times, than the same appreciation clothed in the highest cultivation."[19]

By the time she finished her long run of World's Fair columns in the fall of 1893, Dean had attracted so many readers that the *Inter Ocean* devoted a column to some of the letters she had received from people eager to know more about her. "My Dear Friend," began a letter from Harriet Sutter, "We are a large family of nine: parents, four sisters, and three brothers, all grown except for one." Every morning "there is a scramble for the paper to see what 'Teresa Dean' had to say, and the first one down to breakfast usually tells the story." Sutter was especially curious about Dean's identity, telling her, "I have sat on Midway, where you often rest, and watched the people and wondered if you were near." A reader named Edna wrote that "I must confess that my curiosity is worked up to such a pitch to see you that when I visit the White City, instead of being wrapped in a transport of delight and amazement at the beauties to be seen there, or trying to store my mind with useful information (which it is badly in need of), I find myself speculating about this or that woman with a notebook." Anna Siwell also wrote to Dean as her "Dear friend," telling her that "I have read with amusement and wonder your curious criticisms of people and things. Sometimes I would picture you as a sweet girl of 16 to 20, when the next 'Chips' would assure me you were a man of mature age and experience. The next one I would be just as sure you were a dear old matronly mother with a few teeth and lots of sense. Still again, I would fancy you an old maid, a broken-down teacher with specs."[20] As such comments suggested, human interest journalism not only piqued readers' curiosity, it gave newspaper women a stylistic freedom that readers occasionally found confusing—especially as newspaper women's writings did not always provide conventional markers of the "feminine" or the "girlish."

Human interest journalism gave newspaper women other freedoms, too, as it reconfigured their relationship to public space. Marking a newly expansive approach to the city, human interest journalism liberated both newspaper men and women to map every corner of the metropolis—including, in the case of the World's Fair, even the Midway Plaisance and its many dancers, who were not deemed "respectable" by many. It allowed reporters to find "stories" anywhere and everywhere, to write about all aspects of human experience, to range freely through the public spaces of the city, observing people and their "quirks." Jessie Wood, for one, wrote numerous stories that explored an urban public world of boardinghouses, apartments for single women, the theater, dime shows, streetcars, the el (elevated railroad), department stores, cafés and restaurants. Human interest journalism allowed her to shine a spotlight on "ordinary" spaces and incidents, making them "news."

Human interest journalism also permitted newspaper men and women to experiment with style—even to the point, as we have seen with Teresa Dean, of confusing readers about the writer's gender and age. Newspapers that featured human interest writing—especially the great mass-circulation papers—encouraged and accepted a range of individual writing styles; style, after all, was another means of creating interest. By contrast, more staid and reserved (and respected) papers, such as the *New York Evening Post*, at first eschewed most human interest writing, focusing instead on "straight" reporting. Lincoln Steffens, who joined the *Post* in 1892, later bemoaned the fact that the paper expected reporters "to report the news as it happened, like machines, without prejudice, color, and without style; all alike. Humor or any sign of personality in our reports was caught, rebuked, and in time, suppressed." Steffens claimed that he had been "permanently hurt" as a writer by his years at the *Post*. "The editorial page and, to some extent, the book, theater, and music reviews, were the only departments which were really written," he complained.[21]

Human interest journalism was different. With its catholic interest in all phases of human life, with its openness to fresh styles of writing, human interest journalism allowed newspaper women to explore modes of expression that were typically discouraged in other venues that published women's writings, such as women's magazines. A writer for the *Ladies' Home Journal* knew better than to be caustic, urbane, witty: a didactic and maternal sentimentality was preferred. By contrast, human interest writing allowed women a new latitude in both subject matter and expression, permitting them to move beyond the maternal and domestic into realms of wit, satire, and sarcasm.

Jessie Wood, for example, enjoyed poking fun at the posturing and preening she saw around her; she was intensely interested in the "little dramas" she witnessed in public, in the theatricality of modern life. In an early column on the "poses" struck by many people, she quickly sketched several types of urban "posers" through text and illustration, including "over-dressed women, flashing with diamonds," sitting "in the boxes at the opera or at the theatres," who "look as though they have suddenly been paralyzed into effective attitudes." She lampooned "painters who wear velvet coats and long hair, who give afternoon teas but can't paint," yet received "orders for pictures from millionaires." She skewered the pretensions of a saleswoman who pretended to be "at least a nobleman's daughter in disguise" but was exposed as affecting false airs of delicacy and refinement when she shook her fist in a coworker's face. "Is life long enough to be perpetually playing at being someone else?" Wood asked.[22]

Wood was interested in a world of workers like herself—a world of salesmen, would-be artists, "literary scribblers," and other new urban "types" living in boardinghouses and the hall bedrooms of the new apartment buildings. Like many other women in this era, Wood used her own experiences as fodder for newspaper stories: she developed a personal style built around mordant observations of incidents in her own daily life. In "A Girl Bachelor Says Don't!" she focused on the financial difficulties of being a bachelor girl: "New recruits" to girl bachelordom, who were "full of bright hopes and ideas for decorating door panels," did not yet see "the rocks ahead," she said—"the stale bread, the gas bill, the amateur upholstering, the burned chops, the platonic friendships—which everybody sneers at—the burning of the midnight oil—generally kerosene." "Where, where will these bright recruits be in another three months?," Wood asked in mock alarm. "Why, in a cheap boarding house" (where women did not have to cook their own meals) "and glad to get there."[23]

Spoofing the well-known attributes of girl bachelordom, from cigarette smoking to constant tea making to male callers to chafing dish cookery (see Chapter 4), Wood satirized herself as a girl bachelor who was struggling to make weekly installment payments for wobbly furniture. As was typical of Wood, she framed her column around a story told in the first person: "I was clearing away the cigarette ends left by a temporary Plato, who had just ended his afternoon call, when a young woman friend came in. I mechanically filled the teapot." The friend was eager to know what the life of a girl bachelor was like—including how much it cost to buy furniture. "What did it cost?" Wood replied, punctuating her tale of woe with dashes to indicate rising hysteria: "Months of suspense, mental worry,—what the green carnation school call 'throbbing nerve centres'—bad dreams—the constant oppression of a continual debt—weekly payment—weekly penury—weekly pain—installments of irritation."[24]

Drily remarking that her friend reacted by handing her smelling salts, Wood confessed that she had gotten her furniture "long, long ago." "I didn't know what a nervous headache was in those bright days," she said, "and the druggist round the corner merely knew me as a person who purchased stamps and brunette powder—now he has asked me to write a testimonial for his patent nerve soothing elixir." Wood concluded her sketch with the arrival of a "smart, common-looking young man" of the "commercial traveler type," someone who would "push his way into the ranks of Paradise with a business card in his hands," and who had called from "Veneer & Co." to ask for the weekly furniture installment. The column included humorous illustrations of herself before she became a girl bachelor (confident, insouciant, hands nonchalantly placed in pockets) and after, when she was concerned about paying her bills (worried, eyes downcast, arms tightly folded across her chest).[25]

Wood exposed "the foibles of her fellow beings" in a "manner inimitable," another newspaper writer later recalled. "Her pen was sharp and the shams of life were laid bare with cutting sarcasm, but at the same time her criticisms were so full of wit and humor that the victims themselves were forced to laugh and enjoy them. She aimed not at persons, but at hypocrisies of human nature common to all."[26] Winifred Black commented that Wood "knew everybody and made fun of everybody—herself included."[27]

The phrase "herself included" gives us an additional clue to the ways in which human interest journalism changed newspaper women's relationship to public space. Such journalism offered Wood and other newspaper women the possibility of self-representation and self-dramatization in a new theater of modern life. Not only could they seek out interesting subjects to write about, but also they could themselves become subjects for self-examination, self-reflection, self-invention. Newspaper women invented witty new personae in their columns, creating themselves as characters in a new public realm. Jessie Wood, Teresa Dean, Kate Carew, Marie Manning, and Nixola Greeley-Smith, among others, revealed newspaper women's pleasure in a new public theatricality and the possibilities it offered for public performance.

While at midcentury an emerging middle class had insisted that "insincere" performances of the self were to be decried, as Karen Halttunen has shown, at the turn of the century many newspaper women subscribed to a different ethos.[28] To be sure, they were still interested in exposing the inauthentic and the insincere; some of Wood's wittiest columns had to do with exposing "posers." But the interest in "posers" clearly came from a broader interest in and celebration of the theatricality of modern life—expressed in Wood's own life not only through participating in, and recounting, the "little dramas" of daily life in her newspaper columns, but also through more direct engagement with the theater. Not only did Wood attend the theater frequently, eventually becoming a theater critic herself, but also she wrote humorously about her participation in amateur theatricals in a world composed of other artists and writers.

By contrast, Wood expressed little interest in the world of middle-class gentility; she did not identify as middle-class and certainly felt no affinity with a world of prosperous middle-class club women. Instead, she identified proudly as a worker because she earned her own living ("we of the masses" was a phrase Wood sometimes used). Yet as a worker she did not identify with factory working girls; nor, despite her work as artist and writer, did she regard herself as "bohemian"—a category she scoffed at as a literary invention.

Wood was part of an emerging world of working women that has been little studied by historians—she was neither a new "professional woman" nor a factory working girl, yet not identifiably part of the new white-collar middle class, either. Wood explained women like herself as "social mongrels" in one column. Rather than being interested in "society buds" or "kitchen maids," as she put it, Wood was interested in "another class of young women" who had "the key to more varied experiences." These young women belonged "to no set—no defined class"; instead, she declared, they were "social mongrels." "This is not as bad as it sounds—in fact, much better," she insisted. "To be a social mongrel means to be something between the Four Hundred and the actual 'great unwashed'—to have the best qualities of both classes. It means to live by your brains, which, you know, is a very different matter from living by your wits. It means to have no social obligations save those prompted by the heart—it means to know humanity and see life!"[29]

As a "social mongrel," Wood had no interest in upholding a standard of middle-class respectability in her newspaper work: she was far more mischievous, far more likely to showcase misbehavior than to celebrate stiff middle-class propriety. In one column, she made an amusing story out of an incident at the theater in which a female friend was slapped by a woman sitting in front of her. Wood opened the column not with the incident itself, but with the sense of freedom she and her friend had felt on payday as two young newspaper women. "We had finished our reporting for the day," she began, "and as it was salary day, we felt that we had not only earned the right to enjoy ourselves but were in a position to do so, which was rather an unusual and blissful combination." With her typically dry sense of humor, Wood said that they first went to a "well-known but overrated table d'hote, where a French spirit of Bohemia and a soupcon of deviltry is supposed to pervade," but were disappointed when "at the first table we passed were seated a clean-faced parson and two healthy looking little boys at the knickerbocker and pudding age." However, the two friends were "in good spirits and hoped for better things, and before dinner was fairly over" Wood noticed "a man who looked like an opium fiend."[30]

Wood and her friend "sat talking over our cheese and coffee, finding ourselves and each other profoundly interesting, as people do who are fond of each other and have dined lightly, chattily, and with a full week's salary in their pockets." Their next stop was the theater, where they "invested in fifty-cent seats" that were "very, very dark and far away from the stage." As Wood commented, "Even with a full salary in one's pocket one has to remember that there is the rest of the week to get through." With a certain "quicksilveriness" of mood, and "moved by a spirit of mischief" that was in part the effect of the cheap wine they had drunk (a "mixture of red ink and vinegar"), they began to talk loudly about the obstructing hat of the woman in front of them. "'Have you noticed,' said the other girl in high, clear tones, 'that all well-bred women are removing their hats in the theatre?'" Actually, "it was not a very large hat, and I felt that we were not justified in all our remarks, but something spurred us on to tease that poor young woman in front." Eventually they complained to an usher, who moved them to new seats. But at the end of the play, they heard "a swirl of skirts down the aisle," and in the silence Wood heard a "sharp smart slap" before seeing the "vanishing petticoats of the girl with the hat whisking around the theatre exit." She had "waited to take her revenge when the lights were turned low." Wood's friend "rubbed her reddened cheek and softly laughed." "'I suppose I deserve it,' she said, 'but it was a cowardly thing to do.'"[31]

Wood's retelling of this incident—complete with caricatures—brought vividly to life a world of single newspaper women who delighted in their new access to public space, including restaurants and theaters. Drawn (both literally and figuratively) from observation, this world was also charged with Wood's irreverent imagination. Her writing offered a double form of representation: the contents of her column offered an imaginative rendering—a representation—of her personal life; but the column itself, printed in the public spaces of the newspaper, also offered an indirect political representation, with the lives of single women given a stamp of public acceptability and legitimacy through public portrayal.

If human interest journalism allowed Wood a form of public representation, it allowed her as well to engage in public commentary on some of the new practices of modern life. She was especially scathing—and witty—on the subject of newspaper publicity, which she took relish in exposing to public view (by using, of course, newspaper publicity to do so). Publicity had multiple emerging meanings at the turn of the century: many journalists defended the "searchlight" of publicity (in the sense of exposure to public view) as a necessary tool of municipal reform. As Nixola Greeley-Smith said in a 1906 article in which she proudly defended her work for the *World*, "yellow journalism" meant "turning the limelight of publicity into the dark and hidden places of graft and oppression and corruption."[32] Such publicity was an important part of "muckraking" and vital to the Progressive movement.[33]

But Wood was not a reformer. As someone fascinated by the theater and public "poses," she was interested in other meanings of "publicity" just emerging in the 1890s—especially the idea that through the publicity purposefully created by a newspaper, a person might gain public notice desired for personal ends, including sheer vanity. Wood understood only too well that newspaper publicity involved both an interaction and a transaction. Newspapers sought to interest the public by disseminating stories about well-known figures such as actors and actresses; for their part, actors and actresses (and other public figures) sought to gain and control public notice on their own terms. What makes Wood's many sharply observed articles on publicity fun to read was her understanding that newspaper women also played a role in this transaction, often in a sort of verbal sparring match with their subjects.

Wood satirized the ways in which newspaper women and their wealthy or famous subjects, swept up in one fad or another, were often in collusion to achieve publicity. In one 1894 article, she made fun of the way in which both newspaper women and society women were temporarily obsessed with Napoleon relics, which were momentarily all the rage. Wood knew "a dozen women" who were writing Napoleon-related articles for the popular press: one of them told Wood that she thought she had a "big field for journalistic enterprise before her," and that "her mind was being improved by every minute she gave to it." Wood "commended this feeling in her," wryly commenting: "I never had it myself, but I recognize that the want of it has shut me out from many great enterprises. She, in time, may run a column of advice in a young ladies' journal. But riches like that are not for all women."[34]

Wood and this friend set off to interview a society woman who was reputed to have "furnished a room with Napoleon (alleged) relics." "By this time," her friend "had come to consider the subject as such a great national want that she simply asked for the society woman's relics as something that the society woman owed to the public and literature." The society woman, however, only "smiled coldly" at this request and said that she had "no wish for notoriety." Wood "wondered how it was that she wasn't in a museum or convent" and was "turning to go" when her friend showed that "she was not so green" by slyly flattering the society woman. "'You remind me so strangely of a friend of mine—a very beautiful woman,'" she said, just before "she moved to the door." Within a quarter of an hour, "the collection had been placed entirely at the disposal of my friend."

"What strange ideas you have on beauty," Wood remarked to her friend after they left. "Now, I didn't consider her good-looking."

"Why, neither did I, you goose," her friend said, "but I had to get those Napoleon relics somehow."

"But that's humbug."

"Come off!—that's diplomacy."[35]

As Wood made only too clear, diplomacy and humbug were deeply intertwined in the new world of publicity. And newspaper women were far from immune from humbug in attempting to get their stories.

Wood tackled the subject of publicity in several columns. For the *New York Evening Journal* in 1898, she wrote a lengthy sketch of the wealthy summer colony at Newport, Rhode Island—from the vantage point of a "hack" (inexpensive hired cab) rather than a carriage, she made clear. But it was not the wealthy she was interested in so much as the public's fascination with wealth. In a pair of cartoons accompanying her piece, Wood first showed Newport as the newspaper "society writers" had led her "to believe it looks—all diamonds, Greek profiles, roses, dignified dowagers, sunshine, picturesque sea bathing and the revelation of goddess-like figures in the surf—a sort of Olympia, with a flavor of Paris." In the second cartoon, Wood sketched the "real shapes and styles" of the wealthy in a ludicrous array of scrawny and obese figures, commenting, "Alas, it is not so." Newport "was simply a beautiful spot where ladies and gentlemen go to preserve themselves for the coming winter" and where they pursued "health feverishly." "Ladies bicycle all day there to get thin, and then spoil the effect by feeding up at night."[36]

Wood scoffed at what she found to be an absurd reverence for Newport. "Newport is regarded, almost unconsciously, in the minds of New Yorkers, as a revered spot. Flippancy, satire and scorn are leveled at it, but the fashion in which its chroniclers and reporters correct one another in their accounts of it, shows a deep and jealous respect for it. For instance, one writer will say that it is the habit of Mr. Oliver Belmont's second under gardener to eat radishes for lunch. Another in a rival next week's paper will hold this assertion up to derision, and say that every one who knows anything about Mr. O. H. P. Belmont's gardener knows that he is a confirmed dyspeptic."[37]

She noted that anyone in this "gold fish set" who was "homely or bourgeois in appearance" was described as "intensely democratic," whereas "we of the working class would call him common looking." But newspaper society writers were not alone to blame for feeding the "great and consuming" interest in the wealthy: ordinary people were complicit, too. "Tourists" came from "miles around" to see the rich, crowding the porches of boardinghouses and hotels to watch the wealthy drive by. "A man or woman who has to think hard how to spend his or her money is for some reason considered an interesting sight."[38]

"The traditions of the 'Four Hundred' grow up thickly and indisputably in every boarding house and flat," she noted, "and the great growing interest in mere wealth is handed down from each generation, as surely as the claim to descent from the Pilgrim Fathers. This is the reason that the millionaires in Newport have a regular audience." If they were a "colony of poets or a colony of artists, the interest in them would be explainable." But, in fact, society in Newport was "like an opening of the Grand Opera, without the opera."[39]

Wood's commentary offered a sharp dissection of an emerging celebrity culture, in which fame itself had become of so much glittering interest, and was so industriously spread by newspapers, that it obscured the dullness of many of the famous. Making clear that she found the wealthy themselves quite insipid—they had a "uniform grave placidity"—Wood remarked that the wealthy colony was "like a huge bowl of goldfish—costly, but monotonous, they pass and repass one another year after year." They were "shining, well fed, and inoffensive. Like the goldfish they have all the luxuries of life without an effort. Also like the goldfish they sometimes die of overfeeding and are replaced by other goldfish. But it cannot be said that goldfish are interesting." Tongue in cheek, she imagined the way of life of this "gold fish set" as appropriate preparation for their inevitable future life in hell: "If this colony of millionaires believes in the Bible and have studied the difficult problem which is promised them when the time comes for settling permanently in an everlasting Summer resort, then you must admit that their behavior is very logical. Their future prospects being so bad, they are making themselves just as comfortable as possible for the present. Their plan of marble palaces and lots of ice is very sensible in consideration of the future heat that they have been threatened with."[40]

Omnivorous public curiosity about the lives of the rich and famous—

(Drawn by Jessie Wood.)

This is Newport, as the society writers have led me to believe it looks—all diamonds, Greek profiles, roses, dignified dowagers, sunshine, picturesque sea bathing and the revelation of goddess-like figures in the surf—a sort of Olympia, with a flavor of Paris.

(Drawn by Jessie Wood.)

Alas, it is not so. It is simply a beautiful spot where ladies and gentlemen go to preserve themselves for the coming Winter. The signs of the masseur, the manicure, the hair doctor, the chiropodist and the ordinary all-round doctor adorn its streets. Ladies bicycle all day there to get thin, and then spoil the effect by feeding up at night. They have their bodies rubbed and their heads rubbed, and pursue health feverishly. Young men are very scarce there, and they have to be satisfied with little boys and old men, most of the time. People come from miles around to see these little boys and old men and the ladies who employ so many kinds of doctors. They are interesting to these tourists because they are thinking hard all the time of new ways to spend their money, and hiring other people to think, too. A man or woman who has to think hard how to spend his or her money is for some reason considered an interesting sight. In the diagram I have shown Newport in a fog—as it sometimes is—and the real shapes and styles of the people whom other people go miles to see.

Drawings by "Miss Jessie Wood at Newport," New York Journal, August 3, 1898. "This is Newport, as the society writers have led me to believe it looks," Wood wrote of her first drawing, "—all diamonds, Greek profiles, roses, dignified dowagers, sunshine, picturesque sea bathing and the revelation of goddess-like figures in the surf—a sort of Olympia, with a flavor of Paris." "Alas, it is not so," she commented on her second drawing. "I have shown Newport in a fog—as it sometimes is—and the real shapes and styles of the people whom other people go miles to see." (General Research Division, The New York Public Library, Astor, Lenox and Tilden Foundations) part of the wider cultural curiosity that lay behind human interest journalism in general—fueled countless articles at the turn of the century. But as Wood's example shows, newspaper women who wrote about the rich and the famous did not necessarily offer up only obsequious flattery and celebration; even as Wood shone a spotlight on the wealthy at Newport, she offered up a damning critique. She claimed to find the rich themselves "inoffensive" because they were so boring, but she was quick to criticize both the press and the public for their ravenous interest in wealth, which helped to fuel celebrity culture. Hers was a "disruptive act": inhabiting the public space of the newspaper very much on her own terms, she offered a distinctive individual voice as she created an imagined public world of celebrity for her readers. Even as she provided publicity for Newport—which was her assignment as a newspaper woman, after all—she also publicized the individuality and independence of one newspaper woman.[41]

As an acute observer of the new realm of newspaper publicity, Wood made particular fun of a form of human interest newspaper writing that came roaring into its own in the 1880s and 1890s: the interview. As a genre, the interview had emerged in the era of the Civil War, with Horace Greeley often credited with the first published interview (using a question-and-answer format) of Brigham Young in 1859. A distinctly American phenomenon—many British journalists, for instance, were scandalized by the rude pushiness involved in asking unsolicited questions of public figures—the interview quickly became a tool of newspaper reporting about politicians and just as quickly attracted the attention of critics. In the *Nation*, E. L. Godkin called the interview the "joint production of some humbug of a hack politician and another humbug of a newspaper reporter."[42]

Interviewing techniques quickly migrated to human interest stories, and by the 1890s the feature "interview" of a celebrity—an entire article based on questions and answers—had become immensely popular. Such interviews rapidly developed their own formulas—and it was these formulas that attracted Wood's sarcasm. "They are all so charming, these interviewed people," she wrote in one article. "They are never more than 26, although they have been 26 in every interview that has been published about them for the last ten years. They are all so good looking. They all have dulcet voices. They are always caught by the interviewer writing letters on monogrammed note paper, and when they are thus caught they are always dressed in rare tea gowns or velvet coats. They always order tea for the interviewer. There is a dreadfully sweet uniformity about them all." She concluded that "reading one of the polite interviews of the day is like eating a pot of honey without any bread."[43]

Sycophantic flattery indeed characterized many interviews of celebrities, whether written by newspaper men or women. Wood imagined "what a relief" it would be to the readers of interviews "when some noted person is discovered counting his pawn tickets" or "mending his socks or chasing cats out of his back yard." Perhaps "some time an interviewer will risk the consequences of daring to say that the noted person is not young and beautiful."[44]

But Wood—who described herself as a reporter in several articles and who clearly carried out assignments that included interviewing for the *Recorder*[45]—understood firsthand the particular pressures on the interviewer, who often succumbed to the desire to please prominent interview subjects. In "The Art of Interviewing," Wood observed that "the trouble with most interviewers" was that they were so "palpably careful" that what they wrote should be "pleasing and acceptable in the eyes of the person interviewed instead of pleasing and acceptable in the eyes of the public."

Wood knew that the public was curious to discover the human being behind the image. "Now, it is the public that the interviewer has to please," she said. "Strange as it may seem, the public likes to learn that Senators have pimples, and actresses corns, and that poet laureates wear trousers like those seen on the public statues. The public is not as young as it used to be, and even if the polite interviewer tells it that every one who struts a few paces on the stages of publicity is young and beautiful and wears pretty tea gowns and sits in 'cozy corners,' why the public is not going to swallow it."[46]

Yet as Wood indicated, discovering *too* much about the human being behind the image was fraught with peril for the newspaper woman, especially in the case of popular figures like "matinee idols." In "A Woman Interviewer," Wood drolly told a story of trying to interview "the kind of young actor that is an idol with the women—tall, romantic looking—with a lovely, soft voice, and large pathetic eyes." This young actor was "the fashion: every girl has his photograph on her mantel shelf—and he's the matinee pet—and there's a burning desire with the feminine public to know about him. Of course, the press anticipates the burning desires of the public."[47]

Directed by her editor to "go and interview Galahad Braithwaite," the "man who is christened 'The Woman's Idol,'" Wood was horrified when Braithwaite "insists on telling" her "that he wears a wig, is 53, has a 'game leg,' digs for clams," and "plays an accordion." His wife turned out not to be a "sweet-faced girl wife, such as a man of his reputation ought to have," but instead a "corpulent woman in a wrapper who puts her face in at the door and says, 'Popper, you're wanted.'" He in turn calls her "'mommer,'" and "you go away with all your hopes destroyed, your illusions blasted and not one single fact that will please the public and your editor." Wood concluded in mock despair: "Now, what, I ask, is the reporter to do?"[48]

The temptation for many newspaper men and women was to create a "fake interview"—a journalistic practice often decried at the turn of the century. The accusation of "fakery" did not refer to inexact transcription of the interviewee's remarks; in fact, reporters of this period did not use notebooks, which were thought to be inappropriate and intrusive. "To use a note-book is to destroy the freedom of expression of the person" being interviewed, a prominent journalist wrote in 1890, asserting that "this kills the interesting personality which should pervade every interview."[49] Working entirely from memory, reporters of course got many things wrong, as their subjects sometimes indignantly protested. Still, their resulting interviews were not considered "fake." "A 'fake' interview," as Jessie Wood explained, was "where the reporter makes the victim say all the things she wants him to—in print. Where the soubrette declares that she has a ton of caramels sent in every day; where the tough swears that he wants to go to night school; where the Irishman says, with tears in his eyes, that he longs for the old cabin at home—those are 'fake' interviews."[50]

Other interviews were not so much out-and-out fake as dishonest, often flattering their subjects in absurd ways. Wood spoofed the conventions of such interviews—and the ways in which celebrity culture reached into every corner of a subject's life—in a set of brief parodies for *Life* titled "Unknown Domestics of Well-Known Men." Capturing the sententious, sycophantic, and often gaseous style of such interviews, Wood first profiled "John Blenheim Blobbs, the faithful and interesting butler" of novelist "W. D. H." (readers would have recognized the initials of William Dean Howells, the most prominent novelist of Wood's day). "Mr. Blobbs's conversation is deeply interesting," Wood intoned, "as the conversation of the butler of a noted novelist would naturally be." Blobbs had been "very helpful to Mr. Howells in assisting him in those well-known descriptions of dinner tables and candelabra, which have thrilled all the novel-reading public. Those dainty word-pastels of almost supernatural and dazzling accuracy, dealing with portieres and leather chairs, which have sent many a hungry novel reader into a profound and healthful sleep, are due to the direct influence of Mr. Blobbs."[51] In a second parody, involving "the kitchen maid of the Rev. Charles W. Parkhurst," a vice reformer who was constantly interviewed at the time, Wood noted that "her personal appearance is such that even a *Morning Journal* reporter—weaned on fulsome flattering descriptiveness—would abstain from the adjectives that his soul loves and describe her as 'interesting, rather than strictly beautiful.' She is regarded with favor by ladies with susceptible husbands."[52]

As Wood commented in the *New York Recorder*, "The interviewer either paints the noted person in such pen strokes that he gives an honest sketch of the celebrity 'as others see him,' or else he gives a dishonest sketch of the sitter as the sitter sees himself. The honest sketch invariably makes the better reading, though I own that it doesn't make for the interviewer the most friends. But, though flattery may make popularity, it doesn't make literature."[53]

Wood warned that there were public perils in interviewing: "The thoroughly honest interviewer must not expect to interview his subjects twice. Personally, I always retire to the New York suburbs after interviewing a celebrity. I cross the road when I see Paderewski coming, and I don't much care about riding in the same elevated car as Dr. Parkhurst's chambermaid. You see I interviewed them once. And what is more, I gave my honest impressions. The public chuckles over honest impressions, but the public idol uses cursory language over them."[54]

As Wood knew, newspaper women who became public figures sometimes became interview subjects themselves. With her characteristic wry humor, Wood described her own experience as an interviewee. "You didn't know that I had been interviewed, perhaps?" she wrote in one column. "Well, I own that I am not a celebrity, but that doesn't cut any ice. Interviewing is really for mediocrities."[55]

"The morning that my interview came out—it was a flattering interview—my head was nearly turned," Wood said. "I read that I was a 'sparkling brunette,' that I had a 'ringing laugh,' and my views on athletic sports were given in full, though a trifle obscure. The writer even credited me with cozy corners. I lived in a hall bedroom. It was all corners, but it never before occurred to me that they were cozy."[56]

"However," she continued, "the circulation of the paper that exploited me went up ten copies that day, and I read the article over and over again, until I felt myself a professional beauty, a public person of great importance. About two days later a sweet woman friend suddenly turned to me and said with unusual asperity (I had been giving some of my views): 'You are quite unfit to live with since that interview about you appeared in the paper. I never saw such a change in any one.' Another suggested bandaging my head with a 'cold compress' to keep it from swelling any more."[57]

Wood concluded with a "tip": "It really is best, when a celebrity wants a flattering interview, to ask him to write what he wishes known about himself, and into this fit some questions and cozy corners, and there you are!" "When I have done this," she declared, "celebrities have kissed me, and sent me cards for their receptions, and remarked what a clever writer I am. When I write the interview myself they don't seem to notice what a clever writer I am. When I am a celebrity I shall write my own interviews."[58]

Wood made a joke out of being a public figure as an interviewee, but several newspaper women *did* become famous and thus the subject of interviews themselves. Most renowned in her day was the witty, sophisticated artist Kate Carew (Mary Chambers), who, like Jessie Wood just before her, illustrated her articles with her own caricatures. Like Wood, too, Carew has been virtually lost to history. Rediscovered briefly in 1998, Carew was called "Celebrity's Midwife" by the *New Yorker* because of her many illustrated interviews of prominent political, literary, and artistic figures.[59]

But the joke is that Kate Carew was not just a midwife to celebrity — she herself was a celebrity in the early twentieth century. Carew's closely observed and perceptive interviews, written in a playful, humorous style, focused on the relationship between interviewer and interviewee — with the result that Carew herself became an important subject of each interview. While her first interviews included only caricatures of her subjects, over the course of her career she developed several witty caricatures of herself, always with a hat and clutching a sketch pad, that she inserted into each interview. Featured prominently by the *New York World*, Carew added to newspaper women's publicity — to their acknowledged presence in modern public life. Her prominence brings to mind E. L. Godkin's early concerns about the emergence of the interview as a newspaper genre: it "tended to increase the independence of the reporter from editorial control."[60]

In 1904 the editor of *Pearson's Magazine* described her as "the pioneer of interviewing as a woman's profession," claiming that "to-day she holds the position of being the only prominent lady interviewer in the world." This was not exactly true — there was another prominent interviewer, as we shall see, at the *World*, and of course previous newspaper women had interviewed both celebrities and politicians. But the editor of *Pearson's* did suggest an important truth: at the turn of the century the feature interview, one presented for entertainment, for human interest, and as a source of education, suddenly became an area in which newspaper women specialized and gained new publicity and independence for themselves.[61]

Like so many newspaper women in New York, Carew began her career elsewhere. She started as "illustrator and drama critic" for the *San Francisco Examiner* in 1889, having been suggested for the position by author and "renowned aphorist" Ambrose Bierce — they met when Carew taught Bierce's

Drawing of Kate Carew with Harriot Stanton Blatch. Over the course of her career Carew sketched a number of caricatures of herself as interviewer. (New-York Tribune, June 9, 1912, ProQuest Historical Newspapers, New-York Tribune [1841–1922])

son art at her studio. Her job at the *Examiner* "was to cover all the theatrical premieres, make sketches of the actors and actresses, and write up my interviews," which required filing her stories "in the wee hours of the morning." She worked at "the only all-night spot in San Francisco," mingling with the "after-theater crowd." Carew was one of "seventeen staff artists at the *Examiner*" until "one fine day" they all found themselves "relieved of their employment" because "the introduction of photogravure had made newspaper illustrators obsolete."[62]

As Carew remembered, "It was 1900, the dawn of a new century" and she was "thirty years old with a decade in the newspaper trade and little to fall back on but my skills as a painter." A friend suggested that she pursue a career in portraiture in New York. There she was "a comparatively harmless painter person" who "set up a studio" with a "single eye to serious work— art with a capital 'A,' you know." But during a "mischievous moment" (and no doubt in an attempt to make additional money), she "inked over some grotesque sketches of an actor" she had made on the "margin of a theatre programme" and sent them to the *World*. She hardly expected to "hear of them again."[63]

But a "hunger for novelty" was the "ruling passion of the bright young editors trained up by Mr. Joseph Pulitzer," and her sketches "fell into the hands of an editor whose hunger for novelty was especially poignant." Within two days she "was engaged, at what to a lowly painter of portraits seemed a ridiculously handsome figure, to supply the paper twice a week with two columns of theatrical caricature seasoned with frivolous comment."[64]

The *New York World* featured the first set of caricatures by Carew on its theater page on September 15, 1900, trumpeting them as "First of a Series of Saturday Studies of Stage Celebrities by a New Woman Caricaturist." Just as Wood's articles had been bylined "Miss Jessie Wood," Carew's work was now bylined "Miss Kate Carew"—clearly Wood's work as a theater critic and caricaturist for the *World* and *Journal* had paved the way for Carew. But Jessie Wood had died suddenly of pneumonia in October 1899, at only thirty-four—leaving the position of "woman caricaturist" open for the great New York City mass-circulation newspapers.[65]

Carew "awoke to find" herself "pseudonymously famous." "The alias with which I had signed the sketches—I had selected it at random—shouted at me from advertisements and posters, and 'The Only Woman Caricaturist' was flaunted before the public with a persistence which made me thank my stars I had not signed my real name."[66]

Carew's "two columns" of theatrical caricatures were only the beginning. Her editor had "a new idea—twenty new ideas, for that matter, but one in particular: illustrated interviews by 'The Only,' etc. And my resolve to be drawn no more from the narrow path of art with a capital 'A' was smashed to smithereens beneath the dynamic force of his authority." "One broiled lived [*sic*] celebrity per week was the diet prescribed and rigorously inforced by my uncompromising editor," she declared, "and he organized a staff of one, whose duty it was to hunt down the designated victims. The staff would make an appointment, and I would follow with the instruments of torture, consisting of an inquiring eye and a stub of pencil."[67]

If Carew's early work for the *New York World* consisted mainly of quick, humorous sketches of actors with a few lines of droll commentary, by 1901 she had been given her head in terms of space allotted—and allowed to experiment with a more spacious writing style, as well. Carew, it turned out, was no less than brilliant at profiles: her work was a good example of the synergy that could occasionally result when the press recognized and supported exceptional talent in newspaper women.

Carew's secret was the creation of herself as a character in all of her interviews, so that each profile became the story of "getting" the interview itself. This technique of writing stories was not her own invention — within a New Journalism focused on human interest, other interviewers had also explored making themselves part of the narrative of an interview. But Carew had extraordinary gifts as writer and artist — she could make an interview amusing and interesting even with monosyllabic answers from her subjects, while her keen visual observation brought the physicality of her subjects to life. She was a perfect fit for the new human interest journalism: Joseph Pulitzer might as well have had Carew in mind when he instructed his editors to "please impress on the men who write our interviews with prominent men, the importance of giving a striking, vivid pen sketch of the subject: also a vivid picture of the domestic environment, his wife, his children, his animal pets, etc. Those are the things that will bring him more clearly home to the average reader than would his most imposing thoughts, purposes or statements."[68]

Carew's first interview for the *World* — with no less a personage than Mark Twain, a triumph for a novice interviewer — involved deception. As Carew told it, "Mark Twain had just returned to his native land after many years of absence. His publishers were paying him a princely retainer for the exclusive rights to his every word, spoken as well as written, and under this contract he steadfastly refused to be interviewed, which seemed to my editor a good reason why Mark Twain should be marked as the first victim" of Carew's new interviewing assignment.[69]

"Poor Mark Twain!" Carew recalled in 1904. "Can you wonder that he has fled again from the land of his birth? If I had known about the publishers and the contract and the rest of it," she explained, "there would be no story to tell, but the sagacious editor merely remarked that he would like me to make some sketches of the great humorist and would send an intermediary to ask his consent and introduce me to him. And, as if by way of afterthought, he muttered that whatever I might induce Mark Twain to say would be of value to the paper."[70]

The interview itself, published on October 21, 1900, had as its central "plot" Carew's attempts to obtain as much material from Twain as possible. She began with a sketch of herself as "an exceedingly embarrassed young woman" sitting at "breakfast opposite" Twain, "taking pains to keep her pencil and sketch book below the level of the table." Carew had caught

Twain in the lobby of his New York hotel as he "meandered" toward the dining room, describing him as a "fresh, spotless little old man" who suggested "spring water and much soap." She admired his hands—"delicate, pinky-white hands" that matched his "pinky-white cheeks." Twain, making desultory conversation with her while he drank his coffee—all of which Carew put into her interview—thought she was simply making a sketch of him, per their prior agreement.[71]

"Listening too hard to do much work, though there was never a more tempting head for pencil or brush than this silver-crowned one," Carew was startled when Twain asked her, "with a touch of fatherly reproof" at her apparent "inertia," whether she was getting what she wanted. "Only a few notes" an embarrassed Carew said, at which Twain "half rose from his chair," exclaiming "'Notes!'" with a "sudden drawing down of his shaggy eyebrows." Carew hastily explained that all she meant was "an artist's notes, you know" — "just scratchings on the paper—an eyebrow, a wrinkle, a coat collar."[72]

Twain "sank back, much relieved. 'Make all the notes—that kind of notes—you want to,'" he said. "'So long as—you—don't interview me, I—don't care. I won't be interviewed. I don't approve—of interviews; don't like them—on—principle.'" As Carew wryly reported, "This was not a very good omen for further conversation."[73]

But it was a very good omen for an interview that met Pulitzer's demands, allowed readers to glimpse the individuality of a much-beloved public figure, and, not coincidentally, moved Carew herself to center stage as a public figure. Later she would say wittily that since then she had not "interviewed a man without his knowledge."[74] Whatever one makes of the *World*'s—and Carew's—methods there is no question that the Twain interview launched her career as an interviewer.

As numerous historians have correctly pointed out, a new culture of publicity, shaped and disseminated by human interest journalism, had many exploitative elements. If a fascination with celebrities arose in part from a new "democratization of culture" — an intense new curiosity to read about all aspects of human life — it also included an accelerated invasion of celebrities' private lives. Yet the deplorable loss of privacy for a figure like Twain is only one of the stories to be told about the rise of a culture of publicity.[75]

For women—whose private lives had always, after all, been the subject of public scrutiny—a new culture of publicity had benefits as well as drawbacks. Newspaper women's work, including interviews of celebrities, extended women's presence in public life. It gave them a form of virtual representation in print that, as Michael Schudson and others have argued, is essential to both creating and belonging to a public sphere. Such print representation was an important undergirding of eventual direct political representation.

To be sure, women's interviews did not have a direct democratic function. The truth was that interviewing, a technique that some enthusiastic idealists initially thought would help to both fight corruption and educate the masses, eventually became more "a tool of politicians and celebrities." But as Schudson has noted, the informal back-and-forth of interviewing was "consonant with democratic social and cultural style,"[76] elevating the interviewer to a position of equality with the interviewee. Moreover, interviewing was a means by which newspaper women could participate directly in public life—with such participation an important precursor to direct political representation. As we shall see, a number of women would later use their experience in newspaper work to advocate directly for woman suffrage.

We can see the ways in which human interest interviewing became a means of participating in, as well as gaining experience of, public life by examining the career of one of the most prominent newspaper interviewers of her day: Nixola Greeley-Smith, the granddaughter of Horace Greeley. Greeley-Smith is often remembered merely as one of the "sob sisters" who covered the notorious Harry K. Thaw trials of 1907–8 for the murder of Stanford White. But we should be suspicious of the false and derogatory term "sob sister," often used to stigmatize and stereotype *all* newspaper women's writings retrospectively. It would be a serious mistake to reduce Nixola Greeley-Smith's newspaper career—which spanned decades and literally thousands of columns, and led to extensive advocacy of woman suffrage—to her writings in the famous Thaw case.[77]

There were, of course, newspaper women who did qualify as "sob sisters" in the sense of producing emotionally excessive, adjective-littered, and breathless writing. Jessie Wood made sly fun of Ella Wheeler Wilcox, for instance, the self-styled "poetess of passion." For years Wilcox ran an overheated column of commentary and advice, in addition to writing reams of bad poetry, for both the *New York World* and the *New York Journal*.[78]

But Nixola Greeley-Smith was known in her own day for *not* being an emotional writer. As an admiring—if stereotype-ridden—male interviewer wrote of her in 1906 (a year before the first Thaw trial), "Nixola Greeley is not of the weepy kind. They are not popular in metropolitan newspaper offices. She believes in the economic independence of women and is no more likely to burst into tears than were those fierce visaged and bespectacled females who used to haunt the editorial sanctum in her grandfather Greeley's day."[79]

It was Greeley-Smith "who popularized the better type of interview for newspaper women and made it one of their most useful functions on a paper," according to Ishbel Ross. "Every visiting celebrity for nearly two decades was done" by her. "She went after people that no one had dreamed of interviewing before." Her 1906 interviewer commented that "there is a tradition in Park row that Nixola Greeley-Smith can 'get at' anybody, that she can 'break in' where angels fear to tread. No secret service corps is vigilant enough to keep her away from president, prince, or potentate whom she sets out to interview." Fellow newspaper woman Mary Heaton Vorse concurred: "I pity the unwary who are interviewed by Nixola Greeley-Smith," she said.[80]

Greeley-Smith's very first interview for the *New York World* in early May 1901 revealed the probing intelligence with which she approached her work. Assigned to interview the wife of famed New York vice reformer and minister Charles Parkhurst (newspaper women were always being assigned to interview the wives of prominent men), she asked an especially pointed question. Charles Parkhurst was known as an antiprostitution advocate whose idea of reform was to have brothels raided by the police and prostitutes arrested and thrown in jail.[81] Greeley-Smith, on the other hand, was clearly aware of a contrasting European approach, which sought to regulate prostitution rather than punish prostitutes. She asked Mrs. Parkhurst: "What do you think of the theory that it is not the bad women who are responsible for present conditions, but the good women, who, by their opposition to the methods employed by European cities to regulate vice, have made New York worse than any of them?" It was a question that not only revealed Greeley-Smith's progressive views but also suggested her future embrace of feminism.[82]

In response, Mrs. Parkhurst "gasped," Greeley-Smith reported. "She was silent for a moment, and then said, 'I don't feel that I have studied the question thoroughly enough to answer you. But you may say emphatically that I am opposed to legalization of vice in any form.'"

"To the licensing of saloons?" Greeley-Smith followed up. "'Yes, indeed,'" said Mrs. Parkhurst.[83]

Obviously, Greeley-Smith was not afraid to ask tough questions. And even in her relatively gentle summing up of Mrs. Parkhurst as a wholly domestic woman, she managed to sneak in her own progressive views. "While there may be some who will not sympathize with her opposition to higher education," Greeley-Smith concluded in the last paragraph of her interview, "they will be gratified to learn that she is possibly one of the best arguments in its favor. Mrs. Parkhurst has read much—has travelled widely. She is thoroughly familiar with current topics and discusses them with ease and originality. In effect, she blends the delicacy and refinement of a lady of a hundred years ago with the high intelligence, the perfect poise of the modern woman."[84] Such a comment, with its advocacy of the "modern woman," its barely disguised contempt for merely domestic (and outdated) "ladyhood," helps us to make sense of Mary Heaton Vorse's initially puzzling remarks about Greeley-Smith: "She has the smile of a happy child, the inscrutability of a sphinx; she has wisdom and philosophy, yet behind the sweetest smile she hides a disdain and a bitterness that in point and scope can surpass anything I have ever known."[85]

Ishbel Ross insisted that Greeley-Smith "was not in any sense of the word a sob sister." Instead, "her mind was essentially sharp and creative"; she was "an intellectual."[86] Although "essentially a woman's writer"—in the sense that her assignments were human interest features such as interviews and advice columns—Greeley-Smith was "analytical and editorial": "When she encountered a fruitful mind, she stripped it bare and turned out an interview of depth and subtlety. Her questions were intelligent, amusing, surprising and sometimes impertinent."[87] Greeley-Smith "was not afraid to take an academic subject and make it good newspaper reading,"[88] Ross pointed out.

After Greeley-Smith's first interview in May, the *World* marked her success by adding the boast "Granddaughter of Horace Greeley" under her byline. At the beginning of June, in an interview with Mrs. Richard Croker, wife of the corrupt Tammany boss, again there was a notable edge in Greeley-Smith's questions. After a round of easy domestic queries about Croker's daily life, Greeley "suddenly" asked, "What do you think of the reform movement?" (She was referring to the reform movement that aimed to replace Croker's powerful and corrupt husband.)[89]

"'Why, I don't know anything about it,'" Croker responded.

"I mean," Greeley-Smith asked again, "what do you think of the effort to make New York a better city?"

"Mrs. Croker was silent a moment," Greeley-Smith reported. "Then she leaned forward and said with impressive earnestness: 'There is one reform which I would like to see the city adopt.'"

"What is it?" Greeley-Smith asked with "breathless interest." That word "breathless" had a decidedly cynical edge in the face of Croker's utterly conventional and bourgeois views.[90]

"'I want the city to build and maintain a training school for servants,'" Croker said, declaring that "'every unskilled female immigrant who wishes to become a servant in an American household should be obliged to attend the training school.'" After Croker explained this "reform," Greeley-Smith asked, "But Mrs. Croker, why should the city do this? Don't you think that your plan savors of paternalism?"[91]

Croker defended her idea: "'What affects the interests of every home in New York City so closely as this servant-girl problem?'" But Greeley-Smith again responded with a pointed question: "Have you heard anything, Mrs. Croker, of the servant girls' unions now being formed by 'Mother Jones'?"[92] (Mother Jones, of course, was the famous labor radical.)

This was no sycophantic interview. Greeley-Smith's questions not only cleverly sketched her more progressive perspective; they also helped to reveal Croker's views as hopelessly out of touch with the interests of the working classes. Greeley-Smith was clearly both politically informed and engaged.

This probing interview style was far different from the humorous approach of Kate Carew, who primarily sought to reveal the "human foibles" and unique individuality of her subjects. In her first newspaper job at the *San Francisco Examiner*, Carew remembered, she had "enjoyed watching people, getting their character by talking informally to them. Especially was I fond of my assignments to cover prisoners—there were so many interesting types."[93]

Later, at the *New York World*, Carew was assigned to interview a number of politicians. "Knowing nothing of politics and caring less," she had the "proverbial luck of the beginner" when "the Governor of the State of New York waxed confidential with me at a time of great political excitement arising from his having apparently overthrown and usurped the 'Boss' of his party." She treasured "a souvenir of the occasion in the shape of a handsome ring sent to me with a letter of commendation by Mr. Pulitzer, the unseen but very-much-felt power behind his great newspaper." But "only in the rarest cases"—as with an artist like Sarah Bernhardt—did she feel "really interested in my subject or his pursuits." Instead, "the history of most of" her interviews had been "a frantic effort to penetrate beneath the crust of the politician in search of the man. In this process," she had "discovered many public men to have something almost human about them."[94] Carew's gifts were in observation and in creating an interaction that would reveal something unique about each individual she interviewed; she brought to life the distinctive physicality of each of her subjects through both word and sketch.

Although Greeley-Smith could create vivid enough characters with her prose, her real gifts as an interviewer lay in probing and exploring ideas, in revealing with sharp-edged clarity the complexities and inconsistencies of her subjects' thoughts. Despite this talent (by 1919, the year of her death, she had become probably the country's most famous newspaper interviewer on a wide range of topics), in the early years of her career the *New York World* limited her to interviews with women. This was the fate of most newspaper women, who were usually assigned to "women's topics"—with Kate Carew a prominent exception. There are, of course, multiple ironies in the fact that the *World* assigned Carew, who had no interest in politics, to do political interviews and assigned Greeley-Smith, who was fiercely dedicated to woman's rights and to politics in general, to cover bland domestic women. But at least the *World* did quickly recognize Greeley-Smith's gift for expressing opinions—a gift the newspaper employed in a wide variety of new human interest writing, including advice columns.

# # #

Advice columns of the period, like most other aspects of women's human interest work, have received remarkably little attention—usually dismissed as too silly to deserve much notice. But like other human interest writing, advice columns allowed female journalists to assume new public roles, to create new personae, and to establish new public spaces in print. What is more, they enabled newspaper women to interact directly with the public in their columns. For these reasons alone, they deserve a second look.

At the turn of the century advice columns emerged as a new way for newspapers to reach out to their readers. Newspapers had long provided bits of advice for readers: etiquette columns, for example, were a staple in nineteenth-century newspapers and magazines. Most newspapers also invited readers to send letters to the editor or to participate in such editorial page features as "People's Forums."

But inviting readers to share intimate details of their love lives in "confessionals" was something new in newspaper work. The first of these features was the Beatrice Fairfax column, written by Marie Manning of the *New York Journal*.[95] In her memoirs, Manning vividly recalled her part in inventing this long-lived column. One summer day in 1898, she said, she had been sitting in the "Hen Coop" with her colleague Anne O'Hagan when both heard editor Arthur Brisbane's "footstep coming down the hall." They could "always recognize his approach": "He walked staccato, he talked staccato, and most characteristic of all was his way of putting a sentence across breathlessly, as though he grudged the time wasted by a period at the end of it, or indeed by any punctuation in between." Now he "waved three letters" at them, explaining in his "tumbling speech" that none of these letters "fitted into the 'People's Forum'"—which Manning characterized as a "free-for-all where citizens with writers' itch could either plead for woman suffrage, or beg to be protected from its evils," or perhaps complain about "those meddlesome warnings against spitting" on the elevated trains.[96]

The three letters "had genuine human appeal." The first "came from a deserted wife with three children, who had lost her philandering husband to a vampire. The children were hungry; she wanted to know where she could get a job." The second was from "a desperate girl, forsaken by the lover who should have stood by," who "thought suicide was the only way." The third letter was "from a woman whose son-in-law had been systematically robbing her and beating up his wife if the mother-in-law refused to sign notes for him."[97]

All of this was "'excellent woman's page material,'" Brisbane said, telling Manning and O'Hagan to "'talk the letters over'" and answer them on the woman's page. But Marie Manning, who in her twenties "was youthful enough to rush in with a greater courage than the angels, promptly broached a new idea." Instead of "further cluttering up the miscellany of the woman's page, why not inaugurate a new department? Why not establish a public confessional, inviting unhappy people to write" to the newspaper about their "personal troubles, love problems and domestic difficulties, promising them unbiased opinions and friendly advice?" Most of the letters would "be from women" and would "have to do with affairs of the heart." Therefore "it should be a woman who would answer them"; the column should have a "touch of the maternal" as well as of "the sibyl." "Wasn't there something in this notion?" Manning asked. If she had "been ten years older," she wryly remembered, she "might have hesitated at the Frankensteinian monster" she was invoking.[98]

Brisbane was "immediately impressed" by the "possibilities of this suggestion." (He was the editor Manning had said could "humanize a weather report.") Manning had been "busy assembling those perennial and indestructible features of all women's pages—cooking, etiquette and some very naïve beauty hints, in which soap and water were urged as the best cosmetics." But Brisbane now insisted that she "turn at once from beauty

Drawing of Beatrice Fairfax [Marie Manning] by Jessie Wood. In this caricature, Wood (seated) is offering tea to the Minerva-like figure of Manning, who is surrounded by letters from readers. (Beatrice Fairfax [Marie Manning], Ladies Now and Then [New York: E. P. Dutton, 1944], p. 37)

hints" to the new column and its soon-to-be-named pseudonymous columnist. Within days, Manning had named a new alter ego: Beatrice Fairfax. Manning would remain intermittently connected with the Beatrice Fairfax column—"Fairfaxing" she called her contributions in the 1940s—for over forty years.[99]

As Manning remembered, "The column, which finally appeared on July 20, 1898, bore a far from literal pen-and-ink drawing of me in the upper left-hand corner. The portrait was flattering but recognizable. As an oracle, I was grimly tailor-made, with a black satin bow tie which suggested an iron-mold casting. Over this deceptive portrait was the name 'Beatrice Fairfax,' and under it: 'She will advise you on the troubles of your heart.' (HEART was written in very large capitals.)"[100]

The column was an instant success. "Before long," Manning "began to dread the sight of the office boys, straining under mail sacks." "Circulation zoomed like an ascending airplane," she boasted. "Heartthrobs helped to outdistance the *New York Journal*'s old rival, the *Evening World*, leaving its figures far behind." Soon the *World* "started heart-throbbing on its own, with Harriet Hubbard Ayer at the stethoscope. Editors all over the country, amazed at the pulling power of the 'lovelorn,' founded heart clinics."[101]

Providing public advice about ordinary people's private lives—not to mention inviting readers to share intimate details of their love lives in "confessionals"—marked a change in the relationship between public and private life in American popular culture. Newspapers shone a new light of publicity on private life, lessening the distance between the two realms. But we should be careful in assuming that advice columns necessarily involved the "invasion of privacy" that some critics have charged. As revealed by their extraordinary popularity, such columns did not so much invade readers' lives as they were invited into them. Clearly readers enjoyed engaging in "conversation" with the newspaper women who acted as columnists. Advice columns were part of the new, participatory, interactive world of human interest journalism.[102]

"Privacy" was a fraught term at the turn of the century. Primarily a bourgeois concept in American culture, it was articulated through the construction of a private sphere for middle-class women starting in mid-nineteenth-century America and upheld through a vast print literature, among other cultural institutions, including the law. But many female readers of newspapers like the *World* did not live the genteel private lives that were supposed to be the hallmark of bourgeois culture. Judging from letters to Beatrice Fairfax, the participants in her advice column were often working girls or working women who, as Christine Stansell, Nan Enstad, and others have pointed out, lived lives of public sociability both in their neighborhoods and in their workplaces.[103]

Many newspaper women did not live lives of bourgeois privacy, either, and sometimes they understood firsthand that domestic space was far from a "sacred" private realm. Some newspaper women had tumultuous private lives that flamed up into public view. In this they were like the rest of the population, of course—only possibly more so, given that they not only were public figures, but also lived "advanced" lives in a time when most men expected traditional marriages. In 1896, for instance, Teresa Dean's husband, physician W. Lewis Tallman, created a newspaper sensation by "disappearing"—although he was soon discovered to have eloped with another woman (whom he would later marry, then try to gain an annulment by claiming he had been drunk when he married her).[104] In 1902 Margherita Hamm divorced "Billy" Fales—they seemingly had been separated for some time, although the immediate cause of the divorce was supposed to have been his affair with an actress.[105] In both cases the newspaper exposure of broken private lives must have been unwelcome, painful—certainly Dean's 1900 novel *Reveries of a Widow* bore the marks of her marital experiences (she had been divorced twice, and possibly widowed once, when the book was published). Critic Richard Henry Stoddard commented in the *New York Mail and Express* that hers was a "clever" but "cynical" book. "Its wisdom is hard as steel," he wrote, "disagreeable with the bitterness of disillusion, and it is tolerantly amused by things that shock the majority of us."[106]

Surely, newspaper women did not want to have their own fractured private lives exposed to public view; they must have found it ironic when they appeared in the newspapers in this unwelcome light. But many female reporters certainly understood that within the private spaces of the home, problems and abuses occurred that deserved not only the light of day, but also assistance. Marie Manning looked back on her Beatrice Fairfax column not as an invasion of privacy but as a form of public service: men and women often needed advice about private problems and could not easily obtain it. "At that time," she observed, "there were no generally accepted commonsense solutions to certain eternally familiar problems, as the deserted wife, abandoned children, or the girl who had loved well and unwisely. To a multitude of correspondents, the Beatrice Fairfax column represented the only medium through which they could discuss their perplexities and get an impartial answer from an unknown and unprejudiced person."[107]

Manning's formulation reversed conventional ideas about privacy. Privacy was the problem, not a realm being "invaded": in a world of privacy, women (and men) were often isolated, without access to the help they needed. But Manning's retrospective insistence on the public service her column provided should be taken with a grain of salt, too. Although it was true that by World War II the Beatrice Fairfax column offered a social service as a clearinghouse of information about a wide variety of problems, the early Beatrice Fairfax column was far different—it offered both assistance *and* entertainment through lively published exchanges between columnist and reader.

The fact that the Fairfax column was in part entertainment is immediately apparently in her early columns: Manning's delight in the creation of her new persona—brisk, sassy, strongly opinionated, anything but sentimental—was obvious. So, too, was the fun that readers (mostly teenagers) had in writing to her. More than acting as a public service, these columns articulated a new form of theatrical public engagement, one in which reader and writer were bound up together more closely than in the past.

In an early August 1898 column, for instance, two teenaged girls, Ada W. and Lucy M., wrote to Fairfax:

Dear Madam—We are two refined and accomplished young ladies of sixteen and seventeen years. We wish to gain the affection of some worthy young men. Please advise us why we fail every time. If you know any good love potions that will surely work, please inform us, for we are becoming discouraged. ADA W. and LUCY M.[108]

It is easy to imagine Ada and Lucy giggling together—perhaps at work in a garment factory—as they composed this mock-serious letter. Fairfax's answer was a scolding delivered in a severely lofty style:

You have failed to win love so far, my dear children, because you should be in the nursery and not in the matrimonial marketplace. Men, even young men, don't want the "love" of pert, silly little school-girls.

Give up thinking about sentiment and romance for three years.[109]

Readers delighted in such schoolmarmish severity, judging by the letters that continued to pour in. Of course, not all problems were teenaged love problems. As Manning reminded the readers of her memoir, "Woman suffrage was taken more or less as a joke, except by its ardent proponents, and laws relating to women in many of the states were monstrously unjust." In the character of Fairfax, Manning energetically demanded that individual women stand up for themselves, as seen in the following exchange:

Dear Madam—I am a married woman and wish to ask your advice as to what I should do. My husband has not given me any money to buy clothes for the last five years. He even quarrels when I ask for clothes for the children. He has three bank books and is not a poor man.

Fairfax responded:

My Dear Mrs. S. G.:

For five years, apparently, you have been a very foolish little woman—or may be it is only a very patient one. Whichever it is, folly or patience, the time has certainly come for you to adopt new measures.

Your husband is obliged to pay your reasonable debts for the necessaries of life. Lose no time in contracting those reasonable debts. He is obliged to clothe you as befits his income.

Go to the dry goods stores, the milliner's and shoe dealers. Buy carefully, not too lavishly, but not too economically. Have the bills made out to the creature whom you were unfortunate enough to marry.

Undoubtedly he will make a row. But I dare say he misses few opportunities of doing that as it is. Men of his stamp seldom do. And in this case you will be able to stand the fuss, being sustained and cheered by the thought of your new clothes. Perhaps a little independence of this sort will bring him to his senses. Some men have to be fairly clubbed into decency and need highwayman methods practiced upon them at home.[110]

This was not simply the eminently practical advice, the "large doses of COMMON SENSE," that Manning later remembered giving in the character of Beatrice Fairfax.[111] It was incendiary, rebellious, fun to read. No wonder that Manning remembered that even "reticent people, who ordinarily would not have confided in anyone, enjoyed seeing their own experiences mirrored in the columns of Beatrice Fairfax and her imitators. That old, never-quenched curiosity about the secret springs of other people's lives got us hundreds of thousands of readers."[112]

But Manning also recognized her lack of qualifications to advise the many readers who wrote of "genuine tragedies" and found a partial solution to this dilemma in consulting "Judge Morris," her "old guardian." As she recalled, "Writers of letters with real problems, who enclosed stamped, self-addressed envelopes for personal replies, must have wondered sometimes at the excellence of the legal advice they received from the very young girl whose picture headed the column." Morris used to threaten her with "dire happenings" if she did not "stop asking him for legal advice," but he never turned her down.[113]

The appeal of advice columns for readers was obvious. By 1901, when Nixola Greeley-Smith went to work for the *New York World*, advice columns had spread from newspaper to newspaper—as happened with any successful new human interest feature. At the *World*, beauty editor Harriet Hubbard Ayer began to write an occasional column of "advice to the lovelorn" in addition to her various beauty columns, though her advice was more soothing than the bracing splash of cold water offered by Beatrice Fairfax. Cloyingly sentimental advice columns quickly proliferated, so much so that the *World* itself ran several brilliant parodies of advice columns (part of a series of parodies of the new human interest features) on its own editorial page in 1901. May Irwin's "New Department of Heart-to-Heart Blitherings," for instance, was pitch-perfect: "You must call me 'Auntie May,'" the parody began, "and come to me with all your little worries and vexations. I will help you. That's what I'm here for. Some days a whole frolicking, laughing crowd of you—bless your bright faces!—will flock around my chair. . . . So write your heart worries to Auntie May, and she will answer you and toss great bunches of sunshine into your darkened little lives." This parody sounded suspiciously like the style of the *World*'s own Harriet Hubbard Ayer—or perhaps Marion Harland.[114]

In 1902 Greeley-Smith began her own bylined column of thoughts on modern women, marriage, and the relations between men and women. She would eventually produce hundreds of these columns, which in the 1910s moved increasingly toward an openly feminist viewpoint. Greeley-Smith also wrote an advice column for the *World* beginning in 1905 (Harriet Hubbard Ayer had died in 1903). "Betty's Balm for Lovers" reached out to young people, making the case that the friendly counsel of a modern newspaper could step in where family failed. Such a column was part of the Progressive Era advocacy of the need for "experts" in American life, as we have already seen with the woman's page.

"When young men or young women are in love," "Betty" said in her first column, "it very often happens that the fathers and mothers, to whom they would turn naturally for advice on other problems, are so very unsympathetic in their attitude toward what is really the greatest problem of all, that they are obliged to seek advice elsewhere. Many of these perplexed lovers need only a word of kindly sympathy or caution at the critical moments of their lives, and many take steps that lead to lifelong unhappiness for the lack of it. Scores of letters reach me from young people in love whose hearts are heavy with problems too great for their inexperience to deal with, but who have not in their own environment a sympathetic heart to understand them."[115]

As this surprisingly stiff, formal prose suggests, "Betty" lacked the zest of "Beatrice Fairfax." But in their prosaic way, Greeley-Smith's columns, too, provided an interesting index over time of the concerns of both young women and men. An early letter asked:

> Dear Betty:
> I am on merely friendly terms with a girl. She seems to show a great fondness for me and she has told several of my friends that she loves me. Now, how can I explain to her that my regard for her is merely friendship?
> CHRISTOPHER

Betty responded:

> Probably the girl is not as much smitten as you think. But you might tell her of some friend of yours who has just married, and how foolish you think him for doing so.[116]

Another exchange read:

> Dear Betty:
> I am engaged to a young lady, but she has taken a dislike to me. Would I better break the engagement or try to win back her love?
> J. P.

Betty offered this advice:

> I would ask her to explain the reason of her dislike. Possibly you only imagine she dislikes you. If she says she no longer loves you ask her to break the engagement and she may change her mind.[117]

As these two exchanges suggest, many of Greeley-Smith's correspondents were young men. In fact, in 1906 she commented that "men are much more prone to confide their troubles to me than women are. Where we get one letter from a woman we get 10 from men, and you would also be surprised if you could know how cultivated and intelligent a class of men they are who write me to find out whether I think this girl loves him because of his money. Many people suppose that it is only the young and silly, and unusually [sic] of the female sex, who resort to such sources of information, but, seriously, there could be no greater mistake."[118]

Over the course of her newspaper career, Greeley-Smith wrote hundreds of advice columns such as "Betty's Balm for Lovers," "Hints and Helps for Lovers," and "Sage Advice to Distressed Husbands." As her 1906 interviewer commented, it was "as an authority upon love and marriage that Miss Greeley Smith, under various nom de plumes and in divers delightful vehicles, conveys the greatest amount of help and inspiration to the reading public."[119]

Ironically, although Greeley-Smith and Manning were both dubbed "authorities" on love and marriage, neither was married—nor even much of an adult when she embarked on her newspaper career (both were in their early twenties when they began working for the *World* and the *Journal*).[120] But whether or not readers realized that such columnists were merely a façade or a charade, they obviously enjoyed reading about ordinary life—that extensive world of "human interest"—in the newspaper.

In 1906 a skeptical interviewer asked Greeley-Smith what she thought her grandfather might say about "a newspaper opening its columns to helps and hints for sweethearts and Betty's Balm for Lovers?" Wasn't she "afraid that he might think it just—well, just a little bit frivolous in comparison with the stately journalism of his day?" Wasn't she afraid "he might compare his granddaughter a little—well, a little, just a little unfavorably against his famous feature writer, Margaret Fuller?"[121]

But Greeley-Smith stoutly defended this line of newspaper work. If Margaret Fuller were to come back to Park Row, she said, "She would find that people are much more interested in every day things, in things that intimately affect their lives and their mundane happiness, than they are in transcendentalism and the other dull things she wrote about in the Tribune 50 odd years ago."[122] Proud of what she had accomplished, Greeley-Smith said that all of her columns she had "enjoyed doing with all my heart and soul. My Hints and Helps for Lovers, my Sage Advice to Distressed Husbands and Wives, all the things I have done in my five years of work on the New York World I personally consider worth while. I would not be so egotistical as to be quoted saying that necessarily my way of doing it has been the greatest ever. You see I may as well confess that I take my work seriously, and I have no respect for a newspaper writer, or anybody else, who does not believe in the ultimate value of what he is doing."[123]

# # #

In its insistence on interactions with readers—whether directly through advice columns or indirectly through narrators who drew close to readers in intimate first-person accounts—human interest journalism helped to redefine both writers' and readers' relationships to urban public and private space. Whereas newspapers had once been primarily assemblages of advertisements and foreign news (in the early American period), they now encouraged active curiosity about every aspect of metropolitan life, attempting to enfold all readers within an ephemeral daily community that shimmered with the continuing promise of tomorrow's exciting features. Reaching out through space, newspapers reached forward through time, as well.

Human interest writing was part of the expansionist aims of newspapers at the turn of the century. Paradoxically, however, this expansionism was founded on new ideas of intimacy—through the call for individual relationships between readers and writers that were to be mediated, and then circulated, by the newspaper itself. We can see some of the potentially transformative power of this call for intimacy in the reminiscences of Rose

Pastor Stokes. Her experiences also show us that "human interest" was a mode of newspaper style that spilled over into ethnic newspapers as well as metropolitan mass-circulation newspapers.

In 1901 Pastor was working in a cigar factory in Cleveland when a neighbor gave her mother copies of the *New York Jewish Daily News*: "The editor of its English page was calling for suggestions from his readers. IF YOU ARE IN BUSINESS, WRITE A LETTER! DO YOU WORK IN AN OFFICE? WRITE A LETTER! DO YOU WORK IN THE FACTORY? WRITE A LETTER! In arresting type at the ends of columns, between articles, between short items the invitation went forth in bold-faced type to all and sundry: WRITE A LETTER! WRITE A LETTER! WRITE A LETTER!"[124] Answering this call for reader response, Pastor wrote a letter "in the factory during the lunch hour, addressed it to the editor, and posted it in the spirit of a lark."[125]

Pastor's extraordinary letter, published a few days later, was nothing like the other cautious, carefully worded letters the *Jewish Daily News* had recently printed from readers. It revealed an ardent spirit, swept up by the possibilities of public communication in a newspaper. Pastor talked of not being able to get those words, "Write a Letter," out of her mind: "Readers, — (I address the readers; I risk the almost impossible chance of the publication of this letter), I say, Readers, if you value your peace of mind, your hours of sweet repose — if you value your health and happiness — and say, who does not value that — *do not look at the heading of this column!* Why? You ask, and 'how ridiculous,' you say!" Pastor explained that the words "Write a Letter" had been a torment, giving her no peace: "I bravely pushed the thought from me and went to my work. To keep it away, I sang, laughed and talked all day, but to no purpose. There it was — your blessed paper! — right before my mental vision, with '*Letters! Letters! Letters!*'" She *had* to write a letter, she told the editor and readers of the *Jewish Daily News* — even though it had meant that she had "made two hundred less to-day on account of this letter — not two hundred dollars, but two hundred stogies." "I work in a cigar factory," she confided.[126]

"Here's a Gem" was the subhead the editor of the *Jewish Daily News* gave Pastor's letter. Soon he wrote to her, inviting her to contribute regularly, "preferably talks to the girls." The "invitation pleased and excited me," Pastor later remembered. She became a columnist writing in the character of "Zelda," with the two dollars she received for each column "big as cartwheels in the eyes of my Need" — though far less than she needed to support herself and her family. She continued working in the cigar factory and "burnt the candle at both ends." When she was unable to keep up with the demands of producing a column in addition to her factory work, the editor (who had developed a romantic interest in Pastor) offered her a permanent position on the newspaper. At a time when she faced "sickness, semi-starvation, despair," the newspaper transformed her life, lifting her out of factory work and into the metropolitan world of New York.[127]

This was not a fairy tale ending, however. Like many other women, Pastor grew to see the newspaper as exploitative, the work as never-ending. She had been "sucked up into a maw hungrier than that of the factory," with "no free hours" and with "all thought in my so-called free time" to be "utilized for my columns."[128] Yet there is no question that the strangely intimate world of turn-of-the-century journalism, with its new emphasis on interaction, had reached out from New York to Cleveland, directly altering one woman's life and giving her new possibilities for public self-invention and self-expression.

chapter four **Bachelor Girls**

In the late 1890s Marie Manning of the *New York Journal*, Olivia Dunbar of the *New York World*, and Neith Boyce of the *New York Commercial Advertiser* all lived at the Judson Hotel on Washington Square in Greenwich Village. At the time, the Judson attracted a variety of writers and would-be writers—from poets to playwrights to newspaper men and women. "We became chums," Boyce later remembered of her friendship with the two "other newspaper girls": Dunbar "was the delicate New England type, the most lady-like, reserved and shrinking, exquisite person." Manning, on the other hand, "was a big robust and gay Rabelaisian creature, full of color and laughter telling the funniest stories, amused at herself and her business."[1] The three women "used to get together in the evenings and among other things talk over their respective papers," Boyce recalled. "The Journal was the Yellow Peril, the World the Hellhound of the Opposition," and Boyce's old-fashioned *Commercial Advertiser* "was named 'Grandma' by the irrepressible" Manning, "who gloried in her saffron stories and the screaming headlines which the World was being drawn to imitate." Manning "would take a copy of 'Grandma' and read out what she called the 'prose poems' that appeared as news and go into convulsions of laughter. 'Call that a newspaper' she would cry. She patronized" both Boyce and Dunbar, "though she admitted that the World was a newspaper, but old-fashioned."[2]

Boyce was soon to marry writer Hutchins Hapgood, who visited the Judson regularly. "Probably no girls ever enjoyed themselves more as journalists than these three," he later commented. "They had bid a kindly farewell to their homes, and were tasting economic independence. In the case of Marie Manning, this often went to her head; for no words could have been more highly colored than hers, nor uttered with greater zest."[3] Indeed, Manning was a larger-than-life figure in Boyce's memory: Boyce marveled at her exuberant enjoyment of making a splash, remembering that she had once chosen to wear, for a sedate "literary tea," a "ripe water-

melon red silk" dress, with "heavy rustling taffetas." As Manning explained to her two friends, "'If you have to get a dress, you get something people will look at.'" In the same way, she declared, "'If you write an article, write something people are bound to read and put a shock-head on it. She said the other girls were 'born to blush unseen.'"[4]

Marie Manning and Olivia Dunbar became friends for life, calling each other "Hinky" and "Dinky" (the joke was that Manning, as "Dinky," was exceptionally tall for her day, at five foot eleven) in letters that spanned marriage, children (Manning named one of her sons Oliver), successful writing careers, less successful writing careers, illness, financial troubles, and old age. They remained loyal to each other and visited back and forth as frequently as possible. Dunbar even helped out when Manning needed to pick up "Fairfaxing" again (writing the long-running Beatrice Fairfax advice column) after a hiatus of some years, because she had lost her money on the stock market.[5]

In the late 1890s, however, Manning and Dunbar were still "bachelor girls"—a term that came into vogue in newspapers of the late 1880s to describe independent young women who were living on their own but were

not necessarily the more serious-seeming "New Women" of the mid-1890s. "Bachelor girls" were not necessarily in a hurry to marry. Manning, whose success as Beatrice Fairfax gave her a large salary (and who also had a small independent income), "spoke with pity of the men in her office who were trying to support wives and children on salaries generally less than hers," according to Boyce. "They constantly borrowed of her until pay-day. She viewed family life, which necessitated these borrowings, tolerantly, admitted they couldn't help it; but still thought they might do something about not having so many children. She said she intended to marry herself, 'after a while.' In fact she had a steady suitor, who came from Washington to see her every now and then, and pressed his claim; but Marie was having a very good time as it was."[6]

Manning was still having a good time in 1902, when the *New York World* ran an illustrated feature on the apartment she shared with Dunbar (on West 10th Street in New York City). Focusing on the "evolution" of bachelor girls' "mode of living," and headlined "Made-over Antiques Now the Rage in Home Life of Bachelor Girls," the article explained that "bachelor girl life in New York has become such a joy to so many besides the bachelor girls themselves that nobody ever thinks of it now as freakish. It is what every girl making her own way in New York longs for as much as she used to long for New York itself." Contending that "the whole machinery of bachelor girls' abodes is changed," the writer implied that there was a long history of newspaper articles about bachelor girls—as, indeed, was the case.[7]

Bachelor girl articles, in fact, were a distinctive newspaper phenomenon at the turn of the century: hundreds of them celebrated women's independent new lives, offering an important (if little-known) counterpoint to literature that worried over "women adrift."[8] They also provided what amounted to "how-to" guides for creating a new kind of home. If earlier articles on domesticity explored women's lives within families, stories about bachelor girls celebrated women's abilities to create homes as single women out on their own. This was a new version of domesticity that turned older, mid-nineteenth-century ideas of home on their head: "Home" now meant a realm *away* from family, not the central locus of family. At the same time bachelor girl articles turned the supposedly private realm of the home inside out, creating a new public domesticity that complemented newspaper women's new public lives.

#

In December 1887 newspaper woman Viola Roseboro' wrote to her father that "a newspaper correspondent recently made a great hit, and coined a phrase that has passed into the current vocabulary when he wrote about 'female bachelors.' That filled a long felt want," she added. A female bachelor herself, Roseboro' lived in the late 1880s at the Annex to the Marlboro Arms, a hotel "where an interesting group of newspaper women and artists made her life enjoyable."[9]

Only two months before, the *New York Mail and Express* had noted that "the feminine bachelor" was becoming "a feature of this city." A brief paragraph sketched a set of characteristics that would in fact become the subject of hundreds of articles over the next twenty years: "She is frequently pretty," the article said, "she is always well dressed, and she ranges from 23 to 33 years old. The feminine bachelor is usually a bright girl, and she often comes from the country. She is an art student, a medical student. She is learning music or shorthand. She has literary yearning, and sends manuscripts to all the publishers. She has comparatively few acquaintances of the other sex. Men are apt to like her, and she is apt to like them, but she is too busy to let the association go very far. She can't afford too big a rent bill, and frequently her office or studio or workroom is sitting-room and bedroom in one. She will exercise an ingenuity that stamps her as truly feminine to turn it into a home. Her folding bed doesn't betray that she sleeps there. If she can afford it she goes to a restaurant. If she can't, the possibilities of a gas stove and 'light housekeeping' are boundless."[10]

Like many neologisms that describe an as-yet-unnamed and yet-observable social reality, the term "feminine bachelor" took hold quickly and spread among newspapers in a number of variations. By 1889, a number of newspaper women discussed the "bachelor girl" or "bachelor woman." Mary H. Krout, who wrote the long-running column "Woman's Kingdom" for the *Chicago Inter Ocean* in the late 1880s and 1890s, announced in November 1889 that the "bachelor woman" was a "product of modern opportunity and civilization." There are "thousands of such women in the United States to-day," Krout said. "They crowd the school-room, the colleges, the professions; they make a business of art and literature."[11]

A "bachelor woman" herself, Krout was not just a keen observer of the emergence of "bachelor women"; she actively participated in creating that phenomenon by defining and celebrating bachelor women in her column. Like Krout, newspaper women around the country explored the new topic of the "bachelor girl" or "bachelor woman" (both terms were widely used) in the late 1880s and 1890s, often in feature articles that appeared on the woman's page.[12] The author of the 1889 *New York World*'s "Feminine Bachelor: A Curious Phase of Life among a Certain Type of Self-Reliant New York Woman," for instance, identified herself as a "newspaper woman" and took for granted that others were fascinated by the bachelor girl. "I am a feminine bachelor myself," she said, "and whenever I am associating with any people except other feminine bachelors, they pester me to weariness about the species. They are very conscious that we are not like the familiar household old maid," and "they are devoured with curiosity as to what we are like, and how we contrive to keep so young and jolly and well set up without any visible masculine means of support."[13]

In article after article, newspaper women discussed the "feminine bachelor" who worked for a living. Not only did they sketch where she lived or her movements around the city, but they also wrote her into a new public life by explicitly claiming the unaccompanied bachelor woman's right to a variety of public spaces. In the 1889 syndicated article "Just Like Men: Feminine Bachelors and Their Homes," Eliza Putnam Heaton rapidly outlined the activities of the New York "girl bachelor," one of "the novel developments of life in the city." At the theater, the girl bachelor was the "young woman" who walked "quietly" and "all alone down to an aisle seat in the front row of orchestra chairs; invited to a party out of town, she was the young woman who "rings your cottage bell modestly but unabashed, party bag on arm, without so much as a lady's maid" as "escort to impress the servant who opens the door." She was "the young woman who tramps, detective camera in hand, up and down the mountain roads of the Catskills." She was the "young woman, who, when in New York, composedly takes her place at a French or Italian table d'hote of good class and expects and receives every consideration, though no male creature" vouched "for her respectability."

"Last but not least," she was "the young woman who says to you, 'Keep your seat, sir; I've been seated all day,' when you rise to give her your place in horse car or elevated train, and she says it so simply, so politely and withal in such a matter-of-course tone that you waste no time urging her, but settle back and open your newspaper."[14] And, of course, she was the newspaper writer—Heaton herself—who provided quick sketches and "glimpses" of bachelor girls' public and private lives.

As Heaton's article showed, bachelor girl articles often held up a mirror (admittedly sometimes distorted) to newspaper women's own lives: after all, newspaper women were not only observers of, but also actors in, a new drama of independent urban life. They not only wrote about the new phenomenon of the bachelor girl, thus helping to bring her into public awareness, they also were bachelor girls themselves. Margherita Arlina Hamm made this point explicitly in her column "Among the Newspaper Women" in 1892. "A very bright newspaper woman whom I know has been dubbed by her friends 'that bachelor girl,'" Hamm said, "and I think it seems very appropriate to all or nearly all the newspaper women I know. They live alone, depend upon no one for livelihood, mentality, or entertainment, and in fact paddle their own canoe with all the nerve and independence of a full-fledged bachelor."[15] It is no wonder that bachelor girls' lives received celebratory coverage on woman's pages.

Who counted as a "bachelor girl"? A number of newspaper writers puzzled over the exact answer to this question: according to the 1898 *Chicago Daily Tribune* article "Where and How Chicago's Bachelor Girls Live," "Many persons would find it difficult, if not impossible, to return a definite answer to the question, 'What is a bachelor girl?'"[16] She was unmarried, of course. But at first different writers highlighted different qualities of the bachelor girl—her work, or the fact that she lived on her own, or her age, or even her supposed refinement. Quickly a consensus developed, however. First and foremost, as the *Tribune* said, she was "almost always a worker."[17] Indeed, many commentators made clear from the outset that "bachelor girls" worked out of necessity. As a woman's page article in the *New York Herald* in 1895 commented, "Necessity is in most cases the cause which compels the girl to leave her own roof."[18] Mary Gay Humphreys observed that bachelor girls had begun to work after the panic of 1873, which "literally turned out of doors thousands of women from homes grown luxurious in the exceptional prosperity that followed the war."[19] Although Humphreys published her analysis in *Scribner's Magazine* in 1896, she—like so many magazine writers—had started her career as a newspaper woman. She had received "her newspaper training on The World under the old regime," before also working for the *Daily Graphic* and as a syndicated columnist on decorating.[20]

For some writers, the need to work also marked a difference between the bachelor girl and the "New Woman" in the same period: the "so-called 'bachelor girl'" was "quite a different individual from the 'new woman,'" newspaper and magazine writer Olga Stanley [Lila Woolfall] asserted, "although in many of their interests" they were "closely allied."[21] For Stanley, the "new woman" was someone with more financial resources than the "bachelor girl," but not all commentators would have agreed with her. Still, the New Woman seemed different from the "bachelor girl." While the term "New Woman" captured middle-class women's changing status, including their entrance into professions, sports, and higher education, the term "bachelor girl" increasingly focused on single women's living arrangements and lifestyle.

At the same time, a number of observers believed that the "bachelor girl" was not to be confused with the "working girl." Mary Gay Humphreys, for example, wrote separate articles on "The New York Working-Girl" and "Women Bachelors of New York" for *Scribner's*, in which she described the occupations of "working-girls" as shirtmakers, feather workers, and boxmakers—that is, factory workers—while "women bachelors" were artists, teachers, and newspaper workers. (One newspaper writer in 1894 referred to the latter trio of women's occupations as "the higher professions.")[22] Other occupations of the bachelor girl sometimes included stenographer and typewriter—the new clerical work of women in this period.[23]

"Bachelor girl" also meant something different from "professional woman" and "business girl," terms that were increasingly used in the 1890s to describe women's rapidly changing lives. "Business girl" and "professional woman" generally indicated interest in women's new jobs and careers, and could apply to both married and unmarried women. "Bachelor girl," on the other hand, focused primarily on an unmarried working woman's living arrangements, behavior, and personal appearance—an intimate interest fueling numerous articles describing what she looked like, where she lived, how she dressed, what she ate, how she cooked, and, especially, how she furnished her living space. These various terms were not mutually exclusive—after all, a "bachelor girl" living in her own apartment was also a "business girl" once she was at the office. But the use of "bachelor girl" invited readers to peer into the intimacies of a woman's home life, as well as to imagine themselves in her shoes when she was out in public.

The term "bachelor girl" (or "bachelor woman") also allowed newspaper women to disavow the dreaded stereotype "old maid." In the *Chicago Inter*

Ocean, Mary Krout declared that the "old maid" was now hopelessly old-fashioned and out-of-date—a "race" that thankfully "had become extinct" now that the bachelor woman had replaced her. Some "twenty or thirty years ago," Krout said, the "old maid" had been a "thin, pale, silent type of melancholy failure." She had been "usually poor," "untrained though intelligent," and "had no active part in the affairs of life" and "no especial place in the world." Krout's "old maid" inspired nothing but pity: "She dressed in dull colors and the materials called 'durable,' and if a poor little purple flower bloomed on her best bonnet it was looked at like a winter blossom which had budded out of due season." She had "nothing in the future to anticipate but monotonous days, a succession of seasons, without events or possibilities, and which were frequently clouded by the dread of helpless, poverty-stricken old age."[24]

This exaggerated portrait of the "old maid" (which surely would have been unrecognizable to the many single women of the previous era engaged in benevolent work, teaching, and other occupations) allowed Krout to create a stark contrast between women's present and past lives. If the "old maid" had "vanished" during what was the "woman's century," as Krout asserted, what had come "in her stead" was a "cheering and inspiring product of a broader civilization whom the newspapers gracefully and commandingly call the 'bachelor woman.'" She was "well bred, well trained, and with brain and hands has made her way to success in the calling she has chosen." She was also happy in her work: "Congenial work, a definite aim in life leave no room for impotent regrets: and have kept her temper sweet, her feelings tender, and her sympathies alert; so that she has not lapsed into a state of mummification, as her prototype was apt to do thirty or forty years ago."[25]

"The day of the antediluvian spinster has vanished," a *Chicago Daily Tribune* article asserted in 1897. The "lady with the corkscrew curls, sharp tongue, and long nose, poking into every one's affairs, is now only seen upon the stage." The "old-maid aunt who was relegated to the furthest [*sic*] seat from the family fireplace, and who spent her life in mending and darning for her nephews and nieces, is no more."[26] The *New York Herald* presented a shorthand version of the same points in its headlines for an 1895 woman's page article: "NOT ANY MORE OLD MAIDS. The Bachelor Girl Lives So Happily the Sneer Is Lost. Even With Small Incomes. Make the Best of Everything Is the Secret of Her Charm."[27]

The "old maid," writers agreed, had been a "generous, self-sacrificing type," who had been "expected by all her friends to efface herself."[28] But no one described the "bachelor girl" as self-effacing. On the contrary, she was a "crisp, self-sufficient woman," said Emilie Ruck de Schell, who noted

"'Old Maids' No More—All 'Girl Bachelors' Now," Chicago Daily Tribune, September 26, 1897. This article, contrasting the "Old Maid of 50 50 Years Ago" with the "Maid of 50 Today," explains in the subtitle that "The Creature of Corkscrew Curls, Sour Visage, and Funny Furbelows Is Superseded by a Dainty, Bright-Faced Woman of Nimble Wit, Independent of Horrid Man and His Equal in Social, Business, and Professional Life." (Chicago Daily Tribune, September 26, 1897, ProQuest Historical Newspapers, Chicago Tribune [1894–1987])

that she herself was "doing space work for a daily newspaper at four dollars a column" while she got her "novel ready for publication."[29] The "bachelor girl" was a "wholly emancipated woman" who was, "at least in her own estimation," the "backbone of society."[30]

Many bachelor women achieved success without husbands, writers asserted. "Favored Spinsters," a woman's page article in the *Chicago Daily Tribune* in 1895, took as its subject "clever women" who "have won fortune without a husband." Whereas "it used to be the fashion, and until very recently, to style unmarried ladies past a certain age as old maids," now they desired "to be called women bachelors, whether they be 25 or 55." Including a number of prominent women—among them, journalist Kate Field—in a list of "feminine bachelors," the article made the point that "many women have earned fame and fortune unfettered or unaided by husbands."[31]

But why wasn't the "bachelor girl" married? It was a "notorious fact," explained an article in the *Chicago Daily Tribune*, "that many of our most cultivated and our brightest women remain single from choice." Among their reasons was the fact that it "has become both necessity and custom in families of moderate means for the daughters to enter some occupation that will render them independent and self-supporting." But such self-support could have unintended consequences. A "clever, well-educated woman" could not only earn "her own bread and butter and even preserves," but also make "enough to occasionally taste of the world's free air."[32]

The "bachelor girl," in fact, could savor an independence not available to the married woman. "She can enjoy and pay for an evening's lecture, or theater, without the escort of a cane and crush hat. She and her friends can travel all over the country without the protection of some masculine who is always missing checks and fussing with conductors. She comes to see matrimony through other women's eyes, and the matrimonial experience of friends and relatives makes her look askance at it." In contrast, "she finds that by some strange legal hocus-pocus the marriage ceremony transforms in a twinkling an independent, judicious woman in to a legal nonentity." Being single gave her a "taste for independence."[33]

A newspaper woman who signed herself "Peggy's Partner" in the 1889 *New York World* left no doubt that she valued this independence. "A poor benighted male idiot, on making a first visit to my place the other day," "gazed about at my pretty little place," "drank my exquisite tea," and "chatted with two or three bright people who happened in"—then "suddenly exclaimed in a bewildered sort of way: 'Well, the lonely, unprotected female has a good deal of misplaced sympathy wasted upon her, as nearly as I can make out.'"[34]

"I should think so," Peggy's Partner declared. "I and my kind have just the same reasons for not getting married till we are so much in love we can't help it, as the usual man has, and when there are more women similarly situated there won't be so much need of asking whether or not marriage is a failure. Marriage will be greatly more successful when the women are under less pressure to marry for purposes of convenience."[35]

Part of a larger critique of marriage at the turn of the century, the bachelor girl became a figure of fantasy through which many writers imagined independent new lives for women—with an emphasis on the freedom that such independence allowed.[36] The bachelor girl "has no desire to marry," asserted an article in the *Chicago Daily Tribune.* "Not she. She revels in her absolute freedom. When she comes home from an art reception, a dinner party, a club symposium, a theater party, she finds no husband to growl over her late arrival, no babies to yell and keep her awake through the night. She has all the independence of the married woman and none of her responsibilities."[37]

Olga Stanley emphasized the importance of freedom to bachelor girls. "Probably the thing which first appeals to us is our absolute freedom, the ability to plan our time as we will," Stanley said in a magazine piece titled "Some Reflections on the Life of a 'Bachelor Girl.'" While admitting that there were happy marriages, and that sometimes "we turn with a little sigh towards our little room and our little grate-fire and our little bubbling kettle (all little to accord with the little income, except the girl, who, no doubt, fills most of the space in her domicile)," Stanley still insisted that, when she thought of the unhappy marriages she knew, "We emit a sigh of thankfulness this time, draw nearer to the fire, and, resting our toes on the fender, lean back in our easy chair and congratulate ourselves upon our good fortune."[38]

It is telling that Stanley imagined the bachelor girl at her own hearth, in her own easy chair. For writer after writer, bachelor girls' apartments and living arrangements—the spaces they inhabited and the homes they created—exerted a powerful fascination. Not coincidentally, interest in bachelor girls fit well with the conventional concerns of the woman's page, where newspaper women were beginning to explore the domestic spaces of bachelor girls.

In 1896 Kate Kensington (Cynthia Westover Alden) wrote an affectionate and humorous profile of a woman's page staff member for the *New York Recorder*—part of a series in which she gently teased her female coworkers. Taking the reader for an inside glimpse of "Miriam Dudley in Her Den," Kensington wrote that "Miriam began housekeeping with her sister," who was "a bachelor girl with her," in a "cozy flat on Columbus avenue two years ago, when driven half crazy with boarding life." All the property they possessed consisted of a statue of the Venus de Milo, "a fur rug, a box of books, two knives, a cup and the quilt they hooked to do them up in."[39]

Dudley was "almost a 'blue stocking,'" Kensington said, tongue in cheek. She had not only graduated from college but also was taking a course in law offered for women at the University of the City of New York. She also sought some distance from the "typical" woman's realm of decorative clutter.

"There is not a bit of bric-a-brac to be seen in her den, nor a thread of fancy work." Kensington wrote.

"'Oh, I can't bear it,' she cried when questioned.

"'Why, what a funny girl you are!' I cried in amazement.

"'Don't call me a girl, if you please; I am a woman—been one some time.'

"'New one?'

"'Well, I don't know about that,' and she sent a merry peal of laughter through the room that vied in brightness with the sunshine. 'If disliking a lot of things that you call feminine defines the "new woman," then I may be one,' she added."

Kensington noted that "although her den is so destitute of those 'feminine touches' always looked for in a woman's room, one glance about would make one want to meet the inmate. Books in many languages are scattered everywhere, as if everyday utensils in that quarter. Comfort is marked in every corner, but luxury finds no place there." In sketching the furnishings of Dudley's life, Kensington depicted the furnishings of her mind, as well. "She is a natural philosopher," Kensington said, "and capable of reaching great heights as a writer."[40]

As Kensington indicated, the style of a bachelor girl's home was linked to her new independence. For many writers, in fact, independence and home were so intertwined as to be inseparable—yet another reason for the fascination with bachelor girls' living arrangements. As Mary Gay Humphreys put it, "In the measure that women are determining their own lives, they want their own homes."[41] Humphreys found that desire "entirely reasonable": "The woman who is occupied with daily work needs greater freedom of movement, more isolation, more personal comforts, and the exemption, moreover, from being agreeable at all times and places. She wants to be able to shut her doors against the world, and not to be confined within four walls herself; and she wants to open her doors when it pleases her, and to exercise the rites of hospitality unquestioned."[42]

Freedom and privacy were central requirements of the new bachelor woman, yet both were in short supply in most housing available to metropolitan women. The late 1880s and 1890s saw a rapid increase in bachelor housing for men but no equivalent accommodations for the many independent women arriving in cities. In 1889, for example, Humphreys explored a variety of the new apartment buildings for bachelors in New York—from the Benedict on Washington Square, to the Cumberland on Fifth Avenue, to the Alpine on Broadway. In these buildings the standard bachelor apartment was "understood to be a sitting-room, bed-room and bath"—enough space to give men the valued independence that women also desired. Women felt only "envy" of these new accommodations, Humphreys commented; after all, they were "equally interested" in independent living quarters. But urban apartment living was still a rarity for women.[43]

In writing about bachelor girls, many newspaper women took readers through a litany of complaints about each of the options open to them.

Peggy's Partner, for instance, recounted fleeing a "nasty boarding house" ("I hate all boarding houses," she added) in order to try a "lodging house for women only, established on philanthropic principles." "We had a suite of rooms that pleased us very much for $5 a week apiece," she said, "but the philanthropical principles were too much for us. The nice old hens that found their *raison d'etre* in running the place, felt as if they owned us, despite the fact that we paid for all we got; and having no other amusement, spent their days in making rules for us until life became unendurable."[44]

Such metropolitan lodging houses or "homes" for women were often run by Christian organizations, including the YWCA. As newspaper woman Mary C. Francis noted, such homes at least provided a temporary stopping place for the "struggling young art or musical student, the unfledged newspaper woman deluded with vain hopes of the magazine, the great army of eager, anxious aspirants of all ranks and professions."[45] Margherita Hamm more optimistically commented in 1892 that "quite a large number of newspaper women live at the Margaret Louisa Shepard Home on Sixteenth street, a branch of the Young Women's Christian Association; and it is the home of all homes for newspaper women." Not only was there "a grand library, a fine parlor," and "an excellent office, where numerous desks are open for use," but it also had a "telegraph and telephone connection, and in fact everything the newspaper woman could wish." Hamm had lived there herself and could "conscientiously indorse its perfect harmony and happy associations." The "only drawback" was "the smallness of the rooms."[46]

Yet there were other drawbacks to living at the YWCA home, as Peggy's Partner had revealed: too many rules and restrictions, part of the surveillance of women's lives by those who ran the homes.[47] The Margaret Louisa Home accepted only Protestant women. And while it prided itself on providing "sympathetic home influence" for "women transients," the women who stayed there—for a maximum of five weeks, according to the *Chicago Daily Tribune*—often rebelled against its many regulations, which included a curfew and nightly voluntary prayer meeting.[48]

Many women saw the YWCA as a charitable institution and wanted none of it. As one 1893 *Chicago Daily Tribune* article said, "There must be nothing to stamp it [the ideal apartment house] as a home or charity or Christian Association affair, or the business women will not go into it. They are jealous of giving up one iota of their deserved independence, and previous plans have gone to pieces because of the red tape that impractical philanthropists wished to tie around them."[49] In particular, there should be no curfews or limitations on their company. "The working woman, intelligent enough to do a man's work, insists on a man's privileges and boldly announces that she will have none of the cut and dried routine for her out-goings and comings in. She will pay for her accommodations, and her room must be her castle: she will stand no meddling in her personal affairs. The actress and the newspaper woman go everywhere at all hours, and why should not the other independent women?"[50]

The Margaret Louisa Shepard Home, and others like it, were never meant to be more than temporary stopgaps for self-supporting women. But the problem was, as Mary Gay Humphreys noted, that in New York no other "preparations" had been "made for the indwelling of a number of young women without homes." As a result, one of their few options was the small "hall bedroom" to be found in boardinghouses. The typical New York boardinghouse had five such hall bedrooms, Humphreys said, adding that "there would be six, but that the space for one has been appropriated by the bath-room." Boardinghouses with hall bedrooms were densely layered in the city. Humphreys estimated that "there are three hundred on each cross-town block. In a solid section extending from Washington Square to Fifty-ninth Street, and within the limited confines of Fifth and Sixth Avenues," she calculated that there were "roughly, fifteen thousand hall bed-rooms.[51]

This cramped "hall bedroom" was a prominent feature of bachelor women's lives—and of newspaper articles about bachelor girls. "As necessity is in most cases the cause which compels the girl to leave her own roof," the New York Herald said in 1895, "her expenses must be kept down to the minimum, and thus it happens that the bachelor girl can seldom afford any more spacious quarters than the hall bedrooms in a good boarding house in the metropolis."[52] Rheta Dorr followed the path of many other newspaper women in renting one of these rooms upon her arrival in New York. Before obtaining a staff position at the Evening Post, she lived "in a dimly lighted hall bedroom, so cold that I could write only when wrapped in a dingy red blanket from the cot bed. Over the one gas-jet I cooked most of the food I ate."[53] Such rooms were so small that they allowed a woman to "sit on the bed and wield a brush while confronting the mirror, and at the same time remove a garment from a peg behind the door."[54] In summer the hall room was "hot and stifling" and in winter, "cold and cheerless"; in all seasons it was "either unventilated or swept by perilous draughts." It was, as Humphreys put it, "the Pariah of the community of rooms, the Cinderella of the domestic roof." In it were collected the "weak-kneed chairs, the superannuated springs, the cracked pitchers, the murky mirrors, the knobless bureaus, the darned lace curtains, the cordless shades, the faded stripes of Brussels carpets."[55]

No wonder that throughout the 1890s, newspaper women confronted the issue of housing for bachelor women in articles on the woman's page. In 1896 Mary Francis wrote in the *Milwaukee Sentinel* that "apartment life for women wage-earners" in large cities was a "problem not yet solved." "At first thought one would imagine that proper accommodations for self-supporting and self-respecting women would long ere this have been the natural outgrowth of the influx of women into business and the professions." Instead, she found "on investigation that the contrary is true."[56] "Reflect," she sternly told the reader, "on the life that thousands of women lead on a slender salary, or a precarious income of uncertain amount. Thousands upon thousands of women have these conditions staring them in the face." As for the individual woman, "she must live, she must succeed, she must remain honest and self-supporting. What, then, can she do?" Francis demanded. "How will she live? How does she live?"[57]

Even for women who earned "good salaries" and were in "prosperous circumstances," there were few options. In New York, Francis pointed out, the "problem of living" related "almost as much to an ordinary income as to actual poverty."[58] Other than the YWCA, there was "no apartment house for women, or any accommodation whatever beyond the ordinary boarding house." And in the ordinary boardinghouse, she drily noted, women paid "liberally for doing without any of the comforts of home."[59]

Hotels offered an appealing alternative to boardinghouses—but at a cost. Viola Roseboro' found her own hotel "a pleasant contrast to the misery she had endured in boarding houses for women."[60] Yet only a few newspaper women could afford the spaciousness of hotel life, with the luxury of hot meals served in a dining room. Besides, many wanted more independence and privacy than hotel living permitted. "Some newspaper women prefer the hotel life," Margherita Hamm commented in 1892, "but very few they are."[61]

Obviously new housing options were needed, and over the course of the late 1880s and 1890s numerous newspaper articles discussed schemes in the works for apartment houses for women. In 1893, for instance, the *Chicago Daily Tribune* optimistically telegraphed the news of a new apartment house in New York planned for women: "A Long-Felt Need Is at Last Supplied by New York Capitalists—Women Who Are Engaged in Professions, Trades, and Studies Will No Longer Be Obliged to Live in Lodging and Boarding Houses—Rooms as Comfortable as Those of Any Bachelor in Town."[62] "It was a peculiar fact," this article observed, "that while all avenues of work and study have been opened up to woman, and she has demonstrated her ability to earn her own living and take care of herself, there never has been any cognizance taken of her individuality, no place provided for her to live. Considering the 5,000 women artists, musicians, journalists, bookkeepers, stenographers, and students scattered around in dingy boarding-houses and dark flats," the writer argued, "there is certainly great need of at least one commodious structure that shall be well lighted, well ventilated, and well appointed, where womankind can have freedom and comfort at a moderate cost."[63] To meet this need, "once a woman is admitted there will be no espionage. Their friends, both men and women, may be entertained in their rooms as in their own homes—something that is not permitted in the average boarding-house."[64]

This project, which apparently never materialized, was only one among many discussed on the woman's page. In one article in 1894, titled "Rooms for Girl Bachelors," the *New York Herald* pointed out that a number of "philanthropists" had attempted to fill the void during the late 1880s and 1890s, including "millionaire merchant prince A. T. Stewart," who put up "the big, handsome building at the corner of Fourth avenue [*sic*] and Thirty-second street in the belief that the self-supporting women of New York wanted a place where they could obtain good rooms, pure air and plenty of sunshine and be certain of the eminent respectability of their neighbors." But Stewart's apartment house had been "too grand. Rents were too high for the majority of women who earn their own way."[65]

In the *Herald*'s view, philanthropists like Stewart failed to appreciate women's desire for independence. A "strong reason for the failure of the philanthropists" when "they attempt to deal with the woman's apartment idea is the ease with which they disregard the very first idea that enters the mind of the self-supporting woman."[66] It was "independence, an abomination of the spirit of dependence and its depressing effects," that drove "women to seek a living in the professional and commercial world," and "yet all these so called women's boarding houses have hitherto been conducted on a code of rules and regulations as strict and confining as an orphan asylum or a house of correction."[67]

Year after year, newspaper writers discussed the need for apartment houses for women that would provide this independence, indulging in fantasies that rarely came to fruition. Along with a number of other newspaper writers, Mary Francis approved of the project undertaken by "Miss Janet C. Lewis, a well known business woman of New York, who has for years devoted herself to investigations of a sociological nature." Lewis had organized a "Woman's Building Stock Company," and "architect's plans" had been drawn for "a fine apartment house to be erected at a cost of $700,000."[68] But Lewis's apartment house—considered for several years an exciting new venture—was never built.

As new apartment buildings were rapidly built in New York, however, women began to make inroads into buildings that might formerly have accepted only men or families. One way to do so was to live in small enclaves or groups—and to establish innovative cooperative living arrangements. Cooperative living and "cooperative housekeeping" in apartment houses were new to the 1890s. Such "communal feminine flats"—or "'girl bachelor apartments,' in the execrable phrase of the 'woman's page,'" according to Anne O'Hagan—were a subject of fascination for the woman's page.[69] "Bachelor Girl Plan," an 1895 article on the woman's page of the *Chicago Daily Tribune*, had as its subhead "Professional Women of New York Cooperate in Living: Apartment House So Arranged That a Woman May Have One or More Rooms and the Privilege of Cooking in a Common Kitchen—Scheme Is Rather Bohemian and Suits the Independent Woman of Today." The article featured "that interesting apartment house, the Windemere [*sic*]," which was the "home of dozens of independent young women—artists, poets, disciples of physical culture, illustrators, newspaper women, and students—who have made cooperative housekeeping a success."[70] In the Windermere "women have sought that condition of life which is so hard to find even in liberal America, embracing perfect freedom, bachelor apartments, respectability, and the possibilities of home comforts at a reasonable expense."[71]

Built in 1881 during a wave of large new apartment houses in New York, the Windermere is an interesting example of how "bachelor girls" gained a foothold in New York apartment living. Until 1890, the Windermere had been primarily home to families and single men, who rented whole apartments consisting of five to thirteen rooms.[72] But by 1895 "bachelor women" predominated in the building, many renting single rooms within larger apartments. The rent rolls, which had contained an estimated thirty-five names only a few years before, suddenly contained some two hundred names instead. This changed landscape reflected not only the surge of women workers to New York, but also the unusually benevolent attitude of the Windermere's agent, a man of "artistic tastes" whose own daughters were poets.[73] An 1898 *New York Times* woman's page feature on the Windermere, "Sacred to the New Woman," commented that when "women alone in the city" came to the agent "with their requests for one room and two and three rooms, he decided to let them have them." (In this he was unusual among agents of the time, many of whom disapproved of women living away from their families.) The "new-comers were grouped in small families, five people in an eight-room apartment, seven in ten rooms, and so on, but all absolutely independent of each other." By 1898, this newspaper writer estimated, "eight-tenths of the occupants" of the Windermere were women.[74]

"It is a great deal better than a boarding house," said one female artist interviewed in 1895. Each woman could "have the kitchen to herself at a certain time," since they were all in "different professions." It was a "great privilege," she added, to be able to have "a cup of really good coffee and a nicely broiled steak for breakfast" rather than having to depend on boardinghouse fare and strict mealtime schedules.[75]

While some women lived independently in these apartments, crossing paths perhaps only rarely, others set up cooperative arrangements. In one apartment "a student, a black-and-white illustrator, and a musician made up a common household, with the mother of one of the girls as housekeeper." All contributed to "a common fund, and the work was portioned out so that one girl went to market one week and another the next."[76] In another case, two women "took one of the smaller apartments" and "set up real housekeeping"—meaning that "one girl" went "to business every day" and earned "the money for the expenses," while the other did "all the housekeeping." This arrangement had "given the most satisfaction," as it allowed them to "have their meals at regular hours and sit down to them in a dignified and decorous fashion at a table complete in its appointments of silver, china, and linen."[77]

One of the women living in the Windermere in 1895 was Mary Gay Humphreys.[78] Interviewed for the *Chicago Daily Tribune*, Humphreys declared that a cooperative arrangement was "'a sensible way to live'" for the sake of both "'comfort and health.'" Humphreys herself had a "charming studio in the Windemere [*sic*] on the top floor," from which she could "escape" by means of a "steep ladder" to the roof, where she had "a real summer cottage, with couches, awnings, and easy chairs." There she managed "to keep cool even on a broiling day, for there" was "sure to be a breeze," and there she did "most of her writing with a typewriter beside the couch."[79]

Humphreys was "really the pioneer in cooperative housekeeping," the *Tribune* article noted, "because she, in conjunction with three others," had "lived upon that plan in Fifth Avenue" a few years before. "The quartet prepared their own breakfasts, and then a woman came in, put the house in order, and went home. At dinner time she sent in a well-cooked dinner by a man, who waited upon the table, and after the meal took everything away with him." They had "lived well, at a small expense," Humphreys commented."[80]

In her own 1896 article for *Scribner's*, Humphreys noted that "in its best aspect this new development [cooperative living] in women's lives is worthy of admiration." As she explained, "Since the initial effort tiny households have sprung up all over town. These are as well ordered and the rent as promptly paid as that of other and older households. These women rarely live alone. They combine against burglars, out of congeniality, and to save expense. But their domestic lives are neither adhesive nor entangled. They have common points of interest, but these are surrounded by large areas of unencumbered space, in which each moves freely and without interruption."[81]

Peggy's Partner stressed the practical nature of her own cooperative arrangement: "Peggy and I did not come together because our fine souls felt a mutual attraction on lofty grounds," she said. "We came together because we hated the nasty boarding house," and each believed the other to be a "nice, sensible girl of fairly congenial tastes, and the order of things is such that two women together can live much better for less money than can one woman."[82]

But other writers, including Humphreys, were interested in the new types of friendships that might exist between women who lived together. As Humphreys wrote, out of cooperative living had "arisen a new order of feminine friendship that combines independence, *camaraderie*, frank disagreement, wise reticence, large patience, mutual respect, amiable blindness, consideration in illness, sympathy in joy and sorrow, and the possibility of borrowing money from one another when necessary."[83] In 1894 Isabel Mallon (Bab) also wrote approvingly of the close friendships of bachelor women who lived together. "There was a time when the woman who did not marry was supposed to be a subject for a jest," Mallon pointed out, but now the world had "improved in one respect." The woman who did not marry had a "recognized position socially." Then, too, "the beautiful friendships that may exist between women are recognized, and the possibility of a home being made without a man in it is a certainty."[84]

The *Chicago Daily Tribune* woman's page, too, ran an approving article in 1896 about the friendships between women made possible because of their new independence. "The healthy latter-day independence of women is more closely connected with their friendship than most people recognize," it said. "The latter part of this age has seen many unexpected developments for the sex. There is the bachelor woman, the club woman, and the bicycling woman, not to mention many others," with "varied occupations" as well as "interest in some calling or profession." They had learned to look on "matrimony as a beautiful incident, which occurs in some lives, not necessarily theirs," and which was not "demanded for their happiness, prosperity, or general contentment."[85]

Instead, "many clear-headed girls have found a cordial friendship for one of their sex, if not a substitute" for marriage, "an excellent institution." "Such a friendship" had "something exhilarating and healthy in it. Each acts as a stimulus to the other. There is companionship without the ties that bind the wife and mother so firmly." The "healthy, cheerful woman, who dwells with her friend, who thinks naught of going alone with her to theater or reception, who earns a pleasant livelihood," is "not a being to be tenderly pitied." The "single woman, the recognized 'bachelor woman,' who in our mental fancy is distinct from the slightly-described 'spinster,' makes the best friend and confidante. She it is who stands by her friend 'in sickness and in sorrow,' helps her through the dark days, aspirations, and loves as Jonathan loved David."[86]

Isabel Mallon observed that "in flats, in dainty little houses, two or more bachelor women (they don't call themselves girls), whose lives are so arranged that one can be the housekeeper while the other is out in the world, are happy and comfortable from day to day." One such flat, "a very abode of beauty, is the home of two women friends, one a well-known actress, the other the only woman-dealer in plays in this country."[87] Mallon was referring to Elsie DeWolfe and Elisabeth Marbury, whose partnership—widely recognized as lesbian today—excited much newspaper interest in the 1890s and early 1900s. DeWolfe would later become a famous interior decorator; DeWolfe and Marbury's various apartments together were repeatedly profiled on the woman's page, often in glowing terms. "It is not often two women live together who bear no relation toward each other, and yet share all the pleasures, trials, and struggles of life in harmony," the article "Two Girl Bachelors" declared, before giving a vivid inside glimpse of the "cheery domicile," where each day friends were invited to tea and "the teakettle is always in readiness with its pretty array of cups and saucers and plates of thin bread and butter."[88]

Even in a day when periodicals worried over the "masculine" or "mannish" New Woman, newspaper discussions of bachelor girls who lived together rarely veered off into alarm over women's close friendships; instead, the hundreds of articles about bachelor women were notable for their primarily celebratory tone. Given that most of these stories were probably written by newspaper women who were bachelor girls themselves, this is perhaps not surprising. But it is a significant contrast to the severe stereotyping and lampooning of the New Woman that developed in periodical literature as she became a figure of controversy in the mid-1890s.

In conservative periodical literature, too, the bachelor girl sometimes caused alarm. "You hear of her everywhere," said Ruth Ashmore (probably editor Edward Bok, who often wrote the column—although possibly Isabel Mallon in her double identity) in the *Ladies' Home Journal* in 1898. "You think of her as bright, industrious, neat, quick to speak, equally quick to act, and quite old enough to have decided what she wishes to make of her life." But this positive description was soon revealed as merely a cover for the dark message Ashmore wanted to convey: "Sometimes she is overflowing with vitality, so that she wearies you, and you find yourself wishing unconsciously that she were more feminine and less like a bachelor." Ashmore concluded that "I am forced to wonder with all seriousness, and with all respect to her, whether, after all, the bachelor girl is the best successor of the unmarried woman or not."[89]

It was true, Ashmore admitted, that the "old maid" was "more dependent" than the bachelor girl and "not so well educated." She was indeed "very different from the bachelor girl." But the "old maid" had also been "kindly, loving, tender, with a halo of romance about her." She had a "greater respect for mankind" than the bachelor girl, and although "she had, perhaps, no special home of her own," she "was a power in many homes. She was a mother to the orphans, a nurse to the sick, and a tender friend to whoever was in affliction." Ashmore confessed that "when I look at the bachelor girl I long to say to her, 'Study the spinster maiden of long ago; copy her virtues, imitate her graces.'" [90]

Ashmore printed a letter in "clear, bold handwriting" she supposedly had received from a bachelor girl, but which sounded suspiciously like editor Bok himself: "Is it not a fact that we American girls are growing day by day more masculine in our games, attire and amusements? And do we command the same respect from the opposite sex that was given to the unmarried woman in the days of our forefathers?" The answer was clearly no. "It seems to me," Ashmore concluded, "that the bachelor girls take too much interest, first of all in business, then in base-ball and foot-ball games, yachting, bicycling and lawn tennis, and have not enough interest in the home."[91]

But newspaper articles about bachelor girls were an obvious counterargument to this last point. After all, over and over they made clear that bachelor girls were actually forming a new *kind* of home. Far from abjuring home, they sought to reinvent it—and, of course, redecorate it, as well.

Woman's pages were especially fascinated by the question of exactly how bachelor girls managed in their new living spaces. "How-to" decorating articles appeared by the hundreds, offering fantasies of transformation not just for apartments but also for "dingy" hall bedrooms, to be made new through a variety of "tips" and "hints." As Mary Gay Humphreys observed,

"Of late years there has arisen a Society for the Amelioration of the Hall-Room. Its efforts have been principally directed toward the introduction of beds disguised as sofas, buffets, and decorative mantels, of washstands masquerading as writing-desks, with which to give hall-rooms a delusive air of spaciousness and respectability."[92] Humphreys's comments may have attempted light humor, but in fact they fairly accurately described dozens of articles on decorating the small spaces of hall rooms. "Hints for the Bachelor Girl," an 1894 *Chicago Daily Tribune* article, advised that "a very pretty effect has been produced in a room where the cot divan" was "used as a bed at night." Cushions in "various colorings," along with a "few light pieces of bric-a-brac that do not beget a fear of cracked cranium should they fall," produced a "most attractive cozy corner, inexpensive and tasteful, whose good effect is not marred by any hint of its nightly utilitarianism."[93]

The "cozy corner" (often spelled "cosey corner") became a newspaper trope, repeated as a kind of mantra establishing the bachelor girl's inventiveness as part of her domesticity. The woman's page of the *New York Recorder*, "In Woman's Realm," held a "Cozy Corner Contest" in 1893, promising a "seventy-dollar prize" for the "prettiest corner in the most artistic home in New York city" and inviting readers to send photographs of their decorating efforts.[94] The *New York Herald*'s "Bachelor Girl's Cosey Corner Novelty" described "an ingenious bachelor girl" who had achieved "striking effects" by putting some trunks in "a corner of her den." Then "she threw some soft mats over them and a big cover over them, and over all a few brilliant lounge pillows. Now she has a billowy, cosey corner which makes her the envy of all her uninitiated callers."[95]

Of course, whether trunks covered with pillows truly constituted a "cozy corner" is subject to debate. Still, numerous newspaper articles emphasized the bachelor girl's ingenuity in creating her living space. A *New York Herald* article admitted that she could "seldom afford any more spacious quarters than the hall bedroom in a good boarding house in the metropolis." But this article insisted that it was "the bachelor girl of small income whose life" was "most interesting, because it" developed "all of her womanly ingenuity to get the most out of a little." Offering a "peep into her sanctum," the article described the ingenuity of one bachelor girl who had given "full vent to her artistic instincts" in decorating her room in the "gable of a well located east side boarding house" (in other words, the attic), with "a Japanese rug in which blue and gold predominate," "bits of her own china" as ornaments on a shelf, a window "curtained prettily," and a "few potted plants" to "give the touch which nothing but living green can supply." The "whole environment" was "one of refinement and good taste."[96]

Like so many other bachelor girl articles, the text then indulged in a fantasy of happy, independent living. "This independent creature cooks her own breakfasts and lunches" on a small gas stove, "and best of all, prepares little Bohemian suppers for the favored few who are bidden to her sanctum these cold nights. Sometimes it is a Welsh rarebit, served steaming hot on the pretty plates, which are kept in the hanging cabinet on the wall. Again it is a caramel stew or a taffy boiling. On snappy afternoons the hot water kettle is kept singing on the hob, and if another bachelor girl chum happens in, a pot of tea brewed or a cup of beef tea is made from the little jar of extract always on hand in the closet."[97]

The article drew to its happy conclusion: "Who can say the girl is not happy who can call such a snug spot her own, with its possibilities of cheerful, if not lavish, hospitality? The bachelor girl is happier than many women of larger means, for her life is full of purpose, and while she has time for recreation she has none for idle repinings and vain longings." The elements of this fantasy—the tea kettle, the Welsh rarebit cooked in a chafing dish (chafing dishes became a motif of bachelor girl living), the bohemian suppers, the chums dropping in—were repeated in dozens of articles. So common were these that "Of Course, the Tea Kettle" said the subhead of one article on the bachelor girl.[98]

Almost all writers discussing the "bachelor girl" noted the "bohemian" aspects of her new life. "HER BOHEMIAN EXISTENCE" trumpeted the subhead for the *New York Times* article on bachelor women living at the Windermere.[99] In the late 1880s and early 1890s the idea of living a bohemian existence captured the imagination of numerous young men and women moving to the city. Associated "with revolt against bourgeois convention," bohemia was as much a particular "narrative of urban life" as it was an actual place or set of places. To be sure, to be "bohemian" involved going to certain restaurants, living in certain places, cooking certain foods. But it also involved an act of imagination, as Christine Stansell has pointed out. Would-be bohemians of the 1890s "called up an imagery of art, hedonism, and dissent from bourgeois life," invoking bohemia even as they lived it. Whereas bohemia "in its original incarnation had been all male," at the turn of the century bachelor women "added a sense of themselves as heroines in a new story to bohemia's increasing store of plots."[100]

No one was more important than newspaper women in creating and circulating images of a so-called feminine bohemia. But they did not simply publicize bohemia in their articles. Newspaper women themselves were often figures of bohemia—mentioned over and over again in newspaper articles and magazine fiction. Many woman's page articles on bachelor girls' lives offered tours of "feminine bohemias"—a form of literary tourism that built upon the long tradition of urban "walks" to see the "lights and shadows" of urban life.[101] Not only could readers become flaneurs in these articles, "strolling" through the new apartment houses in which bachelor women lived, they could sometimes catch quick glimpses of women specifically identified as newspaper women.

The 1895 article "Bachelor Girl Plan," which led the reader on a walk through the Windermere apartment building, not only mimicked a tourist guidebook but also created an intimate connection with the reader, who was encouraged to imagine being along for the tour. "To one permitted to walk at leisure through the building interesting views of life present themselves," the article suggested. "From the halls one catches glimpses of studios hung in dull green and Venetian red, with bronzes and friezes and pots and kettles of a charmingly delightful Bohemian character, and at any turn you may come unexpectedly upon a woman whose name is well known in newspaperdom holding a cup of chocolate in one hand and petting a 'tramp' dog with the other. And while you chat with her a door may open and a vision of health in yellow silk flowing draperies burst upon you like a ray of sunshine just escaped from behind a dark-rimmed cloud."[102] The idea that you could "catch glimpses of studios," or could "come unexpectedly upon" a well-known newspaper woman, or could have a "door open" and a "vision" in "yellow silk flowing draperies" be revealed all reduced the imagined distance between public and private life, making the new private spaces of bachelor girls' lives a theatrical public realm that readers were invited over and over again to see for themselves in a form of voyeurism.

Such "glimpses" became a motif of "bachelor girl" newspaper literature. The 1898 New York Herald's "Glimpses into a Feminine Bohemia: Studios in the Bachelor Maids' Colony at Carnegie Hall" informed the reader that "More Than a Hundred Young Women Live in Carnegie Hall Bachelor Apartments." It was "Where Bachelor Maids Reign in Feminine Seclusion." Richly illustrated, this article depicted several "bachelor maids'" studios, shown like cutaways of stage sets whose curtains had just been lifted. The article celebrated the spontaneous "glimpse": "To rush in unannounced and not expected, to catch them at odd moments, that is the fun of it! In this way I have seen a girl who writes the most delicious sonnets you ever read actually frying beefsteak and onions over a greasy oil stove. How we laughed about it!"[103]

Only women—including women newspaper writers—were said to be allowed in this bohemia. "Should you drop into one of those busy studios of a midnight—provided, of course, that you are a woman, for men are strictly tabooed—you would find that there are jolly times among the bachelor maids. There are studio spreads, rarebit parties when the chafing dish and gas stove are brought into play, and when everybody helps fix things and cooks and fetches cups and forks and pans from various quarters."[104]

As with so much bachelor girl literature, the reader was invited to take part in the imagined joys of bohemia. "Fancy the fluttering in and out of a dozen or more bachelor maids under curtained doorways and soft lights, not a vestige of a man anywhere. Now and again an imploring rap on the door discloses a more venturesome spirit of masculinity, who is politely told that men are not wanted. . . . Such wonderful omelettes and creamed oysters that some specially gifted bachelor browns on a most insignificant looking alcohol fixture! Such cheese sandwiches and toothsome salads, which have a way of popping into view from behind wonderful color schemes in hangings and screens!"[105]

In thus rapidly (and somewhat feverishly) recycling the numerous markers of the "bachelor girl" life—the chafing dish, the rarebit, the screens, the gas stove, the "jolly" time—this article was almost a parody of itself. Indeed, given the typological aspects of bohemia—its many conventional elements that were recycled over and over in a steady stream of newspaper (and by the mid-1890s, magazine) articles—it is not surprising that such articles became the subject of sometimes brilliant parody.

A 1904 satire by Mrs. Wilson Woodrow in *Life* perfectly limned the more absurd elements of bachelor girl articles. "There was once a woman who religiously read all of the woman's magazines and Sunday supplements," the piece began, "because they were so full of practical helps and hints." "Especially was she interested," Woodrow continued, "in the gay, mirthful tales of joyous, lighthearted bachelor maids who lived in one large room, which they had secured in a delightful but unfashionable part of town for $1.49 a week, and which they had transformed into a bower of beauty at a net cost of seventeen cents. The walls were rendered so artistic with Sunday newspapers and a small pot of paint that great artists traveled miles to view them. With equal skill the maids converted fruit baskets into exquisite jardinières, and manufactured rare tapestries and hangings from old rain coats. They slept in folding pianos and bookcases and made a roof-garden of the fire-escape."[106]

"To complete the correct mise en scene of a real bachelor maid's home," Woodrow said, "they cooked and washed dishes behind a screen of embroidered flannel petticoats in one end of the room, and delighted their friends with little dinners and breakfasts on all occasions. In ten minutes after vanishing behind the screen, the one who officiated at the stove would have a dainty, epicurean meal ready to serve. When not engaged in the restful recreations of cooking and washing dishes, one of the bachelor maids wrote brilliant bits of fiction, the sale of which afforded her a handsome income; the other painted water-colors, which people came from Japan and San Francisco to buy."[107]

Woodrow ended this sketch by imagining a woman reader who tried to follow woman's page and woman's magazine advice. "'How simple, how easy, how cheap!' said the woman reader. 'I too can paper a room with Sunday newspapers and have no end of fun in trying those delicious recipes the magazines so kindly give'" — such as "'that prune and tomato soufflé served with whipped cream and minced bananas.'" After one month of her "experiment," she ended in the hospital, "bruised and battered from sleeping in a folding automobile, burned to a crisp from cooking behind a screen, starved in body, dazed and confused in mind." The "hospital surgeon wept at the sight" of her: "'Oh, woman's page, woman's page,'" he cried, "'what crimes are committed in thy name!'"[108]

Such an article may have laughed at bachelor girl literature, but it also revealed a presumption that bachelor girl stories powerfully affected their readers. Winifred Sothern's critical 1901 *Munsey's* article, "The Truth about the Bachelor Girl," made the same assumption. Her stern subtitle was "The False Glamour That Has Been Thrown around an Individual Who in Reality Is Merely a Single Woman Living Alone in a City in Order to Work There."[109]

Sothern did not mince words: "Of all the fakes of the present day," she began, "the bachelor girl fake is the most persistent. The plain fact is that the bachelor girl is merely a single woman of small means, pursuing an art or earning her living." Yet this truth was "ignored by a delusion loving world," which insisted, "without regard to the facts of the case, on puffing her condition as a happy blend of gaiety, freedom, and romance," with the adjectives "jaunty, winsome, mischievous, gay, arch, trim, trig, saucy, pert, and — God forgive us all! — bohemian" all hovering "about her course like attendant butterflies."[110]

The reality was far from this ideal, Sothern argued. "It does not add charm and merriment to life to keep the wash basin in the desk and the pickles under the bed," she admonished. "It may be humorous to tell of, but in daily life it is inconvenient as well as sordid. Nothing can be more trying than the compact and circumspect living necessary when all the needs of a home must be met by one room, and appearances are a matter of importance." Sothern concluded that "all the silly glamour that space writers have shed on the subject must be abandoned for an honest view of her life as it is, not as she would like it to be."[111]

Yet ironically, in offering her own parody of such writing, Sothern continued to circulate all the "fake" elements of bachelor girl writing: "In the world's eye," she said, the bachelor girl was "in a perpetual state of Welsh rabbit and 'Oh, girls!' Her one room apartment is a mass of delightful contrivances whereby her gowns inhabit the window seat and her frying pan the bookcase. When she makes the gleeful discovery that she has only thirty cents with which to get through the week, she perches on her table and consults with her chum, and then they dine so hilariously on toasted crackers and cheese that those condemned to roast beef and pudding in the family circle feel a little cheated in their life's allotment."[112]

Sothern admitted that "this roseate view of her state has been so persistent that it has come to affect the bachelor girl herself, the genuine article." Underlining the power of newspapers to shape women's images of themselves, Sothern asserted that the bachelor girl "might never have discovered the charm of her condition if it had not been pointed out to her daily and weekly by enterprising journalism." As the bachelor girl reflected, and reflected upon, her own image in the popular press, "she began to swagger a trifle, to play the part assigned her, to refer self consciously to the chafing dish informality that marked the distinction of her good times."[113]

Sothern imagined the bachelor girl in the role she had learned from the press: "'You'll find us terrible bohemians' she would boast, her claim to that title being based on the fact that she fried chops in her bedroom and did not always wash the dishes. 'This is Liberty Hall; every one does just what he likes here,' grew to be her stereotyped idea of entertainment, and if a guest put his feet on the window sill, or took a nap on her divan, she felt that she was achieving the popular ideal. The thicker the tobacco smoke grew in her one room, the deeper she breathed satisfaction, and nothing gave her such a sense of being the real thing as to know that she could smoke a cigarette just as if she liked it."[114]

This was a dangerously seductive delusion, Sothern indicated, which could easily influence other young women. When the bachelor girl "went back home to visit," she wrote, the "dawning bachelor girls of the locality discovered in her corroboration of all they had read—never dreaming that she was but a product of that same reading." The danger was that "all the freedom and the gaiety of the great city seemed to shine through her novel slang, her audacious opinions, her tales of lively suppers where the glasses were supplemented by tooth mugs and one spoon did for three. 'That's life,'" sighed young girls listening to such talk and "fluttered their rudimentary wings harder than ever, yearning for the glitter with a force that spoiled all their daily life, even though they lived where there was room for gardens and babies and sunshine and all the living pleasures about which the bachelor girl does not say much."[115]

Yet Sothern did not say much about the pleasures of babies and gardens, either, after having made this perfunctory gesture to more conventional womanhood. Instead, the end of her article recovered some of the positive aspects of "girl bachelorhood." "Pages could be written on what a woman gains with the freedom to live her own life in her own way," Sothern admitted. "There is no desire to cry down the real value; only to take off the false glamour." She concluded that "work and freedom alone are perhaps worth the price the bachelor girl pays; only let her in all honesty recognize that there is a price before she sets out for the city of her dreams."[116]

# # #

By 1902, when Marie Manning and Olivia Dunbar's new "bachelor girl" apartment was profiled in the *New York Evening World*, hundreds, if not thousands, of articles about bachelor girls had already been published in newspapers.[117] But the supposedly "false glamour" of being a bachelor girl had clearly not worn off for Manning, who exuberantly recalled the time she and Dunbar had sublet an apartment "in one of the big uptown studio buildings" and had "one palatial room, high and airy and charmingly furnished, with a little one adjoining." In one corner, she remembered, "was a great couch, swathed and draped and covered with cushions, and when we examined into the processes of the couch, we found that it was the bath-tub in a costume of gorgeous velours." Her relish in the story was obvious.[118]

But now Manning's life had changed. A successful newspaper woman on the verge of publishing a novel, Manning was on an ascending curve in her career. The focus of the 1902 *Evening World* article was change, too: the "changes in character" of bachelor girls' apartments in recent years, as they became more sophisticated and left behind the "barrel and dry-goods box stage of ingenuity." In the "last two years, and even in the last year," the article said, "the bachelor girls' apartment" had "changed its character." It was "no more a place of flowered chintz and cheap little prints and bazaar signs, like a college girl's room. It is no longer a place where every innocent piece of furniture is a suppressed wardrobe or a misjudged kitchen. You may sit on any of its chairs without danger of being hurled in the centre of a double-duty medicine chest or precipitated in upon your hostess's most exclusive hat."[119]

Not only were Manning and Dunbar using antiques rather than old barrels to decorate, the article explained, they now had three rooms instead of one. "The three-room apartment home is, however, not the rule among New York bachelor girls," the *Evening World* cautioned, "most of whose apartments consist of one room." Nevertheless, that one room still offered freedom, while the three-room apartment offered even more: "One room and its latch-key make emancipation; two rooms are the wildest luxury; and three rooms and some old furniture are regarded as a close second to the franchise."[120]

An apartment and suffrage: the link was metaphorical but powerful. Newspapers' fascination with the new interiors of bachelor girls' domestic lives, in fact, had political implications. By enabling women to imagine themselves as independent actors in metropolitan life, by sharing the interior details of the homes they had made, bachelor girl articles created a shared public space of independence within the pages of newspapers. The creation of that shared cultural world can indeed be seen as part of the suffrage movement, if we expand our definition of the wider movement of suffrage to include the fight for the representation of independent women in culture as well as politics. Bachelor girl articles — even the silliest "cozy corner" pieces — articulated a world in which women were no longer dependent on men, but rather independent actors, creating a new public realm out of the domestic interiors of their private lives. They opened up a terrain through which other women could imagine independent lives, as well.

chapter five **Adventure**

The headline running across an entire two-page spread of the *New York Sunday World* on March 8, 1896, read "Daring Deeds by the Sunday World's Intrepid Woman Reporters"; immediately underneath was the story "Nellie Bly Proposes to Fight for Cuba." In a splashy illustration accompanying the article, Bly, who was described as a "Fin de Siecle Joan of Arc," wore a costume reminiscent of a theatrical production of the "Daughter of the Regiment," with epaulettes on her shoulders, a stylish helmet with a feather, and a sword brandished in the air. Bly reportedly had said that "Women Have More Courage Than Men and Would Make Braver Officers"; she was "ready to recruit volunteers for her first regiment" of women. A bemused male reporter who had interviewed Bly voiced his incredulity ("Women! Women officers?"), but Bly held her own, declaring that women had "more of the qualities essential to great military leaders than men." One of those qualities was bravery, and, according to Bly, "You have only to read the newspapers from day to day to learn that women are braver than men."[1]

In fact, you had only to read the facing page, where three additional articles explored newspaper women's bravery. On the left was the pseudonymous "Dorothy Dare's Wild Night on a Lightship," described as an experience in "the recent storm when even stout hearts of sea-faring men beat with alarm." On the right was "One Woman as a Barber for a Day," in which an anonymous newspaper woman "shaved a good-natured man, who had patience and a tough skin." In the center was "Kate Swan a Fairy Bareback Rider," detailing her "thrilling experiences in the tan-bark ring, poised on a trained, galloping steed."[2] Taken together, the three stories sketched a map of adventurous experiences that focused on newspaper women's daring, bravery, and transgression of accepted norms. All three pieces were figuratively miles away from the woman's page—even if literally separated by only a few pages.

As Bly's biographer has drily pointed out, after the publication of the spectacularly over-the-top article about Nellie Bly's "regiment"—an obvious attempt by Bly and the *World* to capitalize on her continuing fame—"No more was heard of the plan, nor of Bly for quite some time."[3] After all, no women-only regiment was sent to Cuba; the article was more theater than news.

But that is precisely why this article, as well as the sensational two-page spread of which it was a part, deserves our attention. Both have much to tell us about changing ideas of physical courage for women at the turn of the century, as well as the ways in which newspapers became a new public space of adventure for newspaper women. Newspapers—especially sensational papers like the *World*—offered a public space in the late 1880s and the 1890s in which newspaper women explored adventures of many kinds, including physical feats of daring, "slumming," undercover exposés, and theatrical public performances in the character of working girls, servants, and other urban "types." Such exploits formed an important subgenre of the new human interest journalism, focusing on the dramatic and "thrilling" sight of women out of their accustomed sphere. Nellie Bly had pioneered this subgenre with her undercover work at Blackwell's Island Insane Asylum, her trip around the world, and other stunts, but by the mid-1890s numerous newspaper women were engaged in such work. They were "plucky," "adventurous," "intrepid," "daring."

While Bly's exploits have attracted sustained attention, the work of the many newspaper women who followed her has not. In part this has to do with the contemporary attack on sensational journalism, which set terms of discussion that still hold to this day. "The contest in sensationalism so-called—that is, the furious exploitation of crime, vulgarity and squalid enterprises of women reporters—continues between the New York World and its new and rich rival, the Morning Journal," the *Chicago Times-Herald* trumpeted in a March 1896 article that specifically mentioned several "Kate Swan" pieces. "So far as we are able to reckon hitherto undiscovered depths of degradation, the World thus far has held its own in nastiness. The illustrations in the last two numbers of the Sunday World are vicious beyond anything ever dreamed of in sensational journalism."[4] This language was no stronger than the words used by a 1990 historian of "sob sister journalism," who called the "general effect" of sensational journalism "grotesque and vicious."[5]

Women's stunt journalism mortified and infuriated many newspaper women. Some felt it was a betrayal of the "delicacy" of womanhood, a view clearly articulated by Haryot Holt Cahoon. Others were concerned less with the "violation" of standards of womanhood than with the professional setback they believed accompanied sensationalism. Women who had fought hard for "regular" places on newspapers were dismayed by the lack of dignity in sensational journalism of all kinds, as well as by its blatant exploitation of women. Florence Finch Kelly, a book reviewer for the *New York Times* in the early twentieth century, argued that yellow journalism's "use of women reporters and writers in its emotional, spectacular and scandalous methods and purposes dealt a serious blow to the progress women were making in the profession." Editors were "revolted by the spectacle of these stunting, shrieking and sobbing young women of the yellow press," and their attitude toward women seeking employment "stiffened into antagonism."[6] (There is little evidence, however, that Kelly was right about this new "antagonism.")

Other critics were embarrassed by the sheer absurdity of many sensational articles by newspaper women, as they described dangling from bridges, spending the night in haunted houses, pretending to be factory girls, and handling large snakes. Such stories were clearly not front-page material; they were, in fact, only distantly related to "news." This embarrassment holds true today. One historian has noted that "the stunt reporters' sillier articles—Bly's stint as an elephant trainer comes to mind—can still make readers cringe, even at a century's distance."[7]

Only film historians seem not to be embarrassed by sensational journalism, finding in the exploits of newspaper women a fascinating precursor to popular film melodramas of the 1910s, with their emphasis on adventurous and daring heroines. As Ben Singer has commented, "The serial-queen melodrama clearly extended an image already constructed in the urban mythology of popular entertainment," which included newspaper stories recounting the "exploits contrived by daring women reporters."[8]

Singer's astute analysis allows us to view newspaper women's sensational journalism in a different light: as part of an emerging culture of entertainment and leisure, one that included the thrills and excitement—the sensations—provided by amusement parks and nickelodeons, as well as other popular entertainments.[9] Newspapers were arguably both the fulcrum and the centerpiece of this new culture, providing not only widespread publicity for various popular attractions but also their own set of entertainments. The *Sunday World* magazine, for instance, offered a series of "acts" as much as serious articles. It takes only a quick glance through the magazine in 1896, with its vividly illustrated talking chimpanzees, "tiniest" babies in the world, sea monsters, and weekly "freaks," to see that Sunday newspapers were closely related to the circus, as well as to vaudeville and other forms of popular theater. Offering staged performances of the marvelous, inviting readers to share exciting adventures, newspapers were an arena of urban amusements. If we stop criticizing the sensational writings of newspaper women for *not* being serious news, and instead begin to take them seriously as entertainment, an interesting world opens up to us.

To enter that world, let us start with Kate Swan. In the winter and spring of 1896, the *World* printed numerous sensational articles featuring Swan—including stories the *Chicago Times-Herald* had excoriated, such as "Kate Swan's Two Views of Death: Gliding into the Crematory Resort on the Iron Cradle: Her Awful Night in the Burial Vault." Other articles in the series included "Kate Swan Scales Harlem River Bridge," "Kate Swan as a Snake Charmer," "Kate Swan at Table with Women Convicts," "Kate Swan's Night on Ellis Island," and "Kate Swan's Wrestling Bout with Champion Leonard." The novelty of these pieces lay in their public exposure of Swan in situations usually off-limits to her (such as a wrestling bout), or carrying a wider cultural taboo (such as entering a crematorium); their offense lay in that same exposure.

It is likely that most, if not all, of these articles were written by Kate Swan McGuirk—who during the 1890s signed herself "Kate Swan," "Kate Swan McGuirk," and "Mrs. McGuirk." Like Margherita Hamm, McGuirk had had a "lucky" break that jump-started her newspaper career. Hailing from Fall River, Massachusetts, she apparently knew the notorious Lizzie Borden, and after the murder of Borden's parents she was able to place several newspaper reports about the famous case. By 1891 she also wrote a regular column, called "Capital Chatter," for the weekly *Kate Field's Washington*. From there McGuirk at some point moved to the *New York Journal*. Margherita Hamm spoke of "Mrs. McGuirk in the editorial chair" of the *Journal*'s woman's page in 1895: McGuirk had "newspaper talent of a high order, and is very original and clever in her appropriation and creation of ideas for the woman's page which she edits."[10] Finally, McGuirk emerged at the *New York World* in 1896: we know that she and Kate Swan were the same person because a few of her articles were captioned or headlined "Kate Swan" but carried the signature "Mrs. McGuirk." (In some of the articles, illustrations drawn from photographs show the same woman, with a strong jaw and long face.)

As far as her editors were concerned, the primary purpose of the "Kate Swan" articles was to build circulation for the *World*—a point later made by Arthur Brisbane, editor of the *Sunday World* in 1896. Looking back over his years of working for owner Joseph Pulitzer, Brisbane said that "only success appealed to him, and his idea of success was results, circulation. You could not tell Joseph Pulitzer: 'We are holier and purer than our competitors. That's why they have more circulation than we have.'" At the time, Brisbane remembered, "our readers were increasing at an average rate of 11,000 a Sunday."[11]

Although "Pulitzer's delight was intense" at this increase in circulation, he suddenly had "an attack of 'respectability.'" As Brisbane noted drily, this sometimes happened "with owners" when "circulation came so easily." Pulitzer wrote to Brisbane to "please have on the front page of the magazine in next Sunday's World a fine portrait of General O. O. Howard" (the famous Civil War general and head of the Freedmen's Bureau during Reconstruction). Brisbane privately thought that Howard "would have talked fine platitudes" but would certainly not increase circulation. The following Monday he "sent Mr. Pulitzer this telegram: 'Sorry we did not have that O. O. Howard picture and interview. Instead, on the front page, I had a wonderful picture of Kate Swan in the electric chair and circulation is up 15,000.' Mr. Pulitzer telegraphed back: 'You know perfectly well I am blind, and must rely on you. Congratulations.'"[12]

The article Brisbane was so proud of, featuring Kate Swan in the electric chair, is worth taking a look at—and not just because it was startling enough to increase circulation. As Ben Singer has pointed out, newspaper women's "stunt articles" placed an "extraordinary emphasis on female heroism," giving "narrative preeminence to an intrepid young heroine who exhibited a variety of traditionally 'masculine' qualities: physical strength and endurance, self-reliance, courage, social authority, and freedom to explore novel experiences outside the domestic sphere."[13] Although such popular female heroism is usually associated with the 1910s and 1920s, sensational newspapers actually began developing this "revised femininity" in the late 1880s and 1890s, exploring and celebrating a new version of "female power." Focusing on the "intrepid pursuit of physical peril and kinesthetic excitement," stunt articles "extended the experiential sphere of women."[14] Simultaneously, they also extended the representational sphere of women—not only how women were portrayed in the public spaces of the newspaper, but also the types of experiences newspaper women could write about.

The February 12, 1896, article, "A Woman in the Death Chair," featured "Kate Swan, a Plucky Woman Reporter of the World," and, just as Arthur Brisbane recalled, included a vivid engraving of a blindfolded Swan, hair streaming to her waist, strapped into the electric chair. The article itself did not so much involve an intrepid physical feat, however, as an imaginative feat in which Swan left her own "self" behind to "become" a criminal and "experience" electrocution through a tour of Dannemora Prison, in New

"Kate Swan in the Death Chair," New York World, *February 16, 1896. (General Research Division, The New York Public Library, Astor, Lenox and Tilden Foundations)*

York State, where famed prisoner Bartholomew "Bat" Shea had just been put to death.

"This history shall tell what a woman would undergo if condemned to die by modern law," Swan began. "I have been through the entire routine of an electrocution up to the critical turning on of the current, and if I were to be the legal victim of the official executioner to-morrow I could not experience keener sensations than those I have already undergone." Throughout the article, she emphasized her imagined invasion of a terrain of experience previously off-limits to women, offering up a form of literary imperialism to her readers in which she crossed established boundaries of gendered selfhood.[15]

Taking the reader step by step into prison, Swan transformed what was

adventure {167

essentially just a tour conducted by a warden into a personal journey in which she entered new realms of experience for women. "I had determined to put myself, as far as one person can assume a character, in the place of a woman being electrocuted," Swan declared. "When I passed through the prison proper and through the great iron doors into the section of the condemned cells I left my own self behind. I became for the time a criminal. In my own mind I knew I had taken life. I felt it in every vein. I was an outlaw from society and all else there was for me in this world lay within forty feet of where I stood. I should never draw a breath of clean air again. I told myself all these things until in truth I could believe that I really was a miserable unfortunate with but an hour to live and but one more walk before me."[16]

Using this breathless prose throughout, and keeping the focus entirely on her own subjectivity and the imagined boundary-crossings she was performing, Swan took the reader from the experience of being in the condemned prisoner's cell ("the atmosphere of the cell helped increase my feeling that I was about to die") to the "Walk" down the corridor to the death chamber ("The Warden had agreed to act as though I were really going to death. He acted well. I really felt that death was coming."), to sitting in the chair ("I still had a little control left, but it seemed to me as if it didn't need any application of electric currents to finish me."). Sitting in the chair, she said disingenuously, "it flashed over me that this was only an experiment and not real"—and she "sprang from the chair feeling as if I had barely escaped with my life."[17]

Like a piece of theater, Swan's article asked readers to suspend disbelief, to invest themselves in an imagined "adventure"—even as Swan also continually reminded readers through phrases such as "I felt as though," "I felt as if," that it was she who was performing this imaginative "stunt." Swan offered up an expanded terrain of selfhood with her article as she "invaded" a public space seen as off-limits to women. She also, of course, simultaneously created a new public realm of sensation within the pages of the newspaper.

Kate Swan would write several more of these imaginative adventures, in which she steered readers to fantasize along with her about experiences that were well outside respectable domestic norms for women—and that sometimes broke taboos for both men and women. Her transgressive "With the Dead in Grave and Furnace," for instance, offered a comparison of cremation versus burial through the first-person "experience" of each. In an article that might be called newspaper gothic, Swan visited a crematorium and described the experience of lying down on the iron "cradle" and being pushed into the "retort," or oven. ("I closed my eyes. The heat radiating about me made me half unconscious. I began to feel strangely light. I seemed to feel my body leaving me, floating upward.") Not a particularly gifted writer in this vein, Swan did her workmanlike best to create an "uncanny" atmosphere. ("Separated from the body the spirit hovered over the place. Still the strange dissolution was going on. I seemed to have lost all shape and form, and no longer bore any resemblance to man. There was only matter.") She then visited a tomb, attempting to suffuse her prose with dark foreboding and fear, as well as produce the abjection that came through the gothic's contact with the loathsome. ("Something cold jumped. Then I knew it wasn't a snake. It must be toads. I heard little patters on the floor. More toads. The cold mouldy air made me gasp. As I tried to rise from the floor one hand slipped in damp mould.") Ultimately declaring in favor of cremation, Swan said that becoming "clean white flakes" was "infinitely preferable to a coffin disappearing into the ground."[18]

Such imaginative adventures, complete with vivid illustrations (such as a drawing of Kate Swan looking horrified as she was about to enter the oven or "retort"), used the spectacle of a woman's body in a dangerous or taboo situation to shock and thrill readers. That spectacle, as many critics have pointed out, exploited women, making their embodiment — the display of their bodies — the centerpiece of their articles.

Yet the underlying logic of sensational literature also created new access to public space for newspaper women, making that space a source of possible adventure. By its very definition, a "thrilling" experience could only be one that was not made too familiar through repetition — the "thrilling" demanded novelty, surprise. (Even a roller coaster ride eventually becomes humdrum if repeated often enough, after all.) Sensational journalism continually demanded new sensation, in other words — and therefore new experiences of women's bodies in public. Many critics then and now saw sensational work merely as an exploitation of women, as newspapers sent their female reporters on a variety of wild stunts and undercover assignments. The *Journalist*, for instance, printed a telling joke in 1894:

First Female Reporter. — That Minnie Scribes was always a stupid, disappointing thing. The editor was awfully mad, too. He delayed the forms a full day; but her copy didn't arrive.
Second Female Reporter. — What happened to her?
Oh, she was assigned to write up "How It Feels to Commit Suicide;" she took some rat poison and —
And?
She died. The editor was awfully mad, too![19]

Yet the very real exploitation of newspaper women by newspapers is only one part of the story of their sensational work. Adventurous assignments often put women in settings that would otherwise have been off-limits to them, allowing them to observe and write about a wider range of metropolitan life. These venues were not necessarily "degraded" settings—such as the police court or an opium den—that critics of women's sensational work worried about. But they were certainly "racier" venues than those that came under the purview of most women who wrote for the woman's page.

In one case in 1896, "Lady Kate" (her identity is unclear) undertook a series of assignments for the *New York Recorder* that involved briefly working as a fortune teller, a waitress, a hotel clerk, a cloakroom model, and a domestic servant. On one level these were rather tame "adventures"—Lady Kate simply sat at the front desk and checked in guests during her one evening as a hotel clerk, for instance—but the *Recorder* nevertheless called this "An Exciting Evening for That Adventuresome Young Lady." The excitement came not just from the "queer characters" who "got rooms," but also from the frisson of sexual innuendo attached to hotel work. One guest with "adjusted mustaches" approached her desk and stood "feasting on the outlines of the new night clerk." Later in the evening, Lady Kate decided not to admit one couple as guests because she misjudged the "fine-looking woman": "There was a conscious telltale sort of flush on her cheeks, which might have been natural, or might have been rouge." Lady Kate said, "'I fear we can't accommodate you,'" and glanced "meaningfully and reproachfully at the blond head that was peeping from behind" the young man's shoulder. But the couple were actually newlyweds, as proven by luggage that had already arrived at the hotel, "all done up in bows of white satin ribbon." Kate "made haste to add her congratulations, and gave them the bridal suite to ease her conscience."[20]

In another such adventure, Lady Kate acted as a fortune-teller in a "little back room on Sixth avenue, which was sufficiently dirty and sufficiently badly lighted" for her purpose. Late in the day, as "the street lights were being lighted, and the 'evening editions' were being called," a "poor, shabby, wan-faced, red-eyed girl came in. Her clothes had once been stylish, but her boots were parting sole from uppers, and her finery had been rained on, until all the style had been rained out. A world of misery was in her poor, foolish, pretty face." She wanted to know, Kate said, "if he had really deserted her."[21] Such a character—a deserted woman, possibly a prostitute—rarely appeared on the woman's page.

We do not know whether these "Lady Kate" adventures actually occurred; there is always the possibility they were "faked" in some way or perhaps written by a man. Yet even if the Lady Kate series was not "real," these articles imaginatively placed newspaper women in a variety of new, public, urban settings—they expanded the public terrain available to women for representation.

Newspapers' demand for sensational "adventures" also placed women in a variety of new public settings requiring physical courage—a trait that had rarely before been associated in a sustained way with the appearance of women in public.[22] Numerous articles by Kate Swan McGuirk appearing in 1896 explored and celebrated women's feats of physical bravery—a subject we know was already of interest to McGuirk. In 1892 she had published a celebratory article in the *Washington Post* about "three brave women" who had been awarded "gold medals by the government." Writing in a dashing, energized, gripping style familiar from popular literature, McGuirk told the story of how one woman, a Mrs. White, had saved the lives of several drowning men: "Suddenly in the surf she caught sight of a man. He seemed almost unconscious, and without a second's hesitation Mrs. White dashed into the surf, out beyond her depth, till she reached the sailor and drew him to land." Realizing that a second man needed rescuing, "again she plunged in, discovered when she reached him that he was unconscious, and floated him to land with great exertion. She had only time to lay him on the beach, when, turning, she discovered another body. She stopped only long enough to divest herself of a portion of her clothing, and then, exhausted as she was, plunged for the third time into the boiling surf." McGuirk concluded that "these are the deeds that make a woman glow with pride for her sex."[23]

Perhaps it was natural, then, that in her character as "Kate Swan," McGuirk would want to engage in such exploits herself—or at least be a witness to the feats of others. In "Kate Swan Rides with the Life-Savers," with the subhead "Covered with Ice and Nearly Frozen, She Shares Danger with the Crew of Seabright Station," she related her harrowing experience as a passenger in an oceangoing lifeboat. (A sample: "We were rowing up the coast, but the wind was driving us off shore and out among the white-caps. Water was dashing steadily into the boat and freezing immediately.")[24]

There were more personally daring adventures, as well, such as her stint learning to be a bareback rider. Swan experienced "a sense of elation" when she first managed to get to her knees while galloping around the ring on a "slippery horse's back." When she was able to stand up "with the white reins taut and Duke going proudly around the ring," she felt "just like the winner of the chariot race in Ben Hur."[25] In "Kate Swan Scales Harlem River Bridge," Swan, "pluckily clinging to a rope," was hoisted in a rigger's sling to the "very topmost point—97¼ feet above the water—of the great

Kate Swan at a Dizzy Height.

PLUCKILY CLINGING TO A ROPE, SHE WAS SWIFTLY LIFTED TO THE TOP BRIDGE GIRDER.

"Kate Swan Scales Harlem River Bridge," New York World, *April 19, 1896. (General Research Division, The New York Public Library, Astor, Lenox and Tilden Foundations)*

new drawbridge." The accompanying illustration showed her dangling high above the city. In "Kate Swan Paddles through Hell Gate [a narrow tidal strait in New York City's East River]," she took a "Midnight Ride through the Mad Whirlpool."[26]

In recounting these stunts, Swan often mentioned (or claimed) that men had congratulated or praised her: at the Harlem River Bridge, one of the builders of the span told her: "I wish we had brought a flag. I should have been proud to have had a flag that a woman had waved over the bridge placed up there." (It was "A Dizzy, Difficult Ascent to a Spot No Woman's Foot Ever Before Trod.") After she paddled through Hell Gate, the male canoeist who was her companion applauded her, saying, "You're the first woman to go through Hell Gate."[27] Men's "congratulations" were used to provide authority for Swan's accounts, giving readers permission to approve of her actions in occupying a new public space.

At the same time, the repeated trope of being the "first" woman to accomplish a (supposedly) daring stunt revealed a similarity between the developing genre of women's adventure narratives and accounts of men's exploits climbing mountains, exploring Arctic regions, and undertaking other strenuous deeds. In exploring the terrain of female bravery, Kate Swan chronicled exploits that required physical stamina and courage, qualities that pushed against the boundaries of the conventionally acceptable.

Swan's articles tended to "imagine" danger. But some women's acts of derring-do involved substantial physical risk. A pair of notices in Margherita Hamm's column "Among the Newspaper Women," for instance, told a poignant story. In October 1894 she noted: "Some one writes us that Lottie Germaine is Meg Merrilles of the World, if so, then that accounts for the good story on hospital life in last Sunday's World."[28] Near the end of November, however, the paper told a different tale: "Miss Germaine has not yet fully recovered from the effects of her fall while making a balloon ascension for the *World*, but is well on the way to regain her old-time physical vigor. She is no longer connected with that paper, being engaged on special work for other journals."[29]

But even newspaper women who did not themselves undertake "daring" physical feats sometimes helped to further the new culture of physical adventure. Elizabeth Jordan, for instance, helped to promote an exploit by mountain climber Annie Peck in 1897, although that feat was more fizzle than triumph—"one of the most amusing episodes of my years on the *World*," Jordan recalled. Peck was "America's most distinguished mountain climber." When "it occurred to her to climb" Mount Popocatépetl in Mexico, "the idea also struck her that she would ask the *Sunday World* to finance the adventure." She thought the paper might be interested because "no woman had yet reached the top"; it "would be a brilliant feather in the *Sunday World*'s cap" to "have its banner planted on that terrific peak." Peck met with the three-person staff of the *Sunday World* to make her case, and editor Arthur Brisbane, for whom Jordan worked as an "admiring assistant," was "immediately interested in the project." The "matter was settled before Miss Peck had talked ten minutes"; "she went out triumphant, with her contract and a good advance payment in her pocket."[30]

Clearly it was the adventurous aspects of her climb that the *World* wanted to emphasize. "It was plain to us," Jordan commented, "and we assumed it was to her, that the nerve-racking [*sic*] perils of the climb would be what most interested the public, and that these must be dramatically played up in her story—*if* she survived to write that story." At the time Popocatépetl "had been constantly erupting streams of fire and lava, and the habit had discouraged climbers." As we "bade her good-by we wondered if we would ever see her again. We even wondered—and this thought is the last to lodge in the minds of newspaper editors," Jordan said, "whether we were justified in letting a woman take such risks."[31]

In "preliminary advertising," the *World* "did ample justice" to the "appalling risks of the expedition." The climb "was to be made on a Thursday," and "Miss Peck promised to put the story on the wires the same night, that it might be in ample time, with its illustrations, for the Sunday supplement that carried the account of the unparalleled achievement, and which must go to press on Friday."[32]

"That Thursday" Jordan was at her desk "all night." Most of the "Popocatepetl material was already in the forms," with "stories and legends about Popocatepetl itself, stories about the previous efforts of other climbers to reach the top," and stories about "Miss Peck's mountain-climbing career." The "leading story, of course, was to be Miss Peck's vivid recital of her appalling difficulties, her hair-raising perils, her final triumphant climax." But when the story finally came in over the wires, "shock and incredulity" swept over Jordan "in waves," as she read a tale quite different from what she had hoped, told with "utmost simplicity." The weather had been perfect. Several guests at the hotel where Peck was staying accompanied her on the climb; they had picnicked along the way. A small boy who longed to accompany them had been sent home by his mother, one of the party; but when Miss Peck reached the top of Popocatépetl, the small boy was already there, having disobeyed his mother, found a shorter route, and finally "planted himself on the top of Popocatepetl as a human banner, waving a triumphant greeting to late comers."[33]

Jordan took Peck's account to her editor "and sat down to watch his reaction as he read" it. "At the end of the reading, when he was able to articulate, he spoke in a strangled voice: 'You're going to fix this thing, aren't you?' he asked." "Of course," Jordan answered. She recalled that she went back to her desk and "took out the picnic party, the lunch baskets, the joyous stroll up the mountain side, the pleasant camaraderie. Last of all, and with the most poignant regret, I took out the little boy on the crater. I sent Annie Peck to the top of that fiery citadel dauntless and alone. I made the Sunday World's banner of triumph wave in the evening breeze. But then and later, I sympathized deeply with Miss Peck's disappointment over the published version of her adventure." "'I thought you would want the facts,'" Peck later told Jordan, "sadly and with mild surprise." But, of course, the *World* did not want mere "facts" in its adventure pieces: it wished to create a heightened reality for its audience. Jordan may not have undertaken actual mountain climbing in her work on Peck's article, but she did engage in her own version of a "daring" exploit by inventing ("I took out," "I sent," "I made") an imagined adventure for readers.[34]

As assistant editor of the *Sunday World*, Jordan not only helped to chronicle newspaper women's "daring deeds," but also glorified the "doings" of the New Woman. The years 1895 and 1896 marked the height of the popular cultural fascination with the emergence of the New Woman as a subject of celebration (and derision).[35] In the same Sunday issues that featured Kate Swan articles, there were often full two-page spreads devoted to the New Woman. The April 26, 1896, full-page feature "New Women and Their Doings," for instance, included a variety of articles about the accomplishments of New Women—"The Champion Woman Fencer" even celebrated the achievements of a woman at the Olympic games. The full-page spread of May 10, titled "The New Woman—What She Is Doing, Wearing and Saying," included an illustration, captioned "Miss Allen's Latest Feat," of a woman dangling from a balloon; showed a woman courageously attacking a burglar; and featured the "bicycle girl" in an article that explored "Novel Underwear Designed to Give Comfort to the Jaunty and Up-to-Date Bicycle Girl."[36] This structured miscellany was similar to that of the woman's page—but without the domestic focus.

New Woman articles in sensational newspapers sought to chronicle a wide array of nondomestic "women's doings," including brief mentions of feats of daring. But lengthy "stunt" articles, such as the Kate Swan stories, were different: they spotlighted the newspaper woman's own subjectivity in the midst of an exploit or daredevil feat, letting the reader know how it felt, moment by moment, to engage in a hitherto taboo activity. Focused on daring exploits, stunt articles thus offered a daring form of selfhood as well—one centered around women's independence, individuality, and hunger for adventure. Taken together, such stunts also spelled out a bold new athleticism that was substantially different from the athleticism of the New Woman who was celebrated playing golf, bicycling, or engaged in other sports like swimming or tennis.

But how adventurous was a feat that had been *assigned* to a newspaper woman? One myth of women's adventurous newspaper work is that they were always victims of their editors—that in "choosing" to take on sensational assignments they were never making a "real" choice, especially if they wanted to keep their jobs. While there is no question that newspapers were exploitative, and that newspaper women (like newspaper men) had a limited range of choices in their work, it is too simple to say that these women gained nothing from their sensational work or were merely victims. Such a calculus reduces a complex set of exposures and interactions to an "either-or" binary that has little to do with women's changing experiences of newspaper work.

Newspaper women's valuing of their work could change assignment by assignment—or over the course of weeks, months, or years. Critics of sensational stories like Haryot Holt Cahoon (herself a respected woman's page editor) charged that "in the world of modern wild-cat journalism the woman reporter lasts about four years"—a shrewd assessment with which many newspaper women concurred.[37] But though adventurous assignments may have been a young woman's "game," demanding a level of stamina and athleticism that few women could maintain over the long term, some women thrived on the excitement of such work in the short run.

One of them was Ada Patterson, who celebrated her "yellow" work (see Introduction). After a stint in San Francisco, Patterson joined Pulitzer's *St. Louis Republican* and from there went to New York. In later describing her career, she stressed the connecting thread of adventure. "I came to New York from St. Louis," she remembered, "because the *American* needed a woman to go to the bottom of the East River bridge. They thought I was the woman to do it because I had gone to a fire with the fire department chief in a swiftly moving vehicle that seemed to me to be propelled by the rapid revolutions of one red wheel; had walked on a plank ninety feet above ground to get the first view of St. Louis from the prospective roof of its new city hall; had ridden in the engine of the midnight express from St. Louis to Chicago; had witnessed the execution of a millionaire who murdered his wife. They had named me, for this and similar escapades, 'The Nellie Bly of the West.'" "Yes, I am a yellow journalist," Patterson declared. "No, I make no apology for the fact." ("Yellow journals are the 'movies' of metropolitan life," she commented. "Everybody sees the movies and everybody reads the yellow journals. Even though they deny it.")[38]

In contrast, Elizabeth L. Banks—whose transatlantic career took her back and forth from America to England—stated emphatically that "I have yet to meet the woman engaged even in the mildest sort of sensational journalism who loved, indeed, who did not hate her work!"[39] Yet Banks's declaration needs to be taken with a healthy dose of skepticism, given that her own career famously involved numerous undercover adventures in which she impersonated working-class women—different sorts of adventures about which she sometimes waxed rhapsodic. Banks was one of many newspaper women for whom impersonations of working-class

Elizabeth L. Banks and her poodle, Judge (Elizabeth L. Banks, The Autobiography of a "Newspaper Girl" *[London: Methuen & Co., 1902])*

women offered a rich vein of newspaper work—a form of public theater in which they could not only be actresses, but write about the experience of acting, too.[40]

Nellie Bly had pioneered this work with her dramatic 1887 stunt for the *World* pretending to be insane. But numerous women followed suit in the late 1880s, 1890s, and early 1900s. As Mark Pittenger has written, such exploits allowed them to escape "the confines of the women's page by writing about their brief experiences as flower vendors, beggars, and ballerinas."[41] But Pittenger has assumed that the "stunt girls' moment was fleeting," that the "fad" of stunt assignments "subsided in the early 1890s when such assignments came to be seen as overdone and trivial."[42] On the contrary, stunt work remained an important part of women's reporting well into the early twentieth century, when it was adopted by a widespread popular culture, including film, that spread the image of the adventurous woman reporter.

In the early 1890s, following in the wake of Nellie Bly, Banks had made a name for herself in London by introducing American methods of yellow journalism to English newspapers. Going undercover as a housemaid, parlor maid, street sweeper, and laundry girl (among other disguises), she had written up her experiences as a series of "campaigns of curiosity" under the title "In Cap and Apron." Attracted to public performance—like so many adventurous newspaper women—Banks was delighted with the attention she received as the "American newspaper girl." But she also recognized that she could easily be dismissed as no more than an "adventuress" if she was not seen as respectable and "womanly." Thus Banks often made a rather tortured argument that the kind of undercover work she did in London was not, in fact, sensational or "yellow."[43]

Banks was well aware that in London, where yellow journalism had not yet made significant inroads, such "escapades" as hers were viewed askance. In an 1896 *Pearson's* article on the "leading lady journalists" of England, M. F. (Maud) Billington commented that "a point on which we may congratulate ourselves so far, I think, is, that English lady journalists have not so far descended to any of the vulgar sensationalism and semi-detective business which has discredited the American reporteresses in too many instances." In rather plummy tones Billington noted that "happily our editorial methods and our own instincts as gentlewomen do not lead us to try being barmaids, or going out with costermongers on a bank holiday for the purpose of 'getting copy,' and we very much repudiate anything of the kind as unworthy of the dignity and traditions of our profession."[44] Billington may well have had Banks in mind in making these remarks. Certainly Banks was not included among Billington's list of "leading lady journalists"—although she did mention another, much-less-famous American then working in England.

In England, just as in America, the late 1880s and early 1890s saw a surge of attention to the "problem" of the working classes—or "dangerous classes," to use Charles Loring Brace's term—as numerous middle-class observers "studied" the urban poor in order to provide reform. Such study fueled the settlement movement in both England and America; it inspired a generation of reformers to attempt a wide variety of improvements, from eradication of tenements (Jacob Riis) to education in American culture (Jane Addams) to reform of urban sanitation and health. Reform became an acceptable middle-class activity as genteel observers sought to "improve" the lives of the poor—and, as several historians have pointed out, shore up their own class and race identities in the process of studying the "other."[45]

But Banks made clear she was not a reformer—an admission that she claimed marked her as suspect in genteel reformers' eyes. At a time when numerous middle-class writers on both sides of the Atlantic justified "slumming" as part of a larger reform agenda, Banks insisted that she did not do her "detective work" (going undercover as a working girl) for philanthropic reasons. Seth Koven has pointed to the "indignant rhetoric" of passages in her 1902 *Autobiography*, in which she allowed herself the "dramatic license" of an imagined conversation with a member of an English woman's club. Banks reported that "a woman writer" had asked her:

"'Now, tell me exactly, what was your aim and object—your serious one, I mean—in going out to service and writing about it? It is a question we are all asking.'"

"'I did it for copy,'" Banks answered, "'to earn my living, you know. I knew it was a subject that would interest everybody.'" Banks said she would "never forget the shocked expression on that woman's face nor fail to remember her exclamation of surprise and disgust, as she replied:—'Copy! You mean to confess you had no philanthropic aim, that you did it for mercenary reasons, merely to earn your living?'"

"'Yes,'" Banks returned, "looking her squarely in the face. 'I'm not a hypocrite and won't pose as a reformer.'"

"'Oh! I really never thought any journalist would sink to such a level, or make such a confession,'" the woman replied, "'even if it were true! I must say I have never written anything except with the object of benefiting somebody by it.'"

"'Perhaps you have an income aside from your writing, which I have not,'" Banks retorted.[46]

Having made a name for herself in England, Banks returned to New York in late 1896 intending to "write up the presidential campaign from a British as well as from a woman's point of view."[47] Banks was well-known enough to be both the subject of interviews herself as well as an interviewer for various newspapers: "Photographed, written about, and interviewed right and left, I began myself to write and interview for various papers," she said. "Orders and requests for special articles followed one another in quick succession, and terms considerably higher than those ordinarily paid, were offered me, and I rejoiced exceedingly."[48] In early 1897 the *Washington Post* published several of Banks's feature articles about President William McKinley.[49]

At first Banks did not intend to work for sensational papers. But even for an established newspaper woman who could trade on her own fame, freelancing was "an unsatisfactory and irregular way of earning a living," as Banks put it. Moreover, she "had not been back in my native land more than a few months" when a "financial catastrophe befell me, from the effects of which, I knew, no amount of 'free-lance' work could deliver me." Unable to find a position at a "regular weekly salary" on "one of New York's high-class newspapers," she received advice from an editor at one of those papers to look for work at a sensational newspaper.[50]

Remembering (or, more likely, inventing) her conversation with this editor, Banks recorded her own reaction: "'You mean,'" she said in amazement, "'that I must become a "yellow journalist"'?'" "'Oh, I couldn't!'" she protested. "'You don't know how hard I've worked over in London to get up the few rungs of the ladder I've already climbed! Why, I write for the best magazines and reviews! I look forward to a career in the literary world; even to the time when I may be able to stop writing pot-boilers. I've heard of this terrible "yellow journalism" of my own country, and have been ashamed. I could not be associated, even anonymously, with a "yellow journal." It would ruin my whole future career.'"[51]

But the editor disagreed with her, telling her about other newspaper women who worked for sensational journals: they were, he said, "'writers of the highest talents.'" Indeed, "'some of the most brilliant, most honest, most pure and upright women'" he had "'ever known'" had "'been employed on the "yellow journals."'" Some of them could "'write things worthy to be handed down to the coming generations, poems and prose that should be bound in fine leather and kept among the standard works'"; they had "'brilliancy and wit and humor.'" But they had to "'have money just now.'" By going to work on yellow journals, they had done "'their duty without so much as a whimper.'" He expected they had "'obligations to meet, and they're honest women.'"[52]

In Banks's telling, the editor pointed out his office window to a nearby newspaper building, indicating where she should go: "I looked," Banks said, "and the sunlight, sparkling on a dome of gold, almost blinded my eyes." There was only one gold dome in New York newspaperdom: the Pulitzer building, home of the *World*—where Banks was working in 1898 (see Chapter 6).[53]

Whether or not this conversation actually occurred, Banks's reporting of it accomplished several personal goals. It reinterpreted her sensational undercover work for London newspapers as an entirely respectable career path, one supposedly distinct from the practices of American yellow journalism. It also gave her entry into the world of American sensational newspaper work a patina of respectability through the "wise advice" of the respected editor. Throughout her career, Banks anxiously sought to maintain her status as a "respectable" woman—but she also continually embarked on new adventures.

In the two years she worked in New York, from 1896 to 1898, Banks engaged in a variety of newspaper work, including undercover assignments. "Most especially," she remembered, "my duties took me among the lower class of working girls on the East Side of New York. I worked among the

Polish and Russian Jews in the sweat shops, writing up the lives they led and the life I led among them. I picked over refuse with the ragpickers; made artificial flowers for the adornment of the hats of working girls; I worked as a dressmaker's apprentice; applied myself to the tailoring business."[54]

"For some time I hired a room in one of the poorer districts, and furnishing it up cheaply, started out to live on three dollars per week, telling each day in the paper just what I had to eat, and describing all my comforts and discomforts. There were times, too, when I was obliged to visit the morgue, looking at the bodies of the unfortunate unknowns and listening to the stories of the finding of these bodies, told by the keepers. Among the hospitals, too, I went, and sometimes to the jails."[55]

Once again, Banks made no claim to the status of reformer through this work. Instead, she sought to claim "womanliness" for herself at the same time that she celebrated her adventures and other experiences. She first invoked a variety of "feminine" reactions to the offensive aspects of her work. "A great deal of my work was very horrible, very loathsome, to me. I was obliged to run risks and encounter dangers that even now that they are long past make me shudder and wonder how I got through them. I had always to carry with me spirits of camphor and smelling salts, for I was continually feeling ill and faint from the foul odors that assailed me, and there were times when my heart almost stopped beating with fear."[56]

Yet once having established "womanliness" through her ability to be made "faint" by her work, she also celebrated her new experiences: "'The Way of Life!' Truly, I now began to walk in that Way! Truly I began to grow! As the days and the weeks went on I could even feel myself growing, growing in grace, growing in charity, putting aside such narrow creeds and prejudices as had been a part of my up-bringing, and were, perhaps, in their place and time, good and wholesome for the girl, but cramping, distorting, warping to the woman. Life! Life! Seething life was all about me. The life of a great city, its riches, its poverty, its sin, its virtue, its sorrows, its joyousness—there it was, and I was in it."[57]

Like Banks, numerous newspaper women made the point that adventurous assignments offered invaluable experiences. Yet there were also powerful critics of sensationalism among them. In an 1897 article for *Arena* magazine, woman's page editor Haryot Holt Cahoon admitted that "in the sensational newspaper a woman with a love of adventure finds her taste gratified."[58] But Cahoon, who sought to maintain the dignity and propriety of journalism as a genteel profession for women, was, in fact, appalled by "gutter journalism" (see Chapter 1). To showcase its "degrading" effects upon women, Cahoon constructed a story of an inexperienced woman reporter's moral declension that in its broad outlines was familiar from the narratives of "fallen women" and "mysteries of the city" that had been a staple of popular literature in the mid-nineteenth century.

"I can see her now," Cahoon wrote, sketching a scene straight out of sentimental melodrama, "as she is ushered into the editor's presence with her little card of introduction from some well-meaning friend who wants to help her to get a foothold. She is fresh and fair, and her eyes are bright with hope and credulity. Her attire is not of the city type, but it becomes her in spite of that. Nothing can mar her youth, and there is just a shade of anxiety and eagerness, and a brave attempt to overcome shyness, for her heart beats very loudly."[59]

Having established the "fresh" innocence of her imagined reporter, Cahoon then detailed the ways in which adventurous work steadily degraded her. After interviewing a prize-fighter, she had a police court assignment. Although "the police court is brutal, and she winces some under what she hears there," she believes that she "must not be thin-skinned if she wishes to succeed in her chosen vocation" and so "steels herself, and mantles her womanhood with the mud-stained garment of modern gutter journalism." Whatever work "her editor lays out for her, that she stands ready to do, whether it is figuring in a balloon ascension or a fire-escape descent, posing as an artist's model, camping all night on a millionaire's grave," or "doing" slums, brothels, opium dens, and other "mysterious" places.[60]

The imagined reporter next took on a variety of "undercover" stunt work. This included pretending to be a Salvation Army soldier; working as a teacher in a Chinese Sunday school, where "she has to have [a 'Chinaman'] make love to her, or else she would not get the story"; posing "as a sufferer from an incurable disease" to gain access to a particular patient in a charity hospital; and borrowing a child and dressing as a mendicant with "a shawl on her head" and a "basket on her arm" in order "to harangue against the organized charity of the city."[61]

Far from being an exaggeration or a parody of the assignments given to newspaper women, Cahoon's article was relatively accurate in listing the kinds of sensational work they were asked to do. The *New York World* of May 10, 1896, for instance, featured the anonymous article "Dens of Chinatown Explored by a Woman," proclaiming that "Steve Brodie [a celebrity of the day who claimed to have jumped from the Brooklyn Bridge] Takes Her to See a 'Chink' Play, an Opium Joint and the Joss House." "Other women have visited that strange hidden quarter near Chatham Square," the writer admitted, but "none has ever before seen so much of its customs and vices." Despite this claim, the article itself was little different from dozens of other newspaper stories offering a tour of "exotic" Chinatown in the 1890s. "Eats Chop-Suey and Studies Opium Fiends," the subhead promised.[62]

We can only speculate as to why this particular article was not bylined, instead using the name of a (momentary) celebrity, Steve Brodie, to attract readers. But it is possible that none of the more well-known female reporters at the *World*, such as Kate Swan McGuirk, was willing to take on this assignment. Cahoon's worries may have been well-founded: it may have been young, inexperienced newspaper women who were most likely to accept what others saw as compromising assignments.

Experienced newspaper women *did* constantly draw lines between mere "adventure" and something closer in their view to ruinously degrading assignments. Although Elizabeth Banks wrote that in the experiences of sensational journalism she had indeed found "salvation from faults and failings and much short-sightedness," she by no means considered such work appropriate for all women journalists. But "not for all women could the career I then entered upon have become a means of grace," she contended; the implication was that only women of strong character could navigate the shoals of sensational assignments. "Better far it would be for some young women to struggle always, never succeeding, to suffer cold and hunger, and in the end to die, failures, than to become part and parcel of American sensational journalism," she said, using the high-flown rhetoric she attached to the issue of respectability. Banks claimed to be different from these weaker women: "For myself I can thank the fate that sent me back to my native land after my four years' residence in England and made it absolutely necessary for me to become a 'yellow journalist.' But I also thank the fate that endowed me with a certain kind of reasoning power that helped me to distinguish between what I could and could not do, as a 'yellow journalist,' and still retain my womanhood and self-respect."[63]

Banks believed that women in sensational journalism needed to be assertive. She could "especially thank the fate that endowed me at my birth with a particularly prominent self-assertive and combative disposition that enabled me to recognize my rights and then fight to the death, if necessary, to maintain them. These things, combined with the very important fact that I had made for myself something of a name in England, and had returned to my own country as a 'heroine,' made my position a far more independent and endurable one than it could possibly have been in other circumstances."

As Banks told it, "the very first thing" she "was asked to do in the line of 'yellow' work, was to walk along Broadway at midnight and 'allow'" herself "to be arrested and sent to the lock-up as a disreputable character [a prostitute]—all this in order to bring about a reform in certain laws that were obnoxious to many New Yorkers, and to prove without a doubt that a respectable woman walking quietly to her home late at night, was liable to be pounced upon and arrested."

But Banks drew the line at this assignment: "'I can't do that sort of work,'" she reported saying to the editor "who had suggested this brilliant 'scoop.'"

"'You can't do it,' he exclaimed in surprise." It was "'something that ought to be done, and you're the woman to do it. You've got a name and a reputation, and your name signed to an article exposing this great wrong would add prestige.'"

"'I'm afraid I think rather too much of my name to make use of it for that purpose,'" Banks replied. "'If my name would add prestige to your scheme, I'm sure the scheme wouldn't lend prestige to my name! Now, what other work have you got on hand which you would like me to do?'"

"'Other work? You mean to say that you refuse?'"

"'Certainly,'" she reported responding. "'It is indecent, and I refuse to do anything that I consider indecent.'"

"'Well!'" exclaimed the editor, "tilting back in his chair, and eyeing" her "with great curiosity."[64]

Although we cannot be sure that this self-serving account of Banks's refusal was completely (or even partially) truthful, the fact that numerous other newspaper women also described indignantly refusing to go undercover as prostitutes supports the idea that this was a line beyond which "adventure" was seen to become degradation and loss of reputation. But Banks's account suggests something more, too: that part of the "adventure" of newspaper work was the experience of "drawing the line" itself—of testing women's new selfhood within the realm of the workplace. There was triumph to be had in sparring with newspaper editors.

For Cahoon, however, the inevitable result of sensational work was an intertwined moral and physical decline: the loss of "the bloom and delicacy of the womanhood with which the Creator endowed her, and a blunting of her moral sensibilities." It was a view widely shared by critics of women's sensational newspaper work. "Where now is the hopeful, credulous, enthusiastic, ambitious girl who came to the city about four years before, or less?" Cahoon asked rhetorically, before providing the grim answer: "Ill health from exposure, self-neglect, late hours, and weariness stimulated to strength has begun to plough inroads into her system." Indeed, "she has lost all the capital she had when she began,—youth, health, credulity, her ideals, her self-respect, her enthusiasm, and her ambition."[65]

But even as they expressed similar doubts about sensational work, some women writers admitted its manifold attractions. Newspaper woman Edith Sessions Tupper, for instance, wrote several short stories about a young reporter named Miss Hunt, whom she depicted as becoming disillusioned with newspaper work—yet also attracted to its excitement. In "Why Miss Hunt Went Home," published on the woman's page of the *World*, Miss Hunt reflected with trepidation on where she was assigned to go the next day: "The slumming assignment. . . . how I dread it," she said to herself, "and then there's that interview with the woman in the Tombs. . . . horrible. I was in hopes they would never send me there again." Having just received a loving letter from her parents, and despite success, acclaim, and a recent raise in salary, she decided to go home. In a sentimental conclusion, Miss Hunt flung herself "with one big sob" into her parents' arms.[66]

This story aligned nicely with the concerns of Haryot Holt Cahoon. Yet in a follow-up piece, "Miss Hunt's Temptation," Tupper highlighted the excitement of reporting (not to mention the independence it involved). "Miss Hunt had been home for six months" and thought she was contented with her quiet new life. But "one day, on opening the newspaper for which she had worked while in New York, a paragraph caught her eye to the effect that Miss Van Scribble had been sent to India with a celebrated woman explorer to represent the enterprising journal." Immediately jealous, Miss Hunt dropped the paper "with a smothered cry. Little Van Scribble, she who had written nothing but fashion twaddle and gossipy rubbish, to have such luck!"[67]

Then, Tupper wrote, Miss Hunt received a letter: "The envelope bore the well-remembered letter-head of the big New York daily," and her "hands shook as she opened it and read the note from its managing editor. He wished her to return. There was a better chance than ever on the paper for an enterprising woman." Outside, "it was a perfect June evening," and "the perfume of her mother's rose-garden stole upward." But "suddenly on this peaceful scene was borne that rumble and roar of a great city. Again Miss Hunt saw the throng surging up and down in Newspaper Row, and heard the ceaseless tramp of the restless multitude. . . . Out flashed the electric lights. . . . The shrill cries of the newsboys—'Wextra! Wextra!'—came ringing on the air. . . . An ambulance clanged along the street. . . ." The "windows were ablaze. . . . Color light, confusion, work. The scene trembled with movement and vibrated with life."[68]

There was "no help for her. She had smelt printer's ink once more. The feverish influences of her old life came back upon her seven-fold. Yes, she would go. She had wasted time enough. There was work for her to do. Oh, to be back, back in her accustomed haunts, back at her studies of human nature, back at her dissection of human souls." But just as Miss Hunt was writing her acceptance, she heard her mother's voice from below: "Kitty, where are you, dear? Mother needs you." The young woman "turned back to her desk, took up her half-written letter, looked intently at it for a moment, then quietly tore it in two and tossed it in the waste basket." The sacrifice in this gesture was obvious to the reader: Miss Hunt had chosen the path of duty—but not of desire, which would have led her back to newspaper work.[69]

While for many women home exerted a strong pull, the excitement of newspaper work, with its access to the public world of cosmopolitan city life, was also alluring. This was certainly true of Zona Gale, who worked briefly in the late 1890s for the *Milwaukee Evening Wisconsin*, before landing a job at the *New York Evening World*. Gale, who would later become a Pulitzer Prize–winning novelist and playwright, worked in New York for several years before returning home to live with her parents in Portage, Wisconsin. Her closeness to her parents was undoubtedly exceptional—she would later break off an engagement with poet Ridgely Torrence apparently because they wished her to—but it was not the only reason she left New York. She also realized that newspaper work did not allow her enough time to write fiction and poetry—what she considered her real career.[70]

Gale nonetheless later celebrated the thrilling experience of her newspaper work in New York (see Introduction). Haryot Holt Cahoon may have argued that newspaper work left a woman with nothing but ill health and experience—but it was exactly that experience that other newspaper women craved and celebrated, and that made sensational work exciting, at least in the short term.

As an "all-round" reporter for the *World* in 1901, Gale was assigned several "stunts." Trumpeted as the "First Woman to Run a Steam Locomobile in New York," Gale made "an Exciting Run Up Fifth Avenue from the Washington Arch to the Plaza." She concluded that "the thing I want most to do in the world is to run a locomobile every day, always." A few months later she became "the first woman in America to go flying over American roads, seated beside M. Fournier, the famous French chauffeur." The *World* informed readers that Gale would give "a vivid description of her thrilling experience on the snorting gray terror as it whizzed and rumbled and roared with lightning speed for eighteen miles over country roads and fields."[71]

"The daring of it!," Gale wrote. "The sweep and rush of the wind; the awful force of that something under the aluminum plate that racked and pounded and thundered us on our way! And always and always that pale

flood of yellow meadow and brown ground and gray fence that went swirling and swimming by, dim as dreams!"[72]

Most of Gale's stories did not involve "stunts," however. As a "regular" reporter she wrote urban sketches, covered strikes, did interviews, and covered several criminal cases. Her assignments remind us not only that newspaper women on sensational papers often did a mix of "stunt" and "regular" reporting, but also that there was plenty of excitement to be had in regular reporting. In February 1901 Gale wrote excitedly to her parents in Wisconsin about a notable success she had just had with an article on a notorious criminal case, which had immediately earned her another heady assignment. Enclosing a clipping, she told them facetiously that it had "started me on the highroad to something or other—I don't know what yet." She was proud that the *World* was sending her out again "with decent speeches" of praise. Gale's new assignment involved a shooting in Arlington, New Jersey, where a minister accused of sexually attacking a woman in his congregation had been shot by the woman's husband. Gale was to do a feature: "They wanted me to get what I could about the history of the two people."[73]

Gale regaled her parents with an account of her adventures in getting the story: "I got here Wednesday night at 7:30—and tried to get in at the boarding house where the woman was staying, but I couldn't. She was cautious. The whole town was alert and warlike against reporters and detectives. They all acted like idiots—as if the newspaper people were trying to do them harm." (In fact, of course, the townspeople were acting quite sensibly if they did not want public exposure.)[74]

Finding a room at another boardinghouse, Gale announced her "intention of giving some morning talks on Wagner" (the composer—clearly a "cover" to allay any suspicion that she was a reporter). "I didn't sleep any all night," she wrote; "I was worried for fear I wouldn't do it right and would[n't] get anything." The next day, "I made about 20 calls and finally I ended by bringing the confectioner's wife home to dinner with me and pumping her for 2 hours afterward. She is a member of the same guild to which Mrs. Barker [the woman who accused the minister of sexual attack] used to belong in the minister's church. She went home after 9, and I sat up and wrote 17 pages—finished about 11, got up Friday" and "mailed my letter on the 8:30 train to the address of the city editor of the World so not to use the name of the newspaper on the envelope, and went on working scared to death for fear they couldn't use a word I had done and overwhelmed with the responsibility of living up to the $25 they gave me for expenses." The very level of detail in this letter—taking her parents step by step through her reporting—underlined Gale's excitement.[75]

"At 3:30," she continued, "when the afternoon papers came in I slipped down to the newstand [sic] to see if maybe they had used a letter of mine—and when I got an Evening World I saw a story with a head like the Kennedy one clear across the page—saying 'Secrets Laid Bare.' First (underlined) story of the Arlington case. Evening World's special staff correspondent, who has been for several days studying the case from sources of undoubted authority, sends report of true state of affairs—and there was my story—set in two column matter, extra spaced between the lines and covering all the front page excepting the pictures and a little corner bit their man had sent in."[76]

Gale was so thrilled that "I almost fell out of town," she reported. "I tore across to the station—the only safe place to be seen with a paper—and read it, and whooped with glee. I was so delighted."[77]

"Regular" newspaper work—including covering crimes—obviously provided Gale with many exciting experiences. Other women, too, recounted with relish their adventures doing regular newspaper work. Marie Manning remembered being assigned the task of trying to undermine the credibility of a shopkeeper, an important witness in the William Guldensuppe murder case of 1897. Manning was directed to go to the witness's shop twice, the second time in a disguise, to see whether the shopkeeper would remember her (she did not). "To me, it was a grand lark," Manning remembered of this deception, in which she enlisted "the assistance of a young actress of my acquaintance."[78]

At the turn of the century such deception was not yet viewed as inappropriate for journalists: indeed, such "playacting" was simply part of the newspaper woman's arsenal of tools—often described as part of their "resourcefulness." Nixola Greeley-Smith told an interviewer: "I will say that in order to do effective work on a great metropolitan newspaper a woman has got to have brains. Brains, imagination, and resourcefulness—that is the trinity of qualities that go to make up the woman who would succeed in journalism in this town, particularly resourcefulness." Her eyes "dancing with mirth," she then recalled "the story of the Rockefeller baby's layette," one of her early assignments. "That was where I learned my first lesson in the value of resourcefulness as a journalist [sic] asset."[79]

"A short time after I went to work on the World," Greeley-Smith recalled, "a baby was born to the Percy Rockefellers, up at the Rockefeller country estate at Ardsley-on-the-Hudson. Nobody could find out a single thing about it, though the Journal announced authoritatively that it was a boy. I was ordered up to Ardsley to verify this report, if possible, and to bring back a detailed description of the infant's layette. It was also casually suggested by the editor that any little facts pertaining to the color of the child's hair, eyes and complexion would be gratefully received. Likewise it was suggested that an interview with Baby Rockefeller's nurse, with the proud father or any or all of the grandparents would be interesting. I was greatly pleased with my assignment."[80]

But this was an impossible assignment, of course—the kind of "test" that many editors gave to new newspaper women, and that those few who succeeded in "passing" remembered with triumph. "I was young and inexperienced," Greeley-Smith explained, "and little knew when I left the office that it was as impossible to get within a stone's throw of the Rockefeller stronghold as it was to get near the palaze [sic] of the czar of Russia, and that the infant Rockefeller was as jealously guarded from the prying eyes of journalism as the most sacred prince of India." At Grand Central Station she passed "a newspaper man just returning from a fruitless quest on the same mission. 'You'll not get a thing,'" he told her. "'Every newspaper reporter in town has been camping on that trail for the last 24 hours and not a thing to show for it.'"[81]

By the time Greeley-Smith arrived at Ardsley, her "good spirits were much dampened," she said. "I pictured myself 'falling down' and being discharged at the end of the week if I did not get back with a description of that Rockefeller baby's layette, and in sheer desperation I threw myself upon the mercy of the station agent by taking him completely into my confidence. He was young and full of imagination and the idea made an instant appeal to his spirit of adventure."[82]

The Rockefeller brougham happened to be waiting at the station, and the station agent took it upon himself to introduce Greeley-Smith to the coachman as "Miss Hobson—Miss Ella Hobson, who lived down in Brooklyn," Greeley-Smith remembered. "My sister was a nurse girl up at the Rockefeller place, and wouldn't he drive me up." The coachman agreed, and suddenly Greeley-Smith not only had access to the Rockefeller estate but also, on the way up, the coachman told her that the baby was a girl, not a boy— thus giving her a "beat" over the *Journal*, the *World*'s chief rival.[83]

"All this while I was quaking in my shoes, not knowing what minute I might be discovered in the deception which the station agent had forced upon me, although to be sure I was mighty thankful to be party to it." Although Greeley-Smith was not admitted to the servants' quarters—her "sister" was still back in Brooklyn, it turned out—she had already obtained the information she had come for. What is more, on her return to the station, the station agent—against all rules—allowed her to see, by looking over his shoulder, the many telegrams that were arriving for the Rockefellers. "When the down train picked me up half an hour later," Greeley-Smith said, "I had all the news I wanted about the Rockefeller baby and her layette."[84]

If deception provided a source of public adventure for newspaper women, so too did the need to make "stories" out of a range of "daily happenings." In the early 1890s Elizabeth Jordan found adventure in the assignment she received from the *World* "to write a series of half-page daily specials under the standing caption True Stories of the News, such as the *Petit Journal* was publishing in Paris." Jordan's stories "were to be taken from the daily happenings in New York—those bits of drama which are often covered by a few lines in a newspaper. The finding of an unknown body in the river; the suicide of an unknown girl; some pregnant incident in the prisons or courtrooms or hospitals of the big city."[85]

Part of the adventure of Jordan's charge lay in its entrepreneurial nature: she had to find appropriate stories herself by traveling throughout the city. No part of the city was off-limits to her in an assignment that gave her access to a range of public spaces in New York, including hospitals, police courts, and prisons. She became such a familiar presence as she searched for her stories that "friendly men and women in these institutions" phoned her "tips," all of which she followed up.[86]

As Jordan wryly recalled, the assignment turned out to be strenuous and demanding. Her editor, Ballard Smith, "smilingly assured" her that "all" she had to do was "to dig up all the facts back of the news leads and write each story as fiction, hung on its news hook."[87] This editorial instruction reminds us that a strong link existed between fact and fiction in human interest writing at the turn of the century, with both editors and writers assuming that the most appropriate ways in which to bring the "facts" of newspaper "stories" to life was through narrative techniques that, with the ascendancy of "objectivity" as a goal of news reporting, would later be relegated to fiction (only to be resuscitated once again in new ways in the "New Journalism" of the 1960s, as well as in more recent literary journalism).

Centering news stories around "little dramas," adding "color," reproducing dialogue, providing "poetic" details of scenery—all of these techniques were part of the standard repertoire of the human interest writer. Most of all, newspaper women were encouraged to empathize with their subjects in order to create the most compelling stories. Ada Patterson, for instance, vividly remembered her first assignment from editor Arthur Brisbane at the *New York Journal* (where he had moved from the *New York World* in 1897), who gave her explicit instructions in how to create a story based on empathy. Handing her a "four line clip from a news column," he told her: "There's a feature in this. A woman killed herself because she was tired of doing the same thing day after day. She got up in the morning, got the children off to school, cooked her meals, washed her dishes, went to bed and got up the next morning, and did the same things again. Her husband never took her out for amusement. That's the idea. We will illustrate the story by the clock and show what she did every hour of the day."[88]

Patterson recalled that the editor's eyes were "blue and bright as ice" and "sent forth electric shafts as he spoke." As she "started away eagerly," he called out "'Wait!'" Her "hand on the door knob," she "turned back for the final word. 'Don't embroider,'" he said. "'Truth is more dramatic than any fiction ever invented. The truth is enough.'"[89] Yet, as this recollection revealed, "truth" was already wedded to "fiction." Patterson was not sent to investigate the causes of the woman's suicide. Brisbane assumed he already had the "true" interpretation and instead asked her to find "true" details that would flesh out his interpretation and give it the emotional immediacy of "truth."

Adventurous newspaper work required women to create a theater of the real, to produce daily dramas based on a particular form of what might be called "newspaper empathy." It gave them experiences that enlarged their sense of themselves and their understanding of the world around them. As Elizabeth Banks asserted, the "newspaper life" gave women experience that was "wider and broader" than that of the "average woman."[90] "Come and learn, learn better than you can in any other profession open to our sex, what life, great, wide, teeming life, out in the world of men and women, is like," she urged would-be newspaper women at the end of her 1902 autobiography.[91]

But as we shall see, adventurous newspaper work could also create knotty ethical problems for women, especially when they went undercover. It was one thing for women to create entertainments for a wide urban newspaper audience based on a form of public playacting—or even to engage in relatively mild, temporary deceptions in order to obtain information. But as the case of Dorothy Richardson reveals in Chapter 6, it was quite another matter for a newspaper woman to engage in sustained deception of her readers. Although the fictional worlds newspaper women created gave them new and powerful public identities, they sometimes created serious moral quandaries, as well.

chapter six **Work**

In January 1898 an extraordinary group of New York newspaper women descended on New Bedford, Massachusetts, where a major strike was under way among textile workers whose pay had just been cut by 10 percent.[1] This "New England strike" was not just important labor news — it offered human interest opportunities immediately seized upon by the *New York Journal* and the *New York World*. Both papers were sympathetic to workers — at least up to a point. While neither advocated strikes nor was particularly radical in its labor views, each was deliberately sympathetic to "starving workers" on strike: after all, they regarded workers as part of their readership. The *World* assigned Elizabeth Banks and Kate Swan McGuirk to cover the strike; it also took the unusual step of sending a labor leader from the Lower East Side, Minnie Rosen, to write her impressions and engage with workers. The *Journal* dispatched Anne O'Hagan to provide what she later called "newspaper pathos"; it also sent Eva McDonald Valesh, who the previous summer had become an "all-round" reporter for the *Journal* after acquiring an extensive background as labor organizer and journalist in Minnesota and for the national American Federation of Labor (AFL).[2]

For close to a month, this accomplished group of newspaper women filed numerous human interest stories about the strike, not only finding pathos in workers' lives but also, in the case of O'Hagan and Valesh, engaging in a form of newspaper labor activism encouraged by *Journal* owner William Randolph Hearst, whose slogan at the time was the "journalism that acts." The women's stories — interestingly different from one another, even contradictory — allowed them to become a public presence in the strike, giving them new opportunities as public voices and public figures and, in the case of O'Hagan, lifting her from the woman's page, where at one point she had served as beauty editor.

"Working-girl stories" were a significant part of newspaper women's reporting at the turn of the century, especially for "yellow" papers like the *World* and the *Journal*. As Elizabeth Banks observed about her own work at the *World* and other "yellow journals" in 1897 and 1898, women "on the daily and Sunday editions" seemed "to be kept almost exclusively for the purpose of doing 'working-girl stories' and making 'moral exposures.'"[3] These working-girl stories reflected a quickened interest in the problems of labor and capital at a time of substantial economic turmoil and labor activism; a fascination with poverty, expressed in a literature of "slumming" and tenement reform in this period; and an interest in the growing numbers of women working in major cities.[4]

Working-girl stories also drew on a long-lived sentimental literature of "starving seamstresses" that, both before and after the Civil War, invited readers to sympathize with the plight of respectable but downtrodden working women imagined as pale, shivering, and helpless victims.[5] But newspaper women often found that the very process of being out on assignment undercut their initial attempts to imagine workers in these older sentimental terms. The working women they met were not shivering or helpless—far from it. Newspaper women began to reconfigure and reconceptualize the figure of the working woman—especially in conjunction with working women themselves. That this was a complicated process—one characterized by a mutual sense of betrayal as much as sympathetic identification—is the subject of this chapter, which examines two case studies of newspaper women's working-girl stories.

Not the least of the complications involved in writing working-girl stories was the status of newspaper women themselves as women who worked. Unlike clubwomen and middle-class reformers, many of whom did not have to earn a living, newspaper women were often adamant about the fact that they *had* to work. "I knew only that I needed money," Elizabeth Banks said about beginning her job as a "yellow woman journalist" at the *World*. Eva Valesh also came from the working class. But the fact that both newspaper women and other working women had to earn their living did not necessarily create solidarity—nor did it make newspaper women into the factory girls they wrote about.[6]

For working women, there were multiple complications in being the recipients of the publicity that was at the heart of newspaper women's work. What newspaper women had to offer other working women was a public stage, a public arena, from which their own concerns could be voiced and addressed. Working women took strategic advantage of this opportunity when they could. But public exposure could also backfire, quickening resistance—especially by men—to working women's efforts in the public sphere. At the same time, men's resistance to newspaper women themselves could translate into resistance to the working women they "covered."

In the case of the New Bedford strike, the particular needs of human interest journalism at first limited what newspaper women could express and sometimes even what they could see. O'Hagan, for instance, began by telling stories of "starving workers" and their families—a tried-and-true trope of much nineteenth-century literature focused on workers, but a set of characterizations that seemed only lightly tethered to reality at the beginning of the strike, and that local newspapers, labor leaders, and even some workers indignantly objected to as badly overdrawn. For their part, Eva Valesh and Minnie Rosen engaged in public labor activism — including, in the case of Valesh, lobbying the Massachusetts legislature—that caused significant pushback by male labor leaders in New Bedford. At the beginning of the strike, Elizabeth Banks wrote cheery stories of happy workers that seemed to issue entirely from some other planet. Yet all of the women reporters rapidly changed their coverage after contact with the subjects of their stories—working women themselves. As they continued their labor journalism for the *Journal* and the *World*, it became clear that the newspaper women themselves were receiving a significant public education through their work, which gave them more access to, and knowledge of, a wider public sphere.

Despite that public education, however, turn-of-the-century newspaper women were rarely reformers with far-reaching solutions to offer for urban problems; only around 1910 would women reformers like Sophie Irene Loeb enter newspaper work, at the height of the Progressive Era.[7] As urban workers themselves, newspaper women often struggled to make ends meet and were closer in position than they would have liked to the working girls they studied. They frequently offered up only bromides as "solutions" to working women's problems—improved boardinghouses being a favorite cause. They trusted that the exposure of publicity might bring reform in its wake: they tended to see publicity as a positive good. When they discussed reforms, the inadequacy of their ideas was often readily apparent. They provided a form of public representation, but not solutions.

Newspaper women often justified their undercover work—in which they pretended to be working girls—as a valuable means of exposing poor working conditions and abusive employers. But the case of Dorothy Richardson reveals the troubling ethical questions that could result from a newspaper woman going undercover as a working girl. As a reporter for the *New York Herald*, Richardson created a fictional persona for herself as a young girl who had traveled from the country to the "terrible" city of New York to look for a job. Her 1900 and 1901 newspaper stories of working girls were highly popular, and Richardson would later expand them into magazine articles and then a famous book. But as we shall see, they also raised significant questions about one newspaper woman's claim to be a working girl herself.

# # #

Anne O'Hagan later remembered that her part in the 1898 New Bedford strike was to write articles aimed at "stirring heart interest."[8] Tellingly, this comment appeared in a 1905 *New York Times* profile of O'Hagan as a magazine fiction writer—the writing career she entered after leaving newspaper work. Titled "Anne O'Hagan Writes Stories on Business Principles," the profile highlighted her matter-of-fact understanding of the needs and demands of genteel magazines. As O'Hagan explained to her interviewer, "home means refinement" according "to the required proprieties of a magazine story."[9] By 1905 she had built a successful career writing short stories and articles for magazines; she was able to provide exactly what magazines required.

In 1898 O'Hagan also understood exactly what the *Journal* wanted in her accounts of striking workers' lives. Her first stories from New Bedford were positioned within two major literary traditions: first, tenement literature, such as that of Jacob Riis's *How the Other Half Lives* (1890), emphasizing the degraded living conditions of workers in New York; and second, sentimental literature of "starving seamstresses."[10]

"Do you know what $6 will do in New Bedford?" O'Hagan demanded in one of her early strike stories. (Six dollars was the weekly wage for many workers; mill owners were cutting it to $5.40.) "It will hire a tenement for $2," she said, "the dreariest habitation on earth." She explained that "unutterable degradation—the degradation of dinginess, of forlornness, of poverty, of absolute hopelessness, will hang over it. Plaster will fall from its roof. The wind will whistle through its cracks—a cold wind, too, from the bay on which all New Bedford's great mills and miserable homes for mill operatives are built. The sanitary arrangements of the tenements will be disgusting."[11] There was little in O'Hagan's article to indicate that she had actually been inside a two-dollar New Bedford tenement. There was poverty in New Bedford, to be sure, but this was a description drawn as much from imagination as from observation—influenced, no doubt, by "slumming" literature that was a fad among writers and would-be reformers in the 1890s.[12]

If their living conditions were degraded, the workers themselves were equally miserable, according to O'Hagan. "Very many of them [strikers] were out yesterday afternoon," she told her readers, "huddled wretchedly together in front of the offices where the last of their wages was paid to them. The gray rain fell brutally upon their poorly dressed figures, the gray bay stretched in front of them, the grim, ominously silent mills rose pitilessly around them. They shivered beneath their thin shawls; they coughed; their shoes sucked the water in through gaping holes." Turning to individuals, O'Hagan provided a brief profile of a Lancashire weaver named Jesse Simpkins, who planned to leave New Bedford. His "children came into the world, poor wizened bits of humanity," she said, "who closed their tired eyes upon New Bedford—and small blame to them!—almost as soon as they saw it, or who lingered on to be the victims of every ailment and every disease known to pathology." O'Hagan concluded her story with several brief selections from interviews under the heading "New Bedford Women Weavers Tell the Evening Journal of Their Hard Life."[13]

One of those women weavers, however, fifty-seven-year-old Alice Brierly, vigorously disagreed that her life was so hard—and complained about her portrayal to the local newspaper, the *New Bedford Evening Standard*. "Peter and Alice Brierly, residing at 23 Durfee street, are the victims of yellow journalism," the paper said the day after O'Hagan's article appeared. "They called at the Standard office this forenoon bringing with them copies of the New York Journal and the Boston Post, and engaged in a long lament at the injustice which had been done them." O'Hagan had quoted Alice Brierly saying, "I'm old, and sick, and cross. I'm cross to my man. I'm cross to everybody. But anybody would be cross that had worked 60 years and then found nothing but this."[14]

"Sixty years, indeed!" the local newspaper reported Brierly "indignantly" exclaiming. "My son told me when he showed me that piece that I must have been weaving before I was born. It is a shame, the treatment that woman has given us," she asserted. "We have as respectable and comfortable a home as anybody who works in the mills in New Bedford, and when the young woman came in she was treated as politely as we knew how. And then to think that she should go away and write such a pack of lies about us. Why, people ought to be ashamed to so scandalize the poor in New Bedford." With a "fresh burst of indignation" Brierly recalled that "while she was describing us as in the depths of poverty," Brierly's daughter had been "in the front room playing on the piano."[15]

Brierly's offended personal pride found an echo in the pride of the local reporter, who resented the invasion of metropolitan journalism. Indeed, throughout the strike local newspapers in New Bedford and Fall River (where workers were also on strike) complained bitterly about the arrival of "yellow journalism" in their midst. "New Bedford has had its first intro-duction to real sensational journalism this week," said one article, "and it is greatly shocked at it. The strike has attracted the attention of a New York paper, which sent two women here to write up the situation." The "women frankly told the local newspaper men that they wished to be directed to some place where they could find actual starvation and suffering. They went through the average weavers' families and actually found bicycles, which wouldn't do at all. They wanted blanched and sunken cheeks and must have them."[16] Another story complained that "one of the women correspondents said to a newspaper man on Tuesday: 'Where can I find some extreme poverty? I've been through a lot of the tenement houses but that won't do at all. I want some poverty that's picturesque.'"[17]

If Anne O'Hagan had overstretched herself initially in depicting "starv-ing" workers, Elizabeth Banks went to the opposite extreme. One of her early profiles of the strikers could have come from the cheeriest pages of Dickens's *A Christmas Carol*, making any reader wonder why such prosper-ous workers would bother striking at all. In her "Jolly Strikers Who Don't Whine at Woe" of January 24, Banks described William Foley, the vice president of the Weavers' Union, who had "been nicknamed by his associ-ates the 'jolly striker.' Certainly, he is the most contented, well-fed, happy-looking striker that I have seen since I came to New Bedford," Banks com-mented. He was also eager to rebut the portrait of poverty and starvation then appearing in both the *Journal* and Banks's own *World*.[18]

"Write up some of the happy things in New Bedford," Foley urged Banks. "Don't you go to painting this town blacker than it is. Don't send on tales of starvation and freezing till they begin to come—and the Lord grant they won't ever be here for you to write about." As Foley explained, "We're New Bedford folks, we are, and proud of our town—Why, there's some of the happiest homes in New Bedford; and there's clean homes, too! Don't you go to making out New Bedford's a dirty place."[19]

Foley took Banks home to meet his wife—and the result was exactly the shift in newspaper coverage Foley was lobbying for, revealing that workers were far from mere pawns in their dealings with newspaper women. In fact, sometimes they were able to shape coverage to their own ends. In her next article Banks wrote approvingly that "Mr. Foley's house I found to be an especially clean and cozy place. A prettier little sitting-room, with its bright ingrain carpet, pictures, rocking chairs and bric-a-brac, it would be difficult to find in any country village." She asserted that "many of the French and English weavers and spinners live comfortably and cleanly, and to compare their homes and the streets in which they reside to the slums of London and New York is to libel them and bring out their just resentment."[20]

Banks initially had trouble imagining that workers who looked happy and were not obviously starving might have legitimate grievances, as she demonstrated in several early observations about fashionable working girls. "The prettiest, and most stylishly dressed mill girls were probably those seen at the French Catholic Church today," she wrote. "Walking behind some of them as they returned from mass, it was difficult for me to believe that these girls were striking for 'living wages.' Not that they were extravagantly dressed, for they were not, but they looked jaunty and happy."[21]

Like some of her colleagues from New York, Banks also found New Bedford tenement apartments surprisingly roomy when compared with the cramped living arrangements of Manhattan. The model tenements she saw renting for three dollars a week were "much prettier" than a "Harlem flat." "They have as many as seven large rooms, a piano in the drawing-room and a bathtub standing on legs. One wouldn't mind at all spending one's days in one of them," she concluded.[22] Minnie Rosen, hired by the *World* not just to explore working conditions but also apparently to organize workers, similarly commented that "these people had more room for $1.75 a week than we get in New York for $3."[23] One can feel Banks and Rosen's surprise that the "starving" workers might have better living quarters than the typical hall bedroom of the New York newspaper woman.

Although Banks had posed as a working woman in England and specialized in "working-girl stories" in New York, initially she seems to have been little equipped to explore beneath the surface of the New Bedford strike. After all, her best-known newspaper stories were intensely personal, based on playacting; they involved adventure and the excitement of individual public theater. But Banks soon caught up as a labor journalist, providing detailed, vivid sketches of strike meetings. She even provided convincing analyses of the problems of labor and capital that loomed large in the New Bedford strike, as cotton mills increasingly squeezed workers of their pay.

Eva Valesh, on the other hand, already had an extensive background in labor journalism, labor activism, *and* the kind of playacting Banks specialized in by the time she was hired by the *Journal* in the summer of 1897. She immediately brought this experience to bear in her New Bedford assignment. Born in 1866, Valesh had briefly trained as a typesetter, and, through her father, was already closely affiliated with the Knights of Labor before she was hired by the *St. Paul Globe* in 1888 to go undercover as a working girl at a garment factory.[24]

In the spring of 1888 such undercover work was a new and popular innovation in newspaper work, pioneered only months before when Nellie Bly
posed as an insane woman in order to gain admittance to the asylum at
New York's Blackwell's Island. The resulting story created a sensation and
inspired wide imitation. Several newspapers in New York—including the
World—began to send women undercover in a variety of situations. Former
actress Viola Roseboro', for instance, who worked for the *Daily Graphic*, did
a "special" for the *World* in which she posed as a beggar. Bly herself did several new undercover assignments, including, at the end of November 1887,
pretending to be a "white slave" working in a paper box factory.[25]

New York newspapers had long published articles in which female reporters observed working women, but actually playing the part of a working woman was something new and quickly became a fad. A simple but
brilliant expedient, going undercover opened up new journalistic territory
for women at a time of quickened interest in the problems of labor and
capital. It allowed newspaper women dramatic new public roles—first as
workers in a variety of settings that might otherwise have been off-limits
to them; and then as public figures in print, as they reported on their discoveries.

Soon newspapers in other major cities began to employ newspaper
women as undercover working women. For example, Nell Nelson (Helen
Cusack) wrote a series on the "white slave girls of Chicago" (which in this
case meant working women) for the *Chicago Times* in 1888. She "made up
for the role of shop-girl" and then moved from employer to employer, carefully detailing their practices. Nelson's articles were quickly collected in a
book, *The White Slave Girls of Chicago*, which, as advertised, contained her
"startling disclosures of the cruelties and iniquities practiced in the work
shops and factories of a great city." Her success led to a job—also in 1888—
at the *New York World*, where she engaged in undercover work and writing
"slumming" pieces describing tenement life, before being relegated to the
woman's page.[26]

Remarkably, Eva Valesh had no newspaper experience whatsoever when
she was recruited to go undercover as a working girl for the *St. Paul Globe*.
The editor of the paper's Minneapolis edition, John Swift, who wanted to
expand his coverage of workers' concerns, went to her "father's house one
evening" (both Swift and her father belonged to the Knights of Labor as,
soon, would Valesh) and said that he wanted "somebody to go and work in
the factories, live in the homes, and give an all-round picture of how working people live." Swift had seen Valesh "act in the local dramatic society." He
told her father: "'You know, I think your Eva could do it. She's got to act a

little. She's got to wear an old dress, get her face smudged, and so on. I think she could do it.'" Valesh remembered that it was lucky her mother was not at home at the time: "She would have snapped that off quickly." But her father "was a nice easy-going, tolerant man, and he made no objections."[27]

In her first article of the series, "'Mong Girls Who Toil," Valesh carefully gave the rationale for going undercover. Otherwise, why not simply interview working girls and their employers? The subject was "a difficult one to handle," she explained, because "many of the shops and factories are guarded for the one purpose of preventing the outflow of information." At the same time, "fear of discharge prevents the girls themselves from giving any information"; there had been "cases where the very shame for it has prevented these girls from describing the meager pittance they earn." Drawing close to her potential audience, Valesh, in the character of "Eva Gay" and affirming that "this I know by actual word of mouth," proposed "to carry GLOBE readers with me through a series of articles and show the life, home life and shop life, of the working girls and women of Minneapolis."[28]

In her reminiscences Valesh revealed how the newspaper series had worked: "Some of the workers in a laundry, let's say, would come to me and say, 'We have the most terrible place to work.' They would explain the poor ventilation, lack of heat and this and that. I would go there and in some way get a job. I would then work there a little while, in order to be able to say that I personally knew what those conditions were. I wasn't going to take anybody's word for it."[29] Valesh wore old clothes and had her "hair cut very short like a boy. Certainly I didn't look more than twelve or thirteen. I'd get a job perhaps as a little errand girl for a few days. No employer ever discovered me—that was the odd thing—because they were looking for a tall, grimly efficient spinster."[30]

Valesh liked this investigative work, recalling that "I worked awfully hard in those days, and I enjoyed every minute of it."[31] Part of that enjoyment may have come from the unanticipated consequences of her very first article, which led her into labor activism as well as journalism. Valesh had selected a garment factory for her first undercover assignment. Within two weeks, workers there went on strike after a pay cut. Although Valesh had not caused the strike, she instantly became involved in it, supporting the women workers by speaking at a strike meeting. There she caught the attention of a male labor activist, who told her: "I heard your talk to the girls. Now look here, I think you'd make a good speaker. Would you like to try it? I might help you." "Oh yes, I'd love to try it," Valesh remembered responding. This mentor, a member of the Knights of Labor, took her to different union meetings during the week in order to give each "a little pep talk." "My newspaper work really began at about the same time as my training as a public speaker," Valesh noted.[32]

Valesh and her mentor spoke together at various union meetings for the better part of a year. "I couldn't have said why I so eagerly embraced the labor movement," she later wrote, but she found the combination of public speaking and newspaper work "absorbing."[33] Her career as both labor activist and journalist quickly accelerated after this fast start. She became a state lecturer for the Minnesota Farmers' Alliance, she wrote well-received "Eva Gay" pieces for the *St. Paul Globe* for a year, and then became labor editor and a general reporter for the paper. Valesh also began to publish articles in the labor press, including the AFL journal the *American Federationist*. She was a speaker for the Populists in 1891, spoke on "Women and Labor" at the 1891 national convention of the AFL, lectured at the 1893 Labor Congress at the Chicago World's Fair, and spoke at numerous local and state events. A connecting thread in all of her labor activism was an interest in women's labor and women's working conditions.[34]

By the time she and her husband, labor organizer Frank Valesh, traveled to Europe in 1896, Valesh was able to finance the trip in part by writing articles from Europe for newspaper syndicates. As she wrote to a friend, the editor of the *Minneapolis Tribune*, "I think I told you Bacheller & Johnson will take my European letters." She also had "some expectations with the American Press Association" and was "getting excellent column rates for some 'stories' for the New York papers."[35] While in Europe she studied labor conditions and wrote a series of detailed articles for the *American Federationist*.[36]

By the time she returned to Minneapolis from Europe, Valesh was ready for a new phase of her life—as her biographer Elizabeth Faue says, "She longed to move from the confines of Minneapolis labor politics to a wider world."[37] Leaving her husband behind (they would eventually divorce), she decided to try New York newspapers—and in the fall of 1897 managed to land a job as a reporter at the *New York Journal* through her journalism connections. Someone she knew at the *Minneapolis Tribune* knew someone at Hearst's *Journal*. She was told she could be placed "in the city room as a reporter, but I'd be on my own after that; also that a reporter would have to be 'sensationally clever' to stay. A stranger in New York would have a slim chance of making good."[38]

"For the first time," Valesh remembered, "I was a reporter on a regular assignment, and I was paid for what appeared in the paper" (that is, space rates based on her weekly "string"). "I might turn in a good story. If they didn't have room for it and it was out, I didn't get paid for it. Still I earned more money" that "year than I had ever earned any year in my life." But at first she was not overemployed. "I was around the city room for about three months doing trifling assignments that mostly didn't evolve into stories. Charles Edwards, one of the city editors, didn't like me. He said, 'I just don't like a woman on a paper, that's all. I've got nothing against that girl.' He would give me assignments that wouldn't get in the paper, or they'd only get about an inch, which was kind of tough on me. But you couldn't send me out that I didn't come in with a story on my own that I picked up without being assigned to it."[39]

"When I had been with the paper about three months," Valesh wrote, "I began to feel that I wasn't making good according to their standards. I wasn't surprised when one day Mr. Anderson, one of our city editors, called me to the desk and told me I was about to be let out. 'They have ordered an impossible assignment and that will be the excuse. I'm sorry,' he said. 'There was a girl who committed suicide by drinking carbolic acid right on Fourteenth Street the day before yesterday. You are to identify her.'" Other reporters had been unable to make the identification; it was a way of easily letting Valesh go because of the "failure" to get an assigned story.[40]

But based on a lucky tip from a newsboy who happened to have known the woman, Valesh made the identification. Not only did she "make good," she began to be assigned "political news" in the middle of a "hot municipal campaign." This meant that Valesh "came in contact" with "leading club women" who would become important to her when she much later began the *American Clubwoman's Magazine*.[41]

After months of working for the *Journal*, she received her first labor assignment—the New Bedford strike of early 1898. "I was summoned to Mr. Hearst's office," Valesh remembered. "He said, 'Of course, we are a bit sensational. Do you understand enough of the way we run our papers to be able to give us the sort of a story we want?'" "'Yes, sir,' I said."[42]

What Valesh seems to have understood was that she should not just write newspaper stories but also create the news. She quickly embraced Hearst's idea of the "journalism that acts." The *Journal*, which had hardly noticed Valesh before, much less used her considerable talents and expertise to cover labor issues, now trumpeted her labor qualifications (though it managed to spell her name wrong): "Journal Woman with Strikers" read the headline that introduced her to readers; "Eva Macdonald [*sic*] Valesh, International Labor Commissioner, Tells of New England's Fight for Living Wages." "Herself a worker and member of a dozen labor unions," the *Journal* proclaimed, "she brings to her work not only the technical knowledge necessary to an intelligent discussion of the conditions she will find in the disturbed labor centres, but also the skill and tact of a thoroughly trained and brilliant newspaper woman."[43]

Describing Valesh as an "International Labor Commissioner" for the *Journal* was one of Hearst's many attempts to create official-sounding, quasi-governmental roles for correspondents—part of his larger effort to establish a directly political and interventionist role for journalism. Certainly he could not have picked a better person to be the paper's "Labor Commissioner." After years of labor activism, Valesh was hardly content with simply writing stories about "starving workers." Later she recalled: "There was another lady from New York, from the New York *World*. I saw that she sent in stories about the oldest striker, the youngest striker and that sort of thing. I thought, 'Here these people have real grievances.'" (In fact, it was Valesh's own *Journal* colleague Anne O'Hagan who sent in the oldest-youngest striker story, but this memory revealed that there was no automatic sisterhood among newspaper women, even from the same newspaper, who "out on assignment" were often in direct competition with one another.)[44]

Valesh quickly zeroed in on a striker named Harriet Pickering, who sought to be leader of the striking women but faced a number of frustrating obstacles, many of them gender-related. "A Lancashire lass is leading 4,000 women strikers of eighteen cloth mills," Valesh began her first article from New Bedford, describing Pickering as "brave as a lion." As the newspaper women would quickly learn, Pickering also had a serious grievance in addition to the wage cut: the cloth mills in New Bedford engaged in a punitive fining system for supposed "imperfections" in weaving, which reduced the real wages of weavers substantially. This elaborate, secret fining system stripped workers of pay even for "imperfections" over which they had no control—such as cloth damaged as a result of machinery dripping oil or breaking down. Mill owners did not provide any explanation of why women weavers were being fined—the women simply received substantially less pay than they had been expecting. As a large percentage of weavers were women, this was a distinct woman's issue—one that Pickering had been fighting for years.[45]

Valesh had found the heroine on whom she would hang her feminist story of the strike—at least initially. She approvingly highlighted Pickering's activism at a strike meeting:

"Harriet Pickering said that 'We must make the "fining system" an issue just as much as the 10 per cent cut to wages.'"

"'Sit down!' yelled a man, who has no objection to his wife working in the mill with him, but thinks a woman out of place in a public meeting.

"'Not I,' she retorted, her big, gray eyes flashing fire, 'your Executive Committee know I am right, but they have grown timid.'

"The hundreds of women applauded and the men looked doubtful. A secret ballot, however, endorsed the woman leader's point of view, and the weavers will insist that the 'fining system' be materially altered before they go back to work."[46]

Tellingly, over the next days Valesh presented Pickering as in many ways a double of Valesh herself. She focused on the activist's speaking abilities and the fact that she had studied economics (just like Valesh, who had been in an economics study group in Minnesota); she stressed her leadership skills. Undoubtedly Valesh identified with Pickering—even as she used her for her own purposes. But that usage went both ways: Pickering also fastened onto Valesh as someone who might help her change the fining system.

A day after printing Valesh's first article, the *Journal* ran a large illustration of Pickering, with the caption "Harriet Pickering, Leader of the New Bedford Strikers." But the accompanying article began to maneuver Eva Valesh herself, who had no shortage of ego, into position as the strike's real heroine. Valesh had had a new idea: "Why not go to the legislature," she later wrote, "and get it to pass a resolution to appoint a committee to hold hearings of both the workers and the employers, and see if the strike can be settled." She found a member of the legislature willing to sponsor this resolution and with him quickly "drew it up."[47]

Valesh's "legislative committee" was now trumpeted as the "Journal's Plan." In a burst of self-advertisement over the next few weeks, the *Journal* took credit, through Valesh, for successful intervention in the strike (even though the strike still continued). Valesh's resolution to form an investigative committee "was adopted quite readily," she remembered. "The legislators didn't seem to have any objection to it." But the lack of objection probably came from the fact that such a committee had no power whatsoever: merely informational, it had no provisions for enforcement and did not even require employers to furnish any records for inspection. On January 19 Eva Valesh's daily *Journal* article nevertheless was headlined "Journal's Plan to End Strike Gladly Accepted; Introduced To-day in the Massachusetts Legislature; Investigation Asked." The "Legislature of Massachusetts will be asked to mediate in the cotton weavers' strike," Valesh wrote. "Never has there been a more important and far-reaching investigation than this suggested by the Journal and so promptly indorsed by Massachusetts legislators."[48]

This was a heady success for Valesh. But as she grew interested in possible political solutions to the strike, and as she increasingly relished her own prominent public role, her temporary alliance with Harriet Pickering unraveled. Pickering wanted to eradicate fining entirely. This was the issue she cared passionately about, which she brought to the attention of the many newspaper men and women in New Bedford, including reporters from the *Boston Journal* and the *Atlanta Constitution*.[49]

But not all female weavers agreed with Pickering that the issues of fining and wages should both be addressed during the strike: some wanted to concentrate on wages alone. And when Pickering attempted to foreground the issue of fining by holding public meetings of the weavers, she met resistance from both women and men. "Twice now the women strikers have been invited to a meeting to discuss the fines question," Elizabeth Banks noted in an article subtitled "Revolt against the Leadership of Harriet Pickering, the Young English Woman," and "both times there have been hard words and refusals to be 'led around by the nose,' as they express."[50] Banks, who at first had merely seen the strikers as jollier and more fashionable than she expected, had already become an excellent portraitist.

Banks captured some of Pickering's passion: "'Down with the fine system,' she cries, her thin, white face fiercely set and her eyes burning. 'You call yourselves Americans,' she said the other day to a few women who went to the hall for the meeting. 'You are slaves—white slaves, such slaves as nowhere exist in England. I have worked in Lancashire cotton mills and know what I'm talking about. I have become a citizen of the United States and an inhabitant of your town and State, and I am going to do my duty by you and myself and abolish the slavery of the fining system.'"[51]

But many strikers did not support Pickering in her sense of duty. Men in particular opposed a woman speaking in public. Thus, when Pickering attempted to hold a meeting of women weavers, men, who also did not support a woman's independent actions unsanctioned by the weavers' executive committee, created a disturbance. "Hissed a Woman: Mrs. Pickering Driven Off Stage by Weavers," said one newspaper account. Elizabeth Banks reported that when she "reached the hall she found a dozen women and many men and boys, the latter with their hats on and smoking" (signs of disrespect). "Mrs. Picking [sic] asked them to leave the hall. They refused. Then she decided they must stop smoking and remove their hats. They answered her with cat calls and hisses. The table over which she stood was removed from the platform and her gavel taken away, but for a while she continued her speech. Finally she gave up in despair and left the hall, declaring her intention of holding the meeting at another time." Banks observed: "Not all of the striking female weavers sympathize with the Lancashire woman. They know their men do not approve of Harriet Picking's [sic] leadership, and they themselves are inclined to 'give in' on certain points against which she will hold out forever."[52] Banks had become an astute observer of the pushback against female leadership among both men and women.

Meanwhile, Anne O'Hagan had found her own heroine to narrate the story of the strike: "She is the bravest woman in New Bedford," O'Hagan wrote. "Her name is Jane Gallagher. Her occupation is weaving in the cotton mills. Her bravery is not the Boadicean sort, that arms itself with sword and shield and goes out to battle with its foes. It is the rarer, more significant kind that resists oppression strenuously and steadily, and that, without any sounding cymbals, announces its intention never to yield to injustice."[53]

When Gallagher was fined for an imperfection in the cloth she was weaving, she "did not grumble, did not weep, did not seek to ease the sting of rebuke or robbery by any of the customary feminine sedatives." Rather, "she said to the Hathaway corporation: 'I will not be fined.'" At that, "the Hathaway corporation smiled," O'Hagan commented. "It is not to be blamed for that. The Hathaway corporation is very rich; it owns millions of dollars; it controls thousands of laborers. And here was a plain little woman with an Irish face and a Lancashire brogue defying it. The Hathaway corporation leaned back in its big, leather office chair and laughed heartily." But "Jane Gallagher took her hat and shawl off their peg and trotted quietly out into the mill yard and thence to her home. She never even shook her capable, hard little fist at the Hathaway corporation's offices." Instead, Gallagher—supported by the Weavers' Union—sued the Hathaway corporation, although the suit had "dragged through a year."[54]

Only two days after O'Hagan's article appeared, the *Journal* took up Gallagher's cause, offering to pay her legal costs. O'Hagan described Gallagher as "tremulous with excitement" over this news. "'I don't know how I can thank the Evening Journal,'" she reportedly said. "'It is no longer for myself that I care. It was never for that particular fifty cents that I cared. And now no matter how much I should win, they'd never let me work in the mills again. So that winning or losing, doesn't matter to me personally. But if we win—and we will now that the Evening Journal is going to help—they will never be so unjust again. The other women will profit by it.'" O'Hagan sentimentally concluded that the "little, brown haired woman, who does not mind black listing and boycotting for herself, provided that she benefits other working women, smiled happily."[55]

Again, it seemed that newspaper women and working women had used each other to good purpose. Over the next few days O'Hagan provided an informative set of articles on fining, always using Jane Gallagher as her "peg." She explained that "the championship of Jane Gallagher by the Evening Journal has brought out a great many interesting facts concerning the fines system and a great deal of really interesting theory." It was clear that Anne O'Hagan herself was learning a great deal about New Bedford labor practices. She noted that "the corporations of New Bedford save annually from $50,000 to $75,000 by the fines system." She also pointed out that fining had in recent years grown more onerous, according to information provided by "old weavers." "A fine of 30 cents" had once been regarded as "enormous, and was seldom imposed. Now the fines amount to 50 per cent of the price to be paid for a piece of cloth to be woven. That, of course, is outrageous," she declared.[56]

O'Hagan found a former weaver willing to tell her story of being fined. "'I can tell what I know about fines,'" said Lola Minet, "fearlessly." "'I was fined every week I worked in the Hathaway mills last Summer. I could earn over $7 a week but for fines. I never received more than $5. Why am I not afraid to talk? Because I couldn't get work in any mill in this city from now till doom's-day anyhow. I'm blacklisted.'" Through O'Hagan, it seemed, working women were able to find a voice within the public arena of print culture.[57]

In the meantime, Eva Valesh took another path entirely. Fresh from her success in lobbying the Massachusetts legislature, she traveled to Washington, D.C., and using her connections obtained an interview with President McKinley on the strike. The *New York Journal* made the most of this coup by its "Labor Commissioner," with headlines reading "McKinley Talks to the Journal about the Great Strike: He Confers with the Journal Commissioner: An Expert: She Has Just Investigated the District Affected," and "'Restriction [meaning immigration restriction] Is the First Thing to Be Done,' Says President McKinley." Her interview received a full two-page spread, complete with her photograph as well as an illustration of Valesh talking to the president.[58]

"I interviewed President McKinley to-day on the textile strike in New England," Valesh boasted under her byline. "A prominent Senator presented me and informed the President that I have been making a special investigation of the conditions as they actually exist in the principal mill-centres of that section." The bland interview that followed highlighted Valesh's supposed role in the strike: "'So you have been investigating the condition of the strikers in New England?'" the president reportedly asked. "'Tell me about them. I have heard nothing definite.'" Valesh "explained as concisely as possible that the whole trouble seemed to resolve itself into a question of whether the manufacturers were really obliged to cut wages ten per cent and whether the operatives could live on that reduced amount." "'Yes, I suppose that is about the essence of the question,'" said the president "thoughtfully." "'I suppose it is pretty difficult to tell just where the trouble lies. The manufacturers may feel obliged to make the cut in ways to keep their mills going.'"[59]

No matter how innocuous this interview was, Valesh had scored a significant "beat" by interviewing the president—and the *Journal* gave her a splashy spread. Once back in Massachusetts, she continued to perform the "journalism that acts," then followed up by trumpeting her achievements. Valesh next highlighted what she called the "Journal's Bill to Protect the Weavers," a measure written by her that was introduced to the Massachusetts legislature. Meant to address the fining issue, the bill provided that weavers be given advance written notice of their fines—but made no other requirements of mill owners.[60]

On February 10 Valesh reported: "I have been duly registered under the law of Massachusetts as the counsel for the New York Journal to represent it before the Legislature on the measure known as the Weavers' Fines bill." In an article titled "State Listens to a Journal Woman, Labor's Champion: Mrs. Valesh Officially Presents the Journal's Weavers' Bill," Valesh highlighted her own triumphs in acting as "counsel" at a legislative hearing in which she questioned mill owners about the fining system.[61]

But here came a parting of the ways with Pickering. Valesh's proposed bill, after all, did nothing to eliminate the fining system, nor did it provide any sanctions for owners. Pickering wanted fines entirely eliminated; she viewed Valesh's bill as worse than the current system, and threw in her lot, in this one instance, with the opposition—she supported the owners. This could not have been an easy decision: Pickering had fought against the owners for years. Valesh's actions must have felt like a betrayal.

Clearly, however, any perceived betrayal went two ways. In her reminiscences Valesh savagely dismissed Pickering: "The first witness was a woman who had been very vocal in the early days of the strike about the woes of the strikers. She appeared for the employers, said that everything was all right and the employer had no grievance of any sort. Asked if I wanted to cross-examine her, I replied, 'No, I don't think so because I don't think she's mentally capable. I know about her.'"[62]

Yet Valesh *did* cross-examine Pickering in 1898: the evidence is in her own self-promoting article for the *Journal* about the hearing. "Under cross-examination by the Journal's counsel" (meaning herself), Valesh reported, "Mrs. Pickering admitted that she herself had suffered grievously under the fining system." According to Valesh, Pickering had "burst out impetuously" with the admission that she had been "fined so heavily" that she "could not pay the rent and take care of" her child, as she should have been able to do with what she earned—"evidently forgetting the lesson which had been carefully conned for her speech against the bill." Valesh observed that the counsel for the mill owners "looked sad at this outbreak of his principal witness." He asked Pickering: "'Then you believe fining unfair and unjust?'" "'Certainly, it is,'" she answered decisively. Pickering also admitted that she had once supported an antifining bill and had been "blacklisted for it by the mill owners." She had had to change her name to get work.[63]

"It was not necessary to say anything further" was Valesh's comment on this testimony. "A more pitiable subject could scarcely be imagined than this woman who has spent her life at the loom, and now, broken in health and spirits, evidently fears to oppose the mill owners on a measure which she admits would help the weavers."[64]

But of course Pickering did *not* admit that Valesh's bill would help the weavers: quite the contrary, she obviously believed that Valesh's interference might make the fining situation even worse. On behalf of her bill, Valesh argued that written records of "imperfections" in weaving could be useful evidence in court cases, should weavers choose to formally protest fines. But Pickering must surely have felt that a written record of "imperfections" could also be used *against* the weavers, especially given the fact that the powerful Arkwright Trust controlled the cotton mills, and workers had no significant protections against their employers.[65]

In February 1898, a month after the strike began, intensive newspaper coverage of the labor dispute suddenly ended. With the sinking of the USS *Maine* off Cuba on February 16, the attention of the great "yellow" newspapers immediately turned elsewhere. The strike went on, but the newspaper women were pulled from the story; they left New Bedford, never to return. Whatever their sympathies may have been with the striking weavers, newspaper women abandoned them now. The *Journal* withdrew its support from Jane Gallagher, and Harriet Pickering was left to fight unfair fines on her own.

Yet Pickering had learned something from Eva Valesh. Far from being "broken in health and spirits" simply because she disagreed with Valesh, the labor activist continued to fight for a new fines bill. "Mrs. Harriet Pickering has drawn up a new fines bill and means to secure the passage through the legislature if the weavers will turn to and help her," a newspaper reported in February. "I opposed the other bill," she said, "because it wasn't so favorable to the weavers as the one already in existence. But now I have drawn up one which I believe will prove better than the other, and if the 5,000 weavers will take hold with me we can secure its passage." She concluded, "We will never be free from fines till they are abolished once and for all." In March, Pickering appeared at the Massachusetts State House "to champion her fines bill" (it did not pass). Although Eva Valesh's committees and bills had done nothing to help weavers directly, they had given Pickering ideas of new strategies to use in fighting for her cause.[66]

For her part, by championing working women Eva Valesh strengthened her own career—although not at the *Journal*, ironically enough. Back on the job in New York, Valesh slipped off the running board of a streetcar on a rainy day and strained her back, which forced her to remain in the hospital for several weeks. Despite her success as "Labor Commissioner" and the sensations she had created for the *Journal*, she found on returning to work that "they'd filled my place without even notifying me."[67] She decided to move to Washington, D.C., where she freelanced as a journalist before joining forces with a male editor to begin a syndicated letter on politics.

As for Pickering, in May 1898 she decided to leave the "Grinnell Mill in consequence of a deduction from her wages under the grading system." To a newspaper interviewer she commented that "I have always advocated that weavers who do not do satisfactory work should be discharged, not fined. I did not intend to go back on my principles. I don't think the poor work was my fault." Nevertheless, she was "now looking for a situation as a double or single entry bookkeeper."[68]

In the end, it turned out that Valesh and Pickering actually had a great deal in common. They were both strong, forceful personalities; they were both articulate and impassioned public speakers; they were both interested in bettering the lives of working women; they were both public figures. Last but not least, they were both ill-treated in their jobs.

Yet there was also a necessary divide between the two women. The very nature of their work put them fundamentally at odds with one another. For years Pickering had worked as a weaver, as well as dedicating herself to trying to find a solution to the injustice of the fining system. Valesh's job as a journalist, on the other hand, undercut any such steady dedication to one cause. Out on assignment, she needed to do the work her employer asked her to do; to keep her job, she needed to find fresh sensations, to take up fresh assignments. Newspaper work demanded that a reporter move on to the new.

As Elizabeth Banks found out, however, that was not so easy once war loomed. War fever meant that her working-girl stories could no longer find a place in the newspaper. "War! war! war!" she wrote in her autobiography. "Get up something about the war! No use writing about other subjects." Those "who could not do 'war stories' fared not sumptuously," she admitted. "Oh, the scramble after inspirations that had in them the hint of blood and war!" "More than ever in those days space-writers 'lived by their wits,' for it was no easy matter for men and women living in New York, far away from the actual war, to get up a column, or two or three columns every day on some subject" related to war. "God pity those who could not at command turn their thoughts warward and dip their pens into blood!"[69]

Soon Banks returned to England. O'Hagan left newspaper work for magazines. Valesh moved to Washington. Like so many other newspaper women, they had made a journey that took them *through* newspapers—but they found it impossible to stay in newspaper work for the long haul.

# # #

Yet stories of working girls continued to exert a powerful pull in newspapers—and to draw new newspaper women to New York. The case of Dorothy Richardson, who arrived in 1900, enables us to examine the early newspaper culture of going "undercover" as a working girl—and to explore ethical questions involved in such work.

Richardson is famous as the initially anonymous author of the *The Long*

Day: The Story of a New York Working Girl, published in 1905, one of the most prominent examples of the extensive "working-girl" literature published at the turn of the century.[70] The first-person story of a young Pennsylvania schoolteacher forced by circumstances to seek work in the factories of New York, *The Long Day* created a sensation when it was published.

Historians and literary critics have long known that at some point in her career Richardson worked at the *New York Herald*. Indeed, one critic has noted that "while working for the *Herald*" Richardson "did the research for a series on the life of a working girl that she published anonymously as *The Long Day* in 1905."[71] But Richardson did not just do research for a book on working girls while she worked at the *Herald* in 1900 and 1901 she published a series of newspaper articles on working girls. These were, in fact, experimental versions of her 1905 book—in one article, for instance, a few paragraphs are word for word the same as in the later book. Next, she significantly revised and expanded the series, publishing articles in *Frank Leslie's Popular Monthly* in 1903 and 1904. Several of the *Leslie's* articles are exactly the same as chapters of the 1905 book (there are interesting differences between magazine and book, as well).

Although these earlier newspaper and magazine articles were precursors to her famous *The Long Day*, they have escaped the notice of critics. As this book has argued, newspapers (and, for that matter, "cheap" literature) have often been ignored as part of literary history, thus obscuring a literary journey like Richardson's. Yet the path Richardson traveled from newspaper to book has much to tell us not only about the ethical dilemmas involved in going undercover, but also about the ways in which the demands and practices of newspapers could compromise the work of female reporters.

When she began her working-girl series for the *New York Herald*, Richardson built on her own prior interest in, and knowledge of, labor issues. She had started newspaper work at the *Pittsburgh Dispatch* in 1896, then moved to Chicago, where, from 1897 to 1899, she was "engaged on local newspapers and socialist propaganda" and "connected successively with the *Social Democrat*, Eugene V. Debs' organ of Socialism, and the *New Time* magazine."[72] We can probably exactly date the somewhat surprising connection to Debs: on a social visit to Milwaukee in July 1897, while still working for the *Dispatch*, Richardson managed to score a lengthy interview with the union leader and prominent socialist, who happened to be in Milwaukee at the same time.[73]

Richardson's interview, which appeared in the *Milwaukee Sentinel*, revealed her to be a forthright questioner and a strong personality, with an interest in women workers' lives that remained a unifying thread throughout her later work. In "Women in Debs's Colony: There Will Be a Place for Them Later On," Richardson pressed Debs on the question of women's role in his visionary cooperative commonwealth. "But you have not said one word about women or what part they will take in this great cooperative commonwealth that you are about to establish," she exclaimed. "Do you expect to adopt any specific measures toward the emancipation and advancement of wage-earning women?"[74]

"At the mention of the word 'women,'" Richardson wrote, "the clear cut features of the socialist's face assumed an expression half doubtful, yet suffused with a kindly, compassionate light." "'Women, women,' slowly he repeated the word, dropping his face in his hands" and for some time "allowing his eyes to follow the intricate figure of the Wilton velvet on the floor."[75]

"'Women? What part will women play in the Social Democracy?'" Debs continued at last. "'Well, that question is sort of a riddle. To tell you the truth I cannot exactly define the attitude which the Social Democracy will assume toward women,'" Debs said, before then asserting that women would "'stand according to our constitution on a perfect equality with men.'"[76]

"But what about women in the colony you propose establishing in Washington," Richardson quickly followed up. "Have there not been any definite plans laid for giving employment as soon as the colony is established to at least a few of the tens of thousands of unemployed, self-supporting women to be found in the populous cities?"[77]

"'Oh yes; to be sure,' Debs responded, 'but you must remember that Rome was not built in a day. . . . In the beginning there will not be any work that would be at all suited to women, not even to the most advanced of her sex. What we shall require there will be force of rugged, able-bodied men.'" The "'work will be arduous and you will pardon my frankness, but there will be no room for women, nor do we care to be bothered with them.'" But eventually, Debs assured her, "'we expect to have established divers occupations in which women may engage without jeopardy to either the physical or moral nature.'"[78]

Richardson's impatience with this response was clear. She immediately pressed Debs on his attitude toward the "New Woman": "How do you regard the new woman, Mr. Debs, and will she be allowed as many privileges in your colony as she assumes elsewhere?" Debs was evasive and noncommittal. But whether or not he found her a difficult interviewer—and whether or not she found his replies satisfactory—the next year Richardson was in Chicago working on Debs's newspaper.[79]

In 1900 Richardson moved to New York, where she would help to support her younger brother and two younger sisters. "I have Hazel here now, besides my brother and other sister Florence," she wrote to her friend and mentor Wallace Rice, a Chicago writer and newspaper man, "and we are getting along very nicely together. Hazel is going to school and studying very hard." Richardson initially worked as a proofreader, but she also sought newspaper work; and by early January 1901 she was able to tell Rice about a newspaper triumph: "I mailed you this A.M. two copies of the magazine section of the Herald," she wrote. Both copies contained "installments of my 'Adventures of a Country School Teacher in New York.'" Richardson had recently published a series of articles about the struggles of a young woman to find work and lodging in New York. One, titled "Work or Starve: Woman's Heartbreaking Search for Employment in the Great City," revealed "the Bitter Struggle of the Would-be Breadwinner." Another was "The Girl Who Lives on $5 a Week," with a subtitle promising that Richardson "Tries the Experiment and Tells How It Is Done."[80]

Richardson was proud of her work for the *Herald*, informing Rice that "I am getting along very nicely, being kept constantly busy by the Herald." But she also expressed some anxiety about the fact that her "stories" were not being published under her own name: "You will notice that" they "are written over the name of Dorothy Adams," she said. "Please do not think I have adopted a nom de plume, for I have not, but it was deemed expedient by Mr. Reick" (one of her editors) "and by Mr. Dinwiddie, the Sunday editor, that I should sign some fictitious name to these particular stories, and the first name that came into my head was that of Adams."[81]

Using a pseudonym turned out to be a fateful decision, as was Richardson's choice to write her stories as fiction, pretending to be a schoolteacher from Pennsylvania. At the turn of the century a combination of fiction and fact, as in Elizabeth Jordan's "True Stories of the News" for the *New York World*, was common in newspapers. But what was unusual about Richardson's stories was her continued deception of readers, telling them she was a struggling working girl when she was really a newspaper woman out on assignment.

Although other newspaper women had created characters and voices — from "Bab" to "Beatrice Fairfax" to "Ellen Osborne" — they never asked readers to believe lengthy personal stories of hardship that were based on a false premise. Still others, including Eva Valesh (as Eva Gay), Nell Cusack (as Nell Nelson), and Elizabeth Cochrane (as Nellie Bly), had also gone undercover as working women, but they had always tipped their hand to the reader. Indeed, an important part of their working-girl stories was taking the reader with them as they went undercover into different workplaces—that was part of the adventure their articles offered. Readers always knew that they were reading the story of a newspaper woman who had assumed a new identity. Richardson, by contrast, never admitted in her working-girl stories that she was actually a newspaper woman. In some ways this makes Richardson doubly interesting: she crossed a line that had not yet been fully articulated in a newspaper world that still accepted many forms of "faking it." The fact that she may not have *meant* to cross this line—that she was apparently willing to sign her real name to her stories, but was instructed not to do so by her editors—simply adds another layer of complication to her deception.

Later Richardson would insist that her stories were real—that she herself had struggled to find work in New York, after all, just like her alter ego, Dorothy Adams. She maintained that she had engaged in the types of work that she described in her newspaper and magazine articles, as well as in her book—even if only for a week or two. But was a former schoolteacher who temporarily worked in a factory or department store really a working girl? Who could legitimately make that claim? From the start, Richardson's claim to be a working girl, even as she secretly worked as a newspaper woman, complicated the stories she told, making the "reality" of her stories hard to determine.

The fact that Richardson drew heavily on fiction to frame her narrative further clouded the issue of exactly what type of "reality" she offered. As she made clear in an interview published after her success with *The Long Day*, she was inspired by both Charles Dickens and Susan Warner in constructing her working-girl persona. Asked about the genesis of her book, Richardson explained that "it soon fell upon me to go out in the world and seek my fortune, as the story books say. I like that phrase. It had always appealed to my imagination. I had read and wept over such books as 'The Wide, Wide World' and 'David Copperfield.' They were, above all others, the sort of stories I liked best to read. Not only did I love to pore over them on cold winter nights, when the wind howled down the chimneys of our old house, but I used to dream how jolly it would be to actually live such stories myself. David Copperfield, perhaps, made the greatest impression upon me, and when I was a small girl I used to play being David Copperfield."[82]

"The interior of our barn was Darkest London," Richardson continued, "and within its four dusty, cobwebby walls I acted and reacted the hardships and privations of poor David. Sometimes, when I happened to be in a particularly philosophical mood . . . my mind would speculate upon what might have happened if David Copperfield had been born a girl and baptized Betsy Trotwood. A girl was expected, you know, and David's great-aunt, Miss Betsy Trotwood, never quite forgave him for not being a girl. Supposing, then, that David had been a girl doomed to the same hazard of fortune? What would Charles Dickens have written of Betsy Copperfield cast adrift in London at the tender age of ten years? It was my belief that, much as I loved to read of David's hardships, I should have found my mythical Betsy Copperfield even more absorbing. Why did all the great story writers choose to exploit only the boys and young men who went out into the world to seek their fortunes? I had read all the romances of Balzac and Victor Hugo and Eugene Sue and Dumas, and they all glorified the achievements of boys and men, of poor, inexperienced boys who left their homes in the provinces to go up to London or Paris all a-seeking fortune and adventure."[83]

"I made up my mind," Richardson said, "when I grew up I'd go out and seek my fortune, I'd be Betsy Copperfield, and after I had suffered all sorts of hardships, besides which David's would pale into mere temporary discomfort, a handsome banker should fall in love with and marry me, and then I'd write my story just as David Copperfield wrote his. Alas! I little dreamed that some day not many years off I should be obliged to go forth and realize my dream in deadly and terrible earnest."[84]

"That childish fancy dreamed and enacted in the old barn was, however, to become in later years the real animus of my work," Richardson concluded. "I had always wanted to write the story of the feminine David Copperfield, and two years ago when opportunity offered I did so."[85]

There are many interesting aspects of this self-conscious interview, from its startling romanticization of and fascination with poverty (also a major aspect of slumming literature of this period), to its evocation of the happy endings to be found in fairy tales. But most striking is the power that Richardson gave to the act of reading itself, which for her held transformative potential. As she presented it, reading did not just frame her experience; it was itself an experience capable of inspiring action.[86]

In her working-girl stories Richardson reshaped older plots to new ends. Victorian plots of suffering women had often involved involuntary adventures: women who wanted nothing more than a safe domesticity were instead cast into the world for a variety of reasons (think of Jane Eyre, for instance) and underwent great suffering before being restored to their rightful place in society. Richardson provided an updated version of this plot by presenting an initial embrace of adventure followed inevitably by the discovery that the adventure had *not* been an adventure after all. As we have seen, a number of "bachelor girl" stories were also constructed along these lines.

In a paradoxical logic—one that underlay her newspaper articles as well as her later book—it was precisely the discovery that the adventure was *not* an adventure that defined it as an adventure. The importance of this disillusionment and suffering was a connecting thread running throughout her working-girl stories, which provided a new feminine bildungsroman. Embracing an ethos of experience, stories of adventurous suffering offered a mirror image of a masculine literature—most forcefully articulated by Teddy Roosevelt—that stressed the value of the "strenuous life."[87]

Some five years before the publication of her book, Richardson's December 1900 *Herald* article, "Work or Starve," had introduced almost exactly the same themes of adventurous suffering—and in remarkably similar terms. "When I was teaching in the tiny little red school house back among my Pennsylvania hills," Richardson wrote in the character of Dorothy Adams, "I used to love, on the long, cold winter nights, when the wind whistled at every keyhole, and the big, wide mouthed chimney roared like the fiery furnace itself, and my little brothers and sisters studied their lessons and munched big red apples, while Rick, the hired hand, cracked hickory nuts for the whole family on the worn hearthstone: I used to love on such nights to pull my rocking chair into the chimney corner and read magazine stories about girls who lived in hall bedrooms, on little or nothing a week, and of what good times they had, or seemed to have, with never being quite certain where the next meal was coming from, or whether it was coming at all."[88]

"And oh!" Adams exclaimed, "what fun those girls in the magazine stories had washing out their handkerchiefs in the face bowl and plastering them over the looking glass and window panes to dry! How jolly it was to be so poor that they hadn't even street car fare and were obliged to walk all manner of distances in all kinds of unspeakable weather, and how deliciously dreadful it was when they reached the point where it became necessary to cut insoles for their shoes out of blotting paper, or, as was often the case, where one pair of shoes or one jacket had to suffice for two girls until one or the other of them got a job!"[89]

But soon Dorothy Adams discovered that "real life" was not an adventure. "Now I am ashamed to sit here and write it, but it is the honest truth that I used to envy these girls their adventures. I used to wish when I had finished reading such stories that I only had the opportunity. I used to compare their lot with mine. . . . But the real life of the girl who supports herself on $5 a week in a great city like New York is far, very far, from the story book's ideal. The life of such a girl has in it much more of tragedy than it has of comedy. There is nothing jolly about any of it."[90] Yet such a protest, far from simply puncturing the myths surrounding the "life of the girl who supports herself," served to recycle all the elements of the bachelor girl fantasy.

In her *Herald* articles of 1900 and 1901, Richardson took readers on a tour whose highlights had already been well established by newspaper women before her. One article, for instance, discussed going to New York and failing to find lodging; another, trying to find work; and a third, living on five dollars a week. All three of these topics were well-trod ground by 1900; several years earlier Elizabeth Banks had written a series on "how to live on $3 a week."

But Richardson's innovation was the creation of the fictional character Dorothy Adams, and the heart-rending terms in which she was described. The first article in the series was headlined with a question: "Is an Unattended Woman Arriving in New York at Night, Entitled to No Consideration at a Reputable Hotel?" As the subhead put it: "Miss Adams Tried One Broadway Hotel after Another Only to Be Told There Were No Accommodations for Her—How Many Other Women Strangers in This City Have Had Similar Experiences?" Dorothy Adams related that as she entered the city, "a terrible loneliness crept over me. Alone, at midnight, I was approaching for the first time the great, the terrible city of New York. So lonely did I feel that it seemed years since I had left home. Yet in the early dawn of that very morning I had watched the little red schoolhouse on the hill fade away into the grayness of a Western Pennsylvania landscape." (The "little red schoolhouse" was a persistent motif for Richardson.)[91]

The article's plot was a feminine picaresque that took her from one hotel to another, where she was denied a room each time because she was a single woman. Given that the lack of hotels for women was a real problem at the turn of the century, Richardson was careful to cue the reader to the desired emotional response: "When I reached the street again, the tears would insist upon coming into my eyes and trickling down my cheeks," Adams said. Eventually she found her way to the entrance to Central Park, where she slept on a bench. (The article included a photograph of a woman on a bench; Richardson later revealed that her sister had posed for the *Herald* photographer.) Throughout, the article maintained the fiction that Dorothy Adams did not understand why she was continually turned away from hotel after hotel, that she did not know hotels would not admit single women. Adams did "not discover until many days after the true and only reason why I had been compelled to walk the streets of New York all that long, long night." Of course, this was an entirely disingenuous comment: Richardson had either been assigned the subject of this article or had suggested it herself.[92]

In her next article, "Work or Starve," Richardson turned to a "woman's heartbreaking search for employment in the Great City of New York," in which Dorothy Adams laid bare "the bitter struggle of the would-be-bread winner." Once again the "plot" was a feminine picaresque, following Adams's travels as she sought work. First she looked for a newspaper job, but with a "weary look which he did not in the least try to conceal," an editor handed her submission back to her. She tried to be a book agent (selling books on commission) but quickly experienced "bitter humiliation," as "at nearly every place I called the door" was "shut in my face." She tried but failed to "get a position in one of the many big department stores." In the meantime, "as may be easily imagined," she told readers, "my condition grew more and more desperate as each weary day wore itself into a still more weary night. By this time I had trained myself down to getting along reasonably well on only two meals a day, but now I found it necessary to practise a still more rigid economy by eating two meals one day and the next day only one; then two and then one." It was "at this juncture when I began to realize what it means to go to bed hungry," Adams confided. "I wonder how many women and girls there are in New York who know what it feels like to go to bed hungry—I do not mean paupers, but honest, decent women and girls, willing and anxious to work."[93]

Moving through what she presented as a descending evolutionary scale of possible work, Adams eventually attempted to get a job as a cigar roller (Rose Pastor Stokes's work in Cleveland) or paper box maker. But even when she tried to "get work in the factories"—a last resort—she was told that only experienced workers were wanted. (Some of those factories—such as a paper box factory—would become the subject of Richardson's more extended magazine pieces and would appear in her book.) At the end of her article Adams had at last found work as a "super" in a theater—"one of the shouting mob of people who rush in at the end of the play." A subhead explained that she was "employed at last in the ballet." Readers would immediately have understood that this was not respectable work for a former Pennsylvania schoolteacher.[94]

Finally, in "The Girl Who Lives on $5 a Week," Richardson took her working-girl character on a quest for a place to live and gave her a happy ending. Kicked out of her boardinghouse because her landlady objected to her job at a Broadway theater, Adams searched for a new boardinghouse or an apartment. By luck she ran into a "little stenographer" on the street who had been a roommate in one of her previous lodgings. The stenographer "had gotten discouraged trying to live in cheap boarding houses and had taken a tiny furnished room in East Sixteenth street, where she was cooking her own breakfast and dinner over a little oil stove and pasting handkerchiefs over her window panes just like the girls in the story books, and when she asked me to come, right then and there, and keep house with her I linked my arm in hers and walked up Third avenue with a joyous heart."[95] In short, Richardson had come full circle: at the beginning of her series she denied the possibility of a jolly, storybook adventure in real life, yet at the end she provided exactly that storybook adventure—one she explicitly said was like the storybooks.

Richardson's articles provoked an immediate response from *Herald* readers, who believed that Dorothy Adams was a real person—and worried about her. "I hope you and Mrs. Rice will read the two stories I sent you," Richardson wrote in excitement to her friend Wallace Rice, "because I am receiving on an average fifty letters a day from all sorts of people who take them as gospel. A poor mechanic has written offering to marry me, four widows want to adopt me, others write offering me kitchen work, and positions in factories, stores, offices, etc. etc. The St. James press, a new publishing house, and the Lewis Literary Syndicate have both made me propositions to bring the stories out in book form, in cheap edition, for selling on news-stands and on trains. I will soon have enough written to make up a volume, and then I'll try it."[96] Here was the kernel of both her *Leslie's* articles and her eventual book.

Richardson now incorporated readers' responses into a new article. Put in a false position through both her use of a pseudonym and the pretense that she was struggling to find a job rather than already working as a newspaper woman, Richardson sought to reassure readers. She wanted to "set at rest the fears of those kind people who have written expressions of interest in my forlorn condition and who wish me godspeed to future prosperity and happiness."[97]

"Letters, letters, letters!," Adams wrote. "How they have come pouring in to me since the recently published accounts of my struggle to obtain employment and live honestly on $5 a week." They had "come from all manner and condition of people, each and every one impelled by one of two motives—to tender advice or to render material assistance to a poor, friendless, inexperienced country girl who, by force of circumstance, not choice, is compelled to seek her fortune in this vast, bewildering metropolis."[98]

One widow had written: "'After I had finished reading your article,

"Work or Starve," in last Sunday's HERALD, I went to bed, and do you know I simply could not get to sleep for hours, thinking of you and the hard struggle which you are having in this big, wicked city. I am a widow, living alone, and in very straitened circumstances, but I am not too poor, I hope, to be able to be of some assistance to a young girl like you. If you will come at any time I will be glad to give you a comfortable bed to sleep in and three plain home cooked meals a day.'"[99]

In an attempt to reassure her concerned readers, Richardson added one falsehood after another to her persona. She was grateful for this and other offers she had received, Adams said, but "to attempt to answer even a small part of this correspondence would require more postage than I can possibly afford out of my scant earnings as a super in a Broadway theatre, and likewise I cannot afford the street car fare necessary to the acceptance of the numerous invitations that have been showered upon me by those who wish me to call upon them in the hope that they may be able to render me some assistance in the way of more congenial and profitable employment."[100]

Over the next several years, Richardson refined her working-girl character further, renaming her "Rose Fortune" and placing her in a variety of types of factory work for the Leslie's series, including making artificial flowers and paper boxes. In the last article in the Leslie's series, Richardson took Rose Fortune to work at Coney Island—the entrancing and exotic amusement park that had only recently emerged as part of the modern mass culture of leisure, and that often attracted the criticism of middle-class reformers. But far from providing any lessons about the moral dangers of working at an amusement park, Richardson presented Coney Island as a respite from the normal grind of working women's lives during the rest of the year. Matter-of-factly, she acknowledged that it offered working girls the chance to make money "hand over fist" during the summer if they chose to become "Egyptian sorceresses" and palmists. They could use this money to launch the careers they planned "in the great city up the bay," when "Labor Day at last brought an end to our work," she said.[101] In both the Herald and Leslie's, Richardson portrayed women's entrance into new public spaces without attaching an older Victorian rhetoric of moral depravity to an "adventurous" woman.

For her 1905 book, however, Richardson made small but substantial revisions to her Leslie's articles that reflected the perceived gentility of a new audience. The Long Day was published by the Century Company, an elite, conservative firm that carried the gravitas of respectability in turn-of-the-century literary culture. A Century Company book carried a different valence from the flamboyant, street-smart, sensationalism of "yellow" journalism, or the flashy, racy, photographically rich writings to be found in a cheap magazine like *Leslie's*.

For *The Long Day* Richardson dropped Coney Island and the heroine's work as a Broadway dancer. She reordered the story of the heroine's move from job to job so she could tell a familiar Victorian story of a dangerous descent into possible degradation, since the heroine not only moved to more and more difficult, backbreaking work, but also was increasingly pressured by men along the way. And Richardson added a new character, an eminently respectable "friend" named Minnie Plympton, who ultimately rescued the heroine from a downward slide into degrading work. With Minnie clearly an invention tacked onto the book (she appears only at the beginning and end—a bit like the "little stenographer" of Richardson's *Herald* pieces), it is all the more interesting that some critics have explored the potentially homoerotic aspects of Minnie and the heroine's relationship. Homoerotic elements may well be there, but there are autoerotic elements too, as Richardson invented a version of herself in Minnie—a double—not just to rescue herself from the difficult work of a steam laundry, but also to extricate herself from the narrative confines of her Victorian plot.[102]

As a number of critics have observed, Richardson's vision of working women in laundries, sweatshops, and factories was far from positive in *The Long Day*. Gone was the activist heroism of a Harriet Pickering or a Jane Gallagher. On the contrary, as Daniel Rodgers has written, "The culture into which she was thrown, she reported, was made up of frowzy and stained attempts at fashion, of minds crammed with cheap romantic literature and obscenity, of slacked work, quarrelsome tempers, and loose morals, of 'fat, heavy, dough-colored,' and 'stupid' faces and the slouching gait of congenital degeneracy."[103] At the bottom end of that culture was the character Henrietta Manners, described as a "long, slouching, shuffling figure," with a "tallow-colored face" and "bloodless, loose lips," her face "framed by a trashy picture-hat." Henrietta was "one of the earth's unfortunates; a congenital failure; a female creature doomed from her mother's womb—physically, mentally, and morally doomed." In her epilogue Richardson noted that "only in two or three instances—for instance in my account of Henrietta Manners—have I ventured to hint definitely at anything pertaining to the shame and iniquity underlying a discouragingly large part of the work-girls' world." The truth was that the "factories, the workshops, and to some extent the stores, of the kind I have worked in at least, are recruiting-grounds for the Tenderloin and the 'red light' districts."[104]

It was precisely this version of "realism"—the assumption that a middle-class schoolteacher faced degradation in having to take up work in factories—that appealed to many middle-class critics and readers. Indeed, *The Long Day* was an immediate hit, attracting press attention not only in New York but also around the country. Jack London gave the book a fulsome (if somewhat loopy) review in the *San Francisco Examiner*, in which he wandered off into a form of sexualized stream of consciousness about the threatened body of the heroine and race suicide. "Here is a true book," London said. "It is a human document. It should be read by every man, woman and child who cherishes the belief that he or she is not a selfish clod." The book contained "the working out of a problem. Here is a young woman, clean and wholesome, thrown upon the world friendless in New York City. There is nobody to help her. She must depend upon herself. How will she keep that beautiful body of hers beautiful? How will she retain the color in her cheeks? the clearness and frankness in her eyes? How will she keep her springy step? her erect carriage? her delicate poise of head? the resilience of her muscles? How will she keep her flesh undegraded? her mind unsmirched? and, last but not least, how will she keep the strength in her loins, from which, strong or weak, must come the next generation of women and men?"[105]

Richardson also became the subject of interviews—always an odd position for a newspaper woman who was herself an experienced interviewer. At first, however, either other newspaper women did not realize who she was (Dorothy Richardson rather than Rose Fortune), or they coyly agreed to keep her secret. Izola Forrester of the *New York World* made no mention of Richardson's newspaper work in "One Working Girl's Struggles," her feature article on Richardson, commenting only that *The Long Day* was "not written by a masquerader, or a sociological adventurer. The author has been a working girl from simple necessity. She has worked successively in a box factory, a flower factory, an underwear sweatshop, a steam laundry, a dry goods store, a publishing house, and finally as a writer of 'The Long Day.'" At the end of the interview, she reported, Richardson asked her, "'Don't tell who I am, sure, now.'" Forrester told her readers, "And I won't."[106]

But the very publicity Richardson sought through the process of publication meant that she could not remain anonymous for long. As one account put it, "Owing to the wide publicity given her book by pulpit, press and philanthropy, eventually the matter was taken up by various educational institutions, which through Miss Richardson's publishers discovered her identity and invited her to lecture before them." Once she had been exposed as the book's author, her own paper, the *Herald*, interviewed her and addressed what would be a persistent question regarding Richardson's work: How much of her story was her own experience? "In the main the story that Miss Richardson told is largely her own experience," the interviewer hedged, "and entirely founded on her own observations. She came to New York herself a poor girl seeking employment, and the experiences which she so strongly presents in her story have been burned into her own life's history." *The Long Day* was a "frank, truthful statement of the New York working girl."[107]

Clearly the book filled a need—a hunger for what readers could accept was the reality of working girls' experiences and what middle-class observers and reformers wanted to believe was the reality. Richardson herself had anatomized the issue: in the epilogue to *The Long Day*, she commented that the working girl "has become, and is becoming more and more, the object of such an amount of sentimentality on the part of philanthropists, sociological investigators, labor agitators, and yellow journals—and a goodly share of journalism that prides itself upon not being yellow—that the real work-girl has been quite lost sight of."[108] Only in the imaginations of these observers was she "a proud, independent, self-reliant, efficient young woman—a young woman who works for her living and is glad of it."[109]

Yet in many ways Richardson, too, had lost sight of the "real" working girl—something that labor leader Leonora O'Reilly pointed out in a fury. O'Reilly slammed the book in a letter to a friend, calling it "that rank exploitation of working women of New York without one scrap of sympathy or understanding of them."[110] She also sent an angry letter to the *New York Journal*: "The book sells like hot cakes at a fair—Ministers preach sermons on it. Critics vie with each other to review it. It becomes the topic of afternoon teas. . . . [It appeals to those] who could not be paid to listen to the patient, plodding every day life of the working woman until she is made picturesquely immoral, interestingly vulgar, and maudlinly sentimental. . . . No, good Mr. Editor, Mr. Publisher, Mr. Sensational Minister and Lady Bountiful of afternoon teas, you may have paid your money for a real working girl sensation, but you did not get the real thing. No working woman ever wrote like that about her class. . . . No, we do not pull each other's hair and enjoy the fight—Nor do we 'spit in and bloody each other's face something fierce.' Neither do Salvation Army women who are at the same time factory employees drink gin in the corner liquor store and trade on their Redeemer's name generally."[111]

O'Reilly had hit on a central truth of the book: its characterizations of working girls delivered what many middle-class observers *wanted* to believe about them. It provided the "full shock of class encounter," expressed in combined repulsion and fascination.[112] Yet Richardson was quickly marked as an "expert" on the working girl—someone who should give talks and be consulted on the question of the "problem of the working girl." "It is because of her actual experiences as laundry 'shaker' and lodger in one of the so-called Working Girls' Homes while haunted by the terrifying refrain, 'Work or Starve,' that Miss Richardson has been asked repeatedly the past season to speak before the working girls' clubs in settlements and churches," said the writer Maude Dutton. "Her quietly impressive personality and the broad sanity of her ideas for bettering the conditions of the working girl, so tersely set forth in the epilogue to her book, and enlarged upon when she stands before an audience, have put Miss Richardson in the forefront of New York social workers."[113]

There were multiple ironies in Richardson's brief emergence as an expert because of the fictional character she had created. Yet she had clearly channeled her own experiences as a struggling newspaper woman into her articles and eventual book. Did the fact that she had suffered in her search for newspaper work entitle her to write more generally about working girls? Did her brief experiences in factories entitle her to call herself the "working girl" of her subtitle? The question of the truth of her experiences continued to dog her, even as she was called upon to give speeches at Yale University and a variety of other prominent institutions.

"Is it true?" asked the interviewer from her own paper.

"That's a question I've been asked a thousand times," Richardson replied. "Despite the fact that I expressly stated in the epilogue of my book that every word is true, the inquiries keep pouring in by letter and word of mouth. In reply, I can only reiterate that it is true—true, that is, in essentials. I have worked in factories and in department stores."[114] Yet the fact remained that for most of the time she went undercover she had been employed by the *Herald*. And in the epilogue of *The Long Day* she admitted that "for the sake of unity the order of things has been somewhat changed; and no record is given of many weeks, and even months, when life flowed uneventfully, if not smoothly, on."[115] It was this omission of the ordinary daily life of working girls that had so infuriated Leonora O'Reilly.

In the fall of 1906 Richardson gave a brief talk before the American Academy of Political and Social Science at the University of Pennsylvania. The topic under consideration by several speakers was "The Condition of Working Women in the United States," and Richardson spoke on the "Difficulties and Dangers Confronting the Working Woman." Here she reiterated some of the points she had made in the epilogue to *The Long Day*, although even more baldly. "I hope I shall not be charged with heresy to the working woman," she began, "when I say that I believe the greatest dangers and difficulties which confront her to-day in her struggle for industrial equality with man are to a great extent inherent in herself. I believe them to be not so much of an economic or social nature as they are physiologic and temperamental limitations fixed by sex."[116]

"While it may seem harsh and is warranted to bring down upon me a chattering of disapproval," Richardson continued, "I must say that, as I have seen the working woman, her most fundamental difficulty lies in her inability and unfitness for a sustained effort, as compared with her male competitors. Woman is not capable of doing well much of the labor she has essayed. She does not know how to work as men know how to work. She has not been trained in the past. She has no inherited aptitude for doing things with a view to economic ends. She has not the faintest conception of the general rudimentary principles of intelligent labor, of conscious and carefully co-ordinated effort. And until we have learned to be intelligent workers, capable of sustained effort, we are going to confront perpetually that greatest of difficulties—the wage problem and its attendant complications."[117] Tellingly, Richardson cited Booker T. Washington's *Up from Slavery* as an important influence on her thinking about women's need to learn how to work.[118]

Speaking at the same meeting was Rose Pastor Stokes, who only recently had caused a newspaper sensation with her marriage to millionaire James G. Phelps Stokes, whom she had met at the University Settlement when she went to interview him for her newspaper, the *Jewish Daily News*. Upon her engagement Stokes had been typed by the sensational press as a "ghetto girl," whose romance was a Cinderella story. Far from rejecting such publicity, Stokes embraced it, agreeing to "Contribute a Series of Articles on Tenement Life to the Evening World," as the *World* boasted.[119] The subject of intensive press coverage in the early days of her engagement, Stokes allowed reporter after reporter to interview her at her home. When her mother complained that reporters poked "their noses into every corner" of the apartment they shared, Stokes answered: "'That's all right, Mamele. They are workers, too, most of them underpaid and driven by need. It's not their fault. They hate to be a nuisance, but they are sent. Newspapers are no better than factories.'" When her mother persisted—"'But what do they want with our private lives?'"—Stokes told her, "'No life is private, Mother.'"[120] Stokes would embark on a new advice column for Abraham Cahan's *Jewish Daily Forward* in 1907.[121] In her political life, Stokes would become first a socialist, then a communist.

Stokes's view of the working girl could not have been more different from that of Richardson. If Richardson found the blame for working women's

Drawing of Rose Harriet Pastor. Newspapers were fascinated by Rose Pastor after her engagement to James Stokes. This article, which appeared in the New York Evening World *of April 8, 1905, offers a "Study in Pen and Pencil of Rose Harriet Pastor: The Genius of the Ghetto" and boasts that she agreed to write a series of articles for the* World. *(Chronicling America [online database], Library of Congress)*

poverty in the lack of training as an industrial worker and in "inherited sex traits," Stokes instead indicted an economic system that did not give women a fair wage. "The average working woman knows from her own experience, and from that of the workers about her, that under the existing economic system she must ever live at the margin of subsistence, and that through no effort of her own can she rise to a condition of rightful and necessary independence."[122]

"What the working girl wants (like the working man) is fair hours of labor and fair pay for its product," she argued. What Stokes called "welfare work" — including employers' provisions of "comfortable reading rooms, rest rooms, social rooms, game rooms, dining rooms and other facilities" — could only be regarded as a "pacifying measure to secure her good will" unless she received a "fair reward for her labor." Turning to the philanthropic work of the wealthy, Stokes observed that too often "rich women" showed a "patronizing, condescending type of interest" to "working girls' clubs."[123] She pointed out that "not long ago, in one of the principal settlement houses of New York, a very fashionably dressed woman, a lorgnette dangling from her finger tips, opened the door of a working girls' club, uninvited, and raising her lorgnette to her eyes, surveyed the group before her, and, as though desiring to compliment the girls, remarked in the hearing of all, 'What a very attractive looking lot of working girls these are!'"[124] Stokes bristled with indignation at this condescension.

Yet Stokes gave *The Long Day* a positive review — she saw in it a way of arousing "fortunate women" to action. Titling her review of the book for the *Independent* "The Long Day: A Story of Real Life," Stokes declared that "there can be no shadow of a doubt that 'Herself' is a real flesh and blood woman who has known the despair of the stranger in quest of work, and the untold and untellable agonies of 'The Long Day.'" The book bore "the stamp of reality as few stories of today do," she said, adding that "no man or woman interested in bettering the condition of the New York working girl, and no one wishing to know the New York working girl's condition should be without a copy of this book. It is a revelation of 'conditions, not theories,' and ought to arouse women more fortunately circumstanced to organized effort in behalf of those girls who are grinding out their lives in poverty and half-paid toil." Stokes even commended Richardson's suggestions for reform: boardinghouses for working girls and the dissemination of "good" literature. "There is work for women to do," Stokes concluded, "and the writer points out very wisely what some of that work should be."[125]

Doubts as to the truthfulness of *The Long Day* continued to haunt Richardson. "The first question that I asked Miss Dorothy Richardson over a cup of afternoon tea," wrote *New York Times Saturday Review of Books* reviewer Otis Notman in 1907, "was: 'Did you write 'The Long Day'?'" Richardson had "rather bridled up at that," and "the brown eyes looked at me questioningly. 'Isn't that question a bit odd?'" she said.

"'Why, no,'" Notman protested, "'because I have heard so many people say that Rose Pastor Stokes wrote the story.'"

"'Oh, I am the author,'" Richardson responded. "'But it is true that many people have thought Mrs. Stokes was the author. . . . To tell you the truth, I have had numerous persons accuse me of stealing her glory and berate me for posing as the author of a book I did not write. All of which was very distressing. You see the book came out just at the time that Rose Pastor married J. G. Phelps Stokes, and the papers were full of accounts of the wedding and of her previous hard experiences. How she had originally been a cigarettemaker [sic] and supported herself and her family, and that she had then taken up journalistic work, and it had all ended happily in her marriage. When "The Long Day" came out anonymously people just imagined, I suppose, that it was the story of her life.'"

"'But why did you publish it anonymously?'"

"'Because I didn't want the public to think anything about the author, only about the things I had to say.'"

Richardson reflected on the public's acceptance of her first *Herald* story in which she had pretended to be a schoolteacher. "'The letters that came pouring in as a result of the story were wonderful,'" she said. "'Every one believed me a poor little schoolteacher. I received clothes and food and money and no end of advice. One old lady wanted to know if I didn't realize how I had been cheated and another old lady, a Scotch Presbyterian, got so excited about me—she said "I just know that girl is starving"—that she became ill and the editor had to take me up to her to prove that I was really alive and well.'"

"'It's funny,'" Richardson "ended with a smile," that "'the public didn't realize that if I could write a story and get it accepted I must be making a living, not starving.'"

"'Did you do nothing to satisfy your readers of your well-being?'" Notman asked.

"'Yes,'" she "went on reminiscently," "'I told them in another article about the life of the little school teacher. The public is certainly very sympathetic if appealed to in the right way.'"[126]

Richardson did not remain in newspaper work much longer: instead, after eight years on the staff of the *Herald*, she became the "personal literary and press representative" for David Belasco, the most prominent theater owner and producer of his day.[127] It is tempting to think that the falsity of her position as an "expert" on working women at last grew unbearable for her; it seems that she never wrote articles on working girls again. A last portrait of Richardson in her job as press agent comes to us from newspaper woman Mary Isabel Brush, who soon specialized in covering the revitalized suffrage movement. Visiting Richardson's office in 1911, Brush was struck by its luxury, commenting on the "silver tea service" and empire desk "ornamented with gold and painted representations of pompadoured, high heeled court ladies. . . . One's feet sank deep into the thick carpeting."[128] Richardson had finally left the world of working-girl journalism far behind.

# # #

As both the case of the New Bedford strike and the writings of Dorothy Richardson reveal, the contact between newspaper women and working women at the turn of the century rarely was of direct use to working women—although they certainly made strategic use of this contact when they could. Instead, it was newspaper women who gained a new public visibility in American life through their representations of working women—a visibility they would eventually use not for labor activism, ironically, but to achieve their own professional, political, and personal ends. Explorations of labor became a springboard to a new expanded sense of selfhood and, for many, a sense of adventure as urban explorers whose "slumming" provided new modes of identity.[129] There were exceptions, of course, as we have seen. For Rheta Dorr, writing about working girls led to a new involvement with the labor movement and a radicalization of politics (see Chapter 2). For most others, however, writing about working women led not so much to direct agitation on behalf of the labor movement as to their own greater presence in public life.

Throughout the 1890s and early 1900s, many newspapers sought to appeal to popular interest in working women's "real lives," as Nell Nelson had put it. But they also attempted to make direct connections with their working women readers. In 1896, for instance, the *New York World* began an advice column titled "The Interests of Working Women," with the avowed purpose of providing advice to "workingwomen with small capitals" on the "best methods of investment." The readers of this weekly column almost immediately took it in new directions, writing letters about a variety of topics including their love lives, how best to get exercise, and their complaints about work. They began to respond to each other, providing advice to one another about the previous week's letters. The ever-nimble *World* was quick to respond to this interest. Within a few days it announced that the column was "open to every American working woman who has a complaint to make, a question to ask, a grievance to air or interesting information to give to others."[130] In effect, the column became a public space of shared information and conversation. The many readers who wrote in to this column remind us that, whatever the limitations of newspaper women's working-girl stories, the lives of working women themselves were not confined to the stories that had been written about them.

chapter seven *Travel*

Traveling to Mexico with her mother in early 1886, some three years before her famous trip around the world, Nellie Bly (Elizabeth Jane Cochrane) dreamed not only of adventure but also of a possible "beat" as the first woman newspaper correspondent to write from Mexico City. To her chagrin, on arrival she quickly discovered that she was not the first—or even the second, or third, or fourth—woman correspondent in Mexico City: instead, she was part of a virtual colony of American women writers. As she observed with some asperity in her first "letter" from Mexico to the *Pittsburg Dispatch*, "At the present day there are no less than six widows, of the crankiest type, writing up Mexico, each expecting to become a second [Alexander von] Humboldt and have their statues erected on the public square."[1] Bly's biographer, Brooke Kroeger, has perceptively noted that this "sarcasm may have had more to do with her unhappiness at finding she had been beaten to the assignment of female foreign correspondent than with the quality of her competitors' work."[2]

While we cannot be certain exactly to whom Bly was referring (she did not name names), we do know some of the American newspaper women who were in Mexico in 1886. Chicago journalist Margaret F. Sullivan, for instance, traveled to Mexico that year with occasional newspaper woman and poet Mary Elizabeth Blake. Their trip resulted in the coauthored *Mexico: Picturesque, Political, Progressive* (1888), based in part on columns first published in the daily *Boston Journal*. Fannie Brigham Ward was also there, having moved to Mexico in 1883; she eventually wrote hundreds of letters from Mexico and other Latin American countries for over forty newspapers around the United States—all through self-syndication. The field of newspaper correspondence from Mexico was well occupied, if not crowded— perhaps one of the reasons why Bly cut short what she had originally envisioned as an extended stay. After only a few months, Bly and her mother returned home to Pittsburgh. She published a slight volume, *Six Months in Mexico,* but it made disappointingly little impact at the time. She soon moved to New York, eager to seize the greater newspaper opportunities there.[3]

Like Bly, dozens of newspaper women published newspaper "correspondence" as they traveled beyond the borders of the United States in the late nineteenth century. Deliberately mapping the world with their writings, these women not only observed the customs of other countries in ethnographic-style pieces, but also, in a number of intriguing cases, wrote extensively about politics—including both U.S. foreign policy and the internal politics of other nations. Far from "relatively few American journalists, male or female" having "reported from overseas in the nineteenth century," as one literary critic has claimed, numerous American newspaper women eagerly embraced such work.[4]

Newspaper women's work at the turn of the century was in fact part of *expansionism* in several senses of that term. The inherent impulse behind newspaper work, after all, was expansionist—as reflected in such phrases as "out on assignment" and "cover it," both of which expressed the drive to map larger worlds, to "own" them through observation and acquired knowledge, and to write them into fresh new print forms. At the local level, as this book has argued, newspaper women's work was expansionist in occupying new territory for women in the public sphere—whether in urban public spaces or in the public spaces of print culture. But women's newspaper work was also expansionist in a more traditional sense: it was part of the larger American project to expand territory and influence in the late nineteenth century. Newspaper women participated in that expansionism by traveling the world, "mapping" it with their writings, and, especially, arguing for America's right to new territories and "possessions."

It is important to recognize that it was not just through domestic writing and the deployment of domestic ideology that newspaper women helped to shape and support American expansionism. In recent years a rewarding critical literature has addressed American women's domestic roles in expansionism, stressing that immersion in domesticity did not make women "innocent" of imperialism. On the contrary, domesticity acted as an "intimate" set of practices and beliefs that often helped to further an imperialist agenda. American white women, for instance, advanced ideas of white supremacy and the "superiority" of Anglo-Saxon culture by assuming that American practices of domesticity were superior to those of other cultures.[5]

Newspaper women overwhelmingly shared in these mainstream ideals of domesticity, with their connotations of white racial superiority over supposedly less-civilized peoples. Domesticity also provided a means of masking violence against Cubans, Filipinos, Hawaiians, and others at the turn of the century, as the "innocent eye" of domesticity transformed violence into a set of seemingly benign actions and practices that would help to "civilize" presumed "barbarians."[6]

Yet far from engaging with imperialism solely under the aegis of domesticity, newspaper women were often direct and fervent promoters of American expansionism in explicitly political writings. Sometimes widely copied and circulated, their political articles dealt directly with U.S. foreign policy or explored the internal politics and political histories of other countries. These articles are a lost part of women's political voice at the turn of the century, as well as a lost political space within American print culture.

To say that these writings are understudied is an understatement. Women's newspaper travel writings of all kinds have escaped notice, with only a few exceptions. There is a certain irony in this, as, in fact, a rich scholarly literature on women's travel writings has developed over the last two decades.[7] But that literature privileges women's travel books and magazine articles. As one prominent bibliographer of American travel writings explains, the first decision he made in compiling his bibliography "was to limit the list to books, despite the fact that many travelers had written home to the local newspaper that then published their letters."[8] While one can appreciate the necessity of bibliographic limitation, especially given the vast sea of newspaper writing in the late nineteenth century, the fact remains that such bibliographic choices have erased a range of women writers—especially newspaper women.

# # #

In the wake of the Civil War, Americans traveled abroad in unprecedented numbers, especially to Europe. "A passion for travelling has become one of the manias of American civilization," Mary Elizabeth Blake and Margaret Sullivan asserted. "Thousands cross the seas to gain a more or less superficial acquaintance with the main points of European scenery."[9] As the "mania" for European travel gathered steam in the 1860s, 1870s, and 1880s, both men and women found new opportunities for travel writing—especially as "traveling correspondents" for newspapers. Mark Twain, for instance, became a traveling correspondent for the *Daily Alta California* in 1867 when he journeyed to Europe and "the Holy Land," an experience he immortalized in the satirical *Innocents Abroad* (1869). "Every body was going to Europe—I too was going to Europe," Twain said. "Every body was going to the famous Paris Exposition—I, too, was going to the Paris Exposition." He "basked in the happiness of being for once in my life drifting with the tide of a great popular movement."[10]

Newspaper women were part of this "movement" abroad. On board Twain's steamship the *Quaker City* were at least two women newspaper correspondents: Mary Mason Fairbanks, who wrote a series of letters home to the *Cleveland Herald* and would become a lifelong friend of Twain (he nicknamed her "mother"), and Julia Newell, who was a correspondent for her hometown newspaper in Janesville, Wisconsin; later in the century Newell published a travel book on Cuba. As these two examples suggest, "traveling correspondence" offered opportunities for women to publish articles in a variety of newspapers nationwide.

The arrangements female "traveling correspondents" made with newspapers varied widely. Some women wrote correspondence on a one-time-only basis, contracting with newspapers for a single trip. Sometimes newspapers paid only for women's expenses; sometimes they paid for both the cost of travel and a specified number of articles; sometimes they solicited articles but did not print them (or pay for them); and sometimes they offered no payment at all. Given that few women were employed on the regular staff of a newspaper, arrangements could be frustratingly informal—so informal that women correspondents sometimes had no better way of knowing whether they were still employed than by anxiously watching each day's editions of a newspaper. In 1886 Lucy Hamilton Hooper wrote a plaintive letter from Paris to Joseph Pulitzer, saying that she saw "with regret that for several weeks past none of my letters have appeared in the columns of the World, and in fact since the first of last July their insertion has been the exception and their omission the rule." Hooper clearly feared that she had been replaced as a foreign correspondent: she noted the *World*'s "engagement of a new Paris correspondent the Baroness Althea Salvador formerly Miss Kimpson of Chicago," and asked, "Under the circumstances will you not kindly let me know if you wish me to continue my contributions to the World?" She could not keep "writing letters that are never printed and for which I am consequently never paid."[11]

Henry James imagined a more secure arrangement for the fictional newspaper woman Henrietta Stackpole in his 1881 *The Portrait of a Lady*. Henrietta was already "thoroughly launched in journalism"; her "letters to the Interviewer, from Washington, Newport, the White Mountains, and other places, were universally quoted." Her "cherished desire had long been to come to Europe and write a series of letters to the Interviewer"—and she "managed to get off at last," she explained to her friend Isabel Archer, "the Interviewer having come round to my figure." Having settled the payment that would make her trip possible, she "immediately put a few things into a bag, like a veteran journalist, and came down to the steamer in a street-car."[12]

James—always remarkably sensitive to changes in the status of the New Woman—was of two minds about the traveling woman correspondent as a new public figure. On the one hand his protagonist, Isabel Archer, "esteemed the courage, energy, and good-humour" of Henrietta, "who, without parents and without property, had adopted three of the children of an infirm and widowed sister and was paying their school-bills out of the proceeds of her literary labour." But James also made sly fun of Henrietta: her plan to write newspaper correspondence about Europe "from the radical point of view" was "an enterprise the less difficult as she knew perfectly well in advance what her opinions would be and to how many objections most European institutions lay open." Henrietta was "both an adventuress and a bore—adventuresses usually giving one more of a thrill."[13]

Even more damning, in James's hands the figure of the woman traveling correspondent represented an invasion of privacy. Henrietta Stackpole not only wanted to interview the nobility—"I want some introductions to the first people and shall count on you for a few," she told Isabel; "The Interviewer wants some light on the nobility"—but also was guilty of attempting to retail the private events of her stay in her newspaper letters, and had to be admonished by Isabel to stop. Henrietta represented a new—and to James, deplorable—force of publicity in American life.[14]

The figure of the woman "traveling correspondent" was highly visible by the early 1880s. Women writers discussed art, fashion, society, and the "picturesque" in their newspaper letters home from such European capitals as London, Paris, and Rome. This commentary from Europe was already a cliché by the late 1860s, as Mark Twain revealed in his parodies of European newspaper correspondence. By 1883 Marie J. Pitman, who published under the pseudonym "Margery Deane," sheepishly remarked: "Did I not solemnly vow, when I went to Europe, *not* to write a book about it?" She knew that "men and women have long written of all these things"—including "personal incidents" and "some of the ways and manners that to us are strange, of people of other lands." Yet she, too, published a book, *European Breezes*, that had "grown out of some newspaper articles and letters to friends."[15] Who did *not* write about travels to Europe sometimes seemed more to the point.

Yet a number of traveling newspaper women turned in other directions, away from Europe. Mary Elizabeth Blake and Margaret Sullivan, for instance, acknowledged the popular desire to see Europe—there were, after all, many "instincts of love, of remembrance, and of affection" that helped to "increase pilgrimages to the shrines of the Old World." But they argued that even "when every allowance has been made, there still remains an unaccountable lack of curiosity and knowledge concerning that portion of the world which is essentially ours"—by which they meant Mexico. Compared to the thousands traveling to Europe, there were merely hundreds "who become in any degree familiar with the wonderful beauty which Nature has lavished upon our own land." Mexico was "united to portions of our southern country by ties of common origin, customs, and language"; yet it was a "land almost unknown, much misunderstood, and wholly misrepresented."[16]

In writing about a land that was "ours," Blake and Sullivan belonged to a significant group of newspaper women who acted as cultural imperialists in the late nineteenth century. They were not particularly interested in the burnishing of bourgeois identity to be obtained through well-worn pilgrimages to the great cathedrals and museums of Europe. Instead, they wished to closely observe the customs and politics of countries directly affected by American expansionism—especially Mexico, Cuba, Puerto Rico, the Philippines, and Hawaii. To be sure, they did not always talk directly of imperialism. Nevertheless, their published observations acted as a form of cultural possession that undergirded U.S. political and military possession of these lands.[17]

Striking about their writings was a direct interest in politics as well as culture. Blake and Sullivan, for instance, divided their 1888 book into two parts: Blake described "Picturesque Mexico," and Sullivan wrote about "Political and Progressive Mexico." Sullivan in fact was already a well-known political writer. Passionately interested in Irish independence, in 1888 she had published *Ireland of To-day*, a fierce polemic against English colonialism. In her new work Sullivan brought the same sense of advocacy to her discussion of Mexican political history. Over and over, she directly compared Mexican suffering under Spanish rule to Irish suffering under English rule. Indeed, so prominent was this comparison that sometimes it seemed the book was as much about Ireland as Mexico.[18]

But like most American writers in the post–Civil War era, Sullivan did not take the next logical step: she did not draw any parallels between English and American imperialism. She did not see American aggression against Mexico in the war of 1848 as reprehensible in any way, nor did she see that there might be analogies between English treatment of the Irish and American treatment of Mexicans in California and elsewhere. Such analogies remained opaque to cultural imperialists who celebrated U.S. "influence" in Mexico.

Sullivan was unusual among newspaper women for a career that centered around political editorial writing—a fact many of her peers acknowledged with admiration and envy. "Mrs. Sullivan, of the Chicago Herald is conceded to be the ablest woman journalist in the country," wrote Lida Rose McCabe in 1893. Her "most brilliant work" had "appeared in the Chicago Tribune. During the Parnell-Gladstone controversy Mr. Medill sent Mrs. Sullivan to London. Ten days she sat in the House of Commons and studied the 'local coloring' and the personnel." Then "she began writing a series of letters that were not surpassed by any sent from England during that crisis in Irish affairs."[19]

An often-told story (or perhaps a popular myth) underlined Sullivan's forcefulness and resourcefulness—and served as inspiration to other newspaper women. Sent by the Associated Press in 1889 to cover the opening of the Paris Exposition, Sullivan arrived in the city only to learn that "all press favors were exhausted," and that "Minister Reid and the United States commissioners were powerless to secure her admittance to the dedicatory exercises." Sullivan reportedly then went to the French Ministry, explaining that "'I am a representative of the Associated Press that furnishes the telegraphic news to the people of the United States. It is imperative that I should be present at the opening ceremonies. Will you not procure me a seat?'" When the response from the minister was "'Monsieur regrets his inability to serve madam,'" Sullivan demanded pen and paper and quickly wrote two telegrams.[20]

The first, addressed to Secretary of State James G. Blaine, "stated that the French government did not desire the patronage or support of the United States in furthering their exposition, and advised that officer to take measures that the wish of France in the matter be respected." The second "advised the Associated Press that it was the purpose of the exposition authorities to withhold from American readers the news pertaining to the exposition." When she showed these telegrams to the minister, threatening to send them immediately, "in ten minutes Mrs. Sullivan was the recipient of profound apologies and every facility was at her disposal."[21]

Whether or not this story was entirely true, its retelling (by another newspaper woman) captured some of what her peers admired about Sullivan: that she demanded her rights within a mostly masculine world. As another story claimed, when she was first offered a job in a "newspaper office," the "editor asked her what salary she wanted." She "promptly replied, 'Just what you paid the man before me.'"[22] Newspaper women also admired the political assignments and editorial writing at the heart of Sullivan's work—even as they recognized how unusual such assignments were. As Anne O'Hagan ruefully wrote in 1898, women's newspaper work was "not too seriously regarded by the men whose vision must sweep the horizon from Cuba to Cathay for news." But Sullivan remained a proud example of the possibilities in journalism.[23]

Of course, Margaret Sullivan was not the only newspaper woman interested in politics. In selecting highlights from their careers for brief published biographies, female reporters often stressed their pride in political "beats"—just as Margherita Hamm had done with her career-starting "scoop" on the ill health of Vice President Blaine. But with few exceptions, major metropolitan newspapers did not hire women as political reporters, allowing them to cover politics only from the "woman's angle"—by interviewing the president's wife instead of the president, for example, or commenting on so-called woman's issues like suffrage or temperance.

Still, many women were able to leverage the "woman's angle" into general political coverage through astute, even biting observations of the social world of Washington politics. Washington, D.C., was a focal point for many newspaper women in the decades after the Civil War. As Catherine Cole (Martha R. Field) of the *New Orleans Daily Picayune* commented in 1888, Washington was a "sort of life-saving station to which penniless and ambitious women of all classes drift in the hope of bettering their conditions." Not only did many women "muster" in Washington "in the hope of getting government positions," but also "newspaper women" in the city were "as thick as leaves."[24]

Among these newspaper women were Austine Snead ("Miss Grundy" of the *New York World* and *New York Graphic*) and her mother Fayette Snead ("Fay" of the *Louisville Courier-Journal*), an unusual mother-daughter team in newspaper work. By 1870 Austine Snead was mentioned as the "brilliant 'Miss Grundy' of the New York World" in an article on Washington correspondents.[25] "The youngest lady correspondent in Washington," a "girl scarcely out of her teens," she had previously "supported herself as a clerk in the Interior Department." Upon "receiving her discharge," she sent letters to the *New York Post*, "copies of which were afterward sent to the World, and an engagement secured with that paper on an annual salary of $1200."[26]

Austine Snead became especially prominent during the administration of Rutherford B. Hayes: "She was accepted by the Hayes family over any other correspondent" and allowed to "write a room-by-room description of the White House."[27] In 1885 the Sneads even visited the Hayeses in Ohio (and then traveled on vacation with them), with Hayes recording their arrival in his diary of August 31: "Miss Austine Snead and her mother, the well known Washington correspondents, arrived at 7 P.M." In perhaps a sign of the disrepute in which some newspaper women were held, Hayes added a note that they were "Ladies of good character who will regard the proprieties."[28]

A day later Hayes also recorded some of the flattering Washington gossip Miss Snead had shared with him, revealing that Snead was interested in politics as well as White House decoration. "Touching the Potter Committee and the effort to implicate me in the frauds charged in relation to the election in Louisiana, Miss Snead says that she once said [to] Honorable Joe Blackburn, of Kentucky, that she should lose faith in human nature if President Hayes was found guilty." Snead had told Hayes that Blackburn replied, "'You can keep your faith in human nature. We do not expect to connect Hayes with anything wrong. We do expect to show that Republican leaders and managers were guilty.'" "This in 1878," Hayes noted to himself.[29] It was clear that the younger Snead knew how to oil the gears of Washington social life: she was politic as well as political.

Throughout the 1870s, Austine Snead was accredited to sit in what had once been a men-only press gallery of Congress before the Civil War. She was not alone: the number of women correspondents entitled to press gallery privileges (allowing them to watch congressional proceedings) gradually increased year by year. Snead was one of 4 women in 1870, one of 6 in 1872, one of 10 in 1874, one of 11 in 1876, one of 16 in 1878, and one of 19 in 1879.[30] The upward trend was obvious—as was newspaper women's interest in politics.

Among Snead's colleagues in the press gallery was Grace Greenwood (Sara Clarke Lippincott), who wrote for the *New York Times*. While Greenwood has usually been associated with sentimental midcentury literature, she also could be a keen-eyed and acerbic political writer. But when she wrote about politics she was criticized for stepping "out of her sphere"— a fact she was quick to publicize in print. In an 1877 column, she said that "many times in the past six months I have been called to account in various quarters for my political utterances." She had been "roughly reminded that I was a woman, and told that I ought to be sternly remanded by public opinion to woman's proper sphere, where the eternal unbaked pudding and the immemorial unattached shirt-button await my attention."[31]

Greenwood acidly declared that "I can 'rastle' with cooking and sewing as well as any of my gentler sisters, but just at present I confess I prefer serving up a spicy hash of Southern Democratic sentiment to concocting a pudding, and pricking with my pen 'the bubble reputation' of political charlatans to puncturing innocent muslin with my needle." She had been accused, she said, of "making war on the civil service reform." But she denied the charge: "I attack only the poor pretense, the idle parade, the misleading semblance of reform."[32]

An 1879 painting by Cornelia Adèle Strong Fassett captured the presence of newspaper women in the Senate press gallery during the 1870s. A group portrait commemorating the 1876 election hearings of Rutherford B. Hayes, Fassett's *The Florida Case before the Electoral Commission* depicted some three hundred men and women in the Senate chamber, including a number of women in the press gallery. Among them were Grace Greenwood and Austine Snead, as well as Fannie Brigham Ward, who would soon write extensively from Mexico.[33]

Women's increasing press gallery privileges—and therefore increased public visibility—brought a backlash in 1880, when a new rule effectively denied women access to the gallery. Suddenly accreditation for a newspaper was based on the ability of its reporters to cable or telegraph their copy to the newspaper, as opposed to sending it by mail. Access to a cable thus became the "real" marker of a newspaper reporter. Because few newspapers allowed women access to a cable, the inability to cable news became a significant gender barrier in newspaper work.[34] The effects of the new rule were felt immediately: in 1880 not a single woman was listed as having congressional press gallery privileges.

Was it an accident, then, that by 1883 Fannie Brigham Ward began reporting from Mexico? Probably not: denial of press gallery rights may well have been one factor in Ward's decision to report from Mexico instead of from the nation's capital. Certainly the connection between an often-thwarted interest in politics and an interest in travel can be traced in the careers of many newspaper women in the 1880s and 1890s. After all, travel offered some of the best opportunities available to newspaper women to act as political reporters as well as cultural observers: women could use travel to comment on the political systems and governments of the countries they visited in addition to providing domestic "sketches" of foreign life.

Fannie Brigham Ward is a good example of a newspaper woman whose travel gave her the freedom to discuss both culture and politics, as well as the ability to make a substantial living over some twenty years in Latin America and the Caribbean. Born in Michigan, Ward went to Washington in 1874, at around the age of thirty, to take up a temporary appointment in the United States Treasury Department. No doubt necessity played a role in this move: according to the U.S. Census, although in 1870 Ward was living with her husband and three children, by 1880 she was divorced.[35]

Ward soon provided correspondence for a variety of newspapers. In 1875 she captured the experience of being "down in a coal mine" in the kind of personal, even breathless, prose that Nellie Bly would later make famous. In 1876 Ward began an ongoing column for the *Ohio Farmer* titled "Confidential Chats with the Ladies," in which she discussed fashion and other woman's page topics such as "hints on house decoration." She also wrote a few political columns that were published in the *St. Louis Globe-Democrat*. In these she reflected on the 1876 impeachment trial of Senator William W. Belknap, discussed the reputation of Ulysses S. Grant, and gave her impressions of the "new Chinese minister at Washington"—sometimes under the column title "Capital Gossip."

But in 1876 another newspaper woman beat out Fannie Ward as the regular Washington "gossip" columnist for the *St. Louis Globe-Democrat*. Writing under the name "Ruhamah," Eliza Ruhamah Scidmore began a lengthy career with the *Globe-Democrat*, ultimately providing hundreds of columns under the title "Washington Gossip." Scidmore later also became interested in travel and wrote numerous columns about her trips to Alaska, Japan, China, and India. In the 1890s she would leave newspaper work entirely in order to publish well-received books on her travels.[36]

For several reasons, then, Fannie Ward found earning a living by writing about Washington gossip increasingly problematic. Travel beckoned instead. In 1883 Ward left United States–based newspaper work permanently behind to embark on a life of "traveling correspondence" from Mexico and other Latin American countries. By late 1883 she informed the *Milwaukee Sentinel* that she had "spent two thirds of a year" in Mexico, had "mastered the language," and was "studying the home life and social customs of the people."[37] Her exhilaration in this new life was obvious from the first: describing a trip on the Mexican National Railway outside of Monterrey in September 1883, she exclaimed, "O for the pencil of a Nast, the pen of a Dickens, to portray the ever-changing beauty of these Mother Mountains, the Sierra Madre, in the midst of which the city is set!" Like a good impressionist—and a good tourist—she noted that "every change in the atmosphere, every passing cloud, produces a different tint." The "sight of them is a perpetual tonic, a rest, an inspiration."[38] No doubt the ability to live very cheaply in Mexico was a tonic as well.

Ward quickly began to stake out a position of authority as someone more knowledgeable about Mexico than her American audience. But even as she sought both to instruct American readers and to correct misinformation about Mexico, she brought to bear particularly American prejudices in her newspaper writing. She was scornful of the "many blood-curdling reports about highway robberies" in the country; these "originated in the fevered imaginations of certain voluble foreigners." But even as she dismantled one prejudice she succumbed to others: There was less danger in Mexico "than on our own frontier" because "a Mexican is too lazy to steal, except to satisfy his hunger."[39] There was a "wide difference in temperament between this happy-go-lucky Latin race, and the thrifty, saving Anglo-Saxon."[40] Ward was steeped in the racial thinking that prevailed among whites in the late nineteenth century; Anglo-Saxon "superiority" was simply a given for Ward, a lens through which she viewed Mexican society. In this she was very much a woman of her times.

Much of Ward's travel writing was descriptive and exploratory. She tended to produce a regular cycle of articles from each new city or country she visited, starting with an article on her journey and first "impressions," then on the history of each new place, then on its architecture, then a series on social customs, then on politics, and so forth. When she moved on, she would start the cycle all over again, sometimes varying the order. This rhythm no doubt allowed her to collect notes and "write them up" at her own pace, rather than being tied to a schedule of breaking "news." Her approach also marked a difference from travel writing (often by men) that stressed scientific discovery, conquest, and survival. Ward instead followed what Mary Louise Pratt has called a "descriptive agenda" by women travel writers, one that stressed "social and political life" as "centers of personal engagement" and revealed a "strong ethnographic interest."[41]

Ward's stories often combined social and political commentary. She viewed Mexican politics with a jaundiced eye—but hers was an equal-opportunity cynicism that applied to U.S. politics, as well. As she noted, "There are many humbugs in this wicked world—in Mexican as well as in American politics." She had few illusions about the rule of President Porfirio Díaz, for instance, and in one article not-so-implicitly suggested that Díaz had paid off his closest rival so he would leave the presidential race. "General Diaz is extremely popular in southern Mexico," she wrote, "is enormously wealthy, and like our General Grant, has once had a taste for the presidency, and likes it. But General Trevino, having the army of northern Mexico at his command, is a rival not to be sneezed at in this country, which delights in revolutions. Exactly what compromise was effected nobody knows, but General Trevino suddenly blossomed out as a rich man. The 'presidential bee' ceased buzzing in his bonnet, and he is now in Europe."[42]

As she traveled in Mexico — and later throughout Latin America — Ward could be an astute observer of political systems that were nominal republics but whose rulers were virtual dictators. In 1883 she wrote that "the Russians do not live under a more perfectly centralized government than do the Mexicans, and the power controlling the regular army controls the country." Although she had no doubt that President Díaz was corrupt, her tendency to endorse leaders who favored economic development and U.S. commercial interests led her to support him anyway. "Diaz has secured numerous railway and other subventions, by which he has grown immensely wealthy, and will soon be again the acknowledged ruler," she commented. "It is well for the development of Mexico that Diaz should occupy the Presidential chair, though with him at the helm republicanism is a farce."[43]

Indeed, a running theme through Ward's newspaper columns was the assumption of the cultural imperialist that whatever was good for the commercial interests of the United States should be accepted by Mexico. "There is a horse-car line here, built by a well-known Kansas gentleman," Ward asserted in one column, "and the difficulties he has encountered at the hands of the government you will find it hard to believe. One would think so great an improvement would be welcomed, and that any sensible government would favor, instead of discourage, its introduction. On the contrary, though the Mexican 'powers that be' desire to derive all possible benefits and advantages from foreigners, it is extremely jealous of American enterprise, and invariably throws every obstacle in the way."[44]

Even as she supported American trade interests, however, she could bemoan the loss of the "authentic" in Mexico to the onslaught of progress. This, of course, was also a common stance of the cultural imperialist, who often saw no contradiction in wanting commercial access to another country for "development" while simultaneously demanding the preservation of all supposedly timeless "picturesque" elements of "native" culture. "There is much alleged improvement which does not improve," Ward argued, "and when Mexico shall have become thoroughly Americanized — as it will be within the next decade — its chief interest will have departed."[45] She did not attempt to resolve this contradiction in her thinking.

Yet more than many writers, Ward often wavered between a pro-American and a pro-Mexican point of view. Visiting the site of General Zachary Taylor's 1846 invasion of Monterrey, for instance, she observed that it was "difficult to enthuse much over their [the soldiers'] reploits here," in "peaceful, unoffending Monterey [sic]." She returned over and over again to the cruelty and brutality of U.S. forces during the Mexican War. She warned that "under all the suave 'international' talk which to-day prevails in Mexico, runs a current, deep and strong of animosity toward Americans."[46] It was clear that she sometimes felt this animosity was well-deserved.

Certainly the American general Francis E. Pinto took exception to Ward's depiction of the 1847 Mexican battle of Chapultepec. In a 1903 *New-York Tribune* account of the "Storming of the Castle of Chapultepec" by a "participant in a famous episode in United States and Mexican history," Pinto commented that he had "read from time to time what purported to be true accounts of the storming of Chapultepec by a woman who signs herself Fannie B. Ward, wherein she condemns, in strong language, the slaughter of the young [Mexican] cadets." Quoting extensively from her account of the battle, Pinto particularly took issue with the story of a young cadet who wrapped his country's "beloved banner" around him and "fought till his sword was taken, and he himself actually cut to pieces by the Americans."[47]

Pinto scoffed at this account. "The good woman has been imposed upon by the Mexicans," he declaimed—his "good woman" echoing the gendered scorn of the phrase "a woman who signs herself." Focusing on the flag incident—"all nonsense"—Pinto reluctantly conceded that "there is no denying the fact that our men were crazy mad," but, he said, "the Mexicans brought it upon themselves."[48]

Yet if Pinto had reason to question the romanticized flag incident, Ward was correct in calling the battle a "slaughter."[49] Moreover, her overall assessment of the U.S.-Mexican War as unwarranted and unjust has long since become mainstream historical opinion. Even in her own day, many people agreed that, as Ulysses S. Grant wrote in his remarkably honest 1885 memoirs, the Mexican War "was the most unjust ever waged by a stronger against a weaker nation."[50]

Ward was not afraid to voice decided views on political controversies. Thus, in 1886 she warned against a filibustering maneuver for Mexico that she claimed had escaped attention: "Although the new filibustering scheme for revolutionizing Mexico—which is on foot not only in Texas, but extending much further [sic] north than is generally supposed—attracts little attention in the United States, and none whatever in Washington, the matter is really assuming alarming proportions." She argued that "it is quite time that the United States government looked into this secret scheme and interfered by enforcement of her neutrality laws." She reminded her readers of the history of such filibusterers as William Walker and Narciso Lopez.

While their "pretended object" had been "emancipation" of Latin American countries from tyranny, "doubtless the real object of Walker and all of his successors, was their own aggrandizement by reenacting the part of the original Spanish conqueror."[51]

Ward could be a sharp-tongued as well as an astute observer. She was also an indomitable traveler—and adventurer. "'How can you two women make such a wild expedition?'" one acquaintance asked her about a Mexican journey she planned in 1883, probably with her daughter, to the "famous caverns of Pesyneria." "Burning with journalistic enterprise," she set out anyway.[52] In 1884 she described an expedition "on donkey back through the state of Campeche"[53]—one of many arduous trips she recorded, whether by donkey or to climb mountains or explore caverns. Like mountain climber Annie Peck (see Chapter 5), she apparently ascended Mount Popocatépetl with ease.[54] Subsequently Ward visited Guatemala (1885); British Honduras (1888); Chile (1891); the Falkland Islands, Uruguay, Brazil, San Salvador, Venezuela, and Trinidad (all in 1892); Paraguay and Argentina (1893); Nicaragua (1897); Cuba (1898); and Spain and Portugal (1899).

As some of these dates suggest—Chile in 1891 and Cuba in 1895, for instance—Ward, like a number of other traveling newspaper women, was interested in being in the thick of political action, including rebellion and war. In 1891, during the Chilean Civil War, she wrote that "in view of the present serious disturbances," Chile was "neither a safe nor pleasant place for foreigners to visit; but journalistically speaking, is just now a 'seat of war' by no means to be ignored." She informed her readers that "we made a hasty trip down here from Peru last July for the purpose of studying both sides of the questions at issue."[55]

In 1895 Ward managed to arrive in Cuba just before the start of the Cuban war for independence. This was a remarkable accomplishment for a newspaper woman—though Ward may not have recognized it as such, given her extensive Latin American travel and her uncanny ability to find one "seat of war" after another. But we should give her credit. It was virtually impossible for women to gain permission from American newspapers to report from Cuba or other seats of war, though many yearned to do so.

Mary C. Francis, for instance, bitterly remembered her struggles in getting to Cuba—much less obtaining a newspaper assignment. "Intense interest in an heroic people struggling for their liberty had caused my desire to visit the island of Cuba, meet her men and women face to face, study the existing conditions and observe for myself the actual state of affairs," Francis explained. But "it was almost three years after this wish was born that I had the opportunity of gratifying it. During that interval every avenue was blocked by which a woman could have entered the island and made a tour in the interior."[56]

The fact that Francis was an experienced newspaper woman made no difference. "The difficulties and obstacles I encountered were legion," she wrote. "Despite a long and thorough experience in newspaper work, no editor would lend a willing ear to my plans. One and all they listened with compassion and incredulity to the ideas I outlined, and then, declaring that they would not for the world assume the responsibility of sending a woman to Cuba, advised me to drop the matter and take what steps I could to recover my sanity before it would be too late."[57]

Mary H. Krout of the *Chicago Daily Inter Ocean* faced similar frustration in her attempts to travel to Hawaii in 1892. Her imagination had been kindled when a friend, who had recently returned from Hawaii, told her that "a revolution, with a demand for annexation to the United States, was impending."[58] Krout "was immediately inspired with an ardent desire to be present when the crisis came." This was "not the gratification of a nature disposed to bloodshed and violence, but the realisation of the professional opportunity to be the one special correspondent in the field."[59] She wanted "to witness the actual making of history." Her desire was no more than the "natural instinct of a 'newspaper woman'" who had been working for the *Inter Ocean* for years.[60]

But her editor said no. He "looked at me coldly through his spectacles," Krout reported indignantly; "upon his sharply cut features and the tightly compressed lips there was an expression of justifiable weariness." "'Do you think anybody is interested in Hawaiian politics?'" he asked. The interview "was not prolonged," as "it became evident that my speedy withdrawal was urgently desired."[61] She ended up appealing to the wife of another editor— "forced to resort to schemes and conspiracies, to the exercise of so-called 'tact,' as usual when women must deal with men in matters a little out of the common." That editor finally agreed to let her go to Hawaii, but only after she had volunteered to pay her own way.[62] Krout remarked bitterly that "there dwells in the soul of every man living—and from this category not one is exempted—a fixed belief, confessed or unacknowledged, that political problems are wholly beyond the comprehension of the feminine intelligence. It is not in the least worth one's while to combat this inherent and inherited prejudice."[63]

Fannie Ward, however, was in a different position. She did not need to ask an editor whether she could go to Cuba "on assignment": she simply made assignments for herself, selling projected series of letters to newspaper editors whose acquaintance she carefully cultivated. She did not particularly need help in getting to Cuba: she had been traveling for years in Latin America and then the Caribbean. She did not need access to a cable: she simply sent her columns by mail. (In one column from Concepción, Chile, she mentioned that "at least five weeks must elapse before these written words can reach the United States and appear in print.")[64] Her political columns were not "beats" or "scoops"—and thus her reflections may not have attracted the attention of the authorities—or other "war correspondents."

Remarkably, Ward seems never to have been censored—though she often complained of press censorship in the countries she visited. "The press of Mexico is muzzled to an extent which is hard to believe," she declared in an early column, a theme she returned to many times over the course of her career.[65] From Chile in 1891 she remarked that "at first the rebels used to open all letters that fell into their hands," but "that soon grew to be too much trouble." For many weeks, she said, Americans "had been sending their home letters with the consular budget" or "in the private pocket of the northward-bound sea captain."[66] The fact that Ward consistently sent her articles as letters, by regular mail, seems to have protected her.

Ward managed to slip beneath the radar at a time when other women struggled to get to the "seat of war" in a variety of different global locations. She seems to have escaped notice even in wartime Cuba, although she noted that "the censorship of the telegraph" was "rigorously enforced."[67] Amazingly, Ward was already writing from Cuba on February 15, 1895, nine days before the Cuban war for independence began. "If rumors are to be relied on," she observed on the fifteenth, "the royal troops [of the Spanish] will soon have more work to do, for it is whispered that a widespread revolt is brewing—not of blacks against their so-called owners, but of the best citizens of the island," who "feel the Spanish yoke too galling to be longer borne." Such a comment not only echoed widespread popular support in the United States for Cuban independence from Spain, but also the racial prejudice that would soon undercut support for Cubans. White Americans who assumed that the heroic Cubans were white, while the "dastardly" Spanish were "dark-complexioned," began to remove their previous support from Cubans in 1898 once they discovered that, at least to some extent, the reverse was true in the former slave society.[68]

From Cuba, Ward reported that "Spain's armed minions are everywhere," calling them "these miserable hirelings, the scum of the earth." Yet although she believed that "one must feel deep sympathy for a people so oppressed," Ward also thought it "not likely" that Cubans "would be able to govern themselves after so long repression. Were Cuba's independence declared tomorrow and the forces withdrawn, doubtless chaos would ensue, as in unhappy Brazil, and revolution would succeed revolution for a decade or two."[69] Ward cynically concluded: "It will probably end as so many revolutionary attempts in Cuba have done before—in a good deal of bombast and fiery rhetoric, a little powder smoke, and a few more gory executions; for it is one thing to plan a complete overturning of the powers that be at a safe distance from Jamaica, Key West or New York, and quite another thing to carry it out on Cuban soil."[70]

By March 31, 1895, Ward wrote from Havana that "the political temperature of this hotbed of revolution has grown rather too torrid of late to make it a safe or pleasant abiding place for Americans, and the few who yet remain are holding themselves in readiness to depart at a moment's notice." Yet in May she was still in Cuba and obviously proud to report that she had been able to visit "Moro [sic] prison not long ago—a rare favor, in these days of suspicion, to be accorded to an American." Again she was flying beneath the radar as a woman: "Doubtless our harmless-looking petticoats were the open sesame, for a male stranger would hardly have been admitted to those blood-stained precincts, and certainly not a 'newspaper man.'"[71]

Although Ward was anti-Spanish and thus aligned with American popular opinion, she was by no means an enthusiastic supporter of ordinary Cubans. Instead, just as she had done throughout Latin America, Ward threw in her lot with those she considered to be the "best men" and women, writing of the "lower classes" without sympathy. (In this she was ahead of the curve in terms of U.S. public opinion. Ordinary Americans withdrew their support from the Cuban struggle for independence only during and immediately after the War of 1898.) "A good deal of the talk just now so popular in the United States about oppressed Cuba fighting for liberty is nonsense," she wrote. "The majority of substantial citizens are far more troubled about the consequences if Cuba should achieve her independence—unless under the protecting wing and wise direction of the United States." If Spain's soldiers were withdrawn, "the negroes, Chinese and other irresponsible elements would be in overpowering majority." The "substantial citizens," she commented, "deplore a revolution as the worst thing that would happen to Cuba in the present state of her finances."[72]

Fannie Ward left Cuba in May 1895 but returned several times; during the Spanish-American War she worked with founder of the Red Cross Clara Barton in a hospital for injured soldiers. In July 1898 the *Evening Times* of Washington, D.C., noted that Ward was sailing once again for Santiago, where she planned to "join Miss Barton, with whom she spent some times in Havana last winter."[73] Ward later joined Barton in relief work in Galveston, Texas, in 1900.[74]

Barton and Ward became friends—and their correspondence in the early 1900s provides us with rare glimpses of Ward's life as a newspaper woman. "All my life I have gone on my own independent way, regardless of who might disapprove of my course," she declared to Barton in one letter. But that "independent way" also meant unceasing labor: Ward's finances were sometimes precarious, and she had to work as hard in the early 1900s as she had in the 1880s. As she noted ruefully, "In the present way down-at-heel state of my finances, I find that even the matter of my postage is an elephant."[75] ("If *I only had money*!" she exclaimed in another letter.)[76] Her work, she noted, had seasonal rhythms that she found financially difficult. "The worst of the year for me is now," she explained to Barton in July 1904, "when political campaigns and summer-resort news absorbs [*sic*] the papers to the leaving-out of my line." But she put a cheerful face on this difficulty: "However, the old stand-bys remain and I expect to pull through, in spite of the load, as I have done so many years. Don't worry about me, my dear," she told Barton, adding with a bit of wry humor, "I am doing quite enough of that myself."[77]

Ward faced "work piled up mountains high," she noted in another letter. But it was not work she could give up: it meant "the family bread and butter."[78] In her fifties that work was becoming more difficult, as her health was no longer perfect: "Something new for me to be ailing—I, who have always been tough enough to stand anything!" Yet Ward did not lose her wanderlust, proposing in 1904 to go "to the far East" with Barton. She could write newspaper articles along the way: "I have just 42 papers in which to record the doings," she boasted, "or I will drop them all, if you say so. The trip may be hard—at any rate I know it will be anything but a picnic; but it will lift me out of this rut into which I have been sinking over head and ears, and give me a new lease on life."[79]

Before she had left Cuba in 1895, Ward commented on American newspaper coverage during a period of warmongering by many papers, especially Hearst's *New York Journal*. "There are several correspondents here from the United States who are doing themselves and their respective journals proud in the usual energetic American fashion, by sending flamboyant letters from the alleged 'seat of war,'" she noted acerbically. "But, unfortunately, their sources of information are extremely few and not the most reliable in the world; and should one of these gentlemen really hit upon a grain of truth displeasing to the government, he would find himself hustled out of the country without loss of time—if he did not meet with a dagger in some back street."[80]

Ward, however, faced no such danger. Although she had been mentioned in a prominent 1894 guidebook to journalism as a "living example of the fact that women can sometimes make a success of the most difficult kind of travel correspondence,"[81] she received little attention from authorities. And although she criticized the Spanish authorities harshly and implicitly argued that she had more authority and expertise than her fellow male correspondents in Cuba, she remained invisible. Hiding in plain sight, she was a female war correspondent who was never recognized as such, either in Cuba or in the United States.

# # #

Fannie B. Ward never aspired to be called "war correspondent," of course. But a number of newspaper women eagerly sought that label at the turn of the century—perhaps none more so than Margherita Arlina Hamm. Hamm traveled unusually widely, not only to China, Japan, and Korea (or "Corea," as it was often spelled then) in 1894—but also to Cuba, Puerto Rico, the Philippines, and Hawaii, the latter of interest to her as they became targets of U.S. expansionism. In her 1899 article, "Women as Travelers: The American Woman in Action," Hamm identified herself as "War Correspondent in the Chino-Japanese War, and in the late War with Spain."[82] A newspaper account of her 1897 lecture, "Reminiscences of the East," identified her as "the first woman war correspondent in the world and a traveler in China, Japan, and Corea."[83] For her entry in *Who's Who in America*, Hamm described herself as "war corr. Chinese-Japanese War and Spanish-Am. War."[84]

Clearly to be a "war correspondent" was a badge of honor for Hamm; it meant crossing the most intractable gender line of all in newspaper work, as she well knew. Yet her opportunity for the travel that led to a war "beat" came through surprisingly traditional means for a "bachelor girl": marriage. In late 1893 Hamm married William Fales, "one of the most remarkable literary men in New York," a "writer of brilliant verse and a great linguist" who was both a lawyer and a newspaper man. A bohemian of the old school, a man-about-town, and some twenty years older than Hamm, Fales "not only spoke Chinese" but knew "every Chinaman in New York, and every actor and actress in the country." He liked nothing better than "to pilot a party" to Mott Street at midnight for a Chinese supper—there, he was "in his glory."[85] This unlikely marriage "was one of the surprises of Park Row this week," the *Journalist* noted in October; "no one suspected what was on foot until the cards were sent out." But, the *Journalist* hastened to add, "Once over the surprise the boys joined in wishing the couple all possible happiness."[86] (The marriage was not a success: Hamm and Fales divorced in 1902, with Fales's pursuit of actresses apparently proving a fatal flaw.)[87]

In early 1894 Fales took up an appointment as consul at Amoy, China, and Hamm went with him. Before leaving New York "she made arrangements to correspond for the New York Sun and other periodicals"; when they stopped in Philadelphia, she further arranged to send "some of her Oriental sketches" to the "Philadelphia Times."[88] Upon arrival in China she began sending lengthy descriptive pieces to various newspapers and embarked on an ambitious round of travel. Indeed, she "traveled every week of the time spent in the Dragon empire," writing "observantly from Peking to Formosa, and Seoul, Corea, to Kobe, Japan."[89]

She quickly brought a feminist sensibility to bear in her new setting. One of her pieces, for instance, complained bitterly of the lack of morality of "the civilized man" in China—by which she meant "those masculines of the Anglo-Saxon, German, French, Dutch, Hebrew, Swedish, Norwegian, Danish, Russian, Italian, Spanish and Australian races who have been brought up in the nineteenth century schools of liberality and independence," and who had been taught "to revere women and respect her opinion." These were men who did not "dwell in the past" but recognized "that the world is marching on, and everything and everybody in it must march along, too." It was "this type of the male sex" who went out to China "to make his living, and let me state that he makes a good one, too."[90]

Hamm complained that "a civilized man comes out from England or America, leaving a wife behind. He is in a Chinese town about three weeks, when he rents a Chinese girl of eleven years of age for fifty or a hundred dollars per year. She lives with him as his wife, cooks, washes and does all sorts of labor for him, bears him children, as a rule, and grows up in his house to the age of seventeen, when she is dismissed like a worn-out animal, with a series of half-breed off-spring on her hands, to make room for the real wife, who has at last made up her mind to come to the Orient to live. Imagine the feelings of the slave woman of the civilized man!"[91]

This was not the sort of observation, with its direct critique of white men's sexual imperialism, that Hamm could place in a major metropolitan newspaper, where it would have seemed too risqué even for sensational papers. Instead, she placed it in her "home" trade journal, the *Journalist*, where she had been a columnist for several years (and would soon become editor). Even there, it was strikingly direct in an era of genteel obfuscation.

"Is there any way out of this?" Hamm asked. "None," she answered, "as long as civilization has such small effect upon mankind. For, no matter how well educated Chinese women may get, they may still become only civilized after the pattern of the average civilized man in China to day."[92] The position of women globally continued to fascinate her. In another article, no doubt derived from information she herself provided, the *Journalist* mentioned that she had "studied carefully and faithfully the industrial position of woman in the far East and already has an excellent publisher for a book upon the subject."[93] (No such book ever appeared.)

"Travel," she reflected later in *Frank Leslie's Popular Monthly*, "brings out the deep ethical differences between the two sexes." "In London I have often noticed that the average American gentleman makes a beeline for the famous inns, pubs and music halls, while the average American woman goes to Westminster, St. Paul's and the Tower of London." In "China civilized manhood is to be found at the clubs, the race-tracks and other less commendable places of recreation, while womanhood finds amusement in the joss-houses, the curio stores, the pagodas and the social life of the Chinese gentry."[94] Hamm never gave up her belief—common to many women in the 1890s—that American womanhood was of a higher moral order than American manhood. It was on the basis of woman's special nature—her unique gifts and moral sense—that women deserved equal opportunities with men, she argued.[95]

While in China, Hamm wrote about a number of issues of interest to women, including pieces on the Korean empress and a scathing article on the "barbarity" of the practice of foot binding. No doubt she intended to write a book on the "industrial position of women," but her time was cut short by war. When she and Fales arrived in China in early 1894, Hamm had no idea that war was imminent—but, then, the Western press in general had relatively little knowledge of, or even interest in, Korea. As the *Journalist* crudely put it in September 1894, at the height of the Sino-Japanese War, "the eastern war does not excite much concern in journalistic circles. Newspaper men feel as regards Japan and China very much as the man did in the fight between his wife and a bear. He didn't care which won."[96] While this was certainly not true of all newspapers, the *Journalist* did have a point.

Thus it is questionable how much of an impact within journalistic circles, much less a wider public culture, Hamm could make in 1894 with a claim to be the first female war correspondent in Korea. The truth was that Americans would later pay far more attention to newspaper women who became war correspondents in Cuba and the Philippines, where the stakes were obviously higher in terms of direct U.S. acquisition of territory.[97] Neverthe-

less, Hamm, who always sought as much of a public presence as possible and who was adept at self-promotion, attempted to make the most of what she saw as her greatest accomplishment. In several articles she recounted how she had achieved the Korea "beat" that, in her view, entitled her to call herself a "war correspondent." In one interview, for instance, she explained that during her stay in China, she "made maps of Mongolia and Manchuria while traveling there on camels alone, save with an interpreter." It was "during this tedious journey" that she "made her way to Corea and happened there just as the war broke out."[98]

If Fannie Ward had been an invisible war correspondent, Margherita Hamm was an accidental war correspondent. But as the *Journalist* explained, Hamm knew how to seize opportunity, knew exactly what to do with her beat: "She wrote a graphic account of it for a big London paper," sent it "over the cable for which she received $25 per column," took "the steamer China via Nagasaki [*sic*] and Yokohama for San Francisco," then "wired it to The World thus scoring a beat." The same article noted that "in her great story, she had the official papers of Minister Kurino, the new delegate from Japan, whom she travelled with from Tokio [*sic*] to 'Frisco. The act of gaining his official papers for news purposes was worthy of a famous diplomat."[99] Kurino was indeed on the same steamship traveling to San Francisco, and there is little doubt that Hamm would have found a way to talk with him. There is little doubt, too, that Hamm herself wrote most of the self-serving account that appeared under the heading "The Only Woman War Correspondent" in the *Journalist*.

By early September 1894, Fales and Hamm were back in America after only nine months in China. As they traveled from San Francisco to New York, they stopped to give a joint newspaper interview in Denver. The resulting article declared that Hamm had "well-earned the title of the first woman war correspondent upon record"; she had "been in the thick of the fight and written enthusiastically about it." The article also quoted Hamm's thoughts on the probable outcome of the war: "In my opinion the Japanese will win the day," she said. "They have 100,00 [*sic*] magnificently drilled patriotic soldiers, they have fine ships, fine guns, and the very best and latest equipped torpedo boats." Hamm obviously admired the modernizing efforts of post–Meiji Restoration Japan: "By right of commercial relations with Corea, Japan should come out victor, if not by a moral right, which means that Corea will be rid of mediaeval Chinese barbarisms, social and political customs and blossom into a worthy sister in the boquet [*sic*] of civilized powers." China, on the other hand, did not deserve to win, she declared. Like many Americans at this time, she saw China as "backwards" and praised Japan's push toward industrialization.[100]

As these remarks show, Hamm was remarkably self-assured in her views on foreign affairs. Travel had allowed her to position herself as an authority on the Sino-Japanese War and the Far East in general. But the chance to write about international politics did not remain open to her after she returned to the United States. Resuming more traditional newspaper work, Hamm became editor of the woman's department of the *New York Mail and Express*, where she advocated for woman's rights and access to new occupations. A prodigious and indefatigable worker, she also edited the Saturday supplement for the *Mail and Express*, was a woman's commissioner for the Atlanta Exposition of 1895, began a "department" in *Peterson Magazine* called "Woman's Broader Life" (a "suffrage department," according to one newspaper article), and edited the *Journalist*.[101] These were substantial accomplishments—but her war beat did not translate into a wealth of new political opportunities for her.

When the 1895 Cuban war for independence erupted, Hamm again found a cause that would allow her to engage in general-interest political writing—if not exactly war correspondence, as she claimed. Energetically supporting the Cuban people's fight, Hamm by May 1896 was deeply involved in the "Grand Cuban-American Fair" in New York and listed as a chairman of the "Woman's Congress of Patriotism and Independence." She applauded—and no doubt envied—newspaper woman Kate Masterson, who was sent, in a one-time stunt by the *New York Journal* in the spring of 1896, to interview Spanish general Valeriano Weyler, the infamous "Butcher" who had been instrumental in setting up concentration camps for Cubans that ultimately resulted in some 200,000 deaths. Hamm found Masterson's interview "impressive." Masterson "took all the risks of a sea-voyage, of martial law, and of the yellow fever and other diseases of that tropical isle, performed her task in a manner that won the approbation of both the profession and the public, and returned just as if her splendid labor was a mere matter of course."[102] The fact that Masterson's interview was framed as a sensational "stunt" around the novel idea of a woman interviewing Weyler did not affect Hamm's praise—Hamm would have known only too well the limitations placed on newspaper women in any foreign assignment.[103]

Hamm clearly yearned to be officially involved in some capacity during the War of 1898. In July she was "appointed supervisor and inspector of supplies and head nurses' staff in the Red Cross department of the national guard"—at least according to a newspaper article probably based on information provided by Hamm herself. She was to "first visit Tampa, then go to Santiago," and her official title was "inspector," reported the *Bangor Daily Whig & Courier*.[104] There is little record of whether she performed these tasks, although Hamm later claimed to have been decorated by Cuban president T. Estrada Palma.

But the War of 1898 and new U.S. "acquisitions" did provide Hamm with a pretext for a new round of travel.[105] In 1898 and 1899 she traveled to Puerto Rico, the Philippines, and Hawaii, writing newspaper articles about each new place. She again made plans for a book—and this time was able to bring her plans to fruition, publishing over the next two years a series of what one critic has rightly called "ephemeral" volumes that included *Manila and the Philippines*, *Porto Rico and the West Indies*, and *Dewey the Defender*. Compilations of information, these books were based in part on her newspaper articles. As Hamm noted in the preface to *Manila and the Philippines*, "This volume is based upon notes made by the author while a resident and traveler in the Far East. Some have been used in newspaper correspondence for the New York *Mail and Express*, the New York *Sun*, the New York *Herald*, the Baltimore *American*, the Chicago *Inter-Ocean*, the San Francisco *Examiner*, and the Hong Kong *Telegraph*."[106] Travel had not only allowed Hamm to experience far-flung places; it now gave her the chance to disperse information across a far-flung geographic area. She had become a medium for circulating global information.

In this she was not alone. Hamm's several volumes were part of a massive popular literature produced in response to war, including works by other newspaper women. Emma Kaufman and Anne O'Hagan, for instance, jointly wrote *Cuba at a Glance*, published in 1898 with an introduction by President Palma. "Thanks are due the *New York Journal*," they wrote, "for the use of its library and access to the letters of its war correspondents."[107] Obviously this was a project that their employer had endorsed—if not actually assigned to the two women.

Hamm, Kaufman, and O'Hagan all advocated Cuban independence, but it is interesting to see in Hamm's series of books, in particular, how quickly—and seemingly effortlessly—she moved from advocacy of Cuban self-determination during 1896–98 to matter-of-fact acceptance of U.S. domination of the island. In her 1899 *America's New Possessions and Spheres of Influence*, for example, she simply mentioned that "at the present moment Cuba is governed by an American military department, which is busily working to get the Cubans started upon the problem of self-government." Like so many Americans, she had never judged Cuban "self-government" to be a "problem" before the war. Similarly, while her 1898 volume *Manila and the Philippines* had actually been dedicated to Emilio Aguinaldo, by 1899, when Aguinaldo was fighting for Filipino independence, Hamm changed her tune. In *America's New Possessions* Aguinaldo was a "half-breed"—part of a group of "half-breeds" who, "under proper auspices, such as education, moral discipline, and political liberty," could be "developed into a high type of manhood." At the "present time, however," the "leaders in the late Aguinaldo insurrection" were "suffering from hereditary influences, ancient superstitions and three centuries of Spanish oppression and misrule." In another part of the book, Hamm declared that "hybridization, when carried on upon a low plane, brings out the vices of both the parent races."[108]

The War of 1898, in short, firmed up Hamm's racialized sympathies with American imperialism: in 1899 she had "but little patience with the doctrines of what is termed anti-expansion and anti-imperialism." As she put it, "The stronger the tree the larger it is bound to grow. The greater and nobler the civilization, the wider will be its expanse, and the more numerous the peoples gathered beneath its banners." Hamm believed wholeheartedly in national expansion—not so much as a providential aspect of America's Manifest Destiny, but as what she briskly presented as a simple matter of logic and, especially, of commerce. In *America's New Possessions* she provided a startling array of ideas for American commercial development in its new "spheres of influence," including Hawaii, Cuba, and the Philippines (which she called "the Treasure Islands of the Pacific"). Almost all of her ideas, including mining, forestry, and the growing of sugarcane and tobacco, involved intensive resource extraction from these lands on a colonial model. She had no interest in the self-determination of the peoples of these areas.[109]

Hamm even had her sights on more acquisition of territory from Mexico—in particular the states of Chihuahua and Sonora. After all, she blithely wrote, "Sonora passes imperceptibly into Arizona and Chihuahua into New Mexico"; both states were "of the same general character as Arizona." Besides, "scores of mills and factories, farms and plantations" were "owned and conducted by Americans in nearly every province." Based on this extensive U.S. presence, "the entire Republic" was really already "an American protectorate, with absolute home rule." What is more, there were riches to be had if Americans developed the areas' mining resources: "Sonora contains inexhaustible supplies of gold ore, and Chihuahua of silver," not to mention supplies of copper and other minerals. "When the time comes," she said, "the acquisition of these two States will not be difficult. They are of very little importance to the Mexican government." Given that "the policy of Mexico is that of extreme friendship toward the United States," if "its government believed that the sale of the two States would tend to help their own civilization, they would gladly enact the requisite legislation." She concluded that "the irresistible laws of progress are gradually Americanizing our Sister Republic to the South."[110]

There were other irresistible laws at work here as well, however— including the irresistible law of personal desire. It is hard to escape the fact that Hamm's ardent, racialized expansionism, her promotion of American global "progress," lined up neatly with her own personal desires to travel the world, to report from anywhere she chose, and to make the entire world a public sphere available to newspaper women. The choice to be a "war correspondent" for the mainstream press during the War of 1898, in other words, produced an alignment with U.S. military action and policy—not just for men, but also for women. In Hamm's case, it also seems to have produced a form of jingoism.

\# \# \#

Newspaper women's support for the evolving wars of 1898 and 1899 did not ease their acceptance as war correspondents, however—as revealed in a reminiscence of reporting in the Philippines by the famous war correspondent James Creelman. As he made clear, it was not just newspaper editors at home who maintained a gender line by refusing to assign women to cover "seats of war." Male war correspondents in the field played a substantial role, too. The same male colleagues who often treated women as comrades in the newsroom at home, even helping them to obtain their stories, were likely out in the field to react to the arrival of a woman war correspondent with incredulity, ridicule, or horror.

Creelman told an extended anecdote of one night in the Philippines when he, a group of fellow correspondents, and "tired soldiers sprawled on the stone flooring" all shared space together in the "venerable church of La Loma." At the time, he recalled, the U.S. forces had shifted from fighting the Spanish to fighting Aguinaldo's army. "Everywhere" there were "signs of grim preparation for the advance of the whole division at daybreak toward Malolos, the insurgent capital — war correspondents examining their cameras, chatting with their field couriers, or *laughing at the young woman correspondent* who had just appeared, artillerymen carrying ammunition for their batteries, the confused sound of passing men and horses" (emphasis added).[111]

With obvious exasperation, Creelman reported that, despite the warnings there would be "steady fighting" the next day "across the thirty miles between us and Aguinaldo's seat of government," this "young woman persisted in staying" and could not be persuaded to leave. "She had come to see the battle open with the dawn," Creelman wrote, "and nothing could induce her to go back to Manila. No one knew much about her except that she was from San Francisco, and was supposed to write occasionally for a California newspaper. Most of the officers had nodding and some of them a speaking acquaintance with her. But no one could shake her in her determination to stay all night and watch the death-grapple in the morning. Hints were useless. There was no place for her to sleep — she found two chairs and stretched herself out on them. There was nothing for her to eat — she produced a sticky lump of chocolate and munched it. There might be a night attack by the enemy — she drew an army revolver from her pocket. The place was full of tropical fever — she brought forth some quinine pills, and took a sip of brandy from a dainty cut-glass flask."

At last, Creelman said, "a lieutenant approached the young woman" to try to discourage her. "'It will be a frightful sight,'" he said. "'I hope you will go back to your hotel. This is no place for you. It is horrible to think of a woman looking at the slaughter of human beings. You cannot imagine how appalling it will be.'" The young woman "set her hat straight with a coquettish touch and smiled."

"'All the better copy for my paper,'" she answered, with a yawn that showed her pretty teeth. "'Besides, it will be a new experience.'"

The lieutenant persisted. "'But the danger?'"

"'The only serious danger that confronts me is the danger that my paper may be beaten. That would be simply frightful.'" She "drew her mouth up in a dainty moue."

Making a "gesture of despair," the lieutenant asked, "'Have you considered the chances of defeat, of capture?'"

"'Yes,'" the newspaper woman said. "'I have considered all, all, all. If I am captured, I will interview Aguinaldo. If I am killed, my paper will print my portrait and a melting account of my death. You cannot frighten me away. I have come to stay.'"

"'But don't you see'"—and the lieutenant "stamped his foot till the spurs jingled"—that "'you are a source of embarrassment to us all; that we feel ourselves responsible for your safety; that—'"

"'Well, I like that!'" the woman declared, "sitting bolt upright, and tossing her little head back." "'Who asked any one to be responsible for me?'"

Suddenly the young woman saw two rats. "'Oh! oh! oh!'" she "wailed." "'Rats! Two of them! Big, hairy, black rats! There they are now—oh! oh!'"

Only "ten minutes later," Creelman concluded, "we saw her ride out into the road, and turn her horse's head toward Manila" making a hasty retreat back to her hotel.[112]

Creelman's story—or extended yarn—was no doubt meant to confirm that women remained, at heart, merely fearful, irrational creatures, unsuited to provide coverage of war. Yet his story also revealed the opposite: the young woman he described had through stubbornness and determination made her way to the battlefront in the face of great odds. Creelman vacillated between disparagement and grudging respect as he assessed the new women war correspondents. "I have seen women war correspondents on the firing line more than once," he remarked, but "I have never read an account of a battle written by a woman that had anything of the ring and dash of the real fighting." But "curiously enough," he admitted, "women seldom show any signs of timidity or shockability on the battlefield. Once in the presence of an actual conflict, they are as eager as the men to see the slaughter pressed, and it sometimes happens that officers are compelled to restrain them from leaving the trenches and rushing forward with storming parties. The sight of slain men seems to move them no more than others."[113]

Was there a specific model for the woman war correspondent Creelman described? At least one writer has assumed that it was Anna Northend Benjamin, who became a war correspondent in both Cuba and the Philippines while still in her early twenties. A newspaper in 1902 labeled her the "First Woman War Correspondent to Reach Santiago," a characterization that must have galled Margherita Hamm.[114]

But Benjamin's experience of covering the 1898 war in Cuba primarily illuminates the obstacles faced by women war correspondents. Born in 1874, Benjamin arrived in New York in the mid-1890s and "wrote for various newspapers and magazines," according to the *New-York Tribune*. Then the "war with Spain gave her an opportunity of which she took prompt advantage."[115] Independent and entrepreneurial, Benjamin managed to obtain an assignment to cover the war for the popular newspaper *Leslie's Weekly* in the spring of 1898—*Leslie's* called her their "Special Correspondent in the Field."[116] This sponsorship was an unusual coup for a woman; it was also critical for obtaining an official "War Correspondent's Pass" from the War Department. Remarkably, Benjamin received a pass in May.[117] In this she seems to have been unique among American newspaper women.

When Benjamin arrived in Tampa, Florida, where troops embarked for Cuba, she was "unable to get passage on any of the transports." She then "went to Key West, in the hope of making her way to General [William R.] Shafter's army from there." But officials told her "that it would be impossible for her to reach Cuba." Nevertheless, she "persisted in her efforts until she finally managed to get on board a schooner which was loaded with coal for the American fleet."[118] Benjamin finally reached Guantánamo just as most of the male journalists were leaving. "A great many of the war correspondents and artists are going back on returning transports," she wrote. It was "literally the calm here after the storm."[119] Guantánamo had quickly been taken by U.S. troops on June 14; now the seat of war was shifting to Santiago de Cuba. In short, Benjamin had just missed the action.

Next, Benjamin "succeeded in persuading [a] Captain McCalla, of the navy, to allow her to go on board the transport Aransas." But "then there was more weary waiting. The transport remained off the shore of Cuba for some time, and it was not until after the surrender of Santiago [in July] that Miss Benjamin succeeded in getting to the land."[120]

Not surprisingly, given these frustrations, Benjamin wrote a series of feature stories that hovered around the edges of the war. In June, writing from Tampa before troops embarked for Cuba, she explored a controversy over the extent and quality of their rations.[121] In July she did an illustrated piece on "Horses and Mules for the Army,"[122] and reported on a scare over a single case of yellow fever at Key West.[123] Benjamin was not the only newspaper woman doing such work: Teresa Dean also wrote a series of features on the army for *Leslie's Weekly*, including "A Woman in Camp: Teresa Dean

Messes with the Soldiers at Chickamauga and Likes Their Savory Stew and Black Coffee."[124]

But Benjamin was clearly frustrated at not being able to get to Cuba itself. In an article titled "A Woman's Point of View," *Leslie's* described Benjamin as "our correspondent" who "follows in the army's bloody trail and tells what she sees." This was only too true: Benjamin followed in the wake of—not with—the army. On July 19, when she was finally able to write from Santiago, the excited prose of "A Woman's Visit to Santiago" demonstrated how much this meant to her.

"The day after the surrender! The American flag waves over Santiago," she wrote. She went inside the "largest Spanish hospital," one of the "most interesting places to visit"; she "also visited the Spanish trenches and picked up a bag-full of Mauser cartridges from freshly-opened boxes which lay on the ground." With these souvenirs in hand, she surveyed the battlefield. "Standing there on a hill-top," she observed, one could "read the tragedy." But now Santiago was a "new American city which lies in peace and dawning prosperity."[125] As with Margherita Hamm, Benjamin's desire to achieve a new professional goal—to become a war correspondent—easily slid into an uncritical celebration of American war aims.[126]

On her return from Cuba, Benjamin began lecturing on her experiences, using lantern slides made from her own photographs.[127] But wanderlust led her to strike out again the next May, when she sailed to the Philippines. This time she spent six months in Manila, and from this experience came a fascinating article for *Outlook* magazine, "Some Filipino Characteristics," in which she tried to work out the complexities of the new U.S. imperial relationship to the Philippines.[128]

On the surface, at least, Benjamin eschewed the easy "barbarism-civilization" dichotomy that dominated American discussions of foreign peoples, attempting instead to acknowledge the complexities of a different culture. "As an unrecognized penalty of our great business success, and the self-centered absorption which it has entailed," she began, "we Americans find it difficult to see from the standpoint of other peoples, or to appreciate standards of civilization different from our own."[129]

Benjamin sought a larger framework for thinking about "the East" than simple clichés. She criticized one author "of a little monograph on the native character" for asserting that "the native is an incomprehensible phenomenon." "So speaks the West of the East," she scoffed; "the time has come when such an attitude of mind should be obsolete." She argued that "our political puzzle in the Philippines, and the industrial and social problems which are to come, have but one key: a comprehension of the native character." What she called "sympathetic study" was a "new sacred duty of the American citizen." "Instinctively realizing this when I went to the Philippines," Benjamin said, "I lived among natives and Spaniards during my half year's stay there, and strove, as far as possible, to view the world with Filipino eyes."[130]

Benjamin started from the relative high ground of acknowledging basic human similarities among cultures—"to a greater extent the people of the East and the people of the West have similar traits," she said. But she quickly drew upon conventional stereotypes to frame her thinking. "We are the most potently aggressive nation of the West," Benjamin declared. "It follows, therefore, that the essence of our institutions is most obviously out of sympathy with the somnolent, contemplative spirit of the East."[131]

The idea of the "contemplative" East was already a well-worn cliché by the time Benjamin used it. But the special irony of her article—which discussed her travels around Manila, her conversations with Americans about their servants, and her relationship with her own servant—was that she provided not one example of anything remotely "somnolent" or "contemplative." Quite the reverse, in fact: she described people who engaged in animated exchanges in markets, in impassioned disputes on roads, and in acts of resistance to domestic orders by Americans.

It was this resistance that seemed to most intrigue her. The "*muchacho* (boy servant) of the officer," with "seeming acquiescence, takes polite note of all his master's instructions," but as soon as "the officer's back is turned" proceeds "to carry out his own previously formed ideas." The "native laundress" could not be made to "wash and iron the clothes according to Yankee precedent." Her own servant was a puzzling conundrum of resistance that Benjamin attempted without much success to understand. "It was a struggle to make Matea abandon any of her traditions of service," Benjamin admitted. "But her intelligence was above the average, and once convinced that my way was really the best, the innovation became sacred in her eyes, and she took great pride in it; still, I was always feeling the strain of her will against mine." Benjamin concluded that "this is how the little people in the Philippines are apt to get ahead of the big, aggressive, impatient Americans."[132]

In short, the complex "Filipino character" had been reduced to that old chestnut, the "servant problem"—to be "proven" by the accumulated complaints of American employers about their employees. Perhaps it is not surprising, then, that Benjamin even included in her article on "Filipino characteristics" some of the stories she had been told of stealing by servants. "Hardly a day passed while I was in the Philippines that I did not hear of some minor lapse from the narrow path of honesty on the part of native servants." Benjamin concluded with a comparison to African Americans. "As a rule," she said, the "pilfering is cunningly done, and it must be admitted that the manner indicates a preconceived intention rather than the giving way to sudden temptation and impulse like the American negro."[133]

Here, in what amounted to a throwaway line, was the real heart of Benjamin's article: her assumption of fixed racial characteristics among African Americans, who functioned as the "still point" of her analysis and against whom she compared all other peoples. By the end of the article Benjamin was arguing that "in the Filipino 'pickaninnies' lies the promise of the future. They are responsive and quick to learn, these little brown boys and girls."[134]

The truth was that no matter how broadening they found travel, newspaper women often held fixed racial attitudes—especially regarding the place of African Americans in American culture—that they used to examine other cultures. Those who rhapsodized the most about the life-changing nature of travel, or considered themselves the most "progressive" on racial questions, were sometimes the quickest to devolve into racist stereotypes. This was certainly true of Mary Krout, who finally did get to Hawaii in 1893, after the overthrow of the queen. Krout argued for the value of travel in her *Chicago Inter Ocean* column, "The Home Circle." The "best companions, the best citizens—because the most enlightened—are not those who have lived a lifetime under one roof or spend most of their time within doors," she said. "Next to the university, and rivaling it in some essentials, the world is the greatest of educators." Travel was a means of liberal education: "The citizen of the world learns, as none other ever can learn, how much excellence there is in humanity at large—that even those condemned as hopelessly barbarous show virtues that the civilized might imitate with profit."[135]

But for Krout, as for so many others, travel confirmed her own racial prejudices. As she commented in her 1898 *Hawaii and a Revolution*, "The native Hawaiian has been an object of much misplaced sympathy on the part of those who know nothing of Hawaiian affairs." Krout explained: "When I visited the Islands first, in 1893, I went prejudiced in favour of the natives, deeply sympathising with them because they had been dispossessed of their lawful possessions. A careful and conscientious study of the situation on the spot led me to change my views absolutely, and I perceived whatever had been done had been done of necessity and with wisdom and forbearance."[136] But that "careful and conscientious study" had been conducted entirely among the white elite of the island who had wined and dined her. In some sense Krout had been putty in the hands of the planter class, just as Benjamin reflected the complaints of a white American elite in Manila.

Krout argued that whites were "native" to Hawaii: after all, "the President of the Hawaiian Republic (Mr. Dole)," as well as others "who finally approved the abrogation of the monarchy, were all Hawaiian born." It was "their country, therefore, as much as it was that of any descendent of the Kamehamehas. All that it possesses to-day of worth" was "due to their labour and to no other influence." Krout "frankly" confessed that "before arriving in Honolulu" her "sympathies were wholly with the natives; I took the view—so easy to acquire from books and from other sentimentalists like myself—that the natives were being robbed of their birthright by the relentless whites, who, in their greed and with their superior cunning, had seized and held the balance of power." This "was a fixed hallucination which it took sometime to clear away." But "at the end of a fortnight the question ceased to be one of sentiment; it became simply . . . one more ethnological illustration of that relentless law, the survival of the fittest."[137]

Krout's adherence to ideas of evolutionary racial hierarchy in Hawaii paralleled her views of race in the United States—although, as a progressive Republican who considered herself to be an advanced thinker in her racial politics, she might have protested such a characterization. But such parallels are transparent when we consider a public dispute between Krout and Ida B. Wells-Barnett in 1895, one that revolved around interlinked issues: the responsibility of the North for Southern lynching, the role of race in Civil War memory, and the roles of African Americans in American society.

In December 1895 Mary Krout was living in London and sending "weekly correspondence" to the *Chicago Inter Ocean*. In an article headlined "Negro Is Discussed," Krout reported that she had visited a settlement house in London where one "Mr. Williams, a colored man," had given a speech on "Negro Lynching." Krout was indignant that Williams "made no discrimination whatever between the North and the South" in his account, leaving "the impression upon the minds of his hearers that the outrages which are not only a disgrace to the country but to civilization were of as frequent occurrence in the North as in the South." Williams had made "disjointed, rambling remarks," according to Krout, and "repeatedly dropped into glaring inaccuracies of grammar and pronunciation." What is more, he had given his own race "the entire credit" for the "successful issue" of the "war of the rebellion; and he dilated upon the schools" African Americans "had established without a word of reference to the thousands of dollars contributed by the Republicans of the North, who have always been the black man's friend, and toward whom he has not always been unswervingly loyal."[138]

Not shy about showcasing herself when an opportunity arose, Krout had responded in London to Williams point by point—then gave her own reported remarks much more space and weight in her column than those of Williams. "Throughout the North," she quoted herself saying, "everything had been done for the negro that could be done: the public schools were open to him, the colleges and universities, and every opportunity given him to engage in any business or profession he might select." She especially objected "to having the North held responsible for the barbarism of the South." She acknowledged the South's "fiendish cruelty to those whom she still oppressed" but asserted that white men and white women of the North would see to it that the South "would be called to account." In the meantime, "the negro" in the South "must learn to defend himself." Krout was pleased to report that her speech had "produced a profound impression," with the speaker "frequently interrupted with cries of 'hear! hear!' and its conclusion" followed by "prolonged applause."[139]

Only a few days after this self-congratulatory report appeared in the *Inter Ocean*, Ida B. Wells-Barnett wrote a stinging rebuke in a letter to the newspaper, exposing Krout's complacency. Krout and Wells-Barnett knew each other personally. In fact, only six months before, Krout had attended the June wedding of Wells and Ferdinand L. Barnett; she was one of several members of the "Woman's Republican State central committee" who were wedding guests.[140] It is hard to believe that Krout was unaware of Wells-Barnett's extensive newspaper campaigns against lynching, first waged in the United States and then, in 1893 and 1894, in England. Indeed, Wells-Barnett must have felt as though Krout were issuing a personal challenge that could not go unanswered.[141]

In any event, Wells-Barnett now took Krout to task. "I do not know the Mr. Williams to whom she refers," she began, "but I do know Miss Krout, and it is because I believe she would not be guilty knowingly of the same error of which she accuses her colored brother that I beg leave to make a few remarks." She then proceeded to dismantle Krout's case point by point. Krout's first accusation, that Williams was guilty of "glaring inaccuracies of grammar and pronunciation," was "generally considered a misfortune, rather than a fault, when it is known that the negro's parents, through circumstances over which they had no control, were deprived of liberty, and the fruits of their labor went for the education of the white offspring of their masters."[142]

Next, Wells-Barnett asserted that "Miss Krout is grievously in error when she states that 'throughout the North everything has been done for the Negro that could be done.'" It was not true, she said, that "'every opportunity is given him to engage in any business or profession he may select.'" On the contrary, "economic conditions force him to become a railway porter, hotel waiter, or boot black; the trades unions, by law, have shut him out from the trades and factories and stores of the North." The North was "as cruel to the negro as the South, because the North educated him and then proscribed him."[143]

As for lynching, "It may be true" that "'whenever a lynching occurs it calls forth an outburst of public indignation throughout the entire North from Boston to San Francisco,' that the press, pulpit, and population are of one opinion and unanimous in the open and fearless expression of that opinion." But it was "strange that the negro knows nothing of such unanimity." Nor had "the systematic hanging, shooting, and burning alive of men, women, and children in this country, called forth one-hundredth part of the protest or interest that the woes of Armenia have called forth from press, pulpit, and philanthropist of the entire country." Was not "the North by its seeming acquiescence as responsible morally as the South is criminally for the awful lynching record of the past thirteen years?"[144]

Wells-Barnett's scathing remarks enable us to see the links between Krout's domestic and international writings. Krout's uncomprehending approach to American domestic racial politics was, in fact, the twin image of her global racial views; the two were inextricably bound together. Though she may have traveled the world, that travel always revolved around the fixed point of her own racial compass.

Yet there was at least one newspaper woman who traveled a different path. In California, Mabel Clare Craft, who wrote for the *San Francisco Chronicle*, experienced a different Hawaii, as well as a different relationship to issues of race.[145] Thirty years younger than Krout, Craft had the highest grade point average—albeit by a tiny percentage—in her graduating class of 1892 at the University of California, Berkeley. This was a first for women and for coeducation at the university. She thus deserved to receive the University Medal—the highest award given to a graduating senior. But at first professors had given the medal to a male student—until Craft protested, not only to university authorities, but also in a remarkably brave letter to the *Chronicle*. She made clear her fierce sense of injustice based on this perceived discrimination against women.[146] She received the medal.

Laboring under a similar sense of gendered injustice, Krout argued for the racial superiority of white women. Craft, on the other hand, seems to have used her own experience of injustice to empathize across racial lines.

Employed by the *Chronicle* shortly after college and quickly becoming an all-around reporter, Craft was assigned to cover the formal transfer of Hawaii to American sovereignty in 1898.[147]

Unlike Mary Krout, however, Mabel Craft was not sympathetic to American annexation of Hawaii. Indeed, she was highly critical of the Hawaiian republic under Sanford B. Dole and other white planters, and she especially objected to their overturning of the monarchy. "The looting of the Hawaiian monarchy by a few Americans," she said sarcastically, was "not an exploit over which any American need thrill with pride." She knew that such comments would not please the white elite in Hawaii: "I am aware that my criticism of the Hawaiian republic will not be received with favor in Honolulu's narrow governmental circles," she wrote. "I do not believe that might necessarily makes right, and I have but reflected the political sentiments of the majority of Hawaiians as I found them during the summer of annexation, when hearts were peculiarly stirred by the culmination of an injustice that amounted to crime. The Hawaiian republic knew nothing of the 'consent of the governed.'" "In Hawaii," she declared, "is the old spirit that abides in unhappy Poland, that burns in the breasts of Alsace-Lorraine."[148] Such a comparison between Hawaii and Europe was in itself remarkable when so many writers, including newspaper women, framed discussions of Hawaii around a dichotomy that privileged white "civilization" over "native barbarism."

Remarkably, Craft took this same sense of injustice into her reporting on the Philippines; she was unique among newspaper women for writing an extended profile of "colored troops." "Sailing now to the Philippines goes one of the four regiments with the best right to the title of 'American' of all the troops in the service of these United States—the Twenty-fourth Infantry, most distinguished of the negro regiments in the country and, possibly, the most renowned infantry regiment in the Army," she declared. "Other regiments may take to themselves the American name, but examine the roll and you will find them mixed as the colors of Joseph's coat—Irish, German, French, Italian—all the strains under the sun. The enlisted negro proclaims proudly the fact that he is the only Simon-pure American child of the soil for more generations than he can count. The only naturalization record in his family was written more than thirty years ago from Sumter to Appomattox."[149]

"It seemed strange," Craft wrote, "when these veterans marched San Francisco streets on Decoration day that there was so little enthusiasm over them—strange that any American should not know the inspiring story of how these dark-skinned, white-souled men fought up the stubborn hill of

San Juan; how a color sergeant of the Twenty-fourth was the first to plant the flag on the heights of the hill." In contrast to white soldiers "reeling along the street" or involved in "saloon brawls and street-car rows," "each [African American] soldier behaves as though he were upon his honor never to cast reproach upon the uniform he wears, the flag he serves or the race to which he belongs."[150]

Craft was not without racial prejudice, as her description of the "white-souled" African American soldiers reveals. Yet she was unique among newspaper women for insisting on the patriotism of the black soldier: "To the flag he serves he bears an intense personal loyalty that is a passion. He is grateful with a gratitude that no other American citizen even approaches." His "bondage is too recent to be forgotten. In that sense also the negro is the best American of us all."[151]

In 1901 Craft carried her progressive racial beliefs into a dispute among California clubwomen over the "color line." The previous year African American journalist Josephine St. Pierre Ruffin had attempted to have her Woman's New Era Club admitted to the General Federation of Women's Clubs—without success (see Chapter 2). Now the color line became an issue in California, as the state's women's clubs addressed the question of whether African American women's clubs should be allowed into the General Federation. Within San Francisco's elite Forum Club, the *San Francisco Examiner* noted, "Miss Mabel Craft stood forth as the champion of the social equality of colored women." In a speech at a club meeting, Craft had declared that "as a citizen of America, Booker T. Washington and others of his race should have entrée into all polite circles—white black or yellow."[152]

Her "stand for the negro caused quite a flutter among the ladies," the *Examiner* reported. Some club members agreed with her, but others spoke out openly against the admission of African American women. One member stated that "I am not prepared to accept the negro on equal terms with the whites, and do not admit their social equality."[153] Craft, described by the *Examiner* as a "young woman of advanced ideas" as well as the "leader of the liberalists among local clubwomen," insisted that the "recognition of the social rights of any race" was "not a matter of sympathy, but of justice." She asserted that "I have traveled among the dark races in the South, in Mexico and in Hawaii, and I found these people are human. They have human impulses and ambitions; their affections are human, though their ideals may differ in a minor way from ours." Affirming that "the color line is drawn by prejudice," she admitted that "many ladies who are intellectual, sympathetic and lovable have an inherent prejudice against the negro." But she could not "reconcile this prejudice with twentieth century logic or our boasted progress in civilization."[154] But Craft had little impact beyond the local arena: at the national convention of the General Federation of Women's Clubs a few months later, the issue of the color line was never even brought to the floor, enabling Northern and Southern women to do what they pleased in their own sections.

# # #

At the turn of the century numerous newspaper women ventured beyond the borders of the United States, engaging in a form of print expansionism. Once embarked on extensive travel, some of them never looked back. In 1901 the woman's page of the *New York Sun* profiled Mary Krout as a "woman globe trotter," announcing that "Miss Krout Has a Record of 50,000 Miles in a Single Year."[155] After her stay in the Philippines, Anna Northend Benjamin traveled to Japan, Korea, and China, with a "number of her letters" printed in the *New-York Tribune*. By 1901, when she went to Russia, she carried with her a note from the *Tribune*'s news editor explaining to U.S. consuls that she was "abroad for the purpose of writing articles for the New York Tribune and other American publications."[156] At the time of her death in 1902, at age twenty-seven, apparently from cancer, Benjamin was working on a book about her travels.[157] The *New York World* remarked that "she had done more war correspondence and travelled over more of the world than most men of twice her years."[158]

Nellie Bly's swift travels of late 1889 and 1890—in which she had triumphantly circumnavigated the world in seventy-two days in a "stunt" for the *World*—arose not only out of a larger cultural interest in travel at the turn of the century (especially when undertaken by a woman alone), but also from a new interest in mechanized speed and motion. Hers was a technological triumph in an era that celebrated faster steamships, instant telegraphic connections, more powerful railroads, and, increasingly, the automobile.

But the global race that Bly engaged in was fundamentally different from the travel of the expansionist newspaper women. They sought not to get from place to place as swiftly as possible, but to spend enough time in foreign locations that they could claim to understand—and write about for publication—other places in the world. They brought a form of internationalism to their travels—a genuine curiosity about how other peoples lived, as well as the political situation of other countries.

Whether they *did* understand other cultures is another question entirely, as we have seen. Certainly they viewed other peoples through the lens of their own racial prejudices and, in most cases, were uncritical supporters of—indeed, enthusiastic boosters of—American expansionist aims. In the midst of their global movement, an assumption of racial hierarchy remained a fixed point of reference. Nevertheless, they saw their travel as personally broadening. An article that described Anna Northend Benjamin as "making a tour of the world alone" commented that she had "returned with a fund of experience." Benjamin herself was quoted as saying she had "come back with a broader outlook on life."[159]

Travel not only gave newspaper women an expanded sense of self, it gave them new possibilities for publication. This was a point Margherita Hamm stressed in her 1899 magazine article "Women as Travelers," in which she asserted that travel offered "new opportunities for ambitious women." Arguing that "travel and literature combined present a fine industrial field for the educated woman," Hamm noted that "the encroachments of civilization upon the wilds are bringing into notice and making of interest scores of places which heretofore were of no account excepting to the map-maker or strategist." She saw a "noble field in upper Egypt" for such literary work, not to mention Khartoum—"especially in regard to the domestic life of the Baggarans and other ethnic types"—Uganda, Tanganyika, Rhodesia, and the Congo basin. These were places that offered "rich harvests to the observer and writer." They were "but a few of the long list of places and peoples" that were "waiting for students, and especially women students" to describe them "for the benefit of the great reading public."[160] An expanded sense of the self, an expanded sense of the world—the two went hand in hand for the newspaper women who ventured forth as print expansionists equipped with Hamm's helpful suggestions—a "pair of good field glasses and a medium-sized light-weight typewriter."[161] With such equipment newspaper women were sure they could map the globe.

epilogue *Toward Suffrage*

In 1906 Nixola Greeley-Smith had exuberantly affirmed her work for a "yellow" newspaper—and in fact she remained with the *New York World* for her entire career, except for a brief (and unhappy) period writing for a syndicate. But by 1915 Greeley-Smith, a committed feminist as well as suffrage supporter, was clear-eyed in her assessment of the limited opportunities for women in newspaper work—not to mention the prejudices of male editors. In an article titled "Professional Women Tell of Handicaps: Feminists Who Tell of Their Uphill Struggle to Success," she outlined the barriers newspaper women still faced. "There are no city editors, there are no managing editors, and there are no editorial writers among women. Why?" she asked. "Why, because they are women. That is all. Women who write must write about love, and pour out sweet sugary stuff. That is the only sort that man likes to receive from them." Greeley-Smith patently resented the "sob sister" stereotype and turned it on its head: "You know man is of the sentimental sex," she said. "The best sob-sister is always the man. The woman sees the facts and the real truth of the matter."[1]

In 1917 Greeley-Smith filled out a "Questionnaire for Newspaper Women" administered by the Bureau of Vocational Information. Asked to indicate "Nature of Work," she explained in a handwritten scrawl that "I write interviews on every conceivable subject with experts, with visitors of distinction, write editorial articles which in my case express the feminist point of view—write comments on great murder trials." In answer to the question "What limitations and disadvantages would you point out?" Greeley-Smith was blunt: "A woman cannot get beyond a certain point in New York." There "are no women editors on N.Y. papers," she added.[2]

Greeley-Smith would not live to see the day when there were women city editors and managing editors in New York; she died in 1919, at age thirty-nine, of complications from appendicitis.[3] It would be another sixty years before women occupied top editorial positions at newspapers such as the

New York Times, although they fared better as editors at the tabloids that sprang up in the 1920s as the descendants of the earlier sensational papers.[4] Newspaper women did make substantial gains in reporting assignments during World War I, but their "progress" was again more fitful in the 1920s.

Thus this is far from a story of women's inevitable professional triumphs in newspaper work beginning at the turn of the century; instead, their small gains often needed to be laboriously remade, over and over. When Clara Savage, fresh out of Smith College, began work at the *New York Evening Post* in 1913, she did not even realize that her predecessor was Rheta Dorr — Savage sometimes described herself as the first woman ever to work for the *Post*.

But if turn-of-the-century journalism did not lead women directly upward into editorial positions at newspapers, it did lead women expansively *outward* — out into the world they "covered," out into new experiences in cities and beyond the borders of the United States, out into new careers like magazine work. Newspaper work substantially expanded what we can claim as women's public sphere in this era.

One of the public worlds inhabited and shaped by newspaper women was the suffrage movement. We do not ordinarily think of female journalists in connection with the fight for suffrage — but this is a mistake. *Publicity*, after all, became a central strategy of the suffrage movement by the turn of the century; and the chief vehicle for publicity in this era was the newspaper. Though rarely acknowledged, newspaper women's role in providing that publicity was crucial — as we can see by looking at almost any turn-of-the-century metropolitan newspaper. Before British suffragettes made suffrage a front-page story starting in 1905, suffrage news appeared on the woman's page — the purview of newspaper women. The woman's page of the *Chicago Daily Tribune* on February 8, 1900, is one example out of hundreds. The lead article, "Opens Women's Meeting: Miss Susan B. Anthony Presides for the Last Time,"[5] provided a full account of the opening session of the annual National American Woman Suffrage Association meeting. The woman's page was one of the public spaces of the suffrage movement, where female reporters were able to provide regular, continuing news of suffrage activism.

Even when newspaper editors were indifferent or actively hostile to suffrage coverage, women were sometimes able to use subterfuge to sneak in suffrage news. As Marie Manning remembered of her work in the Hen Coop at the *New York Journal*, "We girls were all confirmed suffragists," but the "big shots on the paper were not interested in woman suffrage in the beginning of the 1900's." It was a period in which the movement was in the "doldrums," with endless small "parlor meetings" that hardly seemed newsworthy. Although Manning and her female colleagues "religiously followed up" these meetings and took "enormous pains" with their reports, they found that "if they weren't discarded altogether," their stories were "always boiled down to a sentence." The managing editor "often said that the majority of women didn't want to vote"; the city editor was only "lukewarm on the subject." The result was that "so far as writing about the subject went, our hands were largely tied."[6]

Yet Manning occasionally managed to slip more extensive suffrage news into the paper, and she later gleefully recounted some of the stratagems newspaper women used to do so. "It was pure chance," she said, "that pointed out to us a crafty and guileful route to use, in order to land such pieces in the paper." At one parlor meeting on suffrage, "some sort of altercation" occurred. Although "it didn't amount to anything," and to the women reporters present it "scarcely seemed worth mentioning," to the "masculine hierarchy it seemed to be amusing and they published it in full." The next time the women reporters "got suffrage assignments to cover," they were told "to watch out for 'fights'"—their editors found the "spectacle" of women arguing entertaining. Manning quickly devised a strategy that played to—and subversively with—this male prejudice. She declared with obvious pride that "not only did we watch out for" fights, "but we actually created them, aided and abetted by those splendid pioneer suffragists who had been working for the amendment for nearly fifty years."[7]

"Wholly imaginary" altercations about "millinery, length of skirts, Republican or Democratic nominees, popular novels, or what not, would be cooked up by the best of friends with a dash of acrimony," Manning said, "and at the end of the row we would manage to get across some scrap of news advantageous to suffrage." Best of all, "the moguls never caught on." Although Manning admitted that "doubtless these innocent prevarications never got the movement very far," they "helped to keep our spirits up in the Hen Coop," and they "mightily amused those splendid old high priestesses of the movement."[8]

Newspaper women supported suffrage in multiple other ways as well. Margherita Hamm, for instance, founded the short-lived Woman's Suffrage Press Association in 1895. Consisting of "newspaper women—editors, special writers, and correspondents," the membership embraced "many names well known in current literature." Its goal was "to protect in every possible way the cause of equal suffrage as it is set forth before the public in the daily press"; members even took a "pledge" to "use all possible means to further the publication of suffrage news." The organization does not seem to have been productive; there is no trace of its influence beyond Hamm's first promotional announcement. Yet it does remind us that newspaper women had a savvy appreciation of publicity and its importance to the suffrage cause.[9]

Many suffrage leaders grew to recognize that newspaper women's extensive newspaper experience put them in a unique position to be effective "press agents" for suffrage. The "president of the California State Suffrage Association" asked Mabel Craft Deering "several times previous to 1906 to take the press chairmanship as I had been a newspaper woman." Craft had always been too busy to consider this job. But in 1906, after "the earthquake and fire in San Francisco" left her with "more time on my hands than I had ever had before or ever expect to again," Craft recalled, "I said to myself, 'What can I do for suffrage?' and the press work occurred to me." She was "at once appointed press chairman for the entire state."[10]

As Rose Young, chairman of the Press Department of New York's 1915 Empire State Campaign Committee, explained: "If you concede that you want to keep suffrage before the public as a live issue, as the livest issue of the times, you must concede that you've got to keep it in the newspapers. To keep it in the newspapers you must relate it acceptably to the news of the day."[11] Of course, Young understood this point firsthand. During 1912–13 she had worked for the *New York Evening Post* "inaugurating a feature devoted to the activities and interests of 'modern' women."[12] Young moved back and forth between press work and suffrage work, as was true of a number of newspaper women.

Ida Husted Harper, for instance, was both a suffrage activist and newspaper woman. For almost five years she produced a regular suffrage column for the *New York Sun*, "The Cause of Women," before the paper was sold to "an anti-suffragist, who discontinued" the column. Harper later not only wrote a biography of Susan B. Anthony but also was the editor of volumes 5 and 6 of the six-volume *History of Woman Suffrage* (published in 1922). Likewise, Elizabeth Jordan remained a staunch advocate of suffrage after she left newspaper work to become editor of *Harper's Bazar*; she wrote a biography of suffrage leader Anna Howard Shaw, as well as publishing a composite suffrage novel, one of whose contributors was Anne O'Hagan.[13]

After 1905, when the suffrage campaign was newly energized by both the example of British activism and new American leadership, male newspaper editors finally began to focus on the movement.[14] This was sometimes a mixed blessing for newspaper women. When suffrage was a front-page story—as with the emergence of the radical English suffragettes, who smashed glass windows, chained themselves to fences, and disrupted Parliament—suffrage stories were often taken away from newspaper women, which they bitterly resented.

Yet with the rise of interest in the movement fueled by the radicalism of Emmeline and Christabel Pankhurst and by English activism more generally, editors also began to designate newspaper women as regular suffrage reporters and columnists, and even as suffrage editors. At the *Chicago Daily Tribune*, Mary Isabel Brush (who had interviewed Dorothy Richardson in her plush office), moved from writing woman's page "stuff," such as interviews and newspaper contests, to a regular column on suffrage. Linking two very different generations of newspaper women together, the *Tribune* trumpeted her in 1911 as their "expert" on "women's political problems" in an advertisement that also featured Marion Harland as an "expert" on "household topics." Over the next year Brush provided smart, forthright, informative, ardently pro-suffrage coverage in her suffrage columns—in other words, free publicity for the movement.[15]

"Heaven bless the press!" exclaimed suffrage leader Harriot Stanton Blatch in remembering her own use of "effective propaganda" during 1908 and 1909. As her substantial scrapbook collection of newspaper clippings shows, she was only too aware of the importance of newspaper publicity to her cause.[16] Yet Blatch rarely acknowledged newspaper women's role in providing publicity for the suffrage fight. Perhaps seeking to emphasize the importance of her own role as a leader, she spoke merely of "placing" suffrage "propaganda" in newspapers. But in many cases that "placement" was not possible without the work of newspaper women—unacknowledged partners in the long fight for suffrage.

Columnists like Nixola Greeley-Smith wrote frequently in support of suffrage and feminism. Kate Carew not only interviewed suffrage leaders but also wrote an account of marching in the great suffrage parade of May 1912. And a whole new generation of younger newspaper women cut their teeth on covering suffrage. Looking back in 1974 on her suffrage work for the *New York Tribune* during the 1910s, Emma Bugbee remembered somewhat wistfully that there "were more women in journalism at that time than there were ever after," because "there were eleven newspapers and they all had women on the daily staff and on the Sunday staff. There were a *lot* of us. And we *all* covered the votes for women campaign." According to another female reporter, "It was fun covering suffrage for the papers in those days."[17]

As they made a public space for suffrage in their newspapers, these women also created a new (if temporary) community: scattered among the great newspapers of New York, women reporters often met on a daily basis at local suffrage headquarters as they searched out that day's "stories." In 1922 some of them founded the New York Newspaper Women's Club: they missed the camaraderie the suffrage movement had provided.[18]

Newspaper women who covered suffrage practiced a form of politics little addressed in histories of the movement—one that used the modern practices of newspaper publicity to further political ends. In striving for political representation for all women, newspaper women simultaneously created new public representation for themselves: after all, in each fresh article they inhabited a new public space in print. Each of these black-and-white public spaces may have been evanescent, lasting only a day, yet they were also linked backward through time to previous, ongoing newspaper conversations. They were also linked forward—to tomorrow's newspaper, and tomorrow's conversation, in which women would surely continue to move forward into public life.

Notes

introduction

1. Margherita Arlina Hamm, "About Newspaper Women," *Journalist*, November 14, 1891. This was the only column with that title: by the end of November, Hamm changed the name to "Among the Newspaper Women."

2. On American women in public life, a good place to start is Mary Ryan, *Women in Public: Between Banners and Ballots, 1825–1880* (Baltimore: Johns Hopkins University Press, 1990). See also Christine Stansell, *American Moderns: Bohemian New York and the Creation of a New Century* (New York: Metropolitan Books, 2000) and *City of Women: Sex and Class in New York, 1789–1860* (New York: Knopf, 1986). For journalism as a set of public "disruptive acts," see Mary Louise Roberts, *Disruptive Acts: The New Woman in Fin-de-Siècle France* (Chicago: University of Chicago Press, 2002).

3. See Alice Fahs, "Newspaper Women and the Making of the Modern, 1885–1910," *Prospects* 27 (2002): 303–39. Men, too, wrote "specials" for newspapers. See Theodore Dreiser's account of his frustrating New York newspaper work in Dreiser, *Newspaper Days: An Autobiography*, ed. T. D. Nostwich (Santa Rosa, Calif.: Black Sparrow Press, 2000). The difference in the women's case is that there were so few staff positions available to them that turning out "specials" could—of necessity—become a way of life.

4. For Hamm's career, see esp. "The Only Woman War Correspondent: Margherita Arlina Hamm," *Journalist*, September 8, 1894; "An Industrious Correspondent," *Chicago Daily Inter Ocean*, March 2, 1895; "Dr. and Mrs. William E. S. Fales en Route," *Journalist*, February 10, 1894; Hamm, "Women as Travelers: The American Woman in Action," *Frank Leslie's Popular Monthly*, June 1899, 214–18; *Who's Who in America* (Chicago: A. N. Marquis and Co., 1906), 764; "Formerly of Bangor," *Bangor Daily Whig and Courier*, July 11, 1898; "Mrs. Fales Gets a Decree of Divorce," *New York Herald*, July 31, 1902; and "Dies as She Begins New Work," *New York Herald*, December 18, 1907. Hamm's fulfillment of her dream to be published in *Century Magazine* is documented in her correspondence with the magazine's editor. See Hamm to R. U. Johnson, April 5, 30, June 12, July 22, August 25, October 7, 1904, January 5, March 8, June 12, 1905, July 16, n.d., and undated letter, Century Co. Records, New York Public Library. As this correspondence reveals, Hamm was the sole author of her 1902 *Ghetto Silhouettes*; but to her dismay, her publisher added the well-known actor David Warfield as a "co-author" of the book for publicity purposes, without her permission. See Hamm to R. U. Johnson, April 5, 1904. Hamm's numerous magazine and newspaper articles also provide occasional biographic information.

5. As Jean Marie Lutes points out, "Scholarship on journalism and turn-of-the-century fiction in the United States focuses almost exclusively on male authors." Lutes, *Front-Page Girls: Women Journalists in American Culture and Fiction, 1880–1930* (Ithaca: Cornell University Press, 2006), 167. But Lutes herself follows in the footsteps of the few scholars of turn-of-the-century newspaper women by focusing on the most famous journalists of the period: Nellie Bly and the so-called sob sisters. For other general works on newspaper women, see Deborah Chambers, Linda Steiner, and Carole Fleming, *Women in Journalism* (New York: Routledge, 2004); Marion Marzolf, *Up from the Footnote: A History of Women Journalists* (New York: Hastings House, 1977); Ishbel Ross, *Ladies of the Press: The Story of Women in Journalism by an Insider* (New York: Harper and Brothers, 1936); Phyllis Leslie Abramson, *Sob Sister Journalism* (New York: Greenwood Press, 1990); Madelon Golden Schlipp and Sharon M. Murphy, *Great Women of the Press* (Carbondale: Southern Illinois University Press, 1983); Elizabeth V. Burt, ed., *Women's Press Organizations, 1881–1999* (Westport, Conn.: Greenwood, 2000); Maurine H. Beasley and Sheila J. Gibbons, *Taking Their Place: A Documentary History of Women and Journalism* (Washington, D.C.: American University Press, 1993); and Barbara Belford, *Brilliant Bylines: A Biographical Anthology of Notable Newspaperwomen in America* (New York: Columbia University Press, 1986). Some of the best histories of women's newspaper work are contained in individual biographies: see esp. Brooke Kroeger, *Nellie Bly: Daredevil, Reporter, Feminist* (New York: Times Books, 1994), and Elizabeth Faue, *Writing the Wrongs: Eva Valesh and the Rise of Labor Journalism* (Ithaca: Cornell University Press, 2002).

6. Digitization allows us to track this syndication for at least some papers. On the history of newspaper syndication, see Charles A. Johanningsmeier, *Fiction and the American Literary Marketplace: The Role of Newspaper Syndicates in America, 1860–1900* (New York: Cambridge University Press, 1997), and Elmo Scott Watson, *A History of Newspaper Syndicates in the United States, 1865–1935* (Chicago: Elmo Scott Watson, 1936).

7. On changing definitions of publicity, as well as the practices of publicity related to newspapers, see Kevin Stoker and Brad L. Rawlins, "The 'Light' of Publicity in the Progressive Era: From Searchlight to Flashlight," *Journalism History* 30 (Winter 2005): 177–88.

8. On the "net circulation" of the *New York Times* when it was bought by Adolph S. Ochs in 1896, see Frank Luther Mott, *American Journalism: A History of Newspapers in the United States through 260 Years, 1690 to 1950* (New York: Macmillan, 1950), 549. There were 55 daily newspapers in New York City in 1890 and 53 in 1900, although many of these were small. See "Table 30—Statistics Relating to Daily Publications in 27 Cities, 1880–1900," in "Printing and Publishing," *U.S. Bureau of the Census: Twelfth Census of the United States, 1900, Manufacturers*, vol. 9, as quoted in W. Joseph Campbell, *Yellow Journalism: Puncturing the Myths, Defining the Legacies* (Westport, Conn.: Praeger, 2001), 57–58.

9. Frank Luther Mott (*American Journalism*, 546) points out that the combined circulation of the *World*'s morning and evening editions "touched the one million mark" in March 1897. In 1896, the year Adolph Ochs bought the "failing and demoralized" *Times*, its circulation was 9,000, compared with 19,000 for the *Evening Post*, 130,000 for the two editions of the *Sun*, 140,000 for the *Herald*, 430,000 for the *Journal*, and 600,000

for the *World*. See Michael Schudson, *Discovering the News: A Social History of American Newspapers* (New York: Basic Books, 1978), 110–11.

10. On Pulitzer, see James McGrath Morris, *Pulitzer: A Life in Politics, Print, and Power* (New York: Harper, 2010); W. A. Swanberg, *Pulitzer* (New York: Scribner, 1967); and Don C. Seitz, *Joseph Pulitzer: His Life and Letters* (New York: Simon and Schuster, 1924). On Hearst, see esp. David Nasaw, *The Chief: The Life of William Randolph Hearst* (New York: Houghton Mifflin, 2000), and W. A. Swanberg, *Citizen Hearst: A Biography of William Randolph Hearst* (1961; reprint, New York: Galahad Books, 1996).

11. On the penny press of the 1830s, see esp. Patricia Cline Cohen, *The Murder of Helen Jewett* (New York: Knopf, 1998), and Andie Tucher, *Froth and Scum: Truth, Beauty, Goodness, and the Ax Murder in America's First Mass Medium* (Chapel Hill: University of North Carolina Press, 1994). In the antebellum period James Gordon Bennett's *Sun* also had many sensational features, as Tucher and Cohen have pointed out. Reporters of the 1890s similarly noticed a link backward to the famous story papers of the mid-nineteenth century, esp. Robert Bonner's *Ledger*. On this point, see James L. Ford, *The Literary Shop and Other Tales* (New York: Geo. H. Richmond and Co., 1894). In other words, newspapers of the 1890s were hardly entirely new. But they represented a significant expansion—quite literally—of this sensationalist mode, with many more pages of features. See also Larzer Ziff, *The American 1890s: Life and Times of a Lost Generation* (New York: Viking Press, 1966), 146–65.

12. Peter Fritzsche, *Reading Berlin, 1900* (Cambridge: Harvard University Press, 1996).

13. Scholars have argued about the origins of the pejorative term "yellow journalism," which first became popular in 1897. Many have speculated that it was related to the new popularity of the *World*'s comic strip figure, the "Yellow Kid." This is a possible explanation, to be sure. But it seems just as likely, in my view, that "yellow journalism" mirrored "yellow literature," which during the Civil War era had been used as a general term to describe cheap novels, some of which were distinctive for their yellow covers. On such cheap literature, see Alice Fahs, *The Imagined Civil War: Popular Literature of the North and South, 1861–1865* (Chapel Hill: University of North Carolina Press, 2001). For controversies over the term "yellow journalism," see Campbell, *Yellow Journalism*. On the *Recorder*, see Lorna Watson, "The New York Recorder as a Woman's Newspaper, 1891–1894" (M.A. thesis, University of Wisconsin, Madison, 1939).

14. Mary Twombly, "Women in Journalism," *Writer* 3 (August 1889): 169. Newspaper woman Emma B. Kaufman made much the same point in 1895: "With the advent of the 'Woman's Page,'" she said, not to mention "the big Sunday editions of metropolitan papers, the opportunities for women" had increased "ten fold." "It would seem," she commented, "that a clever, energetic, adaptable woman is always needed nowadays to do fashions and household matters." Kaufman, "The Newspaper Woman," *Arthur's Home Magazine* 65 (April 1895): 296–97.

15. Margherita Arlina Hamm, "Among the Newspaper Women," *Journalist*, May 28, 1892.

16. Beatrice Fairfax [Marie Manning], *Ladies Now and Then* (New York: E. P. Dutton, 1944), 23.

17. For an interesting discussion of "New Journalism," see Karen Roggenkamp, *Nar-*

rating the News: New Journalism and Literary Genre in Late Nineteenth-Century Ameri-can Newspapers and Fiction (Kent, Ohio: Kent State University Press, 2005).

18. Helen Hambridge, "Women of the Fourth Estate," *Broadway Magazine* 19 (January 1908): 501.

19. Hamm, "About Newspaper Women," *Journalist*, November 14, 1891, and "Among the Newspaper Women," *Journalist*, May 28, 1892.

20. Fairfax [Manning], *Ladies Now and Then*, 71.

21. For the journalistic uses of women's bodies in public, see Lutes, *Front-Page Girls*.

22. Hambridge, "Women of the Fourth Estate," 503.

23. Ross, *Ladies of the Press*, 69.

24. On this point, see Ben Singer, *Melodrama and Modernity: Early Sensational Cinema and Its Contexts* (New York: Columbia University Press, 2001).

25. The *New York Sun*, March 27, 1896, reprinted an article from the *Chicago Times-Herald* under the headline "Plain Words about Some Disgusting Developments of Sunday Journalism." Noting that the "contest in sensationalism, so called" was continuing between the *World* and "its new and rich rival, the *Morning Journal*," the Chicago paper declared that the "furious exploitation of crime, vulgarity, and squalid enterprises of women reporters" had resulted in "hitherto undiscovered depths of degradation." On Kate Swan McGuirk, see Chapter 5.

26. Hamm, "About Newspaper Women," *Journalist*, November 14, 1891.

27. "Fair Women Rustlers: New York's Galaxy of Feminine Newspaper Reporters," *Milwaukee Sentinel*, May 11, 1891. See also Elizabeth G. Jordan, "A Newspaper Woman's Story," *Lippincott's Monthly Magazine*, March 1893, 344–46.

28. Margaret H. Welch, "Is Newspaper Work Healthful for Women?," *Journal of Social Science* (November 1894): 113.

29. Ida Husted Harper, "The Training of Women Journalists," *Women in Professions: Being the Professional Section of the International Congress of Women, London, July, 1899* (London: T. Fisher Unwin, 1900), 59.

30. Anne O'Hagan, "Women in Journalism," *Munsey's Magazine* 19 (July 1898): 615.

31. Jordan, "Newspaper Woman's Story," 347.

32. On mid-nineteenth-century literary work, see esp. Mary Kelley, *Private Woman, Public Stage: Literary Domesticity in Nineteenth-Century America* (Chapel Hill: University of North Carolina Press, 1984).

33. O'Hagan, "Women in Journalism," 615.

34. Elizabeth G. Jordan, *Three Rousing Cheers* (New York: Appleton-Century, 1938), 49–50.

35. Edna Ferber, *A Peculiar Treasure* (New York: Garden City, 1938), 103.

36. Neith Boyce Hapgood, Draft autobiography, p. 61, Hapgood Family Papers, box 30, Beinecke Rare Book and Manuscript Library, Yale Collection of American Literature. Hapgood was remembering her career at the *New York Commercial Advertiser*.

37. August Derleth, *Still Small Voice: The Biography of Zona Gale* (New York: Appleton-Century, 1940), 64. Gale worked for the *New York World*.

38. See, e.g., Mary White Ovington, "The Penny Paper," *Outlook*, Jan. 30, 1904, 280.

39. Nicholson Baker, *Double Fold: Libraries and the Assault on Paper* (New York: Random House, 2001). See also Nicholson Baker and Margaret Brentano, *The World*

on Sunday: Graphic Art in Joseph Pulitzer's Newspapers, 1898–1911 (New York: Bulfinch Press, 2005).

40. On the late nineteenth-century celebration of masculinized experience in popular literary culture, see Christopher P. Wilson, *The Labor of Words: Literary Professionalism in the Progressive Era* (Athens: University of Georgia Press, 1985).

chapter one

1. Mrs. M. L. [Martha Louise] Rayne, *What Can a Woman Do; or, Her Position in the Business and Literary World* (Detroit: F. B. Dickerson and Co., 1884), 42. Rayne herself was proof of this national trend: she not only wrote for Detroit newspapers but also established a journalism school there for women that operated from 1886 to 1890. See Linda Steiner, *Construction of Gender in Newsreporting Textbooks, 1890–1990* (Columbia, S.C.: Association for Education in Journalism and Mass Communication, 1992), 7.

2. Maurine H. Beasley and Sheila J. Gibbons, *Taking Their Place: A Documentary History of Women and Journalism* (Washington, D.C.: American University Press, 1993), 101.

3. See *Journalist*, January 26, 1889.

4. "A Caustic Critic," *Journalist*, October 3, 1891.

5. Charles A. Dana, *The Art of Newspaper Making: Three Lectures* (1895; reprint, New York: Arno and New York Times, 1970), 94.

6. Joseph A. Hill, *Women in Gainful Occupations, 1870–1920* (Washington, D.C.: Government Printing Office, 1929), 42.

7. Edith May Marken, "Women in American Journalism before 1900" (M.A. thesis, University of Missouri, 1932), 51–54, as quoted in Beasley and Gibbons, *Taking Their Place*, 10.

8. Henry James, *The Bostonians* (1886; reprint, New York: Modern Library, 2003), 122.

9. Kate Masterson, "The Newspaper Woman of To-Day," *Era* 10 (October 1902): 375; Haryot Holt Cahoon, "Women in Gutter Journalism," *Arena* 17 (March 1897): 568–69.

10. Mary Gay Humphreys, "Women Bachelors in New York," *Scribner's Magazine* 19 (August 1896): 627.

11. J. L. H. [Jennie L. Hopkins], "A Woman's Experience of Newspaper Work," *Harper's Weekly*, January 25, 1890, 74–75. On the report of Hopkins as the "smartest reporter in Denver," see "Of Interest to Women," *Boston Daily Advertiser*, October 14, 1887, and "The Smartest Girl Reporter," *Morning Oregonian* (Portland), November 15, 1887. For the New Zealand reference, see "Ladies' Gossip," *Otago Witness*, January 13, 1888.

12. Eliza Putnam Heaton, "Girls Who Write," *Milwaukee Sentinel*, December 25, 1887 (Holloway).

13. Margherita Arlina Hamm, "Among the Newspaper Women," *Journalist*, November 28, 1891.

14. Ibid.

15. Florence Finch Kelly, *Flowing Stream: The Story of Fifty-six Years in American Newspaper Life* (New York: E. P. Dutton, 1939), 121.

16. J. L. H., "Woman's Experience of Newspaper Work," 74–75.

17. See the 1880 Federal Census Record for Fanny B. Ward (her name was spelled

both "Fanny" and "Fannie" in official records), whose home was listed in Ravenna, Portage, Ohio, and whose marital status was "divorced." *1880 United States Federal Census*, http://www.ancestry.com. For her unhappy marriage, see Rheta Childe Dorr, *A Woman of Fifty* (1924; reprint, New York: Arno Press, 1980), 57–72. For Dorothy Richardson, see Richardson to Wallace Rice, January 14, 1901, Wallace Rice Papers, Newberry Library, Chicago.

18. Elizabeth G. Jordan, *Three Rousing Cheers* (New York: Appleton-Century, 1938), 104–6.

19. Mary Gay Humphreys, "Women Bachelors in New York," 627. For Humphreys as "one of the brightest of newspaper writers," see *Literary News* 17 (1896): 344. On "New Women," see esp. Carroll Smith-Rosenberg's classic essay, "The New Woman as Androgyne: Social Disorder and the Gender Crisis, 1870–1936," in her *Disorderly Conduct: Visions of Gender in Victorian America* (New York: Knopf, 1985), 245–96. The first wave of identifications of "New Women" occurred in the mid-1890s and are the subject of this book; the second wave came of age in the 1910s, imbued with the turn to feminism. On this second wave, see Nancy F. Cott, *The Grounding of Modern Feminism* (New Haven: Yale University Press, 1987), and Stansell, *American Moderns*.

20. Hamm, "Among the Newspaper Women," *Journalist*, January 14, 1893.

21. Anne O'Hagan, "Women in Journalism," *Munsey's Magazine* 19 (July 1898): 611.

22. Elizabeth Garver Jordan, "The Newspaper Woman's Story," *Lippincott's Monthly Magazine*, March 1893, 341. On Croly, see "Mrs. Jennie June Croly," *New York Times*, March 11, 1890, and "Mrs. Jennie C. Croly Dead," *New York Times*, December 24, 1901.

23. Helen M. Winslow, "Some Newspaper Women," *Arena* 17 (December 1896): 127. She commented that the noms de plume of Fanny Fern and Jennie June had been signed in earlier years to "contributions on all sorts of interesting and timely topics."

24. Hamm, "Among the Newspaper Women," *Journalist*, April 9, 1892.

25. Ibid.

26. Jennie June's pioneering woman's club Sorosis, begun in 1868, now also sometimes attracted scorn, as in the comments of one *Life* columnist: "There is a lingering suspicion that Sorosis to-day represents the side-curl and woman's-rights era of female emancipation rather than the ideas which go with woman's more recent and present position in the world of affairs." *Life*, June 8, 1893, 21.

27. Ida M. Tarbell, "Women in Journalism," *Chautauquan* 7 (April 1887): 393.

28. When the Press League was founded in Chicago in 1891, it made a point of including only "women engaged in actual newspaper service." The "mere dilettante who effects journalism as a fad or pastime finds the door of admittance barred against her." Meta Wellers, "The Press League," *Journalist*, November 28, 1891.

29. Winslow, "Some Newspaper Women," 127.

30. Jordan, "Newspaper Woman's Story," 341.

31. Winslow, "Some Newspaper Women," 140.

32. "Mrs. Zoe Anderson Norris," *New York Times*, February 14, 1914. On Norris, see also *Richmond Dispatch*, March 30, 1902, as well as her magazine *East Side* and articles for the *New York Times* from 1904 to 1913. In addition, she published in a variety of magazines, including *Cosmopolitan*, *Everybody's Magazine*, and *Harper's Weekly*.

33. On Viola Roseboro', see Jane Kirkland Graham, *Viola: The Duchess of New Dorp: A Biography of Viola Roseboro'* (Danville: Illinois Printing Co., 1955). On Winifred Bonfils Black, see esp. her "Rambles through My Memories," *Good Housekeeping*, January 1936, 18–21, 148–54; February 1936, 36–37, 211–22; March 1936, 44–45, 230–39; April 1936, 84–85, 225–37; and May 1936, 36–37, 253–59. On Kate Field, see Gary Scharnhorst, *Kate Field: The Many Lives of a Nineteenth-Century American Journalist* (Syracuse, N.Y.: Syracuse University Press, 2008).

34. Hamm, "Among the Newspaper Women," *Journalist*, November 28, 1891.

35. "Mrs. Merrill's Debut," *New York World*, February 21, 1892.

36. On the Professional Woman's League, see Eliza Archard Conner, "A Woman's World in Paragraphs," *Atchison Daily Globe*, December 21, 1894.

37. See Elizabeth Faue, *Writing the Wrongs: Eva Valesh and the Rise of Labor Journalism* (Ithaca: Cornell University Press, 2002).

38. On the press's fascination with Stokes's engagement, see, e.g., "From Cigar Roller to Rich Man's Bride," *New York World*, April 9, 1905; and "A Ghetto Romance," *New-York Tribune*, April 16, 1905. On dime novels, see Nan Enstad, *Ladies of Labor, Girls of Adventure: Working Women, Popular Culture, and Labor Politics at the Turn of the Twentieth Century* (New York: Columbia University Press, 1999).

39. Stokes began writing columns for the *Jewish Daily News* in 1902 and was hired as a staff member in 1903. See Rose Pastor Stokes, *"I Belong to the Working Class": The Unfinished Autobiography of Rose Pastor Stokes*, ed. Herbert Shapiro and David L. Sterling (Athens: University of Georgia Press, 1992), and Arthur Zipser and Pearl Zipser, *Fire and Grace: The Life of Rose Pastor Stokes* (Athens: University of Georgia Press, 1989). See also issues of the *Jewish Daily News* for 1902 and 1903.

40. Lucy Wilmot Smith, "Some Female Writers of the Negro Race," *Journalist*, January 26, 1889; Hamm, "About Newspaper Women," *Journalist*, November 14, 1891. On African American women's journalism, see Mrs. N. F. [Gertrude Bustill] Mossell, *The Work of the Afro-American Woman* (1894; reprint, New York: Oxford University Press, 1998); Rodger Streitmatter, *Raising Her Voice: African American Women Journalists Who Changed History* (Lexington: University Press of Kentucky, 1994); Patricia A. Schechter, *Ida B. Wells-Barnett and American Reform, 1880–1930* (Chapel Hill: University of North Carolina Press, 2001); Linda O. McMurry, *To Keep the Waters Troubled: The Life of Ida B. Wells* (New York: Oxford University Press, 1998); I. Garland Penn, *The Afro-American Press and Its Editors* (1891; reprint, New York: Arno Press, 1969); Penelope L. Bullock, *The Afro-American Periodical Press, 1838–1909* (Baton Rouge: Louisiana State University Press, 1981); Shirley Wilson Logan, ed., *With Pen and Voice: A Critical Anthology of Nineteenth-Century American Women* (Carbondale: Southern Illinois University Press, 1995); Rodger Streitmatter, "African American Women Journalists and Their Male Editors: A Tradition of Support," *Journalism Quarterly* 70 (Summer 1993): 276–86, and "Economic Conditions Surrounding Nineteenth-Century African-American Women Journalists: Two Case Studies," *Journalism History* 18 (1992): 33–40; and Elizabeth McHenry, *Forgotten Readers: Recovering the Lost History of African American Literary Societies* (Durham: Duke University Press, 2002).

41. Mary Church Terrell, *A Colored Woman in a White World* (1940; reprint, New York: G. K. Hall and Co., 1996), 228.

42. Mrs. N. F. [Gertrude Bustill] Mossell, "Some Painful Truths," *New York Freeman*, November 20, 1886.

43. Ibid.

44. Ibid.

45. Ibid.

46. On Matthews and the Malby Law, see "Her Views on Malby Law: Mrs. Victoria E. Matthews Believes It Should Be Enforced," *New York Times*, June 22, 1895.

47. Ida B. Wells married Chicago lawyer Ferdinand L. Barnett in 1895.

48. Frances E. Willard, *Occupations for Women: A Book of Practical Suggestions for the Material Advancement, the Mental and Physical Development, and the Moral and Spiritual Uplift of Women* (New York: Success Co., 1897), 286, 291.

49. For examples of occupational advice and journalism guides, see Rayne, *What Can a Woman Do*; Willard, *Occupations for Women*; and Edwin Llewellyn Shuman, *Steps into Journalism: Helps and Hints for Young Writers* (Evanston, Ill.: Correspondence School of Journalism, 1894). For short stories featuring reporters, see the "Miss Hunt" stories by Edith Sessions Tupper in the *New York World*, December 20, 1891, March 13, 1892, and the *Journalist*, March 19, June 4, 1892. See also Elizabeth G. Jordan, *Tales of the City Room* (New York: Scribner, 1898). For "day-in-the life" articles, see "A Newspaper Woman's Work," *Daily Graphic*, December 1887, and "News Hunting: The Day's Work of a Busy Female Reporter," *North American*, March 29, 1890. For examples of the many group articles about newspaper women, see Frances E. Willard, "Women in Journalism," *Chautauquan* 6 (July 1886): 576–79; Tarbell, "Women in Journalism"; Lida Rose McCabe, "Women as Journalists," *Atchison Daily Globe*, August 13, 1891; Jordan, "Newspaper Woman's Story," 340–47; Emma B. Kaufman, "The Newspaper Woman," *Arthur's Home Magazine* 65 (April 1895): 296–301; Margherita Arlina Hamm, "New York Newspaper Women," *Peterson Magazine* 5 (April 1895): 403–14, and "Some Women Editors," *Peterson Magazine* 6 (June 1896): 609–19; Carlotta Perry, "Woman and Her Pen," *Atchison Daily Globe*, January 4, 1896; Winslow, "Some Newspaper Women," 127–42, and "Some Handsome Newspaper Women," *Godey's Magazine*, March 1897, 242–47; O'Hagan, "Women in Journalism," 611–16; and Cynthia Westover Alden, "Women in Journalism," *Frank Leslie's Popular Monthly*, December 1898, 208–12.

50. Hamm, "Among the Newspaper Women," *Journalist*, September 10, 1892.

51. "Margherita Arlina Hamm," *Journalist*, May 7, 1892.

52. Hamm, "Among the Newspaper Women," *Journalist*, November 28, 1891.

53. Dorr, *A Woman of Fifty*, 48. Her fashion articles appeared under her maiden name, Rheta Louise Childe.

54. Rheta Louise Childe to Charles A. Dayton, received December 11, 1893, American Press Association Records, Library of Congress (hereafter cited as APA Records).

55. Dorr, *A Woman of Fifty*, 72, 74.

56. Agnes E. Meyer, *Out of These Roots* (1953; reprint, New York: Arno Press, 1980), 65–74.

57. Dorr, *A Woman of Fifty*, 72, 74.

58. Ibid., 74–75.

59. Ibid., 74, 76–77.

60. Ibid., 77, 91–92, 95.

61. Ibid., 96.

62. Beatrice Fairfax [Marie Manning], *Ladies Now and Then* (New York: E. P. Dutton, 1944), 23.

63. O'Hagan, "Women in Journalism," 611.

64. Ibid. The editorial writer was Margaret Sullivan. It is likely that the New York newspaper O'Hagan was talking about was the short-lived *New York Recorder*.

65. Fairfax [Manning], *Ladies Now and Then*, 56, 158.

66. Dorr, *A Woman of Fifty*, 100.

67. On changing space rates and salaries at the *New York World* and other papers, see *Journalist*. Theodore Dreiser remembered counting the inches of space he had published—his "string." Dreiser, *Newspaper Days: An Autobiography*, ed. T. D. Nostwich (Santa Rosa, Calif.: Black Sparrow Press, 2000).

68. Fairfax [Manning], *Ladies Now and Then*, 15.

69. O'Hagan, "Women in Journalism," 615.

70. Lida Rose McCabe, "Women as Journalists," *Atchison Daily Globe*, August 13, 1891.

71. Ibid.

72. O'Hagan, "Women in Journalism," 615.

73. Alden, "Women in Journalism," 14.

74. Masterson, "Newspaper Woman of To-Day," 377.

75. O'Hagan, "Women in Journalism," 615.

76. Kaufman, "Newspaper Woman," 296.

77. Dorr, *A Woman of Fifty*, 98.

78. O'Hagan, "Women in Journalism," 615.

79. See payroll records of the *New York Mail and Express*, New York Public Library. Zoe Beckley, also employed by the *Mail and Express*, was the highest paid staff member of the newspaper.

80. "Questionnaire for Newspaper Women," 1917, Bureau of Vocational Information Records, Schlesinger Library, Radcliffe Institute for Advanced Study.

81. Hamm, "Among the Newspaper Women," *Journalist*, November 28, 1891.

82. Fannie Edgar Thomas to I. D. Marshall, received February 20, 1892, APA Records.

83. Lida Rose McCabe, "Women as Journalists: Something That Will Interest Girls Who Want to Write," *North American*, August 17, 1891.

84. Emily Verdery-Battey to Mr. Marshall, January 24, 1892, APA Records.

85. The McClure, Bacheller, and APA syndicates were the most prominent, but numerous smaller associations and "literary bureaus" sprang up quickly in the mid-to-late 1880s and early 1890s and often just as quickly vanished. On syndicates, see Charles A. Johanningsmeier, *Fiction and the American Literary Marketplace: The Role of Newspaper Syndicates in America, 1860–1900* (New York: Cambridge University Press, 1997), and Elmo Scott Watson, *A History of Newspaper Syndicates in the United States, 1865–1935* (Chicago: Elmo Scott Watson, 1936).

86. "Eliza Putnam Heaton: A Writer Who Has Made Her Mark in Journalism," *Brooklyn Eagle*, February 8, 1891.

87. Ida A. Harper to Eliza Archard Conner, October 15, 1893, APA Records.

88. Ida A. Harper to A. A. Hill, November 1, 1893, APA Records.

89. On Jennie June Croly and syndication, see "The First Woman Journalist," *Memphis Commercial Appeal*, November 11, 1895, and "Mrs. Jennie C. Croly Dead," *New York Times*, December 24, 1901.

90. On Ward's self-syndication, see Fannie B. Ward to Clara Barton, January 6, 1904, Clara Barton Papers, Library of Congress, Washington, D.C. See also Chapter 7.

91. Ida M. Tarbell, *All in the Day's Work: An Autobiography* (New York: Macmillan, 1939), 87.

92. Ibid., 86–87.

93. Ibid, 96–97. The *Cincinnati Times-Star* raised her pay to $7.50 per article, she said.

94. Edward William Bok, *The Americanization of Edward Bok* (New York: Scribner, 1922), 105. On Mallon's self-syndication, see Jane Devor, "The Late 'Bab' and Her Work," *Weekly News and Courier*, January 21, 1899.

95. "An Overtone: Miss Zona Gale's Entertaining Chat in the Milwaukee Wisconsin," *Wisconsin State Register* (Portage), March 28, 1896.

96. Ida M. Tarbell, "Egg-Shell Trifles: Pretty Things to Make for Easter," *Morning Oregonian* (Portland), March 19, 1893.

97. "Newspaper Women—Nixola Greeley Smith," *Idaho Daily Statesman*, September 9, 1906.

98. O'Hagan, "Women in Journalism," 614–15.

99. Ida Husted Harper, "The Training of Women Journalists," *Women in Professions: Being the Professional Section of the International Congress of Women, London, July, 1899* (London: T. Fisher Unwin, 1900), 56.

100. O'Hagan, "Women in Journalism," 614–15.

101. Jordan, *Tales of the City Room*, 3–4, 74–75.

102. O'Hagan, "Women in Journalism," 611, 615, 614. On neurasthenia, see Gail Bederman, *Manliness and Civilization: A Cultural History of Gender and Race in the United States, 1880–1917* (Chicago: University of Chicago Press, 1995).

103. Emily Wortis Leider, *California's Daughter: Gertrude Atherton and Her Times* (Stanford, Calif.: Stanford University Press, 1991), 145.

104. Jordan, *Three Rousing Cheers*, 87.

105. Margaret H. Welch, "Is Newspaper Work Healthful for Women?," *Journal of Social Science, containing the Proceedings of the American Association* 32 (November 1894): 110.

106. Ibid., 111.

107. Harper, "Training of Women Journalists," 57.

108. On Nellie Bly's early newspaper career, see Brooke Kroeger, *Nellie Bly: Daredevil, Reporter, Feminist* (New York: Times Books, 1994).

109. Nellie Bly, "Woman as a Journalist," *Atchison Daily Champion* (Kansas), September 21, 1887.

110. Hamm, "Among the Newspaper Women," *Journalist*, May 28, 1892.

111. Hamm, "Among the Newspaper Women," *Journalist*, January 9, 1892. The main offices of newspapers in this period were at Park Row.

112. Hamm, "Among the Newspaper Women," *Journalist*, January 9, 1892.

113. Ibid.

114. Ibid. On the mid-nineteenth-century "domestic" writers who publicly critiqued domesticity while claiming to be merely "private" women, see esp. Mary Kelley, *Private Woman, Public Stage: Literary Domesticity in Nineteenth-Century America* (Chapel Hill: University of North Carolina Press, 1984).

115. "Howard," "'Howard' Chats on Girls," *Daily Graphic*, December 10, 1887. See also the discussion of Joe Howard in Lorna Watson, "The New York Recorder as a Woman's Newspaper, 1891–1894" (M.A. thesis, University of Wisconsin, Madison, 1939).

116. *Galveston Daily News*, April 10, 1888.

117. For the best account of Bly's impact, see Kroeger, *Nellie Bly*.

118. *Journalist*, November 7, 1891.

119. Hamm, "Among the Newspaper Women," *Journalist*, December 19, 1891.

120. E. F. J., "She Holds the Reins," *Chicago Daily Inter Ocean*, July 28, 1891.

121. "Margherita Arlina Hamm," *Journalist*, May 7, 1892.

122. "A Decided Sensation," *Morning Oregonian* (Portland), August 3, 1891.

123. "Miss Hamm's Libel Suit," *Raleigh News and Observer*, August 4, 1891.

124. "A Decided Sensation," *Morning Oregonian* (Portland), August 3, 1891.

125. See "Miss Hamm's Libel Suit."

126. According to one biography, "Another well-known achievement was her Bar Harbor interview with Mr. Blaine." Frances E. Willard and Mary A. Livermore, eds., *A Woman of the Century: Fourteen hundred-seventy Biographical Sketches Accompanied by Portraits of Leading American Women in All Walks of Life* (Buffalo: Moulton, 1893), 353.

127. Welch, "Is Newspaper Work Healthful for Women?," 116.

128. Cynthia Westover Alden, "Women in Journalism," *Frank Leslie's Popular Monthly*, December 1898, 209.

129. Haryot Holt Cahoon, "Women in Gutter Journalism," *Arena* 17 (March 1897): 569–70.

130. Ibid., 572–73.

131. Edward Bok, "Is the Newspaper Office the Place for a Girl," *Ladies' Home Journal*, February 1901, 18.

132. O'Hagan, "Women in Journalism," 614–15.

133. Alden, "Women in Journalism," 212.

134. Tarbell, *All in the Day's Work*, 92–93.

135. Hamm, "Among the Newspaper Women," *Journalist*, April 2, 1892.

136. Hamm, "Among the Newspaper Women," *Journalist*, March 5, 1892.

137. O'Hagan, "Women in Journalism," 613.

138. Ibid., 615.

139. Ibid., 616.

140. Jordan, "Newspaper Woman's Story," 340–42.

141. Hamm, "Some Women Editors," *Peterson Magazine* 6 (June 1896): 609.

142. Hamm, "Among the Newspaper Women," *Journalist*, April 9, 1892.

143. Hamm, "About Newspaper Women," *Journalist*, November 14, 1891.

144. Hamm, "Among the Newspaper Women," *Journalist*, April 9, 1892.

1. Marion Harland [Mary Virginia Hawes Terhune], "Gossip and Gleanings for the Family Circle," *Brooklyn Times*, October 23, 1886.

2. On Harland as a "literary domestic," see Mary Kelley, *Private Woman, Public Stage: Literary Domesticity in Nineteenth-Century America* (Chapel Hill: University of North Carolina Press, 1984).

3. Marion Harland, "Professional Women at Home," *Congregationalist*, May 12, 1892.

4. Some of Harland's fiction was sold at the same time through the McClure Syndicate.

5. Marion Harland, *Marion Harland's Autobiography: The Story of a Long Life* (New York: Harper and Brothers, 1910), 483.

6. Ibid.

7. Ibid., 484.

8. Ibid.

9. See Nancy F. Cott, *The Bonds of Womanhood: "Woman's Sphere" in New England, 1780–1835* (New Haven: Yale University Press, 1977). For reinterpretations of "separate spheres" and domesticity in American life, see Cathy N. Davidson and Jessamyn Hatcher, eds., *No More Separate Spheres!* (Durham: Duke University Press, 2002), and Laura Wexler, *Tender Violence: Domestic Visions in an Age of U.S. Imperialism* (Chapel Hill: University of North Carolina Press, 2000).

10. Mary Eleanor O'Donnell, "Marion Harland to Write Exclusively for the Tribune," *Chicago Daily Tribune*, October 29, 1911.

11. Among the most well-known "domestic" columnists were Fanny Fern and Grace Greenwood in the antebellum period and Jennie June Croly [Jane Cunningham Croly] after the war. Margaret Fuller was, of course, also famous.

12. See *New York World*, February 23, March 22, April 5, 19, 26, and May 24, 1896.

13. Examples are the *New-York Daily Tribune*'s "Only Woman's Page" (1900), "Woman's Realm" (1900), "Hearth & Boudoir" (1902), "For and About Women" (1907), and "Of Interest to Women" (1910). Other woman's page titles appearing for an entire year included "For the End of the Century Woman" (*New York Herald*, 1894), "The Woman's Page" (*New York World*, 1894).

14. Its regular placement in the newspaper week after week was another indication that it was the recurring "woman's page."

15. At this point Harland seems to have broken her connection with the Bacheller Syndicate. At any rate, she was no longer a featured columnist.

16. E. P. H. [Eliza Putnam Heaton], "Reading for the Home," *Brooklyn Times*, January 15, 1887.

17. J. Howard Fielding, "Literary Women: Writers Well-Known in the Walks of American Literature," *Morning Oregonian* (Portland), November 8, 1887. See also Margherita Arlina Hamm, "Among the Newspaper Women," *Journalist*, April 9, 1892.

18. "Eliza Putnam Heaton: A Writer Who Has Made Her Mark in Journalism," *Brooklyn Eagle*, February 8, 1891.

19. Hamm, "Among the Newspaper Women," *Journalist*, September 3, 1892.

20. Later spelled "Ellen Osborn." "Osborn" was Heaton's maiden name.

21. Elmo Scott Watson, *A History of Newspaper Syndicates in the United States, 1865–1935* (Chicago: Elmo Scott Watson, 1936), illustration facing p. 44.

22. Fielding, "Literary Women: Writers Well-Known."

23. Hamm, "Among the Newspaper Women," *Journalist*, April 9, 1892. Hamm then launched into a piece of unusual malice: "Mrs. Heaton had a baby once and it was a perfect elephant on her hands. She didn't know where to put, nor what to do with it," she wrote. "Poor Mrs. Heaton. The four walls of a home were never made to enclose her and a nursery was a complete cypher in her ambitions and aims. We need such women as Mrs. Heaton for the kind of work she does, and she does it exceedingly well." Hamm noted that another newspaper woman—Christine Terhune Herrick—was much better suited "for the babies" and for the woman's page of the *Recorder*, which Heaton had just left. Ibid.

24. Hamm, "Among the Newspaper Women," *Journalist*, September 3, 1892.

25. "Eliza Putnam Heaton: A Writer Who Has Made Her Mark."

26. "Only Woman's Page," *New-York Tribune*, January 19, 1900; "Up-to-Date Woman," *Chicago Daily Tribune*, January 12, 1895.

27. "Only Woman's Page," *New-York Tribune*, January 19, 1900.

28. Elizabeth G. Jordan, *Three Rousing Cheers* (New York: Appleton-Century, 1938), 14.

29. Anne O'Hagan, "Women in Journalism," *Munsey's Magazine* 19 (July 1898): 612.

30. Hamm, "Among the Newspaper Women," *Journalist*, January 28, 1893.

31. O'Hagan, "Women in Journalism," 611.

32. Ethel M. Colson Brazelton, *Writing and Editing for Women* (New York: Funk and Wagnalls Co., 1927), 35.

33. Ishbel Ross, *Ladies of the Press: The Story of Women in Journalism by an Insider* (New York: Harper and Brothers, 1936), 427.

34. In the most recent account of "women journalists in American culture and fiction" from 1880 to 1930, the woman's page does not merit an index entry. See Jean Marie Lutes, *Front-Page Girls: Women Journalists in American Culture and Fiction, 1880–1930* (Ithaca: Cornell University Press, 2006).

35. "What Women Will Read," *Chicago Daily Tribune*, July 4, 1891 (Elizabeth Akers), reprinted from *New York Herald*.

36. Ibid. (Helen Watterson). But Watterson defended the *idea* of a woman's page, saying that women indeed had "special interests" such as "the care of the home and of children and the lightening of toil." A 1895 article in the *Chicago Tribune*, on "Up-to-Date Woman," argued that the "woman's page affronts fin de siecle femininity," that "fashion and fads" were "not the all-absorbing theme of modern maids and matrons." The "progressive woman—the new woman, if you please" in Chicago was interested not in woman's page "gush" but in "philanthropies and reforms," as well as "politics and municipal affairs." In contrast to the "insipid 'stuff'" offered on the woman's page, the "real work" of the "woman of today" was "progressive." "Up-to-Date Woman," *Chicago Daily Tribune*, January 12, 1895.

37. Edward William Bok, *The Americanization of Edward Bok* (New York: Scribner, 1922), 106–7.

38. Dorr, *A Woman of Fifty*, 92, 95.

39. Bok, *Americanization of Edward Bok*, 105.

40. Ida Husted Harper, "The Training of Women Journalists," *Women in Professions* (London: T. Fisher Unwin, 1900), 60.

41. E. P. H., "Reading for the Home," *Brooklyn Times*, January 15, 1887.

42. Ibid.

43. E. P. H., "Reading for the Home," *Brooklyn Times*, January 29, 1887.

44. Ibid.

45. Ibid.

46. Campbell published these articles as *Prisoners of Poverty: Women Wage Workers, Their Trades and Their Lives* (Boston: Roberts Bros., 1887).

47. E. P. H., "Reading for the Home," *Brooklyn Times*, January 22, 1887. See also Dolores Hayden, *The Grand Domestic Revolution: A History of Feminist Designs for American Homes, Neighborhoods, and Cities* (Cambridge, Mass.: MIT Press, 1982), and Melusina Fay Peirce, *Cooperative Housekeeping: How Not to Do It and How to Do It: A Study in Sociology* (Boston: James R. Osgood, 1884). On the influence of Peirce's work, see Lisette Nadine Gibson, "A Homely Business: Melusina Fay Peirce and Late-Nineteenth-Century Cooperative Housekeeping," in *Separate Spheres No More: Gender Convergence in American Literature, 1830–1930*, ed. Monika Maria Elbert (Tuscaloosa: University of Alabama Press, 2000).

48. Eliza Putnam Heaton, "Matters Feminine: John Wanamaker's Proposed Hotel for Working Women," *Morning Oregonian* (Portland), March 27, 1887.

49. These columns, unlike others written by Heaton, give no names or specific addresses.

50. On the history of "objectivity" in journalism, see Michael Schudson, *Discovering the News: A Social History of American Newspapers* (New York: Basic Books, 1978).

51. Florence Williams, "The Ways of the World," *New York Age*, March 16, March 23, 1889.

52. Williams's column in the *New York Age* began on February 2, 1889, and ended on March 15, 1890.

53. For a description of Williams as a society editor, see William Gatewood, *Aristocrats of Color: The Black Elite, 1880–1920* (Bloomington: Indiana University Press, 1990), 203. In 1886 and 1887 Mossell's weekly "Our Woman's Department" column in the *New York Freeman* was prefaced by the statement: "The aim of this column will be to promote true womanhood, especially that of the African race."

54. For Williams's attendance at the "Bethel Literary," see *New York Globe*, February 17, 1883. Reportedly, she also appeared at various social events — see, e.g., "Local Gossip," *New York Globe*, August 2, 1884, and "A Thanksgiving Entertainment," *New York Age*, December 3, 1887, in which she was mentioned as one of numerous guests including T. Thomas Fortune, editor of the *New York Age*.

55. See, e.g., *New York Globe*, Aug. 2, 1884, and *New York Freeman*, Oct. 1, 1887.

56. See "Off for the West Indies," *New York Age*, March 22, 1890, and "In the Tropics: The Tennessee Jubilee Singers in the West Indies," *New York Age*, April 5, 1890.

57. Florence Williams, "Social Reflections," *New York Age*, February 2, 1889.

58. Ibid.

59. "Miss Williams' Letters," *New York Age*, February 23, 1889.

60. Williams, "The Ways of the World," *New York Age*, March 2, 1889.

61. Williams, "The Ways of the World," *New York Age*, March 9, 1889.

62. Mrs. N. F. Mossell [Gertrude Bustill], "Our Woman's Department," *New York Freeman* (later *New York Age*), December 4, 1886.

63. See Mrs. N. F. Mossell [Gertrude Bustill], "Our Woman's Department," *New York Freeman* (later *New York Age*), May 8, 1886. In this column Mossell quoted extensively "from a paper prepared by Miss Eliza Archard of the *New York World*, read before the Women's Press Association of Illinois and reported by the *Chicago Inter Ocean*."

64. Mrs. N. F. Mossell [Gertrude Bustill], *The Work of the Afro-American Woman* (1894; reprint, New York: Oxford University Press, 1998), 100–101.

65. See, e.g., Gail Bederman's discussion of Charlotte Perkins Gilman (Chapter 4) in Bederman, *Manliness and Civilization: A Cultural History of Gender and Race in the United States, 1880–1917* (Chicago: University of Chicago Press, 1995).

66. Clara Savage Diary, January 16, April 16, 1914, Clara Savage Littledale Papers, Schlesinger Library, Radcliffe Institute for Advanced Study.

67. On the club movement, see esp. Jacqueline Jones Royster, *Traces of a Stream: Literacy and Social Change among African American Women* (Pittsburgh: University of Pittsburgh Press, 2000); Anne Firor Scott, *Natural Allies: Women's Associations in American History* (Urbana: University of Illinois Press, 1991); and Karen J. Blair, *The Clubwoman as Feminist: True Womanhood Redefined, 1868–1914* (New York: Holmes and Meier Publishers, 1980).

68. On Peattie, see esp. Elia Peattie, *Impertinences: Selected Writings of Elia Peattie: A Journalist in the Gilded Age*, ed. Susanne George Bloomfield (Lincoln: University of Nebraska Press, 2005).

69. Fannie Barrier Williams, "A Northern Negro's Autobiography," *Independent*, July 14, 1904, 94.

70. Ibid., 94, 96. This article also detailed discrimination against African American working women.

71. "Color versus Intelligence," *Chicago Daily Tribune*, January 12, 1895 (Kate Field).

72. "Women of the Press: Many Views of the Future of the Sex in Journalism," *Chicago Daily Tribune*, May 24, 1893.

73. Another newspaper woman, Augusta Prescott, wrote an article giving tips on travel costs associated with the fair. She mentioned that "a newspaper woman" and "an artist friend who illustrates for her" were living cheaply by renting a hall bedroom in a private home. Prescott, "World's Fair Visitors: Concerning the Cost of a Journey to Chicago," *Galveston Daily News*, May 21, 1893. Mary E. Stewart, a book reviewer for the *Milwaukee Journal*, spent the entire summer of 1893 at the fair, paying her way by working in the kitchen of the Woman's Building, as well as by writing a few articles. She carefully recorded her (ecstatically favorable) impressions in one of the many souvenir "journals" on sale at the fair. Stewart saw the fair as an unparalleled educational opportunity, and she soaked up every impression she could. See Mary E. Stewart, "My Record of the World's Columbian Exposition," Isaac N. Stewart and Mary E. Stewart Papers, Wisconsin Historical Society, Madison.

74. Ida B. Wells, "The Brutal Truth: Faithful Story of the Bardwell Lynching," *Chicago Daily Inter Ocean*, July 19, 1893.

75. "Asked to Stay Away: Colored People Will Not Recognize the World's Fair," *Chicago Daily Inter Ocean*, June 28, 1893.

76. Ida B. Wells, Frederick Douglass, Irvine Garland Penn, and Ferdinand L. Barnett, *The Reason Why the Colored American Is Not in the World's Columbian Exposition* (1893; reprint, ed. Robert W. Rydell, Urbana: University of Illinois Press, 1999).

77. "Color Line Will Not Obtrude," *Chicago Daily Tribune*, September 20, 1895.

78. "New-York Women Protest," *New-York Tribune*, May 23, 1900.

79. In 1896, the year Adolph Ochs bought the "failing and demoralized" *Times*, its circulation was 9,000 compared with 19,000 for the *Evening Post*. See Michael Schudson, *Discovering the News: A Social History of American Newspapers* (New York: Basic Books, 1978), 110–11.

80. The index recorded items beginning with "Wo," including "Women Detectives" and "Women Who Are Bored." *New York Evening Post* index, New York Public Library, microfilm. See also similar columns about women's occupations in other newspapers, such as "Occupations for Women" in the 1900 *New-York Tribune*. The *Chicago Tribune* had already printed a column titled "Women and Their Work" for several months in 1886 and 1887.

81. The discussion of the "servant problem" was a means by which middle-class white women asserted their status. See Christine Stansell, *City of Women: Sex and Class in New York, 1789–1860* (New York: Knopf, 1982), esp. Chapter 8.

82. Mrs. Margaret H. Welch, "Is Newspaper Work Healthful for Women?," *Journal of Social Science* (November 1894): 110 ff. See also "Women in Newspaper Work," *New York Times*, September 6, 1894.

83. Dorr, *A Woman of Fifty*, 92–94.

84. Ibid., 95, 96.

85. Ibid., 96–97.

86. Ibid., 103.

87. Ibid.

88. Ibid., 104–5.

89. Ibid., 107.

90. Ibid., 98.

91. Ibid., 126–27.

92. Dorr helped to found and edit *The Suffragist*, in support of Alice Paul's Congressional Union. See Dorr, *A Woman of Fifty*, 288.

93. "Household Hints," *Chicago Daily Tribune*, January 7, 1904. Krecker's first bylined "Household Hints" column was published on December 28, 1903.

94. It also underlined the fact that Chicago newspapers provided more opportunities for women than New York papers—at least up to a point. While newspaper women occasionally wrote editorials for Chicago papers, there was no hope of advancement to the positions of city editor or managing editor.

95. Ada May Krecker, "What Women Are Doing in the World," *Chicago Daily Tribune*, May 5, June 2, 1907.

96. Krecker, "Woman's Rise Parallels Masses," *Chicago Daily Tribune*, December 27, 1908.

97. Krecker, "How the Poorest Families Fight to Keep the Wolf from the Door," *Chicago Daily Tribune*, July 5, 1908.

98. Krecker, "Shall We Fly to Other Worlds?," *Chicago Daily Tribune*, August 6, 1911.

99. Krecker, "The Passing of the Family," *Mother Earth* 7 (October 1912): 263.

100. Fairfax [Manning], *Ladies Now and Then*, 52. The answer, in this case, turned out to be that four young women shared one basement room.

101. *New York World*, January 5, 1899.

102. Untitled advertisements, *New York Times*, October 24, 25, 1912.

103. *New York Press*, November 1, 1914.

104. Abraham Cahan, editor of the *Jewish Daily Forward*, was both a notable exception to and proof of this rule.

105. For information on Yetta Dorothea Geffen, see U.S. Federal Census, 1910, Manhattan Ward 12, New York, N.Y., and U.S. Federal Census, 1920, Manhattan Assembly District 10. See also Geffen's contributions to *Theatre Magazine* in the 1910s.

106. Fanny Butcher, *Many Lives—One Love* (New York: Harper and Row, 1972), 108–9.

107. Ibid., 109–10.

108. Ibid., 110.

109. On Mary King as Sunday editor, see *Women and the Chicago Tribune* (Chicago: Business Survey of the Chicago Tribune, 1925), 10–11. See also Ishbel Ross, *Ladies of the Press* (New York: Harper and Bros., 1936).

110. Butcher, *Many Lives—One Love*, 114.

111. Schudson, *Discovering the News*, 119, 157.

chapter three

1. Jessie M. Wood, "The Newspaper Woman," *Life*, May 7, 1896, 372.

2. Ibid.

3. Patricia Marks, *Bicycles, Bangs, and Bloomers: The New Woman in the Popular Press* (Lexington: University Press of Kentucky, 1990), 85.

4. "Miss Jessie Wood," *New York Evening Journal*, October 30, 1899.

5. Winifred Black, "A Sketch of Jessie Wood," *Denver Evening Post*, October 30, 1899. This account should be taken with a grain of salt; Black's "appreciation" of Wood was wrong about a number of details. Still, at some point Wood left her job at the Redfern dressmaking establishment to become a full-time newspaper woman, first for the *New York Recorder*.

6. Black, "A Sketch of Jessie Wood."

7. Charles A. Dana, *The Art of Newspaper Making: Three Lectures* (1895; reprint, New York: Arno and New York Times, 1970), 11–12.

8. Beatrice Fairfax [Marie Manning], *Ladies Now and Then* (New York: E. P. Dutton, 1944), 34.

9. See, for a starting point, Ben Singer, *Melodrama and Modernity: Early Sensational Cinema and Its Contexts* (New York: Columbia University Press, 2001); John F. Kasson, *Amusing the Million: Coney Island at the Turn of the Century* (New York: Hill

and Wang, 1978); Kathy Peiss, *Cheap Amusements: Working Women and Leisure in Turn-of-the-Century New York* (Philadelphia: Temple University Press, 1986); and David Nasaw, *Going Out: The Rise and Fall of Public Amusements* (New York: Basic Books, 1993).

10. Michael Schudson, *Why Democracies Need an Unlovable Press* (Malden, Mass: Polity Press, 2008), 19–20; Joseph Raz, *Ethics in the Public Domain* (Oxford: Clarendon Press, 1994), 140.

11. Schudson, *Why Democracies Need an Unlovable Press*, 38–39 (Rosenblum).

12. Dean, Unpublished autobiography, Teresa Dean Papers, Charles Deering McCormick Library of Special Collections, Northwestern University Library, 4–7. Later, like so many of her peers, she would move to New York. Initially her family supported her desire to set up an art studio in Chicago—although not wholeheartedly. As she sardonically recalled, "'Art was elevating'—said they—though old-fashioned rigid respectability destined all girls and women of a family to stay within the jurisdiction and protection of its men." Once settled in Chicago, Dean revealed an entrepreneurial streak after she self-published a "booklet" on beauty, which received attention in a "front-page column" and was a minor success. She also made a little money as an artist, as she "could dash off things that sold quickly—fruit, flowers, a wave breaking over a rock, a fishing-shack in the moonlight on Lake Michigan and other trifles." But "all the time" she "was getting nowhere on the climb to the fame of my dreams that awaited me 'out there.'" Ibid., 2–3.

13. Dean, "Snap Shots," *Chicago Daily Inter Ocean*, September 19, 1892.

14. Dean, "Snap Shots," *Chicago Daily Inter Ocean*, August 27, 1892.

15. Dean, "Snap Shots," *Chicago Daily Inter Ocean*, March 12, 1893. The reader was replying to "Teresa Dean's Snap Shots," *Daily Inter Ocean*, March 6, 1893.

16. Dean, "Scorns It No More," *Chicago Daily Inter Ocean*, May 10, 1893.

17. Dean, "White City Chips," *Chicago Daily Inter Ocean*, June 8, 1893.

18. Dean, "White City Chips," *Chicago Daily Inter Ocean*, June 30, 1893.

19. Dean, *White City Chips* (Chicago: Warren Publishing Co., 1895), iii–iv.

20. "Who's Teresa Dean?," *Chicago Daily Inter Ocean*, November 6, 1893.

21. Lincoln Steffens, *The Autobiography of Lincoln Steffens* (New York: Harcourt, Brace, 1931), 179.

22. J. M. W. [Jessie M. Wood], "Some Living Pictures," *New York Recorder*, September 23, 1894.

23. J. M. W., "A Girl Bachelor Says Don't!," *New York Recorder*, December 16, 1894.

24. Ibid.

25. Ibid.

26. "Miss Jessie Wood," *New York Evening Journal*, October 30, 1899.

27. Winifred Black, "A Sketch of Jessie Wood," *Denver Evening Post*, October 30, 1899.

28. See Karen Halttunen, *Confidence Men and Painted Women: A Study of Middle-Class Culture in America, 1830–1870* (New Haven: Yale University Press, 1982).

29. J. M. W., "Theatre-going Ethics," *New York Recorder*, April 15, 1894.

30. J. M. W., "A Woman's Revenge," *New York Recorder*, May 19, 1895.

31. Ibid.

32. "Newspaper Women—Nixola Greeley Smith," *Idaho Daily Statesman*, September 9, 1906.

33. See Kevin Stoker and Brad L. Rawlins, "The 'Light' of Publicity in the Progressive Era: From Searchlight to Flashlight," *Journalism History* 30 (Winter 2005): 177–88.

34. J. M. W., "The Napoleonic Fad," *New York Recorder*, November 25, 1894.

35. Ibid.

36. Jessie M. Wood, "Miss Jessie Wood at Newport," *New York Evening Journal*, August 3, 1898.

37. Ibid.

38. Ibid.

39. Ibid.

40. Ibid.

41. On "disruptive acts," see Mary Louise Roberts, *Disruptive Acts: The New Woman in Fin-de-Siècle France* (Chicago: University of Chicago Press, 2002).

42. This paragraph is based on the chapter "Question Authority: A History of the News Interview" in Michael Schudson, *The Power of News* (Cambridge: Harvard University Press, 1995), 72–93.

43. J. M. W., "The Art of Interviewing," *New York Recorder*, March 1, 1896.

44. Ibid.

45. We cannot trace these articles because they were not bylined.

46. J. M. W., "The Art of Interviewing."

47. J. M. W., "A Woman Interviewer," *New York Recorder*, June 6, 1894.

48. Ibid.

49. Frank A. Burr, as quoted in Christopher Silvester, ed., *The Norton Book of Interviews: An Anthology from 1859 to the Present Day* (New York: Norton, 1996), 28.

50. J. M. W., "A Woman Interviewer," *New York Recorder*, June 6, 1894.

51. Jessie M. Wood, "Unknown Domestics of Well-Known Men," *Life*, June 20, 1895, 408.

52. Wood, "Unknown Domestics of Well-Known Men, No. II," *Life*, June 27, 1895, 426.

53. J. M. W., "The Art of Interviewing."

54. Ibid.

55. Ibid.

56. Ibid.

57. Ibid.

58. Ibid.

59. See Christopher Silvester, "Celebrity's Midwife: The Lost Work of Kate Carew," *New Yorker*, February 9, 1998, 56.

60. Schudson, *Power of News*, 76.

61. Kate Carew [Mary Chambers], "Confessions of an Interviewer," *Pearson's Magazine* 18 (December 1904): 653.

62. "Meet Kate Carew," http://showandtellmovie.com/society.htm (accessed January 9, 2010).

63. Ibid.; Carew, "Confessions of an Interviewer."

64. Carew, "Confessions of an Interviewer," 653.

65. Kate Carew, "John Drew in 'Richard Carvel,'" *New York World*, September 15, 1900. On Wood, see "Miss Jessie Wood," *New York Evening Journal*, October 30, 1899.

66. Carew, "Confessions of an Interviewer," 653.

67. Ibid., 653–54, 655.

68. Silvester, *Norton Book of Interviews*, 9. See also Charles L. Ponce de Leon, *Self-Exposure: Human Interest Journalism and the Emergence of Celebrity in America, 1890–1940* (Chapel Hill: University of North Carolina Press, 2002).

69. Carew, "Confessions of an Interviewer," 654.

70. Ibid.

71. Kate Carew, "'My Impressions of America'—Mark Twain," *New York World*, October 21, 1900.

72. Ibid.

73. Ibid.

74. Carew, "Confessions of an Interviewer," 654.

75. See esp. Ponce de Leon, *Self-Exposure*, and Rochelle Gurstein, *The Repeal of Reticence: A History of America's Cultural and Legal Struggles over Free Speech, Obscenity, Sexual Liberation, and Modern Art* (New York: Hill and Wang, 1996).

76. Schudson, *Why Democracies Need an Unlovable Press*, 14.

77. Thaw's 1907 trial resulted in a hung jury; Thaw was tried again in 1908 and pronounced not guilty by reason of insanity.

78. For one of the columns designating Wilcox the "poetess of passion," see "Poetess of Passion on Saver of Souls," *New York World*, May 10, 1896.

79. "Newspaper Women—Nixola Greeley Smith," *Idaho Daily Statesman*, September 9, 1906.

80. Ishbel Ross, *Ladies of the Press: The Story of Women in Journalism by an Insider* (New York: Harper and Brothers, 1936), 89; "Newspaper Women—Nixola Greeley Smith"; Vorse as quoted in Ross, *Ladies of the Press*, 89.

81. On Parkhurst, see Timothy J. Gilfoyle, *City of Eros: New York City, Prostitution, and the Commercialization of Sex, 1790–1920* (New York: Norton, 1992).

82. Nixola Greeley-Smith, "Mrs. Parkhurst: Interesting Personality of the Wife of New York's Famous Reformer," *New York World*, May 5, 1901.

83. Ibid.

84. Ibid.

85. Ross, *Ladies of the Press*, 89 (Vorse).

86. Ibid., 91.

87. Ibid., 89.

88. Ibid.

89. Nixola Greeley-Smith, "A Talk with Mrs. Richard Croker," *New York World*, June 2, 1901.

90. Ibid.

91. Ibid.

92. Ibid.

93. Silvester, "Celebrity's Midwife," 56.

94. Carew, "Confessions of an Interviewer," 655.

95. Although the famous Dorothy Dix (Elizabeth Meriweather Gilmer) is often credited with being the first advice columnist, her early columns were in the form of "chat" rather than the question-and-answer confessional format that the Beatrice Fairfax columns popularized. Dix started newspaper work at the *New Orleans Picayune* and attracted a wide national audience with her "Dorothy Dix Talks" columns. She was hired by the *New York Journal* in 1901. See Harnett T. Kane, with Ella Bentley Arthur, *Dear Dorothy Dix: The Story of a Compassionate Woman* (New York: Doubleday, 1952).

96. Fairfax [Manning], *Ladies Now and Then*, 33.

97. Ibid., 33–34.

98. Ibid.

99. Ibid., 34–36.

100. Ibid., 35–36.

101. Ibid., 37–38.

102. For a cultural history that takes the opposite point of view and deplores the loss of privacy in this period, see Gurstein, *Repeal of Reticence*.

103. Stansell, *City of Women*; Nan Enstad, *Ladies of Labor, Girls of Adventure: Working Women, Popular Culture, and Labor Politics at the Turn of the Twentieth Century* (New York: Columbia University Press, 1999).

104. See in the *Milwaukee Sentinel*: "Dr. Tallman Missing: The Great Northern Hotel Physician Thought to Have Eloped," November 6, 1896; "Were Married in Fargo," December 20, 1896; "Dr. Tallman Talks: Doesn't Know What He Was Doing When He Wed Mrs. Cannon," January 4, 1897; and "Sues for a Divorce: Dr. Tallman of Chicago Says He Married Jane M. Cannon while He Was Irresponsible Mentally," January 23, 1898.

105. On Hamm's divorce, see "Mrs. Fales Gets Decree of Divorce," *New York Herald*, July 31, 1902.

106. Advertisement for *Reveries of a Widow* in *Smart Set*, April 1900, back cover.

107. Fairfax [Manning], *Ladies Now and Then*, 36.

108. Beatrice Fairfax [Marie Manning], "She Will Advise You on the Troubles of Your Heart," *New York Evening Journal*, August 3, 1898.

109. Ibid.

110. Ibid.

111. Fairfax [Manning], *Ladies Now and Then*, 123.

112. Ibid., 38.

113. Ibid., 36.

114. May Irwin, "Her New Department of Heart-to-Heart Blitherings," *New York World*, February 10, 1901.

115. "Betty's Balm for Lovers," *New York Evening World*, August 15, 1905.

116. "Betty's Balm for Lovers," *New York Evening World*, August 19, 1905.

117. "Betty's Balm for Lovers," *New York Evening World*, August 21, 1905.

118. "Newspaper Women—Nixola Greeley Smith," *Idaho Daily Statesman*, September 9, 1906.

119. Ibid.

120. There is evidence that both women may have shaved a few years from their age—a common practice among newspaper women.

121. "Newspaper Women—Nixola Greeley Smith."

122. Ibid.

123. Ibid.

124. Rose Pastor Stokes, *"I Belong to the Working Class": The Unfinished Autobiography of Rose Pastor Stokes*, ed. Herbert Shapiro and David L. Sterling (Athens: University of Georgia Press, 1992), 79.

125. Ibid. Pastor remembered the exact date she posted the letter: July 16, 1901.

126. "Letters! Letters! Letters!," *Jewish Daily News*, July 22, 1901.

127. Ibid.; Stokes, *"I Belong to the Working Class,"* 80–86.

128. Stokes, *"I Belong to the Working Class,"* 86.

chapter four

1. Neith Boyce Hapgood, Draft autobiography, Hapgood Family Papers, box 30, Yale Collection of American Literature, Beinecke Rare Book and Manuscript Library, Yale University.

2. Ibid.

3. Hutchins Hapgood, *A Victorian in the Modern World* (New York: Harcourt, Brace and Co., 1939), 152.

4. Neith Boyce Hapgood, Draft autobiography, Hapgood Family Papers, box 30, typescript, p. 119. In 1898 Boyce published a series of humorous articles titled "The Bachelor Girl" in *Vogue*: see May 5, 294; May 19, 320–22; June 16, vii; July 7, 6, 10; August 4, 75–76, 78; September 1, 138–39, September 8, 156, September 22, 190; and November 3, 1898, 284. Boyce named one of the characters in these sketches "Olivia."

5. For letters documenting their remarkable friendship, see Marie Manning Papers, Sophia Smith Collection, Smith College Library. See also Ridgely Torrence Papers, Department of Rare Books and Special Collections Library, Princeton University.

6. Neith Boyce Hapgood, Draft autobiography, typescript, p. 120.

7. "Made-Over Antiques Now the Rage in Home Life of Bachelor Girls," *New York Evening World*, January 20, 1902.

8. On middle-class worries over "women adrift," see Joanne Meyerowitz, *Women Adrift: Independent Wage Earners in Chicago, 1880–1930* (Chicago: University of Chicago Press, 1988).

9. Jane Kirkland Graham, *Viola: The Duchess of New Dorp: A Biography of Viola Roseboro'* (Danville: Illinois Printing Co., 1955), 278–79.

10. "The Feminine Bachelor," *Chicago Daily Inter Ocean*, October 23, 1887, reprinted from *New York Mail and Express*.

11. Mary H. Krout, "Woman's Kingdom," *Chicago Daily Inter Ocean*, November 2, 1889, 11.

12. An early discussion of the "bachelor girl" in the late 1880s was "The Ways of the Bachelor Girl," *Frank Leslie's Illustrated Newspaper*, December 8, 1888.

13. "Feminine Bachelor," *Rocky Mountain News* (Denver), May 5, 1889.

14. Eliza Putnam Heaton, "Just Like Men: Feminine Bachelors and Their Homes," *Milwaukee Sentinel*, August 4, 1889. This was a syndicated article.

15. Margherita Arlina Hamm, "Among the Newspaper Women," *Journalist*, Au-

gust 13, 1892. In the original, "think" is spelled "thing." I have corrected this obvious typographical error.

16. "Where and How Chicago's Bachelor Girls Live," *Chicago Daily Tribune*, March 20, 1898.

17. Ibid.

18. "Not Any More Old Maids," *New York Herald*, March 3, 1895. Newspaper and magazine writer Olga Stanley [Lila Woolfall] agreed: "Circumstances, not choice, force many of us to join the ever-increasing army of women." Stanley, "Some Reflections on the Life of a 'Bachelor Girl,'" *Outlook*, November 7, 1896, 830.

19. Mary Gay Humphreys, "Women Bachelors in New York," *Scribner's Magazine* 10 (August 1896): 626.

20. "To Marry or Not: Newspaper Women Discuss the Question," *Milwaukee Sentinel*, April 20, 1890.

21. Stanley, "Reflections on the Life of a 'Bachelor Girl,'" 830.

22. Humphreys, "Women Bachelors in New York," 626; "Here Rest Is Found," *Chicago Daily Tribune*, November 24, 1894 ("the higher professions").

23. On women's office work, see Sharon Hartman Strom, *Beyond the Typewriter: Gender, Class, and the Origins of Modern American Office Work, 1900–1930* (Urbana: University of Illinois Press, 1992). See also Joseph A. Hill, *Women in Gainful Occupations, 1870–1920* (Washington, D.C.: U.S. Government Printing Office, 1929).

24. Mary H. Krout, "Woman's Kingdom," *Chicago Daily Inter Ocean*, November 2, 1889.

25. Ibid.

26. "'Old Maids' No More — All 'Girl Bachelors' Now," *Chicago Daily Tribune*, September 26, 1897.

27. "Not Any More Old Maids."

28. "'Old Maids' No More — All 'Girl Bachelors' Now," 48.

29. Emilie Ruck de Schell, "Is Feminine Bohemianism a Failure?," *Arena* 20 (July 1898): 6. De Schell published the short story "Exile" in the March 1902 issue of *Atlantic* (vol. 89).

30. De Schell, "Is Feminine Bohemianism a Failure?," 6.

31. "Favored Spinsters," *Chicago Daily Tribune*, June 8, 1895.

32. "Why They Do Not Wed," *Chicago Daily Tribune*, January 24, 1896, reprinted from *New Orleans Picayune*.

33. Ibid.

34. "Feminine Bachelor: A Curious Phase of Life among a Certain Type of Self-Reliant New York Woman," *Rocky Mountain News* (Denver), May 5, 1889.

35. Ibid.

36. On the history of marriage, see Nancy Cott, *Public Vows: A History of Marriage and the Nation* (Cambridge: Harvard University Press, 2000), and Hendrik Hartog, *Man and Wife in America: A History* (Cambridge: Harvard University Press, 2000).

37. "'Old Maids' No More — All 'Girl Bachelors' Now," 48.

38. Stanley, "Some Reflections on the Life of a 'Bachelor Girl,'" 830.

39. Kate Kensington, "Miss Miriam Dudley of the Only Woman's Page — Her Peculiarities and Foibles," *New York Recorder*, March 15, 1896.

40. Ibid.

41. Humphreys, "Women Bachelors in New York," 633.

42. Ibid.

43. Mary Gay Humphreys, "Single Blessedness: A New Society in Gotham to Discourage Marriage Builds Bachelor Apartments," *Chicago Daily Inter Ocean*, June 23, 1889.

44. "Feminine Bachelor," *Rocky Mountain News* (Denver), May 5, 1889.

45. Mary C. Francis, "Home for City Women," *Milwaukee Sentinel*, May 17, 1896.

46. Margherita Arlina Hamm, "Among the Newspaper Women," *Journalist*, March 26, 1892.

47. On this point, see also Joanne Meyerowitz, *Women Adrift: Independent Wage Earners in Chicago, 1880–1930* (Chicago: University of Chicago Press, 1988).

48. "Here Rest Is Found," *Chicago Daily Tribune*, November 24, 1894. Such complaints about the rules of "homes" were long-lived. A 1914 study of "organized homes" in New York, including the Margaret Louisa Shepard Home, reported that "the chief reason given by girls for not living in Homes" was "the fear of restrictions." Lack of privacy was another frequent complaint. See Esther Packard, *A Study of Living Conditions of Self-Supporting Women in New York City* (New York: Metropolitan Board of the YWCA, 1915), 24.

49. "For Business Women," *Chicago Daily Tribune*, March 11, 1893.

50. Ibid.

51. Humphreys, "Women Bachelors in New York," 631.

52. "Not Any More Old Maids," *New York Herald*, March 3, 1895.

53. Rheta Childe Dorr, *A Woman of Fifty* (New York: Funk and Wagnalls, 1924), 78, 82.

54. Humphreys, "Women Bachelors in New York," 632.

55. Ibid.

56. Francis, "Home for City Women."

57. Ibid.

58. Ibid.

59. Ibid.

60. Graham, *Viola: The Duchess of New Dorp*, 279.

61. Hamm, "Among the Newspaper Women," *Journalist*, March 26, 1892.

62. "For Business Women," *Chicago Daily Tribune*, March 11, 1893.

63. Ibid.

64. Ibid.

65. "Rooms for Girl Bachelors," *New York Herald*, October 21, 1894.

66. Ibid.

67. Ibid.

68. Francis, "Home for City Women."

69. Anne O'Hagan, "Shall She Come to New York?," *Munsey's Magazine* 26 (January 1902): 555.

70. "Bachelor Girl Plan," *Chicago Daily Tribune*, August 31, 1895. The article misspelled the name of the apartment house: its correct name was the Windermere. For an excellent history of the Windermere, see Michael D. Caratzas, "The Windermere Des-

ignation Report," Landmarks Preservation Commission, New York City, June 28, 2005, www.nyc.gov.

71. "Bachelor Girl Plan."

72. See *New York City Directory* for 1890.

73. "Sacred to the New Woman," *New York Times*, April 10, 1898.

74. Ibid.

75. Ibid.

76. Ibid.

77. Ibid.

78. See *New York City Directory* for 1895. Humphreys was still listed as living at the Windermere in 1914—long after many of her fellow bachelor women had moved elsewhere, including to Brooklyn and Harlem, in search of cheaper rent. For Humphreys' 1914 listing, see *Woman's Who's Who of America: A Biographical Dictionary of Contemporary Women of the United States and Canada, 1914–1915*, ed. John William Leonard (New York: American Commonwealth Co., 1914), 415.

79. "Bachelor Girl Plan," *Chicago Daily Tribune*, August 31, 1895.

80. Ibid.

81. Humphreys, "Women Bachelors in New York," 634. The article's illustrations by W. R. Leigh and Martin Borgood were "drawn from the life." See contents page, *Scribner's Magazine* 10 (August 1896).

82. "Feminine Bachelor," *Rocky Mountain News* (Denver), May 5, 1889.

83. Humphreys, "Women Bachelors in New York," 634.

84. Bab [Mallon], "The World of Woman," *Morning Oregonian* (Portland), October 28, 1894.

85. "Makes Women Close Friends," *Chicago Daily Tribune*, May 30, 1896.

86. Ibid.

87. Bab [Mallon], "The World of Woman," *Morning Oregonian* (Portland), October 28, 1894.

88. "Two Girl Bachelors," *Chicago Daily Tribune*, March 3, 1894.

89. Ruth Ashmore, "The Bachelor Girl," *Ladies' Home Journal*, April 1898, 22.

90. Ibid.

91. Ibid.

92. Humphreys, "Women Bachelors in New York," 632.

93. "Hints for the Bachelor Girl," *Chicago Daily Tribune*, November 28, 1896.

94. "A Cozy Corner Contest," *New York Recorder*, April 9, 1893.

95. "Bachelor Girl's Cosey Corner Novelty," *New York Herald*, April 2, 1899.

96. "Not Any More Old Maids," *New York Herald*, March 3, 1895.

97. Ibid.

98. Ibid.

99. "Sacred to the New Woman," *New York Times*, April 10, 1898.

100. Christine Stansell, *American Moderns: Bohemian New York and the Creation of a New Century* (New York: Metropolitan Books, 2000), 16–17, 26, 28.

101. See, e.g., George G. Foster, *New York by Gas-light and Other Urban Sketches*, ed. Stuart Blumin (1850; reprint, Berkeley: University of California Press, 1990).

102. "Bachelor Girl Plan," *Chicago Daily Tribune*, August 31, 1895.

103. "Where Bachelor Maids Reign in Feminine Seclusion," *New York Herald*, March 6, 1898.

104. Ibid.

105. Ibid.

106. Mrs. Wilson Woodrow, "Let Those Who Will Be Clever," *Life*, February 18, 1904, 162.

107. Ibid.

108. Ibid.

109. Winifred Sothern, "The Truth about the Bachelor Girl: The False Glamour That Has Been Thrown around an Individual Who in Reality Is Merely a Single Woman Living Alone in a City in Order to Work There." *Munsey's Magazine* 25 (May 1901): 282. On bachelor apartments for men in the same period, see Katherine Snyder, "A Paradise of Bachelors: Remodeling Domesticity and Masculinity in the Turn-of-the-Century New York Bachelor Apartment," *Prospects* 23 (1998): 247–84.

110. Sothern, "The Truth about the Bachelor Girl," 282.

111. Ibid., 282–83. With most bachelor girl articles appearing on the woman's page, "space writers" referred primarily to newspaper women.

112. Ibid., 282.

113. Ibid.

114. Ibid.

115. Ibid.

116. Ibid.

117. This was far from the end of the bachelor girl phenomenon, which would be a newspaper staple for another decade.

118. "Made-Over Antiques Now the Rage in Home Life of Bachelor Girls," *New York Evening World*, January 20, 1902.

119. Ibid.

120. Ibid.

chapter five

1. "Nellie Bly Proposes to Fight for Cuba," *New York World*, March 8, 1896.

2. *New York World*, March 8, 1896.

3. Brooke Kroeger, *Nellie Bly: Daredevil, Reporter, Feminist* (New York: Times Books, 1994), 291.

4. "Muck-Rake Journalism," *Morning Oregonian* (Portland), March 31, 1896.

5. Phyllis Leslie Abramson, *Sob Sister Journalism* (New York: Greenwood Press, 1990), 22.

6. Florence Finch Kelly, *Flowing Stream: The Story of Fifty-six Years in American Newspaper Life* (New York: E. P. Dutton, 1939), 458–59. Steady increases in women's employment in journalism belie her assessment, but Kelly's distaste for sensational journalism was unequivocal. By the mid-1890s, she wrote, "women had made good in nearly all kinds of newspaper work—reporting, feature writing, interviews, critical work of all varieties, desk work, editorial writing; and the record was impressive enough to make

the future of women in journalism look secure and promising." But then "came yellow journalism," and "the outlook took on another color."

7. Jean Marie Lutes, *Front-Page Girls: Women Journalists in American Culture and Fiction, 1880–1930* (Ithaca: Cornell University Press, 2006), 38. The idea that stunt reporting was degrading and demeaning dominates the history of newspaper women's work.

8. Ben Singer, *Melodrama and Modernity: Early Sensational Cinema and Its Contexts* (New York: Columbia University Press, 2001), 248–50.

9. On this culture of entertainment, see esp. John F. Kasson, *Amusing the Million: Coney Island at the Turn of the Century* (New York: Hill and Wang, 1978); Kathy Peiss, *Cheap Amusements: Working Women and Leisure in Turn-of-the-Century New York* (Philadelphia: Temple University Press, 1986); David Nasaw, *Going Out: The Rise and Fall of Public Amusements* (New York: Basic Books, 1993); and Miriam Hansen, *Babel and Babylon: Spectatorship and American Silent Film* (Cambridge: Harvard University Press, 1991).

10. Margherita Arlina Hamm, "New York Newspaper Women," *Peterson Magazine* 5 (April 1895): 413–14.

11. Quoted in S. J. Woolf, "An Editor Talks of Papers and People," *New York Times*, April 12, 1931.

12. Quoted in ibid.

13. Singer, *Melodrama and Modernity*, 221.

14. Ibid., 249.

15. Kate Swan, "A Woman in the Death Chair," *New York World*, February 16, 1896.

16. Ibid.

17. Ibid.

18. Kate Swan, "With the Dead in Grave and Furnace," *New York World*, March 22, 1896.

19. *Journalist*, January 26, 1895.

20. Lady Kate, "Lady Kate as a Hotel Clerk," *New York Recorder*, December 1, 1896.

21. Lady Kate, "Lady Kate Tells Fortunes," *New York Recorder*, February 23, 1896.

22. Representations of women in wartime were an exception. For the celebration of women's bravery in Civil War popular literature, for instance, see Alice Fahs, *The Imagined Civil War: Popular Literature of the North and South, 1861–1865* (Chapel Hill: University of North Carolina Press, 2001).

23. Mrs. McGuirk, "Three Brave Women," *Chicago Daily Inter Ocean*, June 27, 1892.

24. Kate Swan, "Kate Swan Rides with the Life-Savers," *New York World*, February 23, 1896.

25. Kate Swan, "Kate Swan a Fairy Bareback Rider," *New York World*, March 8, 1896.

26. Kate Swan, "Kate Swan Scales Harlem River Bridge," *New York World*, April 19, 1896, and "Kate Swan Paddles through Hell Gate," *New York World*, May 17, 1896.

27. Swan, "Kate Swan Scales Harlem River Bridge" and "Kate Swan Paddles through Hell Gate."

28. Margherita Arlina Hamm, "Among the Newspaper Women," *Journalist*, October 20, 1894. Hamm explained that "Lottie Germaine was formerly on the Recorder, and

has done both excellent writing in the literary end of that brilliant paper, and advertising in the business department. She is thoroughly sincere, earnest, trustworthy and ambitious."

29. Hamm, "Among the Newspaper Women," *Journalist*, November 24, 1894. Hamm wrote: "Lottie Germaine, the bright special writer, is just now arranging for the publication of a new magazine of which she will have complete control. To those who know her this means little short of a charming success. The details of the publication cannot be divulged at present, but a surprise is promised."

30. Elizabeth Garver Jordan, *Three Rousing Cheers* (New York: Appleton-Century, 1938), 160–61.

31. Ibid., 161.

32. Ibid., 161–62.

33. Ibid., 162–63.

34. Ibid., 164–65.

35. Newspapers' fascination with the New Woman has been little explored. In fact, there were multiple representations of New Women in both newspapers and magazines. In *Scribner's* and *Cosmopolitan*, among other magazines, women were represented golfing, fencing, playing tennis, swimming, and, especially, bicycling. The national bicycling craze reached a crescendo in the mid-1890s, becoming acceptable for a wide variety of middle-class women. Even Frances Willard, head of the WCTU (Woman's Christian Temperance Union), was an exuberant proponent of bicycling. On bicycling, see esp. Ellen Gruber Garvey, *The Adman in the Parlor: Magazines and the Gendering of Consumer Culture, 1880s to 1910s* (New York: Oxford University Press, 1996). Magazines were also captivated by new athleticism emerging in women's colleges, as the first organized sports and games for women gained ground.

36. "The New Woman—What She Is Doing, Wearing and Saying," *New York World*, May 10, 1896.

37. Haryot Holt Cahoon, "Women in Gutter Journalism," *Arena* 17 (March 1897): 568.

38. *True Story* article, n.d., Ada Patterson File, *New York Journal-American* Morgue, Center for American History, University of Texas Library, Austin.

39. Elizabeth L. Banks, "American 'Yellow Journalism,'" *Nineteenth Century* 44 (August 1898): 338.

40. On Banks's newspaper career in England, see Seth Koven, *Slumming: Sexual and Social Politics in Victorian London* (Princeton: Princeton University Press, 2004).

41. Eliza Putnam Heaton, for instance, briefly left the woman's page behind in 1888 to pose as a "sham immigrant" traveling steerage from Liverpool to New York. Her account of that journey was first published in her hometown newspaper, the *Brooklyn Times*, in October 1888; after Heaton's death, her husband, newspaper man John Langdon Heaton, published the story of this undercover journey as a book. See Eliza Putnam Heaton, *The Steerage: A Sham Immigrant's Voyage to New York in 1888* (Brooklyn: Brooklyn Eagle Press, 1919).

42. Mark Pittenger, "A World of Difference: Constructing the 'Underclass' in Progressive America," *American Quarterly* 49 (March 1997): 26–65.

43. On this point, see Koven, *Slumming*.

44. M. F. Billington, "Leading Lady Journalists," *Pearson's Magazine* 2 (July 1896): 111.

45. See Charles Loring Brace, *The Dangerous Classes of New York and Twenty Years' Work Among Them* (New York: Wynkoop and Hallenbeck, 1872). On the connections between race and reform as mediated through class, see, e.g., Gail Bederman, *Manliness and Civilization: A Cultural History of Gender and Race in the United States, 1880-1917* (Chicago: University of Chicago Press, 1995). See also Matthew Frye Jacobson, *Barbarian Virtues: The United States Encounters Foreign Peoples at Home and Abroad, 1876-1917* (New York: Hill and Wang, 2000).

46. Koven, *Slumming*, 160; Elizabeth L. Banks, *Autobiography of a "Newspaper Girl"* (New York: Dodd, Mead and Co., 1902), 95–96.

47. "Maids and Matrons," *Milwaukee Journal*, August 5, 1896.

48. Banks, *Autobiography of a "Newspaper Girl,"* 199–200.

49. See, e.g., "Small Boy Encouraged: Innocent Fiction concerning McKinley's Boyhood Cheers Him Amazingly," *Milwaukee Journal*, March 13, 1897, reprinted from *Washington Post*.

50. Banks, *Autobiography of a "Newspaper Girl,"* 203.

51. Ibid., 204–5.

52. Ibid., 206.

53. Ibid., 204.

54. Ibid., 220.

55. Ibid., 220–21.

56. Ibid., 221.

57. Ibid., 222.

58. Cahoon, "Women in Gutter Journalism," 568.

59. Ibid., 568–69.

60. Ibid., 569–72.

61. Ibid., 570–71.

62. "Dens of Chinatown Explored by a Woman," *New York World*, May 10, 1896.

63. Banks, *Autobiography of a "Newspaper Girl,"* 211.

64. Ibid., 211–13.

65. Cahoon, "Women in Gutter Journalism," 572–73.

66. Edith Sessions Tupper, "Why Miss Hunt Went Home," *New York World*, March 13, 1892.

67. Edith Sessions Tupper, "Miss Hunt's Temptation," *Journalist*, June 4, 1892.

68. Ibid.

69. Ibid.

70. On Gale, see Elizabeth V. Burt, "Rediscovering Zona Gale: Journalist," *American Journalism* 12 (Fall 1995): 444–61, and August Derleth, *Still Small Voice: The Biography of Zona Gale* (New York: Appleton-Century, 1940).

71. Zona Gale, "First Woman to Run a Steam Locomobile in New York," *New York World*, May 26, 1901, and "First Woman in America to Speed with Fournier in His Gray Terror," *New York World*, October 23, 1901.

72. Ibid.

73. Gale to her parents, n.d., typescript (by Gale biographer August Derleth), Zona Gale Papers, Wisconsin Historical Society, Madison.

74. Ibid.

75. Ibid.

76. Ibid.

77. Ibid.

78. Beatrice Fairfax [Marie Manning], *Ladies Now and Then* (New York: E. P. Dutton, 1944), 24–25.

79. "Newspaper Women—Nixola Greeley Smith," *Idaho Statesman*, September 19, 1906.

80. Ibid.

81. Ibid.

82. Ibid.

83. Ibid.

84. Ibid.

85. Elizabeth Garver Jordan, *Three Rousing Cheers*, 49.

86. Ibid.

87. Ibid.

88. *True Story* article, n.d., Ada Patterson File, *New York Journal-American* Morgue, Center for American History, University of Texas Library, Austin.

89. Ibid.

90. Banks, *Autobiography of a "Newspaper Girl,"* 234.

91. Ibid., 310.

chapter six

1. On December 31, 1897, mill owners had announced a cut in wages of 10 percent to take place in January; this pay cut was on top of a significant cut in wages only two years before. Not only New Bedford, but also the mill town of Fall River, Mass., was affected by what was, in fact, a regional pay cut decided by a powerful mill owners' collective. Many of the workers in the New Bedford cloth mills were French and English (from Lancashire). For the most complete account of the strike, see Mary H. Blewett, *Constant Turmoil: The Politics of Industrial Life in Nineteenth-Century New England* (Amherst: University of Massachusetts Press, 2000), 338–91.

2. Pendennis, "Anne O'Hagan Writes Stories on Business Principles," *New York Times*, June 18, 1905. On Valesh, see Elizabeth Faue, *Writing the Wrongs: Eva Valesh and the Rise of Labor Journalism* (Ithaca: Cornell University Press, 2002).

3. Elizabeth L. Banks, "American 'Yellow Journalism,'" *Nineteenth Century* 44 (August 1898): 333.

4. On the history of working women at the turn of the century, see esp. Alice Kessler-Harris, *Out to Work: A History of Wage-earning Women in the United States* (New York: Oxford University Press, 1982); Nan Enstad, *Ladies of Labor, Girls of Adventure: Working Women, Popular Culture, and Labor Politics at the Turn of the Twentieth Century* (New York: Columbia University Press, 1999); Christine Stansell, *City of Women: Sex and Class in New York, 1789–1860* (New York: Knopf, 1986); and Kathy Peiss, *Cheap Amusements: Working Women and Leisure in Turn-of-the-Century New York* (Philadelphia: Temple

University Press, 1986). See also David Montgomery, *The Fall of the House of Labor: The Workplace, the State, and American Labor Activism, 1865–1925* (New York: Cambridge University Press, 1987), and Roy Rosenzweig, *Eight Hours for What We Will: Workers and Leisure in the Industrial City, 1870–1920* (New York: Cambridge University Press, 1983).

5. On such literature, see esp. Stansell, *City of Women.* Christine Stansell has pointed out that no sympathy was deemed appropriate for women judged to be "disorderly" by bourgeois standards.

6. Banks, "American 'Yellow Journalism,'" 333.

7. See Sophie Irene Loeb's regular columns for the *New York World* (syndicated nationally) beginning in 1909.

8. Pendennis, "Anne O'Hagan Writes Stories on Business Principles."

9. Ibid.

10. These literary traditions remained potent throughout the 1880s and 1890s, influencing magazine and newspaper coverage of working women. For one example among hundreds, see the (unsigned) article titled "Plying Needle and Thread" in the *Daily Graphic* of November 21, 1887, which explored the "Terrible Poverty of the Sewing Women of New York" and a "Cry for Aid." In its broad outline, the article might have been written in 1870, 1860, 1850, or 1840.

11. Anne O'Hagan, "Big Mill Strike Likely to Be a Siege of Many Months," *New York Journal*, dateline January 20, 1898, in New Bedford Strike Scrapbooks, vol. 1, Widener Library, Harvard University.

12. On slumming in England, see esp. Seth Koven, *Slumming: Sexual and Social Politics in Victorian London* (Princeton: Princeton University Press, 2004), and Judith R. Walkowitz, *City of Dreadful Delight: Narratives of Sexual Danger in Late-Victorian London* (Chicago: University of Chicago Press, 1992). For the American version of slumming, see Mark Pittenger, "A World of Difference: Constructing the 'Underclass' in Progressive America," *American Quarterly* 49 (March 1997): 26–65, and Carrie Tirado Bramen, "The Urban Picturesque and the Spectacle of Americanization," *American Quarterly* 52 (September 2000): 444–77.

13. Anne O'Hagan, "Heroines Sustain Men in the Big Cotton Mill Strike," *New York Journal*, dateline January 21, 1898, in New Bedford Strike Scrapbooks, vol. 1.

14. "Victims of the Yellow: Mr. and Mrs. Brierly Scandalized by What Was Said of Them," *New Bedford Evening Standard*, dateline January 22, 1898, in New Bedford Strike Scrapbooks, vol. 1. O'Hagan had also misspelled her name—"Bierly" instead of "Brierly."

15. Ibid.

16. Untitled article in unnamed local newspaper, n.d., in New Bedford Strike Scrapbooks, vol. 1.

17. Untitled article in unnamed local newspaper, n.d., in New Bedford Strike Scrapbooks, vol. 1.

18. Elizabeth L. Banks, "Jolly Strikers Who Don't Whine at Woe," *New York World*, dateline January 24, 1898, in New Bedford Strike Scrapbooks, vol. 2.

19. Ibid.

20. Ibid.

21. Ibid. On the incomprehension of middle-class observers of working-class fashions, see esp. Stansell, *City of Women*, and Nan Enstad, *Ladies of Labor*.

22. Elizabeth L. Banks, "Housewives Who Live on $7 a Week Described by Miss Banks," *New York World*, dateline January 19, 1898, in New Bedford Strike Scrapbooks, vol. 1.

23. Minnie R. Rosen, "Minnie Rosen Finds No Sign of Weakness in the Strike," *New York World*, dateline January 24, 1898, in New Bedford Strike Scrapbooks, vol. 2.

24. Faue, *Writing the Wrongs*.

25. See Brooke Kroeger, *Nellie Bly: Daredevil, Reporter, Feminist* (New York: Times Books, 1994), 101–2.

26. Nell Nelson, *The White Slave Girls of Chicago: Nell Nelson's Startling Disclosures of the Cruelties and Iniquities Practiced in the Workshops and Factories of a Great City* (Chicago: Barkley Publishing Co., 1888), 5.

27. Eva McDonald Valesh, Reminiscences, Oral Histories of Newspaper Women, Columbia University Libraries and Collections, New York, N.Y., 10.

28. Eva Valesh [Eva Gay], "'Mong Girls Who Toil," *St. Paul Daily Globe*, March 25, 1888.

29. Valesh, Reminiscences, 20–21.

30. Ibid., 21.

31. Ibid., 20–21.

32. Ibid., 11–14.

33. Ibid., 19.

34. See Faue, *Writing the Wrongs*.

35. Eva McDonald Valesh to Albert Dollenmayer, 20 December 1895, Albert Dollenmayer and Family Papers, box 4, Minnesota Historical Society, as quoted in Faue, *Writing the Wrongs*, 119.

36. See Faue, *Writing the Wrongs*.

37. Ibid., 116.

38. Valesh, Reminiscences, 51.

39. Ibid., 51–53.

40. Ibid., 54–55.

41. Ibid., 55–58, 60–61.

42. Ibid., 61.

43. Eva McDonald Valesh, "Journal Woman with Strikers," *New York Journal*, dateline January 18, 1898, in New Bedford Strike Scrapbooks, vol. 1.

44. Valesh, Reminiscences, 62.

45. Valesh, "Journal Woman with Strikers." On fining, see Blewett, *Constant Turmoil*, and the contemporary newspaper articles discussed below.

46. Valesh, "Journal Woman with Strikers."

47. Eva McDonald Valesh, "Journal's Plan to End Strike Gladly Accepted," *New York Journal*, dateline January 19, 1898, in New Bedford Strike Scrapbooks, vol. 1; Valesh, Reminiscences, 62.

48. Valesh, "Journal's Plan to End Strike Gladly Accepted."

49. See miscellaneous articles from Boston newspapers and the *Atlanta Constitution* in New Bedford Strike Scrapbooks.

50. Elizabeth L. Banks, "Women in Big Strike Are Losing Heart," *New York World*, dateline January 22, 1898, in New Bedford Strike Scrapbooks, vol. 2.

51. Ibid.

52. "Hissed a Woman: Mrs. Pickering Driven Off Stage by Weavers," newspaper unknown, dateline January 29, 1898, in New Bedford Strike Scrapbooks, vol. 2. Elizabeth L. Banks, "Exodus of New Bedford Strikers," *New York World*, dateline January 28, 1898, in New Bedford Strike Scrapbooks, vol. 2.

53. Anne O'Hagan, "All New England May Be Involved in Mill Strike," *New York Journal*, dateline January 22, 1898, in New Bedford Strike Scrapbooks, vol. 1.

54. Ibid.

55. Anne O'Hagan, untitled article, *New York Journal*, dateline January 24, 1898, New Bedford Strike Scrapbooks, vol. 1.

56. Anne O'Hagan, "Strike Keynote in New Bedford Mill Is Fine System," *New York Journal*, dateline January 26, 1898, in New Bedford Strike Scrapbooks, vol. 2.

57. Anne O'Hagan, "Mill Men Pay Pro Rata Share of Strike," *New York Journal*, dateline January 27, 1898, in New Bedford Strike Scrapbooks, vol. 2.

58. Eva McDonald Valesh, "McKinley Talks to the Journal about the Great Strike," *New York Journal*, January 23, 1898.

59. Ibid.

60. Eva McDonald Valesh, "Journal's Bill for the Weavers," *New York Journal*, dateline January 29, 1898, in New Bedford Strike Scrapbooks, vol. 2.

61. Eva McDonald Valesh, "State Listens to a Journal Woman, Labor's Champion: Mrs. Valesh Officially Presents the Journal's Weavers' Bill," *New York Journal*, dateline February 9, 1898, in New Bedford Strike Scrapbooks, vol. 3.

62. Valesh, Reminiscences, 62–63.

63. Valesh, "State Listens to a Journal Woman."

64. Ibid.

65. Ibid.

66. "A New Fines Bill," newspaper unknown, n.d., "Mrs. Pickering's Plea," newspaper unknown, March 18, 1898, both in New Bedford Strike Scrapbooks, vol. 4.

67. Valesh, Reminiscences, 71–72.

68. "Mrs. Pickering Leaves Work," newspaper unknown, May 1898, in New Bedford Strike Scrapbooks, vol. 4.

69. Elizabeth L. Banks, *The Autobiography of a "Newspaper Girl"* (New York: Dodd, Mead and Co., 1902), 231–33.

70. On "working girl" literature, see esp. Enstad, *Ladies of Labor*, and Laura Hapke, *Tales of the Working Girl: Wage-Earning Women in American Literature, 1890–1925* (New York: Twayne Publishers, 1992).

71. Dorothy Richardson, *The Long Day: The Story of a New York Working Girl*, ed. Cynthia Sondik Aron (1905; reprint, Charlottesville: University Press of Virginia, 1990), x.

72. *Who's Who in America*, vol. 5, 1908–9.

73. In its "Social and Personal" column, the *Sentinel* noted that Richardson had just been feted with a "palm party." Richardson was "known in the East as a young writer of more than ordinary ability, having been connected with the New York newspapers," and was "now on the staff of The Pittsburg Dispatch." "Social and Personal," *Milwaukee Sentinel*, July 18, 1897.

74. Dorothy Richardson, "Women in Debs' Colony: There Will Be a Place for Them Later On," *Milwaukee Sentinel*, July 25, 1897.

75. Ibid.

76. Ibid.

77. Ibid.

78. Ibid.

79. Ibid.

80. Dorothy Richardson to Wallace Rice, January 14, 1901, Wallace Rice Papers, Newberry Library, Chicago.

81. Ibid.

82. "Newspaper Women: Dorothy Richardson," *New York Herald*, September 30, 1906.

83. Ibid.

84. Ibid.

85. Ibid.

86. On reading in this period, see Enstad, *Ladies of Labor*. Also see Joan Shelley Rubin, *The Making of Middlebrow Culture* (Chapel Hill: University of North Carolina Press, 1992), and Barbara Sicherman, *Well-Read Lives: How Books Inspired a Generation of American Women* (Chapel Hill: University of North Carolina Press, 2010).

87. On Roosevelt and the "strenuous life," see esp. Gail Bederman, *Manliness and Civilization*.

88. Dorothy Adams [Dorothy Richardson], "Work or Starve: Woman's Heartbreaking Search for Employment in the Great City of New York: Personal Experience of Dorothy Adams Reveals the Bitter Struggle of the Would-Be-Breadwinners of Her Sex," *New York Herald*, December 23, 1900.

89. Ibid.

90. Ibid.

91. Dorothy Adams [Dorothy Richardson], "Is an Unattended Woman Arriving in New York at Night, Entitled to No Consideration at a Reputable Hotel?," *New York Herald*, November 18, 1900.

92. Ibid.

93. Adams, "Work or Starve."

94. Ibid.

95. Adams, "The Girl Who Lives on $5 a Week," *New York Herald*, January 6, 1901.

96. Dorothy Richardson to Wallace Rice, January 14, 1901.

97. Dorothy Adams [Dorothy Richardson], "One-Room Life of the Working Girl—Its Light and Shadows," *New York Herald*, January 20, 1901.

98. Ibid.

99. Ibid.

100. Ibid.

101. Dorothy Richardson, "Earning a Living at Coney Island," *Frank Leslie's Popular Monthly*, April 1904, 689. See also December 1903 and January and February 1904.

102. On the homoerotic elements of *The Long Day*, see Cathryn Halverson, "The Fascination of the Working Girl: Dorothy Richardson's *The Long Day*," *American Studies* 40 (Spring 1999): 95–115.

103. Daniel T. Rodgers, *The Work Ethic in Industrial America, 1850–1920* (Chicago: University of Chicago Press, 1978), 205–6.

104. Richardson, *The Long Day*, 120, 275.

105. Jack London, Review of *The Long Day*, *San Francisco Examiner*, October 15, 1905.

106. Izola Forrester, "One Working Girl's Struggles," *New York World*, October 15, 1905.

107. "Newspaper Women: Dorothy Richardson," *New York Herald*, September 30, 1906.

108. Richardson, *The Long Day*, 276.

109. Ibid.

110. Nancy Cott, ed., *History of Women in the United States: Historical Articles on Women's Lives and Activities*, vol. 17, *Social and Moral Reform*, pt. 2 (Munich: K. G. Saur, 1994), 483 (Leonora O'Reilly).

111. Leonora O'Reilly, in an unpublished submission to the *New York Journal*, as quoted in Meredith Tax, *The Rising of the Women: Feminist Solidarity and Class Conflict, 1880–1917* (1980; reprint, Urbana: University of Illinois Press, 1998), 117–18.

112. Rodgers, *Work Ethic in Industrial America*, 205.

113. Maude Burrows Dutton, "In New York Literary and Artistic Circles," *Congregationalist and Christian World*, June 16, 1906.

114. "Newspaper Women: Dorothy Richardson," *New York Herald*, September 30, 1906.

115. Richardson, *The Long Day*, 274.

116. Dorothy Richardson, "The Difficulties and Dangers Confronting the Working Woman," *Annals of the American Academy of Political and Social Science* 27 (May 1906): 162.

117. Ibid., 163–64.

118. See Richardson, *The Long Day*, 270, 279.

119. "Daughter of the Ghetto to Write about the East Side," *New York World*, April 9, 1905.

120. Rose Pastor Stokes, *"I Belong to the Working Class,"* 101.

121. "To Advise on Love: Mrs. Rose Pastor Stokes to Answer Questions in Jewish Paper," *New-York Tribune*, August 11, 1907. Her new "department" was to "appear every Saturday under the heading 'Letters from Vorwaerts' readers answered by Rose Pastor Stokes."

122. Rose H. Phelps Stokes, "The Condition of Working Women, from the Working Woman's Standpoint," *Annals of the American Academy of Political and Social Science* 27 (May 1906): 166.

123. Ibid., 173.

124. Ibid.

125. Rose H. Phelps Stokes, "The Long Day: A Story of Real Life," *Independent*, November 16, 1905.

126. Otis Notman, "Writers of Contemporaneous History," *New York Times*, May 25, 1907.

127. For Richardson's connection with Belasco, see Undated notice, box 83, Century Company Records, New York Public Library: "All requests for material, literary or pictorial, regarding Mr. Belasco or his various artists or productions, will, if addressed to Miss Richardson, receive prompt and efficient attention."

128. Mary Isabel Brush, "Trailing Belasco's Thought in His New York Theater," *Chicago Tribune*, April 23, 1911.

129. See Koven, *Slumming*.

130. See "The Interests of Working Women," *New York World*, July 6, 12, 1896. For examples of later advice columns for working women, see both the "For and by Business Girls" column of the *Chicago Tribune* in the 1910s and Sophie Irene Loeb's syndicated columns for working girls in the *World*, beginning in 1909.

chapter seven

1. "Nellie in Mexico," *Pittsburg Dispatch*, February 21, 1886. Alexander von Humboldt (1769–1859), famed German explorer and naturalist, traveled widely in Latin America from 1799 to 1804.

2. Brooke Kroeger, *Nellie Bly: Daredevil, Reporter, Feminist* (New York: Times Books, 1994), 62.

3. Mary Elizabeth Blake and Margaret F. Sullivan, *Mexico: Picturesque, Political, Progressive* (Boston: Lee and Shepard, 1888); Kroeger, *Nellie Bly*.

4. This claim is made by Jean Marie Lutes, "Journalism, Modernity, and the Globe-Trotting Girl Reporter," in *Transatlantic Print Culture, 1880–1940: Emerging Media, Emerging Modernisms*, ed. Ann Ardis and Patrick Collier (New York: Palgrave Macmillan, 2008), 170.

5. See Laura Wexler, *Tender Violence: Domestic Visions in an Age of U.S. Imperialism* (Chapel Hill: University of North Carolina Press, 2000); Kristin Hoganson, *Consumers' Imperium: The Global Production of American Domesticity, 1865–1920* (Chapel Hill: University of North Carolina Press, 2007) and *Fighting for American Manhood: How Gender Politics Provoked the Spanish-American and Philippine-American Wars* (New Haven: Yale University Press, 1998); Ann Laura Stoler, ed., *Haunted by Empire: Geographies of Intimacy in North American History* (Durham: Duke University Press, 2006); Amy Kaplan, *The Anarchy of Empire in the Making of U.S. Culture* (Cambridge: Harvard University Press, 2002); and Amy Kaplan and Donald Pease, eds., *Cultures of United States Imperialism* (Durham: Duke University Press, 1993).

6. On the "innocent eye" of domesticity, see esp. Wexler, *Tender Violence*.

7. See, e.g., Mary Louise Pratt, *Imperial Eyes: Travel Writing and Transculturation* (New York: Routledge, 1992); Sidonie Smith, *Moving Lives: 20th-Century Women's Travel Writing* (Minneapolis: University of Minnesota Press, 2001); Mary Suzanne Schriber, *Writing Home: American Women Abroad, 1830–1902* (Charlottesville: University of Vir-

ginia Press, 1997); and Monica Anderson, *Women and the Politics of Travel, 1870–1914* (Madison: Fairleigh Dickinson University Press, 2006).

8. Quoted from Harold Frederick Smith, *American Travellers Abroad: A Bibliography of Accounts Published before 1900* (1969; reprint, Lanham, Md.: Scarecrow Press, 1999), vii.

9. Blake and Sullivan, *Mexico*, 7.

10. Mark Twain [Samuel Langhorne Clemens], *The Innocents Abroad* (1869; reprint, New York: Penguin Books, 2002), 13.

11. Lucy Hamilton Hooper to Joseph Pulitzer, October 12, 1886, *New York World* Archives, Columbia University Libraries and Collections.

12. Henry James, *The Portrait of a Lady*, Norton Critical Edition (1881; reprint, New York: Norton, 1995), 55, 78.

13. Ibid., 15, 55, 88.

14. Ibid., 78. Tellingly, James made Henrietta an even more unappealing character in a 1908 revision—he had not been won over by the rise of women in journalism. On this point, see Nina Baym, "Revision and Thematic Change in *The Portrait of a Lady*," in James, *Portrait of a Lady*, 620–34.

15. Margery Deane [Marie J. Pitman], *European Breezes* (Boston: Lee and Shepard, 1883), 7–8, 11–12.

16. Blake and Sullivan, *Mexico*, 8.

17. On this point, see Laura Wexler, *Tender Violence*; Emily S. Rosenberg, *Spreading the American Dream: American Economic and Cultural Expansion, 1890–1945* (New York: Hill and Wang, 1982); Stoler, *Haunted by Empire*; Anne McClintock, *Imperial Leather: Race, Gender and Sexuality in the Colonial Context* (New York: Routledge, 1995); and Kaplan, *Anarchy of Empire*.

18. Lida Rose McCabe, "Margaret Sullivan," *Los Angeles Times*, June 4, 1893.

19. Ibid.

20. Ibid.

21. Ibid.

22. "Do Women Lower Men's Wages?," *New York Times*, February 27, 1893.

23. Anne O'Hagan, "Women in Journalism," *Munsey's Magazine* 19 (July 1898): 611. For a mention of Sullivan as an important part of newspaper women's history, see, e.g., Elizabeth G. Jordan, "A Newspaper Woman's Story," *Lippincott's Monthly Magazine*, March 1893, 341.

24. Catherine Cole [Martha R. Field], "National Capital Notes," *New Orleans Daily Picayune*, April 15, 1888.

25. "Washington Correspondence," *Georgia Weekly Telegraph and Georgia Journal & Messenger*, September 6, 1870.

26. "Literary Items," *Milwaukee Sentinel*, February 11, 1871.

27. *Ohio Historical Quarterly*, vol. 68, p. 325.

28. Rutherford Birchard Hayes, Diary, August 31, 1885, *Diary and Letters of Rutherford Birchard Hayes* (Columbus: Ohio State Archaeological and Historical Society, 1922–26).

29. Hayes, Diary, September 1, 1885, ibid.

30. "Appendix: Women Correspondents Entitled to Press Gallery Privileges ac-

cording to Congressional Directory, 1870–1885," in Maurine Hoffman Beasley, *The First Women Washington Correspondents*, George Washington University Washington Studies No. 4 (Washington, D.C.: George Washington University Press, 1976), 25.

31. Grace Greenwood, "The New Order of Things," *New York Times*, July 3, 1877.

32. Ibid.

33. In the late 1870s Ward was listed as an accredited Washington correspondent for the *National Republican* (1877–78) and the *Washington Chronicle* (1879). Beasley, *First Women Washington Correspondents*, 25.

34. Donald A. Ritchie, *Reporting from Washington: The History of the Washington Press Corps* (New York: Oxford University Press, 2005).

35. Loris Troyer, *Portage Pathways* (Kent, Ohio: Kent State University Press, 1998), 126–27; "Mrs. F. B. Ward Dead," *Washington Post*, October 6, 1913. Census records for Fanny B. Ward: 1870 U.S. Federal Census for Ravenna, Portage, Ohio; 1880 U.S. Federal Census for Ravenna, Portage, Ohio, http.ancestry.com.

36. Today Scidmore is remembered only for her travel books—her newspaper writings have received almost no attention.

37. "Personal," *Milwaukee Sentinel*, November 7, 1883.

38. Fannie B. Ward, "Summer Days in Mexico," *Boston Daily Advertiser*, September 1, 1883.

39. Ibid.

40. Fannie B. Ward, "Land of the Palm," *Cleveland Herald*, September 1, 1883.

41. Pratt, *Imperial Eyes*, 155–56.

42. Ward, "Summer Days in Mexico."

43. Fannie B. Ward, "Modern Mexico: The Present Political Situation," *Cleveland Herald*, December 3, 1883.

44. Ward, "Summer Days in Mexico."

45. Ward, "Land of the Palm."

46. Fannie B. Ward, "Monterey: Fanny B. Ward Bids It Farewell," *Cleveland Herald*, September 22, 1883.

47. General Francis E. Pinto, "Storming of the Castle of Chapultepec," *New-York Tribune*, November 1, 1903.

48. Ibid.

49. See, e.g., Robert W. Merry, *A Country of Vast Designs: James K. Polk, the Mexican War, and the Conquest of the American Continent* (New York: Simon and Schuster, 2009), 388.

50. Ulysses S. Grant, *Personal Memoirs of U. S. Grant* (1885, 1886; reprint, New York: Penguin Books, 1999), 25.

51. Fannie B. Ward, "A New Republic," *Milwaukee Sentinel*, December 5, 1886.

52. Fannie B. Ward, "Modern Mexico: Famous Caverns of Pesyneria," November 28, 1883.

53. Fannie Brigham Ward, "In the Mexican Tropics: The Trip of Two Ladies on Donkey Back through the State of Campeche," *Rocky Mountain News* (Denver), November 9, 1884.

54. Fannie B. Ward, "Old Popocatipetl [*sic*]: Two Ladies Ascend to Its Topmost Peak," *Cleveland Herald*, June 5, 1884.

55. Fannie B. Ward, "The Chilian Trouble," *Morning Oregonian* (Portland), March 12, 1891.

56. Mary C. Francis, "How I Carried the Flag to Cuba," *Independent*, March 2, 1899, 601.

57. Ibid.

58. Mary H. Krout, *Hawaii and a Revolution: The Personal Experiences of a Correspondent in the Sandwich Islands during the Crisis of 1893 and Subsequently* (New York: Dodd, Mead and Co., 1898), 33.

59. Ibid., 34.

60. Ibid.

61. Ibid., 37.

62. Ibid., 40.

63. Ibid., 36.

64. Fannie B. Ward, "The Patriots of Chili," *Morning Oregonian* (Portland), September 13, 1891.

65. Fannie B. Ward, "A Living Volcano: The Tendency to Revolution in Mexico," *Los Angeles Daily Times*, December 2, 1884.

66. Ward, "Patriots of Chili."

67. Fannie B. Ward, "War Times in Cuba," *Chicago Daily Inter Ocean*, March 31, 1895.

68. See Gerald F. Linderman, *The Mirror of War: American Society and the Spanish-American War* (Ann Arbor: University of Michigan Press, 1974), 114–47. On the fight for Cuban independence, see esp. Louis A. Pérez Jr., *Cuba: Between Reform and Revolution*, 3rd ed. (New York: Oxford University Press, 2006).

69. Fannie B. Ward, "City of Matanzas," *Morning Oregonian* (Portland), March 17, 1895.

70. Ibid.

71. Fannie B. Ward, "Warm Times in Cuba," *Morning Oregonian* (Portland), March 31, 1895; Ward, "Last Days in Cuba," *Morning Oregonian* (Portland), May 5, 1895.

72. Fannie B. Ward, "The War in Cuba," *Morning Oregonian* (Portland), April 19, 1895.

73. "City Brevities," *Evening Times* (Washington, D.C.), July 23, 1898. See also Fannie B. Ward to Clara Barton, September 15, 1898, Barton Papers, Library of Congress. "I have written you twice since my unpremeditated departure from Santiago," Ward wrote.

74. "Red Cross to the Rescue," *Evening Times* (Washington, D.C.), September 13, 1900. See also "Off for Galveston," *The Times* (Washington, D.C.), September 14, 1900. She was described as "Miss Fanny B. Ward, who did such splendid work in Cuba." Ward may well have "placed" this favorable comment with one of the editors with whom she worked.

75. Fannie B. Ward to Clara Barton, March 22, 1903, Clara Barton Papers, Library of Congress.

76. Ward to Barton, April 8, 1903, ibid.

77. Ward to Barton, July 17, [1904], ibid.

78. Ward to Barton, March 2, 1901, ibid.

79. Ward to Barton, January 6, 1904, ibid.

80. Ward, "War in Cuba."

81. Edwin Llewellyn Shuman, *Steps into Journalism: Helps and Hints for Young Writers* (Evanston, Ill.: Correspondence School of Journalism, 1894), 154.

82. Margherita Arlina Hamm, "Women as Travelers: The American Woman in Action," *Frank Leslie's Popular Monthly*, June 1899, 215.

83. "Reminiscences of the East," *New York Herald*, Brooklyn supp., March 28, 1897.

84. John William Leonard, ed., *Woman's Who's Who of America: A Biographical Dictionary of Contemporary Women of the United States and Canada, 1914–1915* (New York: American Commonwealth Co., 1914), 764. Her entry in this volume (most likely provided by Hamm herself) spelled out her achievements: "Traveled in U.S., Hawaii and W. Indies in '90s for Sun, Herald, and Mail, New York; later visited Japan, China, India, Egypt and Russia for same papers; made maps for Geog. Soc.; war corr. Chinese-Japanese War and Spanish-Am. War; also mil. nurse without salary." According to the *Boston Herald* in 1898, on the eve of her departure for wartime Cuba, "She was a war correspondent in Corea, Japan and China." "Formerly of Bangor," *Bangor Daily Whig & Courier*, July 11, 1898.

85. *Current Literature* 3 (November 1889): 375.

86. *Journalist*, October 14, 1893.

87. For accounts of their divorce and the quoted letter of an actress, see "Mrs. Fales Gets Decree of Divorce," *New York Herald*, July 31, 1902.

88. "Dr. and Mrs. William E. S. Fales en Route," *Journalist*, February 10, 1894.

89. "Russia Is Behind It," *Rocky Mountain News* (Denver), September 5, 1894.

90. Margherita Arlina Hamm, "The Civilized Man in China," *Journalist*, June 9, 1894.

91. Ibid.

92. Ibid.

93. "The Only Woman War Correspondent: Margherita Arlina Hamm," *Journalist*, September 8, 1894.

94. Hamm, "Women as Travelers," 215.

95. On the various strands of feminism, see esp. Nancy F. Cott, *The Grounding of Modern Feminism* (New Haven: Yale University Press, 1987), and Christine Stansell, *The Feminist Promise, 1792 to the Present* (New York: Modern Library, 2010).

96. "Mostly Local and Critical," *Journalist*, September 8, 1894. The *Journalist* also noted that "many journalists are actually more interested in the doings of the giants than they are in the fate of Corea." As Marilyn Young has noted, after Japan's victory in the Sino-Japanese War, popular interest in the Far East increased exponentially. But there seems to have been less knowledge of, or interest in, Korea—at least in the popular press. See Young, *The Rhetoric of Empire: American China Policy, 1895–1901* (Cambridge: Harvard University Press, 1968).

97. This is not to say that there was no interest in the Far East. See Matthew Frye Jacobson, *Barbarian Virtues: The United States Encounters Foreign Peoples at Home and Abroad, 1876–1917* (New York: Hill and Wang, 2000), and Young, *Rhetoric of Empire*.

98. "Formerly of Bangor." Another article explained that she was spending a month visiting Korea "when the attack upon Seoul took place." "The Only Woman War Correspondent."

99. "The Only Woman War Correspondent."

100. "Russia Is Behind It."

101. "An Industrious Correspondent," *Chicago Daily Inter Ocean*, March 2, 1895.

102. Leaflet announcing "Grand Cuban-American Fair," xerxesbooks.com, accessed October 8, 2011. Margherita Arlina Hamm, "Some Women Editors," *Peterson Magazine* 6 (June 1896): 610.

103. Masterson's entire interview was reprinted in a number of the popular books published in response to the Cuban war.

104. "Formerly of Bangor," *Bangor Daily Whig & Courier*, July 11, 1898.

105. On the Spanish-American and American-Philippine wars, see esp. Paul A. Kramer, *The Blood of Government: Race, Empire, the United States, and the Philippines* (Chapel Hill: University of North Carolina Press, 2006); Stuart Creighton Miller, *"Benevolent Assimilation": The American Conquest of the Philippines, 1899–1903* (New Haven: Yale University Press, 1982); Jacobson, *Barbarian Virtues*; Rosenberg, *Spreading the American Dream*; and Linderman, *Mirror of War*.

106. Margherita Arlina Hamm, Preface to *Manila and the Philippines* (New York: F. Tennyson Neely, 1898), n.p.

107. A. O'Hagan and E. B. Kaufman, *Cuba at a Glance* (New York: R. H. Russell, 1898), copyright page.

108. Margherita Arlina Hamm, *America's New Possessions and Spheres of Influence* (New York: F. Tennyson Neely, 1899), 111, 134.

109. Ibid., 30–31.

110. Ibid., 220–21, 211–12.

111. James Creelman, *On the Great Highway* (Boston: Lothrop Publishing Co., 1901), 320–21.

112. Ibid., 321–27.

113. Ibid., 337–38.

114. "Death of Miss Benjamin," *New-York Tribune*, January 22, 1902.

115. Ibid.

116. Anna Northend Benjamin, "The Truth about Army Rations," *Leslie's Weekly*, June 30, 1898.

117. War Correspondent's Pass, Miscellaneous Papers, 1884–1905, box 1, William Dummer Northend Papers, Emory University Library. According to the pass, Benjamin was a correspondent for the Arkell Publishing Company, New York, which in 1898 bought *Leslie's Weekly*.

118. "Death of Miss Benjamin."

119. Anna Northend Benjamin, "A Woman's Point of View," *Leslie's Weekly*, August 18, 1898, 135.

120. "Death of Miss Benjamin."

121. Anna Northend Benjamin, "The Truth about Army Rations," *Leslie's Weekly*, June 30, 1898, 426.

122. Anna Northend Benjamin, "Horses and Mules for the Army," *Leslie's Weekly*, July 7, 1898, 14. Benjamin's article appeared on a page labeled "From the Seat of War"; the movement of troops was covered by male correspondent Gilson Willets.

123. Anna Northend Benjamin, "Yellow Fever at Key West," *Leslie's Weekly*, July 28, 1898, 74.

124. Teresa Dean, "A Woman in Camp," *Leslie's Weekly*, July 28, 1898.

125. Anna Northend Benjamin, "A Woman's Visit to Santiago," *Leslie's Weekly*, August 25, 1898.

126. In this, of course, Benjamin and Hamm were no different from male correspondents.

127. Mary A. Livermore, the famed Civil War nurse and woman's suffrage activist, wrote to Benjamin in September 1898: "Will you deliver your lecture on 'Guantanamo, Santiago, etc.' for the Women's Union of Melrose [Mass.]?" In the spring of 1899, in New Jersey, she gave an "illustrated lecture on Tampa and Key West during the war and Santiago after the war." Benjamin, in addition to her writings, delivered a number of lectures in New York and elsewhere on her war experiences. "Death of Miss Benjamin," *New-York Tribune*, January 22, 1902. Later Benjamin asked for an endorsement from now–Major General Shafter. Shafter replied: "I am trying to recall you to my memory. If you are the young lady that called on me at Tampa, with a companion also from the North, and who was advised by me not to think of going to Cuba, owing to the stormy outlook ahead, then I do recall you very well, and it will give me great pleasure to comply with your request." Major General Shafter to Miss Anna Northend Benjamin, March 15, 1899, William Dummer Northend Papers, Emory University Library.

128. Anna Northend Benjamin, "Some Filipino Characteristics," *Outlook*, August 31, 1901, 1003–8.

129. Ibid., 1003.

130. Ibid.

131. Ibid., 1004, 1003.

132. Ibid., 1004.

133. Ibid., 1005.

134. Ibid., 1008.

135. Mary H. Krout, "The Home Circle: Travel as a Means of Liberal Education," *Chicago Daily Inter Ocean*, July 29, 1893.

136. Mary H. Krout, *Hawaii and a Revolution*, vii, ix.

137. Ibid., viii, 84. On racialized hierarchies in late nineteenth-century thought and practice, see Jacobson, *Barbarian Virtues*, and Gail Bederman, *Manliness and Civilization: A Cultural History of Gender and Race in the United States, 1880–1917* (Chicago: University of Chicago Press, 1995).

138. Mary H. Krout, "Negro Is Discussed: Miss Krout's Weekly Correspondence from London," *Chicago Daily Inter Ocean*, December 30, 1895.

139. Ibid.

140. "Barnett-Wells: Distinguished Defender of the Colored Race Married to a Chicagoan," *Chicago Daily Inter Ocean*, June 28, 1895.

141. On Ida B. Wells's antilynching campaign, see esp. Patricia A. Schechter, *Ida B. Wells-Barnett and American Reform, 1880–1930* (Chapel Hill: University of North Carolina Press, 2001), and Bederman, *Manliness and Civilization*.

142. "Ida Wells-Barnett: Her Comment on Miss Krout's London Letter," *Chicago Daily Inter Ocean*, January 2, 1896.

143. Ibid.

144. Ibid.

145. On Craft, see Rudolph M. Lapp, "Mabel Craft Deering: A Young Woman of Advanced Ideas," *California History* 66 (September 1987): 162–69.

146. No woman had ever won the University Medal. But as Craft sarcastically commented in her letter to the *Chronicle*, "Of course, this would never do, and was a result entirely unexpected by those who had the matter in charge." In order to give the award to a male student, the faculty had readjusted upward, on spurious technical grounds, the grade point average of another male student. Craft immediately petitioned against this patently unfair award. When the regents of the university met to decide on her petition, the president shifted gears in initially arguing that the medal should go to the male student "because the young man possessed a superior mind." "As to the superior mind argument," Craft wrote, "the only test of the ability of the student so long as the present marking system prevails is the marks received, and no professor has any right to say that a student who has not received the highest average is a more distinguished student than the one who received such highest average." "The University Medal," *San Francisco Chronicle*, July 2, 1892.

147. Later Craft published a book, *Hawaii Nei*, that drew on this experience, reprinting columns that had "appeared originally in the San Francisco *Chronicle*, the New York *Sun*, the New York *Tribune*, the Philadelphia *Press*, and other American newspapers, in the form of letters from Honolulu, written on the eve of and immediately following the formal transfer of Hawaii to her new sovereignty." Mabel Clare Craft, *Hawaii Nei* (San Francisco: William Doxey, 1899), viii.

148. Ibid., vii.

149. Mabel Clare Craft, "The Colored Man as a Soldier," *San Francisco Chronicle*, July 2, 1899. Obviously, Craft could not have taken this stance without the support of the progressive *Chronicle*.

150. Ibid.

151. Ibid.

152. "The 'Color Line' Excites the Ladies," *San Francisco Examiner*, November 8, 1901.

153. Ibid.

154. "Agitation Now Worries Leading Club Women," *San Francisco Examiner*, November 9, 1901.

155. "A Woman Globe Trotter," *New York Sun*, April 7, 1901. "For the last six years she has flitted from continent to continent in a way that makes ordinary folks dizzy," the *Sun* commented.

156. James Martin to U.S. Consuls, May 7, 1901, William Dummer Northend Papers, Emory University Library. See also "Death of Miss Benjamin," *New-York Tribune*, January 22, 1902.

157. See "Burial of Miss Benjamin," *New-York Tribune*, January 25, 1902, which states that she had "died from the effects of a tumor."

158. "Girl War Writer Dies in Paris," *New York Evening World*, January 22, 1902.

159. But her broader outlook had been gained, Benjamin said, "from an insight into the cramped methods of the Far East, in comparison with our own. I more than ever appreciate the value of the independence and self-reliance of the American girl, for

everywhere I was treated with the utmost courtesy, and I never once felt the need of a protector." "An Interesting Journey," *New-York Tribune*, August 5, 1900.

160. Margherita Arlina Hamm, "Women as Travelers: The American Woman in Action," *Frank Leslie's Popular Monthly*, June 1899, 13–16.

161. Ibid.

epilogue

1. "Professional Women Tell of Handicaps," *New-York Tribune*, February 21, 1915.

2. Nixola Greeley-Smith, "Questionnaire for Newspaper Women," 1917, Bureau of Vocational Information Records, Schlesinger Library, Radcliffe Institute for Advanced Study.

3. See "Nixola G. Smith Dies under Knife," *New York World*, March 10, 1919.

4. See Nan Robertson, *The Girls in the Balcony: Women, Men, and "The New York Times"* (New York: Random House, 1992).

5. "Opens Women's Meeting: Miss Susan B. Anthony Presides for the Last Time," *Chicago Daily Tribune*, February 8, 1900.

6. Beatrice Fairfax [Marie Manning], *Ladies Now and Then* (New York: E. P. Dutton, 1944), 157. The editors Manning mentions were Arthur Brisbane and Charles Edward Russell.

7. Ibid., 158.

8. Ibid.

9. *New York Sun*, May 27, 1895. Among the newspaper women mentioned in this article were Cynthia Westover, Eliza Archard Conner, Mary C. Francis, and Mary H. Krout. The object of the organization was "the collection and distribution through the press of the country of the latest and most reliable news of all progressive women's clubs, organizations, and societies, and particularly of the National Woman's Suffrage Association."

10. Mabel Craft Deering, in *Winning Equal Suffrage in California: Reports of Committees of the College Equal Suffrage League of Northern California in the Campaign of 1911* (N.p.: National College Equal Suffrage League, 1913), 17. Mabel Clare Craft married Frank P. Deering in 1902.

11. *Annual Report: New York State Woman Suffrage Association*, Forty-seventh Annual Convention, 1915 (New York: New York State Woman Suffrage Association, 1915), 53.

12. See "Miss Rose Young, Author, Ex-Editor," *New York Times*, July 8, 1941. Young had also written novels and features for *Good Housekeeping* before turning to her press work for the suffrage movement.

13. See Ida Husted Harper, ed., *The History of Woman Suffrage*, vols. 5, 6 (New York: National American Woman Suffrage Association, 1922), 5:15. The pro-suffrage editor of the *Sun* was Charles Henry Dana. See Ida Husted Harper, *The Life and Work of Susan B. Anthony*, 3 vols. (Indianapolis: Bowen-Merrill Co., 1899–1908), and Anna Howard Shaw, with Elizabeth Jordan, *The Story of a Pioneer* (New York: Harper and Brothers, 1915). Jordan actually wrote the biography of Shaw, though it is listed as joint authorship. Eliza-

beth G. Jordan, ed., *The Sturdy Oak: A Composite Novel of American Politics by Fourteen American Authors* (New York: Henry Holt and Co., 1917).

14. On the new American leadership, see esp. Ellen Carol DuBois, *Harriot Stanton Blatch and the Winning of Woman Suffrage* (New Haven: Yale University Press, 1997).

15. "What Shall I Do?," *Chicago Daily Tribune*, November 8, 1911. The *Tribune* advertised its list of "the greatest staff of experts ever assembled for the sole purpose of solving every problem of its woman readers." It included not just the usual fare—Marion Harland on "household topics" and Lillian Russell on "beauty problems"—but also Mary Isabel Brush on "women's political problems." This advertisement appeared repeatedly.

16. Harriot Stanton Blatch and Alma Lutz, *Challenging Years: The Memoirs of Harriot Stanton Blatch* (New York: Putnam, 1940), 108. For Blatch's scrapbooks, see Harriot Stanton Blatch Papers, Manuscripts Division, Library of Congress, Washington, D.C.

17. Reminiscences of Emma Bugbee, Oral Histories of Newspaper Women, 1974, Columbia University Libraries and Collections; Eleanor Booth Simmons, "Names of Suffrage Pioneers Not Forgotten in Victory," *New York Sun*, December 9, 1917.

18. On the New York club, see Beverly G. Merrick, "Newswomen's Club of New York, 1922–Present," in *Women's Press Organizations, 1881–1999*, ed. Elizabeth V. Burt (Westport, Conn.: Greenwood Press, 2000). The club still exists. See also Minutes, Newswomen's Club of New York.

Selected Bibliography

archival sources

Brown University Library, Providence, R.I.
    Lucy Larcom Papers
Center for American History, University of Texas Library, Austin
    New York Journal-American Morgue, Ada Patterson File
Columbia University Libraries and Collections, New York, N.Y.
    New York World Archives
    Oral Histories of Newspaper Women—Eva McDonald Valesh, Emma Bugbee
Department of Rare Books and Special Collections, Princeton University Library,
      Princeton, N.J.
    Ridgely Torrence Papers (for Olivia Dunbar)
Emory University Library, Atlanta, Ga.
    William Dummer Northend Papers (for Anna Northend Benjamin)
Huntington Library, San Marino, Calif.
    Elizabeth Boynton Harbert Papers
Library of Congress, Washington, D.C.
    American Press Association Records
    Clara Barton Papers
    Ida Husted Harper Papers
    National American Woman Suffrage Association Papers
Charles Deering McCormick Library of Special Collections, Newberry Library,
      Chicago
    Fanny Butcher Papers
    Wallace Rice Papers
Newswomen's Club of New York (formerly New York Newspaper Women's Club),
      New York, N.Y.
    Newswomen's Club Minutes
New York Public Library, New York, N.Y.
    Century Company Records
    Elizabeth Garver Jordan Papers
    Mail and Express Records
    Angela Morgan Papers
New York University Library, New York, N.Y.

Rose Pastor Stokes Papers
Northwestern University, Evanston, Ill.
   Teresa Dean Papers
Schlesinger Library, Radcliffe Institute for Advanced Study, Cambridge, Mass.
   Bureau of Vocational Information Records, "Questionnaire for Newspaper
      Women"
   Clara Savage Littledale Papers
Sophia Smith Collection, Smith College Library, Northampton, Mass.
   Marie Manning Papers
Widener Library, Harvard University, Cambridge, Mass.
   New Bedford Strike Scrapbooks
Wisconsin Historical Society, Madison
   Zona Gale Papers
   Isaac N. Stewart and Mary E. Stewart Papers
Yale Collection of American Literature, Beinecke Rare Book and Manuscript Library,
      Yale University, New Haven, Conn.
   Hapgood Family Papers (for Neith Boyce)
Yale University Library, New Haven, Conn.
   Rose Pastor Stokes Papers

books, articles, and theses

Abramson, Phyllis Leslie. *Sob Sister Journalism*. New York: Greenwood Press, 1990.
Adams, Katherine H. *A Group of Their Own: College Writing Courses and American
   Women Writers, 1880–1940*. Albany: State University of New York Press, 2001.
Anderson, Margaret. *My Thirty Years' War: An Autobiography*. New York: Covici,
   Friede, Inc., 1930.
Anderson, Monica. *Women and the Politics of Travel, 1870–1914*. Madison, N.J.:
   Fairleigh Dickinson University Press, 2006.
Ardis, Ann, and Patrick Collier, eds. *Transatlantic Print Culture, 1880–1940: Emerging
   Media, Emerging Modernisms*. New York: Palgrave Macmillan, 2008.
Baker, Nicholson. *Double Fold: Libraries and the Assault on Paper*. New York: Random
   House, 2001.
Baker, Nicholson, and Margaret Brentano. *The World on Sunday: Graphic Art in Joseph
   Pulitzer's Newspapers, 1898–1911*. New York: Bulfinch Press, 2005.
Banks, Elizabeth L. *The Autobiography of a "Newspaper Girl."* New York: Dodd, Mead
   and Co., 1902.
———. *Campaigns of Curiosity: Journalistic Adventures of an American Girl in Late
   Victorian London*. Edited by Mary Suzanne Schriber and Abbey Zink. Madison:
   University of Wisconsin Press, 2003.
Beasley, Maurine Hoffman. *The First Women Washington Correspondents*. George
   Washington University, Washington Studies No. 4. Washington, D.C.: George
   Washington University Press, 1976.
Beasley, Maurine H., and Sheila J. Gibbons, *Taking Their Place: A Documentary History
   of Women and Journalism*. Washington, D.C.: American University Press, 1993.

Becker, Jules. *The Course of Exclusion 1882–1924: San Francisco Newspaper Coverage of the Chinese and Japanese in the United States*. San Francisco: Mellen Research University Press, 1991.

Bederman, Gail. *Manliness and Civilization: A Cultural History of Gender and Race in the United States, 1880–1917*. Chicago: University of Chicago Press, 1995.

Belford, Barbara. *Brilliant Bylines: A Biographical Anthology of Notable Newspaperwomen in America*. New York: Columbia University Press, 1986.

Blair, Karen J. *The Clubwoman as Feminist: True Womanhood Redefined, 1868–1914*. New York: Holmes and Meier Publishers, 1980.

Blake, Mary Elizabeth, and Margaret F. Sullivan. *Mexico: Picturesque, Political, Progressive*. Boston: Lee and Shepard, 1888.

Blatch, Harriot Stanton, and Alma Lutz. *Challenging Years: The Memoirs of Harriot Stanton Blatch*. New York: Putnam, 1940.

Blewett, Mary H. *Constant Turmoil: The Politics of Industrial Life in Nineteenth-Century New England*. Amherst: University of Massachusetts Press, 2000.

Bleyer, Willard Grosvenor. *Main Currents in the History of American Journalism*. Boston: Houghton Mifflin, 1927.

Bok, Edward William. *The Americanization of Edward Bok: The Autobiography of a Dutch Boy Fifty Years After*. New York: Scribner, 1922.

Boughner, Genevieve Jackson. *Women in Journalism: A Guide to the Opportunities and a Manual of the Technique of Women's Work for Newspapers and Magazines*. New York: Appleton, 1926.

Boyce, Neith. *The Modern World of Neith Boyce: Autobiography and Diaries*. Edited by Carol DeBoer-Langworthy. Albuquerque: University of New Mexico Press, 2003.

Boyd, Melba Joyce. *Discarded Legacy: Politics and Poetics in the Life of Frances E. W. Harper, 1825–1911*. Detroit: Wayne State University Press, 1994.

Brady, Kathleen. *Ida Tarbell: Portrait of a Muckraker*. New York: Seaview/Putnam, 1984.

Brazelton, Ethel M. Colson. *Writing and Editing for Women*. New York: Funk and Wagnalls Co., 1927.

Britt, George. *Forty Years—Forty Millions: The Career of Frank A. Munsey*. New York: Farrar and Rinehart, 1935.

Brown, Hallie Q. *Homespun Heroines and Other Women of Distinction*. New York: Oxford University Press, 1988.

Buechler, Steven M. *The Transformation of the Woman Suffrage Movement: The Case of Illinois, 1850–1920*. New Brunswick, N.J.: Rutgers University Press, 1986.

Buhle, Mari Jo. *Women and American Socialism, 1870–1920*. Urbana: University of Illinois Press, 1981.

Buhle, Mari Jo, and Paul Buhle, eds. *The Concise History of Woman Suffrage: Selections from the Classic Work of Stanton, Anthony, Gage, and Harper*. Urbana: University of Illinois Press, 1978.

Bullock, Penelope L. *The Afro-American Periodical Press, 1838–1909*. Baton Rouge: Louisiana State University Press, 1981.

Burns, Sarah. *Inventing the Modern Artist: Art and Culture in Gilded Age America*. New Haven: Yale University Press, 1996.

Burt, Elizabeth V., ed. *Women's Press Organizations, 1881-1999*. Westport, Conn.: Greenwood Press, 2000.

Burton, Antoinette, ed. *After the Imperial Turn: Thinking with and through the Nation*. Durham: Duke University Press, 2003.

Butcher, Fanny. *Many Lives—One Love*. New York: Harper and Row, 1972.

Cahoon, Haryot Holt. *What One Woman Thinks: Essays of Haryot Holt Cahoon*. Edited by Cynthia M. Westover. New York: Tait, Sons and Co., 1893.

Cameron, Mabel Ward, comp. *The Biographical Cyclopaedia of American Women*. Vol. 1. New York: Halvord Publishing Co., 1924.

Campbell, W. Joseph. *Yellow Journalism: Puncturing the Myths, Defining the Legacies*. Westport, Conn.: Praeger, 2001.

Cane, Aleta Feinsod, and Alves, Susan, eds. *"The Only Efficient Instrument": American Women Writers and the Periodical, 1837-1916*. Iowa City: University of Iowa Press, 2001.

Chambers, Deborah, Linda Steiner, and Carole Fleming. *Women and Journalism*. New York: Routledge, 2004.

Chapman, John. *Tell It to Sweeney: The Informal History of the New York Daily News*. New York: Doubleday, 1961.

Clifford, Nicholas. *"A Truthful Impression of the Country": British and American Travel Writing in China, 1880-1949*. Ann Arbor: University of Michigan Press, 2001.

Cohen, Patricia Cline. *The Murder of Helen Jewett: The Life and Death of a Prostitute in Nineteenth-Century New York*. New York: Knopf, 1998.

Collins, Gail. *America's Women: 400 Years of Dolls, Drudges, Helpmates, and Heroines*. New York: Harper Perennial, 2007.

Cott, Nancy F. *The Bonds of Womanhood: "Woman's Sphere" in New England, 1780-1835*. New Haven: Yale University Press, 1977.

———. *The Grounding of Modern Feminism*. New Haven: Yale University Press, 1987.

———. *Public Vows: A History of Marriage and the Nation*. Cambridge: Harvard University Press, 2000.

———, ed. *History of Women in the United States: Historical Articles on Women's Lives and Activities*, vol. 17, *Social and Moral Reform*, pt. 2. Munich: K. G. Saur, 1994.

Craft, Mabel Clare. *Hawaii Nei*. San Francisco: William Doxey, 1899.

Creelman, James. *On the Great Highway*. Boston: Lothrop Publishing Co., 1901.

Cummings, Kathleen Sprows. *New Women of the Old Faith: Gender and American Catholicism in the Progressive Era*. Chapel Hill: University of North Carolina Press, 2009.

Czitrom, Daniel J. *Media and the American Mind: From Morse to McLuhan*. Chapel Hill: University of North Carolina Press, 1982.

Dana, Charles A. *The Art of Newspaper Making: Three Lectures*. 1895. Reprint, New York: Arno and New York Times, 1970.

Davidson, Cathy N., and Jessamyn Hatcher, eds. *No More Separate Spheres! A Next Wave American Studies Reader*. Durham: Duke University Press, 2002.

Dean, Teresa H. *How to Be Beautiful: Nature Unmasked: A Book for Every Woman*. Chicago: T. Howard, 1889.

———. *White City Chips*. Chicago: Warren Publishing Co., 1895.

————. *Reveries of a Widow*. New York: Town Topics Publishing, 1899.

Deane, Margery [Marie J. Pitman]. *European Breezes*. Boston: Lee and Shepard, 1883.

Deegan, Mary Jo, ed. *The New Woman of Color: The Collected Writings of Fannie Barrier Williams, 1893–1918*. De Kalb: Northern Illinois University Press, 2002.

Deering, Mabel Craft. In *Winning Equal Suffrage in California: Reports of Committees of the College Equal Suffrage League of Northern California in the Campaign of 1911*. N.p.: National College Equal Suffrage League, 1913.

Dennis, Charles H. *Victor Lawson: His Time and His Work*. Chicago: University of Chicago Press, 1935.

Department of Commerce and Labor. *Statistics of Women at Work. Based on Unpublished Information Derived from the Schedules of the Twelfth Census: 1900*. Washington, D.C.: Government Printing Office, 1907.

Derleth, August. *Still Small Voice: The Biography of Zona Gale*. New York: Appleton-Century, 1940.

Dorr, Rheta Childe. *What Eight Million Women Want*. Boston: Small, Maynard and Co., 1910.

————. *A Woman of Fifty*. New York: Funk and Wagnalls, 1924.

Dreiser, Theodore. *Newspaper Days: An Autobiography*. Edited by T. D. Nostwich. Santa Rosa, Calif.: Black Sparrow Press, 2000.

DuBois, Ellen Carol. *Harriot Stanton Blatch and the Winning of Woman Suffrage*. New Haven: Yale University Press, 1997.

Duggan, Lisa. *Sapphic Slashers: Sex, Violence, and American Modernity*. Durham: Duke University Press, 2000.

Elbert, Monika Maria. *Separate Spheres No More: Gender Convergence in American Literature, 1830–1930*. Tuscaloosa: University of Alabama Press, 2000.

Elshtain, Jean Bethke. *Jane Addams and the Dream of American Democracy: A Life*. New York: Basic Books, 2002.

Enstad, Nan. *Ladies of Labor, Girls of Adventure: Working Women, Popular Culture, and Labor Politics at the Turn of the Twentieth Century*. New York: Columbia University Press, 1999.

Fahs, Alice. *The Imagined Civil War: Popular Literature of the North and South, 1861–1865*. Chapel Hill: University of North Carolina Press, 2001.

————. "Newspaper Women and the Making of the Modern, 1885–1910." *Prospects* 27 (2002): 303–39.

Fairfax, Beatrice [Marie Manning]. *Ladies Now and Then*. New York: E. P. Dutton, 1944.

Farina, Elizabeth L. "Alice Rix in the *San Francisco Examiner*." M.A. thesis, Florida State University College of Arts and Sciences, 1988.

Faue, Elizabeth. *Writing the Wrongs: Eva Valesh and the Rise of Labor Journalism*. Ithaca: Cornell University Press, 2002.

Ferber, Edna. *A Peculiar Treasure*. New York: Doubleday, Doran, 1938.

Field, Kate. *Hap-Hazard*. Boston: James R. Osgood and Co., 1873.

————. *Ten Days in Spain*. Boston: James R. Osgood and Co., 1875.

————. *Selected Letters*. Edited by Carolyn J. Moss. Carbondale: Southern Illinois University Press, 1996.

Finnegan, Margaret. *Selling Suffrage: Consumer Culture and Votes for Women*. New York: Columbia University Press, 1999.

Flanagan, Maureen A. *Seeing with Their Hearts: Chicago Women and the Vision of the Good City, 1871-1933*. Princeton: Princeton University Press, 2002.

Fleischman, Doris E., ed. *An Outline of Careers for Women: A Practical Guide to Achievement*. New York: Doubleday, Doran, 1928.

Flexner, Eleanor. *Century of Struggle: The Woman's Rights Movement in the United States*. Cambridge: Belknap Press of Harvard University Press, 1959.

Foster, Frances Smith, ed. *A Brighter Coming Day: A Frances Ellen Watkins Harper Reader*. New York: Feminist Press, 1990.

Fox, Richard Wightman. *Trials of Intimacy: Love and Loss in the Beecher-Tilton Scandal*. Chicago: University of Chicago Press, 1999.

Fritzsche, Peter. *Reading Berlin, 1900*. Cambridge: Harvard University Press, 1996.

Gallagher, Jean. *The World Wars through the Female Gaze*. Carbondale: Southern Illinois University Press, 1998.

Gamber, Wendy. *The Boardinghouse in Nineteenth-Century America*. Baltimore: Johns Hopkins University Press, 2007.

Gamber, Wendy, Michael Grossberg, and Hendrik Hartog, eds. *American Public Life and the Historical Imagination*. Notre Dame, Ind.: University of Notre Dame Press, 2003.

Garrison, Dee. *Mary Heaton Vorse: The Life of an American Insurgent*. Philadelphia: Temple University Press, 1989.

Garvey, Ellen Gruber. *The Adman in the Parlor: Magazines and the Gendering of Consumer Culture, 1880s to 1910s*. New York: Oxford University Press, 1996.

Gatewood, William. *Aristocrats of Color: The Black Elite, 1880-1920*. Bloomington: Indiana University Press, 1990.

Gere, Anne Ruggles. *Intimate Practices: Literacy and Cultural Work in U.S. Women's Clubs, 1880-1920*. Urbana: University of Illinois Press, 1997.

Gershanek, S., and M. N. Ask, eds., *Who's Who in Journalism*. New York: Journalism Publishing Co., 1925.

Gibson, Lisette Nadine. "A Homely Business: Melusina Fay Peirce and Late-Nineteenth Century Cooperative Housekeeping." In *Separate Spheres No More: Gender Convergence in American Literature, 1830-1930*, edited by Monika Maria Elbert. Tuscaloosa: University of Alabama Press, 2000.

Gilfoyle, Timothy J. *City of Eros: New York City, Prostitution, and the Commercialization of Sex, 1790-1920*. New York: Norton, 1992.

Glenn, Susan. *Female Spectacle: The Theatrical Roots of Modern Feminism*. Cambridge: Harvard University Press, 2000.

Gordon, Ann D., ed., with Bettye Collier-Thomas. *African American Women and the Vote, 1837-1965*. Amherst: University of Massachusetts Press, 1997.

Gottlieb, Agnes Hooper. *Women Journalists and the Municipal Housekeeping Movement, 1868-1914*. Women's Studies, vol. 31. Lewiston, N.Y.: Edwin Mellen Press, 2001.

Graham, Jane Kirkland. *Viola: The Duchess of New Dorp: A Biography of Viola Roseboro'*. Vol. 1. Danville: Illinois Printing Co., 1955.

Graham, Katharine. *Personal History*. New York: Knopf, 1997.

Graham, Sara Hunter. *Woman Suffrage and the New Democracy*. New Haven: Yale University Press, 1996.

Grant, Ulysses S. *Personal Memoirs of U. S. Grant*. 1885, 1886. Reprint, New York: Penguin Books, 1999.

Guglielmo, Jennifer. *Living the Revolution: Italian Women's Resistance and Radicalism in New York City, 1880–1945*. Chapel Hill: University of North Carolina Press, 2010.

Gullett, Gayle. *Becoming Citizens: The Emergence and Development of the California Women's Movement, 1880–1911*. Urbana: University of Illinois Press, 2000.

Gurstein, Rochelle. *The Repeal of Reticence: A History of America's Cultural and Legal Struggles over Free Speech, Obscenity, Sexual Liberation, and Modern Art*. New York: Hill and Wang, 1996.

Halttunen, Karen. *Confidence Men and Painted Women: A Study of Middle-Class Culture in America, 1830–1870*. New Haven: Yale University Press, 1982.

Hamm, Margherita Arlina. *Manila and the Philippines*. New York: F. Tennyson Neely, 1898.

———. *America's New Possessions and Spheres of Influence*. New York: F. Tennyson Neely, 1899.

———. *Dewey, the Defender: A Life Sketch of America's Great Admiral*. New York: F. Tennyson Neely, 1899.

———. *Greater America: Heroes, Battles, Camps: Dewey Islands, Cuba, Porto Rico*. New York: F. Tennyson Neely, 1898.

———. *Porto Rico and the West Indies*. New York: F. Tennyson Neely, 1899.

———. *Builders of the Republic: Some Great Americans Who Have Aided in the Making of the Nation*. New York: James Pott and Co., 1902.

———. *Eminent Actors in Their Homes: Personal Descriptions and Interviews*. New York: James Pott and Co., 1902.

———. *Famous Families of New York: Historical and Biographical Sketches of Families Which in Successive Generations Have Been Identified with the Development of the Nation*. New York: Putnam, 1902.

Hamm, Margherita Arlina, and David Warfield. *Ghetto Silhouettes*. New York: James Pott and Co., 1902.

Hansen, Miriam. *Babel and Babylon: Spectatorship and American Silent Film*. Cambridge: Harvard University Press, 1991.

Hapgood, Hutchins. *A Victorian in the Modern World*. New York: Harcourt, Brace and Co., 1939.

Hapke, Laura. *Tales of the Working Girl: Wage-Earning Women in American Literature, 1890–1925*. New York: Twayne Publishers, 1992.

Harland, Marion [Mary Virginia Hawes Terhune]. *Marion Harland's Autobiography: The Story of a Long Life*. New York: Harper and Brothers, 1910.

Harper, Ida Husted. *The Life and Work of Susan B. Anthony*. 3 vols. Indianapolis: Bowen-Merrill Co., 1898–1908.

———, ed. *The History of Woman Suffrage*. Vols. 5, 6. New York: National American Woman Suffrage Association, 1922.

Hartog, Hendrik. *Man and Wife in America: A History*. Cambridge: Harvard University Press, 2000.

Hartsock, John C. *A History of American Literary Journalism: The Emergence of a Modern Narrative Form*. Amherst: University of Massachusetts Press, 2000.

Hawes, Elizabeth. *New York, New York: How the Apartment House Transformed the Life of the City, 1869–1930*. New York: Knopf, 1993.

Hayden, Dolores. *The Grand Domestic Revolution: A History of Feminist Designs for American Homes, Neighborhoods, and Cities*. Cambridge, Mass.: MIT Press, 1982.

Hayes, Rutherford Birchard. *Diary and Letters of Rutherford Birchard Hayes*. Columbus: Ohio State Archaeological and Historical Society, 1922–26.

Heaton, Eliza Putnam. *The Steerage: A Sham Immigrant's Voyage to New York in 1888*. Brooklyn: Brooklyn Eagle Press, 1919.

———. *By-paths in Sicily*. New York: E. P. Dutton, 1920.

Heller, Adele, and Rudnick, Lois, eds. *1915, the Cultural Moment: The New Politics, the New Woman, the New Psychology, the New Art and the New Theatre in America*. New Brunswick, N.J.: Rutgers University Press, 1991.

Henry, Alice. *Memoirs of Alice Henry*. Edited by Nettie Palmer. Melbourne: N.p., 1944.

Hill, Joseph A. *Women in Gainful Occupations, 1870–1920*. Washington, D.C.: Government Printing Office, 1929.

Hoganson, Kristin L. *Fighting for American Manhood: How Gender Politics Provoked the Spanish-American and Philippine-American Wars*. New Haven: Yale University Press, 1998.

———. *Consumers' Imperium: The Global Production of American Domesticity, 1865–1920*. Chapel Hill: University of North Carolina Press, 2007.

Horowitz, Helen Lefkowitz. *Alma Mater: Design and Experience in the Women's Colleges from Their Nineteenth-Century Beginnings to the 1930s*. New York: Knopf, 1984.

Hughes, Helen MacGill. *News and the Human Interest Story*. 1940. New York: Greenwood Press, 1968.

Hull, Gloria T., ed. *Give Us Each Day: The Diary of Alice Dunbar-Nelson*. New York: Norton, 1984.

Irwin, Inez Haynes. *The Story of the Woman's Party*. New York: Harcourt, Brace, 1921.

Irwin, Will. *The Making of a Reporter*. New York: Putnam, 1942.

Israel, Betsy. *Bachelor Girl: The Secret History of Single Women in the Twentieth Century*. New York: William Morrow, 2002.

Jacobson, Matthew Frye. *Barbarian Virtues: The United States Encounters Foreign Peoples at Home and Abroad, 1876–1917*. New York: Hill and Wang, 2000.

Johanningsmeier, Charles A. *Fiction and the American Literary Marketplace: The Role of Newspaper Syndicates in America, 1860–1900*. New York: Cambridge University Press, 1997.

Jordan, Elizabeth G. *Tales of the City Room*. New York: Scribner, 1898.

———. *Three Rousing Cheers*. New York: Appleton-Century, 1938.

———, ed. *The Sturdy Oak: A Composite Novel of American Politics by Fourteen American Authors*. New York: Henry Holt and Co., 1917.

[Jordan, Elizabeth, co-writer], and Anna Howard Shaw. *The Story of a Pioneer*. New York: Harper and Brothers, 1915.

Kane, Harnett T., with Ella Bentley Arthur. *Dear Dorothy Dix: The Story of a Compassionate Woman*. New York: Doubleday, 1952.

Kaplan, Amy. *The Anarchy of Empire in the Making of U.S. Culture*. Cambridge: Harvard University Press, 2002.

Kaplan, Amy, and Donald Pease, eds. *Cultures of United States Imperialism*. Durham: Duke University Press, 1993.

Kasson, John F. *Amusing the Million: Coney Island at the Turn of the Century*. New York: Hill and Wang, 1978.

Keetley, Dawn, and Pettegrew, John, eds. *Public Women, Public Words: A Documentary History of American Feminism*. Vol. 2: 1900 to 1960. Lanham, Md.: Rowman and Littlefield Publishers, 2002.

Kelley, Mary. *Private Woman, Public Stage: Literary Domesticity in Nineteenth-Century America*. Chapel Hill: University of North Carolina Press, 1984.

Kelly, Florence Finch. *Flowing Stream: The Story of Fifty-six Years in American Newspaper Life*. New York: E. P. Dutton, 1939.

Kessler-Harris, Alice. *Out to Work: A History of Wage-earning Women in the United States*. New York: Oxford University Press, 1982.

Kinsley, Philip. *The Chicago Tribune: Its First Hundred Years*. 3 vols. New York: Knopf, 1943–46.

Kochersberger, Robert C. *More than a Muckraker: Ida Tarbell's Lifetime in Journalism*. Knoxville: University of Tennessee Press, 1994.

Koven, Seth. *Slumming: Sexual and Social Politics in Victorian London*. Princeton: Princeton University Press, 2004.

Kraditor, Aileen S. *The Ideas of the Woman Suffrage Movement, 1890–1920*. New York: Norton, 1981.

Kramer, Paul A. *The Blood of Government: Race, Empire, the United States, and the Philippines*. Chapel Hill: University of North Carolina Press, 2006.

Kroeger, Brooke. *Nellie Bly: Daredevil, Reporter, Feminist*. New York: Times Books, 1994.

Krout, Mary H. *Hawaii and a Revolution: The Personal Experiences of a Newspaper Correspondent in the Sandwich Islands during the Crisis of 1893 and Subsequently*. New York: Dodd, Mead and Co., 1898.

Kurth, Peter. *American Cassandra: The Life of Dorothy Thompson*. Boston: Little, Brown, 1990.

Lancaster, Paul. *Gentleman of the Press: The Life and Times of an Early Reporter: Julian Ralph of the "Sun."* Syracuse, N.Y.: Syracuse University Press, 1992.

Laughlin, Clara E. *Traveling through Life: Being the Autobiography of Clara E. Laughlin*. Boston: Houghton Mifflin, 1934.

Lehuu, Isabelle. *Carnival on the Page: Popular Print Media in Antebellum America*. Chapel Hill: University of North Carolina Press, 2000.

Leider, Emily Wortis. *California's Daughter: Gertrude Atherton and Her Times*. Stanford, Calif.: Stanford University Press, 1991.

Leonard, John William., ed. *Woman's Who's Who of America: A Biographical*

Dictionary of Contemporary Women of the United States and Canada, 1914–1915.
New York: American Commonwealth Co., 1914.

Linderman, Gerald F. *The Mirror of War: American Society and the Spanish-American War.* Ann Arbor: University of Michigan Press, 1974.

Logan, Shirley Wilson, ed. *With Pen and Voice: A Critical Anthology of Nineteenth-Century African-American Women.* Carbondale: Southern Illinois University Press, 1995.

Lumsden, Linda J. *Inez: The Life and Times of Inez Milholland.* Bloomington: Indiana University Press, 2004.

Lutes, Jean Marie. *Front-Page Girls: Women Journalists in American Culture and Fiction, 1880–1930.* Ithaca: Cornell University Press, 2006.

Marks, Patricia. *Bicycles, Bangs, and Bloomers: The New Woman in the Popular Press.* Lexington: University Press of Kentucky, 1990.

Marzolf, Marion. *Up from the Footnote: A History of Women Journalists.* New York: Hastings House, 1977.

Mavity, Nancy Barr. *The Modern Newspaper.* New York: Henry Holt and Co., 1930.

McClintock, Anne. *Imperial Leather: Race, Gender and Sexuality in the Colonial Context.* New York: Routledge, 1995.

McGerr, Michael. *A Fierce Discontent: The Rise and Fall of the Progressive Movement in America.* New York: Oxford University Press, 2003.

McHenry, Elizabeth. *Forgotten Readers: Recovering the Lost History of African American Literary Societies.* Durham: Duke University Press, 2002.

McMurry, Linda O. *To Keep the Waters Troubled: The Life of Ida B. Wells.* New York: Oxford University Press, 1998.

Mead, Rebecca J. *How the Vote Was Won: Woman Suffrage in the Western United States, 1868–1914.* New York: New York University Press, 2004.

Merry, Robert W. *A Country of Vast Designs: James K. Polk, the Mexican War, and the Conquest of the American Continent.* New York: Simon and Schuster, 2009.

Messerli, Douglas. *Djuna Barnes: A Bibliography.* New York: David Lewis, 1975.

Meyer, Agnes E. E. *Out of These Roots.* 1953. Reprint, New York: Arno Press, 1980.

Meyerowitz, Joanne J. *Women Adrift: Independent Wage Earners in Chicago, 1880–1930.* Chicago: University of Chicago Press, 1988.

Miller, Stuart Creighton. *"Benevolent Assimilation": The American Conquest of the Philippines, 1899–1903.* New Haven: Yale University Press, 1982.

Mills, Sara. *Discourses of Difference: An Analysis of Women's Travel Writing and Colonialism.* New York: Routledge, 1993.

Mitchell, Edward P. *Memoirs of an Editor: Fifty Years of American Journalism.* New York: Scribner, 1924.

Mitchell, Sally. *The New Girl: Girls Culture in England, 1880–1915.* New York: Columbia University Press, 1995.

Montgomery, David. *The Fall of the House of Labor: The Workplace, the State, and American Labor Activism, 1865–1925.* New York: Cambridge University Press, 1987.

Morantz-Sanchez, Regina. *Conduct Unbecoming a Woman: Medicine on Trial in Turn-of-the-Century Brooklyn.* New York: Oxford University Press, 1999.

Morris, James McGrath. *Pulitzer: A Life in Politics, Print, and Power*. New York: Harper, 2010.

Mossell, Mrs. N. F. [Gertrude Bustill]. *The Work of the Afro-American Woman*. 1894. Reprint, New York: Oxford University Press, 1988.

Mott, Frank Luther. *American Journalism: A History of Newspapers in the United States through 260 Years, 1690 to 1950*. New York: Macmillan, 1950.

Nasaw, David. *Going Out: The Rise and Fall of Public Amusements*. New York: Basic Books, 1993.

———. *The Chief: The Life of William Randolph Hearst*. New York: Houghton Mifflin, 2000.

Nelson, Nell. *The White Slave Girls of Chicago: Nell Nelson's Startling Disclosures of the Cruelties and Iniquities Practiced in the Workshops and Factories of a Great City*. Chicago: Barkley Publishing Co., 1888.

Newman, Louise Michelle. *White Women's Rights: The Racial Origins of Feminism in the United States*. New York: Oxford University Press, 1999.

Nord, David Paul. *Communities of Journalism: A History of American Newspapers and Their Readers*. Urbana: University of Illinois Press, 2001.

O'Brien, Frank M. *The Story of the Sun: New York, 1833–1918*. New York: George H. Doran Co., 1918.

O'Hagan, A. [Anne], and E. B. Kaufman. *Cuba at a Glance*. New York: Russell, 1898.

Orvell, Miles. *The Real Thing: Imitation and Authenticity in American Culture, 1880–1940*. Chapel Hill: University of North Carolina Press, 1989.

Packard, Esther. *A Study of Living Conditions of Self-Supporting Women in New York City*. New York: Metropolitan Board of the YWCA, 1915.

Parry, Albert. *Garrets and Pretenders: A History of Bohemianism in America*. New York: Covici, Friede, Inc., 1933.

Patterson, Martha H. *Beyond the Gibson Girl: Reimagining the American New Woman, 1895–1915*. Urbana: University of Illinois Press, 2005.

Peattie, Elia. *Impertinences: Selected Writings of Elia Peattie: A Journalist in the Gilded Age*. Edited by Susanne George Bloomfield. Lincoln: University of Nebraska Press, 2005.

Peirce, Melusina Fay. *Cooperative Housekeeping: How Not to Do It and How to Do It: A Study in Sociology*. Boston: James R. Osgood and Co., 1884.

Peiss, Kathy. *Cheap Amusements: Working Women and Leisure in Turn-of-the-Century New York*. Philadelphia: Temple University Press, 1986.

Penn, I. Garland. *The Afro-American Press and Its Editors*. 1891. Reprint, New York: Arno Press, 1969.

Pérez, Louis A., Jr. *Cuba: Between Reform and Revolution*. 3rd ed. New York: Oxford University Press, 2006.

Petty, Leslie. *Romancing the Vote: Feminist Activism in American Fiction, 1870–1920*. Athens: University of Georgia Press, 2006.

Polacheck, Hilda Satt. *I Came a Stranger: The Story of a Hull-House Girl*. Edited by Dena J. Polacheck Epstein. Urbana: University of Illinois Press, 1989.

Ponce de Leon, Charles L. *Self-Exposure: Human Interest Journalism and the*

Emergence of Celebrity in America, 1890–1940. Chapel Hill: University of North Carolina Press, 2002.

Pratt, Mary Louise. *Imperial Eyes: Travel Writing and Transculturation*. New York: Routledge, 1992.

Rascoe, Burton. *We Were Interrupted*. Garden City, N.Y.: Doubleday, 1947.

Rayne, Mrs. M. L. [Martha Louise]. *What Can a Woman Do; or, Her Position in the Business and Literary World*. Detroit: F. B. Dickerson and Co., 1884.

Raz, Joseph. *Ethics in the Public Domain*. Oxford: Clarendon Press, 1994.

Richardson, Anna Steese. *The Girl Who Earns Her Own Living*. New York: B. W. Dodge and Co., 1909.

Richardson, Dorothy. *The Long Day: The Story of a New York Working Girl*. 1905. Reprint, edited by Cindy Sondik Aron, Charlottesville: University Press of Virginia, 1990.

Ritchie, Donald A. *Reporting from Washington: The History of the Washington Press Corps*. New York: Oxford University Press, 2005.

Roberts, Mary Louise. *Disruptive Acts: The New Woman in Fin-de-Siècle France*. Chicago: University of Chicago Press, 2002.

Robertson, Michael. *Stephen Crane, Journalism, and the Making of Modern American Literature*. New York: Columbia University Press, 1997.

Robertson, Nan. *The Girls in the Balcony: Women, Men, and "The New York Times."* New York: Random House, 1992.

Rodgers, Daniel T. *The Work Ethic in Industrial America, 1850–1920*. Chicago: University of Chicago Press, 1978.

Roggenkamp, Karen. *Narrating the News: New Journalism and Literary Genre in Late Nineteenth-Century American Newspapers and Fiction*. Kent, Ohio: Kent State University Press, 2005.

Rooks, Noliwe M. *Ladies' Pages: African American Women's Magazines and the Culture That Made Them*. New Brunswick, N.J.: Rutgers University Press, 2004.

Rosenberg, Emily S. *Spreading the American Dream: American Economic and Cultural Expansion, 1890–1945*. New York: Hill and Wang, 1982.

Rosenzweig, Roy. *Eight Hours for What We Will: Workers and Leisure in the Industrial City, 1870–1920*. New York: Cambridge University Press, 1983.

Ross, Ishbel. *Ladies of the Press: The Story of Women in Journalism by an Insider*. New York: Harper and Brothers, 1936.

Royster, Jacqueline Jones. *Traces of a Stream: Literacy and Social Change among African American Women*. Pittsburgh: University of Pittsburgh Press, 2000.

Rubin, Joan Shelley. *The Making of Middlebrow Culture*. Chapel Hill: University of North Carolina Press, 1992.

Ryan, Mary P. *Women in Public: Between Banners and Ballots, 1825–1880*. Baltimore: Johns Hopkins University Press, 1990.

Rydell, Robert W. *All the World's a Fair*. Chicago: University of Chicago Press, 1984.

Sanders, Marion K. *Dorothy Thompson: A Legend in Her Time*. Boston: Houghton Mifflin, 1973.

Sangster, Margaret E. *From My Youth Up*. New York: Fleming H. Revell Co., 1909.

Scanlon, Jennifer. *Inarticulate Longings: The Ladies' Home Journal, Gender, and the Promises of Consumer Culture*. New York: Routledge, 1995.

Scharnhorst, Gary. *Kate Field: The Many Lives of a Nineteenth-Century American Journalist*. Syracuse, N.Y.: Syracuse University Press, 2008.

Schechter, Patricia A. *Ida B. Wells-Barnett and American Reform, 1880–1930*. Chapel Hill: University of North Carolina Press, 2001.

Schiller, Dan. *Objectivity and the News: The Public and the Rise of Commercial Journalism*. Philadelphia: University of Pennsylvania Press, 1981.

Schlipp, Madelon Golden, and Sharon M. Murphy. *Great Women of the Press*. Carbondale: Southern Illinois University Press, 1983.

Schriber, Mary Suzanne. *Writing Home: American Women Abroad, 1830–1920*. Charlottesville: University of Virginia Press, 1997.

Schudson, Michael. *Discovering the News: A Social History of American Newspapers*. New York: Basic Books, 1978.

———. *The Power of News*. Cambridge: Harvard University Press, 1995.

———. *Why Democracies Need an Unlovable Press*. Malden, Mass.: Polity Press, 2008.

Schwarz, Judith. *Radical Feminists of Heterodoxy: Greenwich Village, 1912–1940*. Norwich, Vt.: New Victoria Publishers, 1986.

Scott, Anne Firor. *Natural Allies: Women's Associations in American History*. Urbana: University of Illinois Press, 1991.

Scott, Bonnie Kime. *The Gender of Modernism: A Critical Anthology*. Bloomington: Indiana University Press, 1990.

Sedgwick, Eve Kosofsky. *The Coherence of Gothic Conventions*. New York: Arno Press, 1980.

Seitz, Don C. *Joseph Pulitzer: His Life and Letters*. New York: Simon and Schuster, 1924.

Shaw, Anna Howard, with Elizabeth Jordan. *The Story of a Pioneer*. New York: Harper and Brothers, 1915.

Showalter, Elaine, ed. *These Modern Women: Autobiographical Essays from the Twenties*. Westbury, N.Y.: Feminist Press, 1978.

Shuman, Edwin Llewellyn. *Steps into Journalism: Helps and Hints for Young Writers*. Evanston, Ill.: Evanston Press Co., 1894.

Sicherman, Barbara. *Well-Read Lives: How Books Inspired a Generation of American Women*. Chapel Hill: University of North Carolina Press, 2010.

Silvester, Christopher. *The Norton Book of Interviews: An Anthology from 1859 to the Present Day*. New York: Norton, 1996.

Singer, Ben. *Melodrama and Modernity: Early Sensational Cinema and Its Contexts*. New York: Columbia University Press, 2001.

Smith, Harold Frederick. *American Travellers Abroad: A Bibliography of Accounts Published before 1900*. 1969. Lanham, Md.: Scarecrow Press, 1999.

Smith, Richard Norton. *The Colonel: The Life and Legend of Robert R. McCormick, 1880–1955*. Boston: Houghton Mifflin, 1997.

Smith, Sidonie. *Moving Lives: 20th-Century Women's Travel Writing*. Minneapolis: University of Minnesota Press, 2001.

Smith-Rosenberg, Carroll. *Disorderly Conduct: Visions of Gender in Victorian America*. New York: Knopf, 1985.

Sneider, Allison L. *Suffragists in an Imperial Age: U.S. Expansion and the Woman Question, 1870–1929*. New York: Oxford University Press, 2008.

Snyder, Katherine V. *Bachelors, Manhood, and the Novel, 1850–1925*. Cambridge: Cambridge University Press, 1999.

Squire, Belle. *The Woman Movement in America: A Short Account of the Struggle for Equal Rights*. Chicago: A. C. McClurg and Co., 1911.

Stansell, Christine. *City of Women: Sex and Class in New York, 1789–1860*. New York: Knopf, 1986.

———. *American Moderns: Bohemian New York and the Creation of a New Century*. New York: Metropolitan Books, 2000.

———. *The Feminist Promise, 1792 to the Present*. New York: Modern Library, 2010.

Steadman, Jennifer Bernhardt. *Traveling Economies: American Women's Travel Writing*. Columbus: Ohio State University Press, 2007.

Steffens, Lincoln. *The Autobiography of Lincoln Steffens*. New York: Harcourt, Brace, 1931.

Steiner, Linda. *Construction of Gender in Newsreporting Textbooks, 1890–1990*. Columbia, S.C.: Association for Education in Journalism and Mass Communication, 1992.

Stoker, Kevin, and Brad L. Rawlins. "The 'Light' of Publicity in the Progressive Era: From Searchlight to Flashlight." *Journalism History* 30 (Winter 2005): 177–88.

Stokes, Rose Pastor. *"I Belong to the Working Class": The Unfinished Autobiography of Rose Pastor Stokes*. Edited by Herbert Shapiro and David L. Sterling. Athens: University of Georgia Press, 1992.

Stoler, Ann Laura, ed. *Haunted by Empire: Geographies of Intimacy in North American History*. Durham: Duke University Press, 2006.

Streeby, Shelley. *American Sensations: Class, Empire, and the Production of Popular Culture*. Berkeley: University of California Press, 2002.

Streitmatter, Rodger. *Raising Her Voice: African-American Women Journalists Who Changed History*. Lexington: University Press of Kentucky, 1994.

Strom, Sharon Hartman. *Beyond the Typewriter: Gender, Class, and the Origins of Modern American Office Work, 1900–1930*. Urbana: University of Illinois Press, 1992.

Sullivan, M. F. *Ireland of To-Day: The Causes and Aims of Irish Agitation*. Philadelphia: J. C. McCurdy and Co., 1881.

Swanberg, W. A. *Pulitzer*. New York: Scribner, 1967.

———. *Citizen Hearst: A Biography of William Randolph Hearst*. 1961. Reprint, New York: Galahad Books, 1996.

Tarbell, Ida M. *All in the Day's Work: An Autobiography*. New York: Macmillan, 1939.

Tate, Claudia. *Domestic Allegories of Political Desire: The Black Heroine's Text at the Turn of the Century*. New York: Oxford University Press, 1992.

Tax, Meredith. *The Rising of the Women: Feminist Solidarity and Class Conflict, 1880–1917*. 1980. Reprint, Urbana: University of Illinois Press, 2000.

Tebbel, John. *An American Dynasty*. New York: Doubleday, 1947.

Terborg-Penn, Rosalyn. *African American Women in the Struggle for the Vote, 1850–1920*. Bloomington: Indiana University Press, 1998.

Terrell, Mary Church. *A Colored Woman in a White World*. 1940. Reprint, New York: G. K. Hall and Co., 1996.

Thornbrough, Emma Lou. *T. Thomas Fortune: Militant Journalist*. Chicago: University of Chicago Press, 1972.

Trachtenberg, Alan. *The Incorporation of America: Culture and Society in the Gilded Age*. New York: Hill and Wang, 1982.

Tucher, Andie. *Froth and Scum: Truth, Beauty, Goodness, and the Ax Murder in America's First Mass Medium*. Chapel Hill: University of North Carolina Press, 1994.

Turnbull, George. "Notes on the History of the Interview." *Journalism Quarterly* 13 (September 1936): 272–79.

Twain, Mark [Samuel Langhorne Clemens]. *The Innocents Abroad*. 1869. Reprint, New York: Penguin Books, 2002.

Vorse, Mary Heaton. *I've Come to Stay: A Love Comedy of Bohemia*. New York: Century Co., 1918.

———. *A Footnote to Folly: Reminiscences of Mary Heaton Vorse*. New York: Farrar and Rinehart, 1935.

Walker, Stanley. *City Editor*. New York: Blue Ribbon Books, 1934.

Walkowitz, Judith R. *City of Dreadful Delight: Narratives of Sexual Danger in Late-Victorian London*. Chicago: University of Chicago Press, 1992.

Watson, Elmo Scott. *A History of Newspaper Syndicates in the United States, 1865–1935*. Chicago: Elmo Scott Watson, 1936.

Watson, Lorna. "The New York Recorder as a Woman's Newspaper, 1891–1894." M.A. thesis, University of Wisconsin, Madison, 1939.

Waugh, Joan. *Unsentimental Reformer: The Life of Josephine Shaw Lowell*. Cambridge: Harvard University Press, 1997.

Wells, Ida B., Frederick Douglass, Irvine Garland Penn, and Ferdinand L. Barnett. *The Reason Why the Colored American Is Not in the World's Columbian Exposition*. 1893. Reprint, edited by Robert W. Rydell. Urbana: University of Illinois Press, 1999.

Wendt, Lloyd. *Chicago Tribune: The Rise of a Great American Newspaper*. Chicago: Rand McNally, 1979.

Wexler, Laura. *Tender Violence: Domestic Visions in an Age of U.S. Imperialism*. Chapel Hill: University of North Carolina Press, 2000.

Whiting, Lilian. *Kate Field: A Record*. Boston: Little, Brown, 1900.

Willard, Frances E. *Occupations for Women: A Book of Practical Suggestions for the Material Advancement, the Mental and Physical Development, and the Moral and Spiritual Uplift of Women*. New York: Success Co., 1897.

Willard, Frances E., and Livermore, Mary A. R., eds. *A Woman of the Century: Fourteen hundred-seventy Biographical Sketches Accompanied by Portraits of Leading American Women in All Walks of Life*. Buffalo: Moulton, 1893.

Wilson, Christopher P. *The Labor of Words: Literary Professionalism in the Progressive Era*. Athens: University of Georgia Press, 1985.

————. *White-Collar Fictions: Class and Social Representation in American Literature, 1885-1925*. Athens: University of Georgia Press, 1992.

Winslow, Thyra. *Picture Frames*. London: Constable and Co., 1924.

Women and the Chicago Tribune. Chicago: Business Survey of the Chicago Tribune, 1925.

Women in Professions: Being the Professional Section of the International Congress of Women, London, July, 1899. London: T. Fisher Unwin, 1900.

Woodress, James. *Willa Cather: A Literary Life*. Lincoln: University of Nebraska Press, 1987.

Wright, Gwendolyn. *Building the Dream: A Social History of Housing in America*. Cambridge, Mass.: MIT Press, 1981.

Yamane, Nancy Ann. "Women, Power, and the Press: The Case of San Francisco, 1868 to 1896." Ph.D. diss., University of California, Los Angeles, 1995.

Young, Marilyn Blatt. *The Rhetoric of Empire: American China Policy, 1895-1901*. Cambridge: Harvard University Press, 1968.

Zipser, Arthur, and Zipser, Pearl. *Fire and Grace: The Life of Rose Pastor Stokes*. Athens: University of Georgia Press, 1989.

Zurier, Rebecca. *Picturing the City: Urban Vision and the Ashcan School*. Berkeley: University of California Press, 2006.

Acknowledgments

It is a pleasure to acknowledge the many sources from which I have received support for this book. Fellowships from the American Council of Learned Societies and the University of California (in the form of a President's Fellowship for Research in the Humanities) allowed me to pursue my research full time in the early stages of this project. My residential fellowship at the Newberry Library during 2007–8 provided me not only with crucial time to write but also with intellectual community and friendship. My warm thanks to Jim Grossman for creating an unparalleled scholarly environment at the Newberry. Thanks as well to Martha Briggs, Diane Dillon, Dick Brown, and Megan Thomas—and especially to Justine Murison and Denver Brunsman, astute readers and great friends.

Fellowships from the Schlesinger Library, the Huntington Library, Smith College, the Newberry Library and the Wisconsin Historical Society also provided support for travel and research. At the Schlesinger Library, Ellen M. Shea located a number of extraordinary resources for me that I would not have found on my own. I am also grateful to the helpful staff of the New York Public Library, where I more or less lived in the microfilm room.

I am grateful for invitations to give talks at Princeton University; the University of California at Los Angeles; Boston College; the University of California, Irvine; and Washington State University, Pullman. My thanks to Christine Stansell, David Quigley, Joan Waugh, Heidi Tinsman, Uli Strasser, Carolyn Boyd, and Jenny Thigpen for making these talks such intellectually rewarding occasions. I am also indebted to Gina Morantz-Sanchez, Rachel Klein, Christopher Wilson, Gayle Gullett, and Vicki Ruiz for their astute comments. I am especially grateful to Jon Wiener for both his expert editorial eye and his friendship.

It has been a great pleasure throughout this project to work with graduate students, a source of inspiration in and out of the classroom. I benefited from expert research assistance provided by several students, including Tracy Sachtjen, Emily Sundstrom, Bethany Sweeney, and Adam Thomas. Also important to this project were ongoing conversations with other students, including Daniel Rood, Matt Mooney, Bill Landis, and Beth Anderson. Special thanks as well to researcher Kate Nicholson.

I am delighted to be publishing my third book with the University of North Carolina Press, and count myself lucky to be working with the Press's director, Kate Torrey, and managing editor, Ron Maner. My deep thanks for their expert editorial advice and guidance. A shout-out, too, to UNC Press staff members Mary Blaine, Dino Battista, and Rachel Surles for their help, as well as to copyeditor Stevie Champion.

I especially appreciate the support of friends and family. Ellen Burt, Joan Ariel, Ellen Broidy, Jane Elkoff, Liz Ezra, Holly Poindexter, Nancy Johnson, Bob Moeller, Lynn Mally, Ted Wright, and Nina Macdonald have lived with this project as long as I have— I am grateful for their encouragement and interest along the way. My family, too, has been immensely supportive. My sister, Mimi Fahs, has a rare gift for being positive, and I deeply appreciate her consistent enthusiasm and interest. My thanks to her, Elizabeth Thompson, and Craig Thompson for their generous hospitality in New York. I am grateful as well to my son-in-law, Chris Douthitt, for his Texas-style hospitality. And as for Trixie: the world would be a dull place without her.

No acknowledgment can quite capture how much the support of Mimi Chubb and Charlie Chubb has meant at every stage of this book. Not only have they been my go-to readers and editors for every single draft, but they have offered the sustaining virtues of wisdom, good advice, and constant encouragement. Plus they are fun to be with. What more can I say? Simply that I have dedicated this book to them, with my deep gratitude.

Index

Note: Pen names of newspaper women appear in quotation marks.

Harper's Weekly, 19

Harrison, Benjamin, 74

Hathaway Corporation, 207–8

Havana, Cuba, 249, 250

Hawaii, 2, 234, 237, 247, 251, 256, 258, 264, 265, 267, 268–69; and Hawaiians, 264–65

Hawaii and a Revolution, 264–65

Hayes, Rutherford B., 239–40, 241

Hearst, William Randolph, 3, 5, 193, 203, 204, 250

Heaton, Eliza Putnam ("Ellen Osborne"), 15, 36, 59–61, 67–68, 69, 70, 74, 137, 138, 215

"Hen Coop," 5, 32, 33, 83, 91, 122, 273, 274

Henry Street Settlement, 83

Herald. See New York Herald

"Her Point of View," 7, 82

Herrick, Christine Terhune, 56

Higher education and New Women, 139. *See also* College women

Holloway, Laura, 19

Home: celebration of on woman's page, 56; changing meanings of, 136; and living arrangements of bachelor girls, 143–61. *See also* Apartments; Bachelor girls; Domesticity; Hall bedroom

Hong Kong Telegraph, 256

Hooper, Lucy Hamilton, 235

Hopkins, Jennie L., 19, 20

Hotels, 28, 69, 116, 133, 136, 147, 219–20

Housekeeping. *See* Cooperative housekeeping/housing

Housing, 144–51, 160–61; working woman's hotel, 69; cooperative ideas of, 149–51; tenement apartments, 178, 196–99, 200, 227. *See also* Apartments

Howard, Joe, 45

Howard, Oliver Otis, 166

Howells, William Dean, 110

How the Other Half Lives, 196

Hugo, Victor, 217

Human interest, 4, 5, 13, 79, 91, 92–132, 163, 191, 193, 195

Humboldt, Alexander von, 232

Humphreys, Mary Gay, 19, 21, 138–39, 144, 146, 150, 151, 153–54

I Belong to the Working Class, 26

Imperialism, 233, 234, 237, 252, 257; literary, 167. *See also* Expansionism

"In Cap and Apron" (Banks), 177

The Innocents Abroad, 234

"The Interests of Working Women," 231

Interviews: as new newspaper genre and form of human interest, 1, 6, 13, 32, 90, 93–94, 108–21; newspaper women as subjects of, 7, 28, 40, 60, 129, 130, 150, 162, 179, 189, 196, 216–17, 225, 226, 227, 254, 255, 276; by newspaper women, 8, 11, 16, 18, 75, 179, 187, 227, 236, 239, 256, 260, 276; by Nellie Bly, 42–43, 44, 45; by Margherita Arlina Hamm, 47–48; as "degrading" assignment, 48, 49, 182, 185; African American women and, 75, 81; by Rheta Dorr, 83–84; by Marie Manning, 86; by Jessie Wood, 109–12; by Kate Carew, 112–16; by Nixola Greeley-Smith, 117–21; by Zona Gale, 187–88; by Anne O'Hagan, 197; by Eva Valesh, 201, 209; by Dorothy Richardson, 213–14

Ireland of To-day, 237

Irwin, Agnes, 88

Irwin, May, 24, 127–28

James, Henry, 18, 36, 235–36

Janesville, Wisc., 235

Japan, 2, 79, 85, 242, 251, 252, 253, 254, 255, 270

Jewish Daily Forward, 227

Jones, Mother (Mary Harris Jones), 120

Jordan, Elizabeth Garver: career of, 7, 8, 20, 21, 24, 34, 173–75, 190–91; on appeal of newspaper work, 8, 40–41; on newspaper women's progress, 22, 54; on definition of "newspaper woman," 24, 54; on woman's page work, 63; and role of fiction in newspaper work, 70, 215; and clubs, 76; and suffrage, 275

Hearst, William Randolph; Medill, Joseph; Pulitzer, Joseph; Rice, Wallace; Smith, Ballard; Swift, John

Newspaper Row, 32, 40, 41, 185

Newspapers: as form of public space, 1, 3, 47, 276; growth of, 3; circulation of, 3, 165–66; and rise of "New Journalism," 3–4; and rivalry between *New York World* and *New York Journal*, 3–4; and "yellow journalism," 4; and attempts to cloister women, 5; fiction for, 5; and development of human interest journalism, 5, 93–95; and new genres of writing at turn of the century, 6, 108, 121; and sensationalism, 7, 11, 48–49, 164–65; and expansive relationship to public space, 8–9, 52; attacks on, 10–11; history of compared to history of film, 10–11; as spaces of popular entertainment, 10–11, 164–65; destruction of paper copies of, 11; databases of, 14–15; as form of popular literature, 16; and racial prejudice, 26; resistance to women, 31, 43–44; differences from magazines, 39; desire for women readers, 59, 64, 65, 66; and development of ideal of "objectivity," 90; as space of public representation, 103; and new culture of publicity, 116–17; expansionist aims, 130; use of sensationalism to build circulation, 155–56; and working-girl stories, 193–94, 231; as political space for newspaper women, 234, 272–77; as important part of suffrage movement, 272–77. *See also* Editors; Human interest; New Journalism; Newspaper women; Publicity; Sensational newspapers and sensationalism; Woman's page; "Yellow journalism"; *individual newspapers*

Newspaper syndicates. *See* Syndicates and syndication

Newspaper women: meeting in public, 1; types of work, 6; public exposure of, 7; and difficulties in obtaining work, 7, 29–32; as public figures, 7, 111–12; and appeal of newspaper work, 7–8; racial privilege of, 9; class status of, 9, 102; erasure of from popular memory, 9–10; "objectivity" and, 12; fame and celebrity of, 12, 18, 46–47; and changing relationship to public space, 12, 98–99, 101; devaluing of own work, 13; and definition of modern gendered selfhood, 14; and rejection of earlier sentimental culture, 14; and advocacy of suffrage, 14, 67, 87, 117, 161, 230, 272–77; and celebration of "experience," 14, 217–18; increasing numbers of, 17; move to New York, 17, 112; as correspondents, 18; and syndication and self-syndication, 18, 35–38, 60–62; participation in public life, 18, 52, 117; Southern and Western, 19, 35; and financial need, 19–20, 35–36, 250; college-educated, 22; and generational shift in 1880s and 1890s, 22–23; and professional organizations, 23; and term "newspaper woman," 23; and pathway into newspaper work from acting, 24; and working-class women, 26, 193–201; and African American women, 26–29, 70–81; need for "pluck" and "push," 30; as suffragists and feminists, 32, 74, 272–77; and pay by "space rates," 33, 34; and newspaper work as springboard to magazine work, 34; salaries of, 35; creation of public personae, 39, 112–16; defense of "yellow journalism," 40; physical demands on, 40; health of, 41–42, 50; and gender barrier in police reporting, 43–44; and creation of new public space in newspapers, 44; sensational exploits, 44–46, 162–92; defense of right to public space, 47; ambition of, 47, 54; as public actors, 48, 102–3; attacks on as public figures, 48–49; controversy over sensational work of, 48–50, 163–64, 178–84; as "Bohemians," 51, 88–89, 155–56; freedom and independence of, 51, 102–3; and observation and active participation as new values, 52–53; and falsity, 53; work on woman's page, 56–91; and coverage of women's progress, 59–60, 62–63, 67–70, 82–88; and criticism of woman's page, 63–65; and coverage of women's clubs, 76; as novelists, 87; experimentation with style, 99; and newspaper work as form of public representation, 103–4; and publicity, 104–7; and celebrity culture, 108–9; and interviews, 108–20; and advice columns, 121–29; notoriety of in private lives, 124–25; and self-invention, 132; as bachelor girls, 133–61; focus on bodies of, 169; exploitation of, 170, 175–76; coverage of working women's lives, 193–231; as travel writers, 232–51; as war correspondents, 251–62. *See also* African American newspaper women; Bachelor girls; Human interest; Sensational newspapers and sensationalism; Suffrage; Travel; Woman's page; Work; Working girls and women

New Time, 213

"New Woman," 14, 21, 24, 59, 63, 88, 135, 139, 144, 149, 152, 175, 214, 236

New York Age, 26, 71, 72, 73, 75

New York City: newspaper women's public life in, 1, 83; fast-changing newspaper world of, 3; culture of entertainment in, 6; excitement of newspaper work in, 9, 185–88, 190–91; large number of newspaper women in, 17, 18; newspaper women move to, 35, 39, 113, 165, 203, 233, 261; police reporting in, 43; advice to come to, 54–55; writings on women's lives in, 67, 68, 219–21, 222; housing in, 69, 146–50; sensational work in, 171–73, 179, 180–81, 182; community of suffrage reporters in, 276–77

New York Commerical Advertiser, 133

New Yorker, 112

New York Evening Journal. See New York Journal

New York Evening Post, 3, 87–88, 239; Rheta Dorr's experiences at, 31, 32, 34, 66, 82–85, 146; Clara Savage at, 76, 273; handwritten index of, 81; Lincoln Steffens's memories of, 99; Rose Young employed by, 275

New York Evening World. See New York World

New York Freeman, 72

New York Globe, 72

New York Graphic. See Daily Graphic

New York Herald, 3; Nellie Bly's interview of editor of, 43, 44; Marion Harland's affiliation with, 57; woman's page articles in, 64, 138; bachelor girl articles in, 140, 146, 148, 154, 156; Dorothy Richardson as reporter for, 195, 213, 215, 218–22, 223, 224; Margherita Hamm writing for, 256

New York Jewish Daily Forward, 227

New York Jewish Daily News, 25, 131, 227

New York Journal, 3, 51, 225; and New Journalism, 3–4; rivalry with *New York World*, 3–4; genteel attacks on, 11; Anne O'Hagan at, 22, 193, 195, 196–97, 198, 207–8, 212, 257; Eva Valesh at, 25, 193, 195, 203–7, 209–12; Marie Manning at, 32, 86, 94, 121–27, 129, 133, 273; newspaper office of, 43; Jessie Wood at, 93, 105, 107, 110; Ella Wheeler Wilcox at, 117; Kate Swan at, 165; Ada Patterson at, 191; warmongering of, 250–51; Kate Masterson at, 256; Emma Kaufman at, 257

New York Mail and Express, 2, 125; Rheta Dorr as highly paid staff member of, 34–35; on "feminine bachelors," 136; Margherita Hamm and, 255, 256

New York Newspaper Women's Club, 277

New York Post. See New York Evening Post

New York Press, 88–89

New York Recorder, 4, 35; Haryot Holt

Sentimentalism and critiques of sentimentalism, 63, 64, 73, 99, 127, 182, 185, 194, 196, 208, 240, 272

Shafter, William R., 261

Shaw, Anna Howard, 83, 275

Shea, Bartholomew "Bat," 167

Shostac, Nancy, 88

Singer, Ben, 164, 166

Sister Carrie, 96

Six Months in Mexico, 232–33

"Slumming" and slumming literature, 163, 178, 185, 194, 196, 200, 217, 231

Smith, Ballard, 191

Smith College, 22, 76, 273

"Snap Shots" (Dean), 95, 96

Snead, Austine ("Miss Grundy"), 239–40, 241

Snead, Fayette, 239

"Sob sisters," 11, 12, 117, 119, 163, 272

Social Democrat, 213

"Social mongrels," 102–3

Society page and writings, 6, 13, 19, 26, 30, 32, 43, 62, 71, 95, 102, 104–5, 106, 107, 236

Sorosis, 76

Sothern, Winifred, 158, 159, 160

Space rates, 17, 18, 29, 31, 33, 34, 203

Space work, 24, 33, 35, 141

Spain, 246, 248, 249, 251, 261

Spanish-American War of 1898, 2, 212, 249, 256–57, 260–62

Sports. *See* Athletes and athleticism

Standard Oil, 39

"Stanley, Olga" (Lila Woolfall), 139, 143

Stansell, Christine, 124, 155

Steffens, Lincoln, 99

Stewart, Alexander T., 69, 148

Stevenson, Robert Louis, 36

Stocker, Corinne, 81

Stoddard, Richard Henry, 125

Stokes, James Graham Phelps, 25, 227, 228, 230

Stokes, Rose Pastor ("Zelda"), 25, 26, 130–32, 220, 227–30

"Strenuous life," 14, 41, 218

Strikes. *See* New Bedford strike

"Strings," 33, 203

Stunt work: and appeal of daredevil feats, 6; as part of popular culture of leisure and entertainment, 6; Ada Patterson and, 6; relation to melodrama, 6; criticism of, 29, 46, 163–64, 182; Nellie Bly and, 163, 177, 270; and emphasis on female heroism, 166; Kate Swan and, 168, 171–73; exploitation of women in, 169; as means of extending women's terrain of experience, 170; creation of daring form of selfhood through, 175; numerous women involved in, 177; Zona Gale and, 186–87; Kate Masterson and, 256

Sue, Eugène, 217

Suffrage, 18, 79, 81, 122, 239; Margherita Hamm and, 2, 255, 274; Nixola Greeley-Smith and, 12, 276; as expression of modern gender identity, 14; Ida Husted Harper and, 37, 66–67, 275; woman's page as site for, 66–67, 87–88, 161; Rheta Dorr and, 83, 85, 89; *New York Times* opposition to, 87–88; advocacy of by newspaper women, 117; Marie Manning on, 126, 273–74; Mary Isabel Brush and, 230, 276; Mabel Craft Deering and, 275; Anne O'Hagan and, 275; Elizabeth Jordan and, 275; Rose Young and, 275; and English radicalism, 275–76; Harriot Stanton Blatch on importance of press in fight for, 276; Emma Bugbee and, 276; New York Newspaper Women's Club and, 277

Suffragettes, British, 273, 275–76

Sullivan, Margaret F., 232, 234, 236–39

Sun. See New York Sun

Sunday World. See New York World

"Swan, Kate" (Kate Swan McGuirk), 6, 7, 162, 163, 165–69, 171–73, 175, 183, 193

Swift, John, 200–201

Syndicates and syndication, 3, 9, 15, 22, 32; as new development at turn of